Think Tank Research Quality

Lessons for Policymakers, the Media, and the Public

Think Tank Research Quality

Lessons for Policymakers, the Media, and the Public

edited by

Kevin G. Welner
University of Colorado at Boulder

Patricia H. Hinchey
Penn State

Alex Molnar
Arizona State University

and

Don Weitzman
Independent Researcher

Information Age Publishing, Inc.
Charlotte, North Carolina • www.infoagepub.com

Library of Congress Cataloging-in-Publication Data

Think tank research quality : lessons for policymakers, the media, and the
public / edited by Kevin G. Welner ... [et al.].
     p. cm.
  Includes bibliographical references.
ISBN 978-1-61735-020-7 (pbk.) -- ISBN 978-1-61735-021-4 (hardcover) --
ISBN 978-1-61735-022-1 (e-book)
  1. Privatization in Education--United States. 2. Education and
state--United States. 3. Education--Research--United States. 4. Research
institutes--United States. I. Welner, Kevin Grant, 1963-
  LB2806.36.T484 2010
  370.7'2--dc22
                              2010010173

Printed in the United States of America

CONTENTS

ACKNOWLEDGMENTS

This book and the underlying Think Tank Review Project are the result of a decade's worth of contributions from a large number of people. The idea of reviewing the research publications of private think tanks first took shape when in 1998 Alex Molnar created the Center for Education Research, Analysis, and Innovation at the University of Wisconsin-Milwaukee. It advanced further and took the form of the Think Tank Review Project when in 2006 the Arizona State University Education Policy Research Unit (EPRU) and the University of Colorado at Boulder Education and the Public Interest Center (EPIC) teamed up and began a collaboration with The Great Lakes Center for Education Research and Practice (GLC). The academic expertise resident in EPRU and EPIC and the funding commitment of the GLC have together made the Think Tank Review Project a nationally recognized voice in support of high-quality research.

Lu Battaglieri, chair of the GLC, and Teri Battaglieri, that Center's executive director, have been steadfast in their support. From the outset they and the GLC Board of Directors have shared our vision of making independent, high-quality, expert reviews of think tank research publications available to policymakers. The reviews we produce are also distributed and republished by the GLC, as part of its "Think Twice" project.

We also owe a large debt of gratitude to Keith Gayler, who contacted us early on to offer his assistance. He has been a wonderful asset and a dear friend, and we very much hope to continue working with him in the future.

For his editing on every review we've published, we thank Erik Gunn, who operates Great Lakes Editorial Services. Special recognition is also due to Wendy Chi, Gary Miron and Bill Mathis, all of whom are mentioned below in their roles as reviewers, but who also have helped us expand the project in managerial roles.

Finally, we offer our most heartfelt thanks to the 45 reviewers who have found time in their hectic lives to answer our calls. These are some of the top scholars in their respective areas, with enormous demands on their time and expertise. When we make our urgent requests for them to set aside their ongoing work to immerse themselves in a new think tank report, the easiest and most understandable response is to politely decline. We are always grateful—and even a little amazed—when they do not. Here's the full list:

- Richard Allington, University of Tennessee
- Brooks Applegate, Western Michigan University
- Bruce Baker, Rutgers University
- Steven Barnett, Rutgers University
- Clive Belfield, Queens College, City University of New York
- Damian Betebenner, The National Center for the Improvement of Educational Assessment
- Robert Bifulco, Syracuse University
- Derek Briggs, University of Colorado at Boulder
- Carol Burris, Rockville Centre School District
- Greg Camilli, University of Colorado at Boulder
- Martin Carnoy, Stanford University
- Wendy Chi, University of Colorado at Boulder
- Casey Cobb, University of Connecticut
- Sean Corcoran, New York University
- Sherman Dorn, University of South Florida
- Anthony Gary Dworkin, University of Houston
- Edward García Fierros, Villanova University
- Bruce Fuller, University of California, Berkeley
- Gene Glass, Arizona State University
- Jennifer Jellison Holme, University of Texas at Austin
- Ernie House, University of Colorado at Boulder
- Ken Howe, University of Colorado at Boulder
- Luis Huerta, Teachers College, Columbia University
- Jennifer Jennings, Columbia University
- Mindy Kornhaber, Pennsylvania State University
- Jaekyung Lee, State University of New York at Buffalo

- Jon Lorence, University of Houston
- Christopher Lubienski, University of Illinois, Urbana Champaign
- Sarah Theule Lubienski, University of Illinois, Urbana-Champaign
- Jeff MacSwan, Arizona State University
- Bill Mathis, University of Colorado at Boulder
- Patrick McEwan, Wellesley College
- Patrick McQuillan, Boston College
- Gary Miron, Western Michigan University
- Lawrence Mishel, Economic Policy Institute
- Raymond Pecheone, Stanford University
- Sean Reardon, Stanford University
- Meredith Richards, University of Texas at Austin
- Gary Ritter, University of Arkansas
- Joydeep Roy, Economic Policy Institute and Georgetown University
- José Luis Santos, UCLA
- Ash Vasudeva, Stanford University
- Ruth Chung Wei, Stanford University
- Ed Wiley, University of Colorado at Boulder
- John Yun, University of California, Santa Barbara

INTRODUCTION

Bringing Think Tank Research Into the Scholarly Debate

Alex Molnar and Kevin G. Welner

Reflecting on what we had learned during the first year of the Think Tank Review Project, we wrote in 2007:

> At a time when America's education policymakers have nominally embraced the idea of tying school reform to "scientifically based research," many of the nation's most influential reports are little more than junk science. A hodgepodge of private "think tanks" at both the state and national levels wield significant and very often undeserved influence in policy discussions by cranking out an array of well-funded and slickly produced—yet ideologically driven—research.[1]

Since that time, the situation hasn't noticeably improved. The Think Tank Review Project (TTRP), a collaboration of the Education and the Public Interest Center (EPIC) at the University of Colorado at Boulder and the Education Policy Research Unit (EPRU) at Arizona State University remains as necessary as ever. In our view, the best ideas emerge from a public process of rigorous critique and debate. We do not consider TTRP reviews the final word or think of the Project as a "watchdog." What we value and attempt to encourage is a public dialogue about the quality of the evidence offered to support education policy proposals.

The value of contributions made by think tank publications to the marketplace of ideas is the subject of dispute. Think tank research has been praised for its introduction and championing of ideas,[2] while critics have pointed to the often misleading and unreliable nature of think tank research and analysis.[3] By providing independent, expert, third-party evaluations of think tank research publications, the TTRP helps policymakers and members of the public draw their own conclusions about the value of a given think tank publication. Since reviews are designed to highlight issues of reliability, accuracy and usefulness, a policymaker or reporter who has read both the think tank report and the Project's review of it is in a much better position to assess the value of the report's findings and make sound use of them. TTRP thereby promotes high-quality research, informed public debate, and research-driven policymaking.

WHY THE THINK TANK REVIEW PROJECT WAS LAUNCHED

We began the Think Tank Review Project because we had, in the course of our scholarly work, come across numerous instances of policymakers and the media citing as authoritative sources think tank reports that did not meet the minimal standards of research quality. Our working assumption was that the non-peer-reviewed reports produced by think tanks were of greatly varying quality, and we were troubled that there was no systematic process for bringing them within the established push and pull of scholarly research discussions. Instead, these reports seemed to influence policy by moving along a parallel track, separate and apart from scholarly research in academic institutions. We reasoned that the Project's review process could, over time, help raise the overall quality of think tank reports by drawing think tank publications into the critical environment of peer-reviewed scholarship.

Since 2006, the TTRP has published 59 reviews of reports from 26 different institutions, most of them free-market think tanks. From the outset, the Project has had a strong focus on self-described "free-market" think tanks, because they have dominated the existing universe of think tanks in terms of both output and resources. However, research published by non-advocacy think tanks such as RAND and Mathematica, as well as moderate- to liberal-leaning organizations such as Brookings, the New Teacher Project and the Center for Education Policy, has also been reviewed.

When reviewing original research, the Project's reviewers adhere to the canons of social science inquiry and ask the kind of questions set forth in the American Psychological Association's research standards:[4]

- Is the research question significant, and is the work original and important?
- Have the instruments used in the research been demonstrated to have satisfactory reliability and validity?
- Are the outcome measures clearly related to the variables with which the investigation is concerned?
- Does the research design fully and unambiguously test the hypothesis?
- Are the participants representative of the population to which the generalizations are made?
- Is the research at a stage advanced enough to make the publication results meaningful?

Most publications produced by advocacy think tanks are not, however, original research. A large number are what we consider policy briefs. High-quality policy briefs can be very helpful to policymakers. Useful briefs generally include a comprehensive consideration of previously published research and accurately synthesize what is known in order to draw out policy implications. In essence, the value of policy briefs in policymaking is strongly dependent upon the adequacy of their reviews of the literature.

For those reports that do offer original analyses of data, questions of research design and methodology come to the fore. Valid research findings require not only that the data are sound but also that the methods used to do the analyses are appropriate, properly executed, and clearly enough described that they can be replicated. As with policy briefs, a research report's practical utility often depends on the authors' carefully and faithfully basing conclusions and recommendations on the empirical evidence presented.

SELECTING PUBLICATIONS TO REVIEW

A Think Tank Review Project researcher visits websites of the most prolific think tanks each day. When a new research report about education is posted, it is flagged for possible review. Also considered for review are reports suggested by readers. The number of reviews conducted is limited by several factors. In general, the TTRP does not review reports that focus on curricular issues or on higher education. Further, budgetary limitations and the limited availability of expert reviewers mean that not every report can be reviewed. Repetitiveness also plays a role; advocacy think tanks sometimes hammer away at key messages, repeating the same arguments and re-using essentially the same evidence in multiple reports. Rather than review each new iteration of such reports, press releases are sometimes used to point out that a given report has been, in essence, assessed by the review of an earlier report. If the topic is of sufficient policy significance, multiple, repetitive reports from the same think tank are sometimes reviewed together.

THE REVIEW PROCESS

The Think Tank Review Project publicly considers the strengths and weaknesses of education-related research reports published by think tanks by using a peer review process. The purpose of peer review is to subject research to the scrutiny of third-party experts. This is the mechanism used by academic journals to determine whether research is of high enough quality to merit publication. Similarly, TTRP reviews provide policymakers and the general public with information that can be used to assess the value of the research being produced by think tanks.

It is the editors' task to keep the reviews focused on substance. Experts often have strong views, but irrespective of reviewers' personal opinions, TTRP reviews are based on the evidence at hand. Reviewers are expected to consistently and appropriately use social scientific principles of analysis. Our highest priority is to publish intellectually honest, academically sound reviews.

In general, we agree with the Friedman Foundation for Educational Choice that in research the "good apples" should be separated from the "bad apples."[5] The Friedman Foundation offers the following questions it believes researchers and their critics should be prepared to answer. We think they are fair questions and are, in fact, the kind of questions our reviewers ask:

Does this study isolate the effects of the factor being studied from the effects of other factors that might influence the results? If so, how and to what extent?

What, specifically, does this study measure? Is that the most appropriate measurement?

Does the study involve measuring one thing as a proxy for something else that can't be measured? If so, how reliable is the proxy?

Do the data raise any issues involving definitions or classifications?

How were the data for this study collected? Are the subjects of the study representative of the whole population? How was this ensured?

Does the study compare groups of students? If so, what were the comparison groups, and are there ways in which they might not be comparable?

How large is the effect identified in this study, in specific numbers? Would you characterize this as small, moderate, or large? Why? How does this effect size compare to the effect sizes in research on other topics?

What alternative explanations might there be for the results of the study?

Is there reason to think the results would have been different if the study had examined a different student group, or a different location, or a different method of implementing a certain policy? If the study examines a pilot project, is there reason to think the project's results would be different if taken to scale?

How does the result of this study compare with the results of other studies of this topic? How does the method of this study compare with the methods of other studies of this topic? What are the limitations of this study? How do the limitations of this study compare with the limitations of other studies of this topic?

To date, the goal of bringing think tank research reports within the broader family of research publications subject to systematic expert review has been only partially met. For the most part the response from authors of think tank reports and from the think tanks themselves has been silence.[6]

THE ASCENDANCE OF MARKET-ORIENTED THINK TANKS

As we noted earlier, the TTRP has devoted much of its attention to the many free-market think tanks that are part of a network of organizations promoting a relatively constrained set of educational policies. As a result, the research reviewed by TTRP has tended to focus on privatization and school choice. About half the reviews in this book address one of these topics in some form or another.

While the policy goals of think tanks do not determine their reports' quality, knowing something about the origins of think tanks is necessary to put the Think Tank Review Project and this book in perspective. Public policy think tanks began fairly modestly with the founding of such institutions as the Brookings Institution (1927), the American Enterprise Institute (1943), and the Hoover Institution (1959). In the 1970s a number of influential think tanks such as the Heritage Foundation (1973) and the Cato Institute (1977) were founded,[7] and since the 1970s the number of think tanks has increased dramatically. The majority of the most visible are free-market think tanks.

In addition to national organizations, a very influential network of state-level free-market think tanks has been built.[8] Some of these can be quite large: Michigan's Mackinac Center in 2006 had a budget of more than $4 million and a staff of 32.[9] Its members echo each other's arguments, cite each other's work, share ideas, and republish each other's work after changing titles and state-specific references.[10] These think tanks have changed the nature of policy discussions. Holly Yettick's recent analysis suggests that, although university- or government-based researchers produce most research, publications of private think tanks are disproportionately represented in the reporting of major national newspapers.[11]

Market-oriented think tanks, in particular, have proliferated because of large gifts by a relatively small number of benefactors.[12] Researchers at the University of Colorado at Boulder found that between 1985 and 2000 more than $100 million in grants were awarded to just 15 market-oriented think tanks by three funders: the Lynde and Harry Bradley Foundation, the Sarah Scaife Foundation, and the John M. Olin Foundation.[13] Similarly, the National Center for Responsive Philanthropy calculated that foundations overall provide grants to conservative school choice organizations amounting to approximately $100 million per year. [14]

The number, size, and reach of market-oriented think tanks, relative to moderate or progressive think tanks, reflects, in some measure, the impact of the divergent funding decisions of donors on the left and right.[15] Conservative donors have demonstrated a greater willingness to spend their money on developing institutions and supporting those who adhere to their ideological premises—and to fund activities that directly engage the political process.[16]

As a result of the focused giving of conservative donors, market-oriented think tanks have been able to engage in aggressive outreach to media and policymakers to promote their favored ideas. This pattern of funding is in contrast to the grant-making of most other foundations, which tend to shy away from politics, focusing instead on charitable work that supports community groups and others.[17] Few progressive foundations fund ongoing institutions with strong strategic communications components and clear public policy goals. Because nonconservative foundations are much more likely to engage in community-based projects, it is not surprising that institutions funded by conservatives produce a much greater level of activity aimed directly at influencing policy—publishing research reports, briefing documents, legislative analyses, and commentaries, as well as organizing briefings for policymakers and reporters.

THE STRATEGIC VALUE OF IDEAS

In a 2005 *Commentary* magazine essay, James Piereson, then the executive director of the John M. Olin Foundation, one of the strongest funders of the free-market think tank network, argued that promoting ideas is vital if conservatism is to remain viable as a governing philosophy.[18] He concluded his essay by declaring,

> [Friedrich] Hayek and the neoconservatives have had it right all along: any movement, if it is to maintain or augment its influence, will need to wage an ongoing battle of ideas. To do so, conservatives, no less than liberals, will need the help of sympathetic foundations.

Piereson recognized that as a governing philosophy, conservatism also necessarily had to incline toward the practical and offer a workable agenda that included "school vouchers, personal retirement accounts, legal reform, elimination of the estate tax, and so forth." This suggests another truth we have come to understand: not only are market-oriented think tanks more numerous, their strategic agenda is more focused and ambitious.

Market-oriented think tanks devote a considerable portion of their efforts toward media coverage, which tends to amplify their impact. In 2001, researchers at the Center for Education Research, Analysis, and Innovation at the University of Wisconsin-Milwaukee contacted seven organizations that regularly publish education policy research: the RAND Corporation, the Consortium for Policy Research in Education, the Brookings Institution, the Heritage Foundation, the Hoover Institution, the Thomas B. Fordham Foundation, and the Economic Policy Institute. Each was asked about their media strategies and whether the documents they published were peer reviewed prior to publication and, if so, what their peer review process was. The three conservative organizations (Heritage, Hoover, and Fordham) responded that they did not have a peer review process. In contrast, the Economic Policy Institute and the three more centrist organizations (the Consortium for Policy Research in Education, RAND and Brookings) described peer review processes but tended to have much less well-developed media strategies for bringing their publications to the attention of policymakers and the public.[19] A rough indicator of the priorities of the Heritage Foundation is that about 35% of its annual budget at the time was devoted to advertising.[20]

Almost a decade ago, one of us (Molnar) coauthored a study that examined the content and production of Michigan's Mackinac Center for Public Policy.[21] The study, discussed in greater detail below, found that between 1990 and 2001, the Mackinac Center published 22 documents it described as "studies." An essay written by Mackinac's Nathan J. Russell in a 2006 publication, *An Introduction to the Overton Window of Political Possibilities* helps explain why Mackinac produced so many reports.[22] Overton, a former Mackinac Center vice president, understood, according to Russell, that "regardless of how persuasive the think tank, lawmakers are constrained by the political climate" and that "to be truly successful, the Mackinac Center should not focus on direct policy advocacy, but instead focus on educating lawmakers and the public in an attempt to change the political climate." Russell concluded, "This is the true influence of a think tank—shaping the political climate of future legislative and legal debates by researching, educating, involving, and inspiring." As stated by Friedrich Hayek, one of the founders of the modern conservative movement, "Those who have concerned themselves exclusively with what seemed practicable in the existing state of opinion have constantly found that even this has rapidly become politically impossible as the result of changes in a public opinion which they have done nothing to guide."[23] Following a mission framed by such thinking, many of the publications of the Mackinac Center and other market-oriented think tanks have become little more than ideological marketing materials relentlessly supplied to policymakers and the public, driven primarily by ideology.

There is nothing necessarily wrong with this strategic vision. It is based on sound premises. In our view, Russell, Overton and Hayek are almost certainly correct in their political analyses. Moreover, we believe that think tank studies, whether or not they are motivated by ideological considerations, could make a genuine contribution to public policy. The integrity of the strategy and its value for public policy hinges, however, on the quality of the studies produced.

Applying the research standards of the American Psychological Association to Mackinac Center research was the focus of the 2001 study referred to earlier. The study revealed that although the Center described itself as committed to delivering "the highest quality and most reliable research on Michigan issues," the research it produced was of low quality.[24] Of the education research reports published by Mackinac between 1990 and May 2001, only one met the standards necessary to be judged of high enough quality to even be considered for publication by a peer-reviewed academic journal.

At the national level, the Friedman Foundation for Educational Choice, which has published 105 reports since 2006, has been among the most prolific national think tanks. On the opening pages of those reports, the Foundation issues a challenge to readers.[25] It begins, "Our research adheres to the highest standards of scientific rigor," and goes on to note that while the Foundation clearly has values and a point of view, "[t]he sensible approach is to accept studies that follow sound scientific methods, and reject those that don't." It concludes,

> So if you're skeptical about our research on school choice, this is our challenge to you: prove us wrong.... But, if you can't find anything scientifically wrong with it, don't complain that our findings can't be true just because we're not neutral. That may make a good sound bite, but what lurks behind it is a flat rejection of science.

Unfortunately, as illustrated by several of the chapters in this book, our reviewers have found a troubling pattern of low-quality research in the Friedman Foundation's research publications. Through 2009, the Think Tank Review Project has reviewed 10 Friedman Foundation reports. Taken together, the expert reviews catalogue a disturbing and consistent pattern of shoddy work. The ideological beliefs of the authors appear at times to have distorted the methods deployed, the literature reviewed, the analyses conducted, and the conclusions offered. We have communicated our responses to the Friedman Foundation "challenge." It has not seen fit to reply.

A BOOK OVERVIEW

This book is presented in 10 parts, the first 5 of which address 6 school choice topics: vouchers, charters, competition effects, private school outcomes, the fiscal impacts of choice, and contracting out of services. The remaining parts cover subjects ranging from preschool to school finance to teacher quality and standards-based accountability. For most of these topics, we present two think tank reviews—21 in all. To present the ideas and themes that emerge from the reviews in each of the subject areas, the sections begin with a brief introduction by the book's editors. In the end, however, the reviews speak for themselves. These are contributions from some of the top scholars in their particular subject areas—researchers who recognize the influence of think tank reports and who have worked with us to produce high-quality reviews, written for both academic and non-academic audiences to help improve the quality of the debate over education policy.

Private think tanks play an influential role in framing and shaping debates over education reform. We believe it is important to bring the research publications of think tanks into the scholarly debate and to provide policymakers and the public with access to independent, expert assessments of the research these think tanks publish. With the help of our scholar-reviewers, we will continue to advance these goals in the years to come.

NOTES AND REFERENCES

1. Welner, K. G,. & Molnar, A. (2007, March 28). Truthiness in education. *Education Week, 26*(25), 32, 44.

2. Ricci, D. M. (2006). *The transformation of american politics: The new Washington and the rise of think tanks.* New Haven, CT: Yale University Press.

3. Haas, E., Molnar, A., & Serrano, R. (2002). *Media impact of think tank education publications 2001.* Tempe, AZ: Education Policy Research Unit. Retrieved December 30, 2009 from http://epicpolicy.org/files/EPSL-0205-115-EPRU.pdf

   Molnar, A. (2001). *The media and educational research: What we know vs. what the public hears.* Tempe, AZ: Education Policy Research Unit. Retrieved December 30, 2009 from http://epicpolicy.org/files/cerai-01-14.htm

   Rich, A. (2005). *Think tanks, public policy, and the politics of expertise.* Cambridge, MA: Cambridge University Press.

4. American Psychological Association (1995). *Publication manual of the American Psychological Association.* Washington, DC: Author.

5. Friedman Foundation for Educational Choice. (n.d.). *Good apples vs. bad apples: The Friedman Foundation's Guide to evaluating the scientific quality of education research.* Indianapolis, IN: Friedman Foundation for Educational Choice.

6. Among the exceptions was a reply by Chester Finn of the Fordham Foundation to the review in chapter eleven of this book by University of Colorado at Boulder Professor Emeritus Ernest House. The review of the Fordham publication as well as the Finn reply and House response are linked at http://epicpolicy.org/thinktank/review-trends-charter-school-authorizing.

7. Abelson, D. E. (2002). *Do think tanks matter? Assessing the impact of public policy institutes.* Montreal, Canada: McGill-Queen's University Press.

8. Cookson, P. W., Molnar, A., & Embree, K. (2001). *Let the buyer beware: An analysis of the social science value and methodological quality of educational studies published by the Mackinac Center for Public Policy (1990-2001).* Tempe, AZ: Education Policy Research Unit. Retrieved December 30, 2009 from http://epicpolicy.org/files/EPSL-0109-102-EPRU.pdf

   DeParle, J. (2006, November 17). Right-of-center guru goes wide with the gospel of small government. *New York Times,* section A, p. 24.

9. DeParle, J. (2006).

10. DeParle, J. (2006).

11. Yettick, H. (2009). *The research that reaches the public: Who produces the educational research mentioned in the News Media?* Boulder, CO and Tempe, AZ: Education and the Public Interest Center & Education Policy Research Unit. Retrieved December 30, 2009 from http://epicpolicy.org/publication/research-that-reaches

12. Rich, A. (2005); see note 3.

    Stefancic, J., & Delgado, R. (1996). *No mercy: How conservative think tanks and foundations changed america's social agenda.* Philadelphia, PA: Temple University Press.

13. Rabin, S., & Chi, W. (2008). *Examining the funding and activities of free market education think tanks.* Unpublished manuscript, University of Colorado at Boulder.

14. Cohen, R. (2007). *Strategic grantmaking: Foundations and the school privatization movement.* Washington DC: National Center for Responsive Philanthropy.

15. Rich, A. (2005b, Spring). War of ideas: Why mainstream and liberal foundations and the think tanks they support are losing in the war of ideas in American politics. *Stanford Social Innovation Review,* 18-25.

16. Rich, A. (2005b).

17. Rich, A. (2005b).

18. Piereson, J. (2005, May 27). Investing in the right ideas: How philanthropists helped make conservatism a governing philosophy. *Commentary Magazine.* Retrieved December 30, 2009 from http://www.opinionjournal.com/extra/?id=110006723

19. Molnar, A. (2001); see note 3.

20. Haas, E., Molnar, A., & Serrano, R. (2002); see note 3.

21. Cookson, P. W., Molnar, A., & Embree, K. (2001); see note 8.

22. Russell, N. J. (n.d.). *An introduction to the overton window of political possibilities.* Mackinac Center for Public Policy. Retrieved December 30, 2009 from http://www.mackinac.org/7504

23. Hayek, F. A. (1949). The Intellectuals and Socialism. *The University of Chicago Law Review, 16*(3). Retrieved December 30, 2009 from http://mises.org/story/2984

24. Cookson, P. W., Molnar, A., & Embree, K. (2001); see note 8.

25. See, for example, DiPerna, P. (2007). *Illinois' opinion on k-12 education and school choice.* Indianapolis, IN: Milton & Rose D. Friedman Foundation. Retrieved December 30, 2009, from http://www.friedmanfoundation.org/downloadFile.do?id=260

PART 1

School Choice and
the Benefits of Competition

Reviews in Part 1 introduce critical themes that appear repeatedly throughout the Think Tank Review Project analyses published over the years: selective use of earlier research to bolster findings; failure to account for selection bias; overstated conclusions and unsupported recommendations; and a conflation of correlation and causation. Two reviews are presented here in their entirety. The first is by Christopher Lubienski, who analyzed Greg Forster's 2009 review of studies on voucher effects, *A Win-Win Solution: The Empirical Evidence on How Vouchers Affect Public Schools*, published by The Friedman Foundation for Educational Choice. The second is John Yun's review of Jay Greene and Marcus Winters' 2008 study *The Effect of Special Education Vouchers on Public School Achievement: Evidence from Florida's McKay Scholarship Program*, published by the Manhattan Institute for Policy Research. As noted below, several other TTRP reviews not included here raised similar concerns, pointing to clear patterns in this body of think tank research and in the reports reviewed.

Voucher advocates argue that financial threats to public schools through increased competition will force improved outcomes even for students who

Think Tank Research Quality: Lessons for Policy Makers, the Media, and the Public, pp. 1–4

choose to remain in those public schools. Skeptics and critics, on the other hand, have worried that vouchers will drain resources and selectively skim students from public schools—the least expensive to educate, the highest achieving, and those with the most engaged parents—worsening conditions for those left behind.

Forster's report examines 17 studies on how vouchers have affected public schools in Florida, Milwaukee and a few other locations and finds what the author considers overwhelming evidence of positive impact. However, Lubienski points to Forster's inferential leap from correlation to causation, noting: "Other factors could also be at play, but these studies generally cannot identify them, since they focus almost exclusively on vouchers as the causal mechanism." Forster acknowledges possible alternative causes for improvements, Lubienski notes, but dismisses them without providing any empirical evidence to bolster his arguments. Moreover, the reviewer notes that reported gains for individual schools are small and disappear at the district level.

Lubienski also highlights the biased nature of the studies included in the review: "the majority of the studies were produced by a very small group of people" with ties to pro-voucher organizations. Although two independent, peer-reviewed studies were included, the reviewer finds that Forster misrepresented the findings of one, ignoring the half of the study that produced a finding contradictory to the case for vouchers. Overall, Lubienski finds Forster's review to constitute "a pro-voucher argument rather than an even-handed presentation of research." According to the reviewer, a more accurate picture of what is known about voucher effects is that "the record is very thin," with little actually known about how public school students are affected by voucher programs.

The Greene and Winters study also examines the possible impact of vouchers on public school outcomes, but it focuses specifically on students enrolled in special education programs. The authors examine the effect of Florida's McKay Scholarships, which provide vouchers to students with learning disabilities, and they find that vouchers have a positive impact on special education students who choose to remain in public schools. Reviewer Yun's characterization of this report echoes Lubienski's assessment of the Forster report: "Without any tests or appropriate literature substantiating [the authors'] assumptions, the report leads the reader down a path with a predetermined conclusion: that vouchers have a positive competition effect." Yun explains that the report fails to factor in the impact of a school's location in either an urban or suburban area; to consider seriously alternative explanations for gains; to specify how exactly reported gains were measured; or to consider the possible impact of testing accommodations. Yun also points out that the report's analysis is based on the number of private schools in a 5- to 10-mile radius of a given public school rather than on the more appropriate number of private school seats available for eligible students. Although he finds the attention to special education students laudable, Yun concludes that "the analyses are so vague and the approach so flawed that their only practical use is as an initial template for addressing the important issues of selection bias for studies such as this."

Our reviewers have documented similar weaknesses in several other think tank reviews of related reports (all available at thinktankreview.org):

- Another Friedman Foundation study by Forster, *Promising Start: An Empirical Analysis of How EdChoice Vouchers Affect Ohio Public Schools* (2008), reports the same finding as the report detailed above: academic gains at public schools exposed to the possibility of losing students to vouchers. We had asked Christopher Lubienski to review this initial report as well, and he found weaknesses similar to those he later identified in Forster's 2009 study: "Despite being presented as scientifically rigorous, the report suffers from serious methodological shortcomings. The analysis uses weak variables and an incorrect approach to measuring academic gains and tries to make claims based on cherry-picking uneven results."

- In *Feeling the Florida Heat? How Low-Performing Schools Respond to Voucher and Accountability Pressure* (2007), from the Urban Institute's National Center for Analysis of Longitudinal Data in Education Research, authors Cecilia Elena Rouse, Jane Hannaway, Dan Goldhaber and David Figlio similarly found that vouchers and other accountability measures sparked changes in school behavior and resulting achievement gains. Reviewer Damian W. Betebenner found, however, that although the study did yield some sound findings, "the report overstates and makes causal claims about the relationship between accountability sanctions and improvements in school achievement." He notes that the data and methods used in this study are not capable of parceling out causal effects to, for instance, changed school practices, test preparation, or any other factors not expressly considered.

- The same conclusion—that the availability of vouchers improved the academic performance of eligible students who did not take advantage of them—is evident in Jay Greene and Ryan Marsh's study *The Effect of Milwaukee's Parental Choice Program on Student Achievement in Milwaukee Public Schools* (2009), from the School Choice Demonstration Project at the University of Arkansas. Reviewer Gregory Camilli found that the report offered fair and thorough accounting of results. However, when methodological weaknesses are considered, "the practical effect of competition through vouchers appears to be small, if not negligible." Therefore, while Camilli found some strengths in this study, he also found reason to be "skeptical" that it provided reliable support for choice mechanisms as the optimal tool for leveraging school reform and improvement.

Overall, our reviewers have concluded that these competition reports' findings are unreliable, suffering from methodological weaknesses, selective use (and misuse) of evidence, and overstated findings. The reports address a very important issue, since many more students potentially experience the impact of competition than do direct users of vouchers. But they fall short in their ability to guide sound policy.

CHAPTER 1

A WIN-WIN SOLUTION

The Empirical Evidence on
How Vouchers Affect Public Schools

Christopher Lubienski

Review of Greg Forster's "A Win-Win Solution: The Empirical Evidence on How Vouchers Affect Public Schools," published by the Friedman Foundation for Educational Choice. This is a modified version of a review originally published on April 27, 2009.

INTRODUCTION

The question of using vouchers to send children to private schools at public expense has been at the center of an ongoing debate in the United States over the use of market mechanisms for organizing public education. Although there has not been the anticipated rush by states to implement vouchers since the 2002 U.S. Supreme Court decision in *Zelman v. Simmons-Harris* affirming the constitutionality of these programs, voucher advocates have been working to highlight evidence of their beneficial effects. In fact, there are data on a number of issues around vouchers,

Think Tank Research Quality: Lessons for Policy Makers, the Media, and the Public, pp. 5–22

from a small handful of voucher programs. Quite often, research has focused on the question of the immediate effects of vouchers on the academic achievement of students who use them to attend private school. This is obviously an important issue, particularly if vouchers are to provide these "choosers" with access to better quality options.

Another key question is the secondary impact of vouchers: how they affect public schools. Critics of vouchers have expressed concern for the non-choosers, the students remaining behind in the public schools. They worry that transferring students and funding to private schools removes resources as well as academic and social capital from schools most in need of them. Supporters, in turn, argue that vouchers will create the competitive incentives necessary to compel these schools to become more effective. That is, the loss of some students, or simply the threat of losing students (and, of course, the government funding they bring), may be enough to force schools to make important instructional improvements, thereby benefiting all students, including those who did not choose to use a voucher.

This second critical question is thus whether voucher programs harm or benefit public schools and their students, a question that is invariably addressed through examinations of achievement data. The answer has serious implications for our understanding of the potential role of voucher programs in American education. Consequently, a number of different individuals and teams—primarily voucher supporters—have attempted to provide some illumination, or at least some evidence, on this question.

A recent report by Greg Forster of the Friedman Foundation for Educational Choice summarized evidence on the competitive effects of vouchers on public schools.[1] The Friedman Foundation for Educational Choice publishes reports to advance the late Milton Friedman's vision of privatized K-12 education.[2] Forster is a senior fellow at the Foundation and has written extensively for policy and popular media outlets on school choice.

This new report selects 17 studies concerning the competitive effects of vouchers in places such as Florida and Milwaukee, finding an overwhelming consensus that vouchers improve academic performance in public schools. It then discusses and dismisses three alternative explanations for the purported improvements in public schools that the author ascribes to competitive effects: that vouchers are "creaming" the best students or "dredging" the worst ones from nearby public schools; that public schools are improving not because of voucher threats, but simply because of the "stigma" of being labeled as low-performing; and that improvements in performance are simply a matter of a statistical artifact known as regression to the mean. The penultimate section of the report asks an eminently sensible question: if vouchers do indeed cause public schools to improve their performance, as the author argues, then why have school systems with voucher programs not witnessed dramatic, or even noticeable, improvements in performance? The report concludes with a brief summary that points to other reasons, in addition to competitive effects, to support vouchers; it re-states the claim that there is a research consensus on evidence of positive secondary effects from vouchers; and it asserts that vouchers have not been shown to cause harm.

FINDINGS AND CONCLUSIONS OF THE REPORT

Based on a review of 17 studies, the report finds a general consensus that the competitive effects of vouchers cause public schools to improve. The report finds only one instance, the District of Columbia, where vouchers did not lead to improved outcomes in public schools. In D.C, no negative effects were found, and, according to the report, the lack of a positive impact was due to "hold-harmless" provisions shielding public schools from financial losses when students used vouchers to leave for private schools.[3]

The report disputes the claim that voucher users are more likely to be higher-achieving, leaving public schools with students who tend to be lower achievers or less motivated. Public schools located near voucher-accepting private schools would not, as others fear, enter into spirals of decline as they lose ground academically due to their more motivated students (as well as resources) leaving.[4] The report instead concludes that the opposite happens. It claims that students of all achievement levels are equally likely to use vouchers to leave public schools. Further, it contends that the real or potential loss of students to vouchers spurred the public schools in these studies to become more effective, as evidenced by their increased test scores.

Notably, the report also concludes that vouchers "can have a significant positive impact on public schools without necessarily producing visible changes in the overall performance of a large city's schools" (p. 5). This is a key assertion, necessary to explain the counter-intuitive twin conclusions drawn from the 17 studies: each of the reports (save one) shows a positive impact from vouchers on the public schools that are studied, but these gains are not apparent on a larger scale in the districts. This is explained as due to the fact that "the overall performance of a school system can never by itself provide a reliable guide to whether any one factor (such as vouchers) is having a positive effect"—too many variables are at play (p. 30). The report therefore concludes that it is necessary to further deregulate and expand voucher programs so that their impact can be enhanced.

Some critics of the studies marshaled in this report have suggested that other factors may also very well be at work and might better explain the academic outcomes sometimes evident in schools near voucher programs.[5] For instance, gains in public schools may be due to changes in student composition, the shame of being classified as a failing school (a key eligibility criterion in Florida), or simply the likelihood that outlying schools on the bottom end of the performance scale are more likely to move up, as a statistical artifact. The report reviews these possibilities, provides arguments to dismiss each alternative theory, and concludes that any positive trends in student achievement must be the result of the competitive effects of vouchers alone.

While the report focuses on 17 studies to highlight the competitive effects of vouchers, it also includes additional assertions that do not directly address the research topic, but rather are used to support the report's conclusions. For instance, it cites additional studies outside the set of 17 for the proposition that "vouchers make public schools better off financially" (p. 11). This is a key claim, since it is used to undergird the contention that there is no evidence "that vouchers harm public schools" (pp. 5, 10, 34). Similarly, although not tested in his report, the author cites his own earlier work to conclude that, even without a competitive effect, vouchers

> provide a better education to those who use them, they provide better services for disabled students, they put students into schools that are more racially integrated, [and] they improve students' civic values. (p. 34)

RATIONALES SUPPORTING THE FINDINGS AND CONCLUSIONS

The conclusions in this report are based on the apparent consensus of the 17 selected studies. The main finding that competition from voucher programs causes public schools to improve is drawn from analyses that show improvements in public school achievement after the introduction of voucher programs in Milwaukee, Florida, and a few other locations.

As noted below, the data available on this question show an association between the emergence of voucher programs and an increase in measures of academic performance in local public schools, but do not demonstrate direct causation. Researchers typically attempt to test for and eliminate other possible explanations for patterns, thereby isolating the role of vouchers as the likely factor leading to the outcome.

It is important to note, however, that neither this report nor almost all of the analyses it draws on identify the ways in which student achievement is improved in public schools, and how related mechanisms and processes may or may not be associated with vouchers. This "black box" approach, which does not empirically consider possible mechanisms for the purported improvement process, leaves open questions about alternative explanations: it is difficult if not impossible to know what contribution to any improvement could be attributed to vouchers (that is, if the schools did in fact improve, and if they did so with the same students—see below). Other factors could also be at play, but these studies generally cannot identify them, since they focus almost exclusively on vouchers as the causal mechanism. This would be critical information, because it could help other schools replicate those improvements. Instead, the report, along with most of the studies cited, makes the logical leap that schools are rather generic organizations, in which changes in external stimuli (such as the introduction of voucher threats) lead to changes in outcomes (test scores) in some automatic yet unspecified way. In short, these studies lack the rigor and curiosity that might bring them to a different conclusion.

The findings in the report are based on at least three other key underlying assumptions, all of which are questionable. First, the report frequently repeats the exaggerated refrain that vouchers bring choice to education, thus creating the "positive incentives we take for granted *everywhere else*…. The same Americans who have difficulty with the idea that competition improves schools have no difficulty applying the same concept *everywhere else*" (p. 12, emphasis added). In making this claim, the author casts education simply as a consumer good, one that he equates with "magazines, haircuts, dry cleaning and video games" (p. 11). He also fails to acknowledge that, while Americans typically choose private consumer goods and services, we do not choose public goods such as national defense providers, sewage systems, or courts.

Second, the report assumes that a very basic conception of the logic of competitive incentives can improve education. It assumes, advancing from the idea that education is simply another consumer good, that vouchers create incentives that force schools to improve—the premise of the report's main finding. "Colleges must provide a good education … or else lose students. Professionals like doctors and lawyers must provide good services or else lose clients. Stores must provide good value or else lose customers" (p. 11). According to this reasoning, schools will react to the competition created by vouchers simply by becoming more effective. This assumption is reflected in the report's findings, filtering out unexplored alternative explanations for those findings. However, the assumption is tenuous when one considers how many people hire charming, well-advertised, but bad lawyers, how many mortgage and derivative brokers *gained* clients while providing toxic products, or how many people pay to see bad movies. The connection between quality and consumer preference is not nearly as simple as this report assumes. There are different types of markets, and the role of consumer information differs greatly among them.[6] In some markets, consumers can easily acquire useful information about the quality of different options, while in others, such information is virtually impossible to obtain. This report makes assumptions, which it fails to support, about what types of information is readily available to education consumers.

Third, the report asserts that private schools are more effective and efficient than public schools: "educating students in private schools rather than public schools not only accomplishes better results, it also costs less" (p. 11). Setting aside the veracity of this claim, it is largely a red herring, since competition felt by public schools could result in academic improvements even if the appeal of private schools was due to some factor unrelated to effectiveness or efficiency, such as religious preference. However, the report offers the assumption as a basis for its contention that because of the competition generated through vouchers, any achievement gains in public schools must result from their trying to emulate the superior achievement in private schools. Yet the report includes no evidence for the assumption that private schools are superior, and there is a growing body of research—much of it peer-reviewed—suggesting that they are not.[7]

THE REPORT'S USE OF RESEARCH LITERATURE

Because the report is a review of other studies, a comprehensive review of the research literature is critical. A review of research that presents only a subset is of little use, and if that subset is biased toward a given finding, it becomes dangerously misleading. At more than one point, the report claims to encompass "all available empirical studies on how vouchers affect academic achievement in public schools" (p. 10). However, the report never describes how studies were collected, or what criteria were used for selecting or rejecting studies from this review.

The programs reviewed in the Friedman report represent an interesting, if odd (given the inclusion of Vermont and Maine, as discussed later), assortment of voucher plans to examine competitive effects. Ten of the reports studied public school achievement in relation to Florida's voucher programs. Nine of those considered Florida's A+ program, which was ruled unconstitutional and ended in 2006[8]; the remaining paper focused on Florida's McKay voucher program for students with disabilities.[9] Five studies examined changes in public school achievement in the wake of the Milwaukee voucher program.[10] The remaining studies focused on the Edgewood District in Texas,[11] the EdChoice program in Ohio,[12] the federally funded voucher program in Washington, DC,[13] and older "tuitioning" programs in Maine and Vermont.[14]

This set of studies includes some rigorous work by respected researchers. But issues of methodology, interpretation, and generalizability emerge when the research is marshaled simply to support a narrow agenda, as with the Friedman Foundation's primary goal of "school choice for all." Then, the temptation for selectively summarizing research can distort the actual findings. Consider one example from the report. As the Friedman report notes, Stanford economist Martin Carnoy and colleagues released a report in 2007 on the possible competitive effects that vouchers had on public schools in Milwaukee. According to the Friedman report's summary, the Carnoy et al. report's findings confirmed the existence of a beneficial competitive effect from the voucher program:

> [T]heir analysis "confirms the earlier results showing a large improvement in Milwaukee in the two years following the 1998 expansion of the voucher plan to religious schools." Before 1998, religious schools were excluded from the Milwaukee program, so many fewer students participated. When religious schools were admitted to the program in 1998, participation increased dramatically. (p. 17)[15]

Although the report quotes Carnoy et al., it does not provide a page number for the quote, so readers are unlikely to read this "finding" in its proper context.[16] In fact, that context offers a different perspective than the one portrayed in the Friedman report.

Carnoy et al. actually conducted two analyses. The first, which the Friedman report highlights and includes among the 17 reviewed, did confirm a competition effect, but the researchers were simply attempting to replicate earlier research. The second, which the Friedman report notes but does not include among the 17, found no competition effect.

The approach used by Carney and his colleagues, replicating an earlier study using the same data, is common, especially when the initial research is controversial or has been conducted by investigators who have drawn criticism in the past for their methodological choices or advocacy positions, as was the case here.[17] But while the report quotes part of Carnoy et al.'s findings, it fails to summarize the complete finding from their first analysis. The two sentences following the passage quoted in the Friedman report would have greatly helped readers understand the conclusions reached by Carnoy and his colleagues:

> *However*, we also confirm that *little positive improvement took place in later years* even as enrollment declined in Milwaukee's neighborhood schools and the number of voucher applications continued to increase. *This raises questions about whether traditional notions of competition among schools* explain these

increased scores in the two years immediately after the voucher plan was expanded.[18]

In other words, the competitive effect posited by voucher advocates did not appear to be having the anticipated impact.

Despite this point, the Friedman report suggests that the researchers need not have gone further with the second part of the study, even though the first analysis was only a replication and the authors explicitly raised questions about the very conclusions that the Friedman report tries to draw from their study.

But Carnoy and his colleagues also offered a second analysis, presenting results from their own original research, which took into account factors such as proximity, supply and demand. That is, instead of simply looking for impact on the entire Milwaukee school system (which the Friedman report later warns against), the researchers took a more sophisticated approach by examining factors thought to be important in creating competitive conditions.[19] The approach used in earlier studies was to compare the school district as a whole to other schools in Wisconsin that did not experience competition from vouchers.[20] Carnoy et al. used a more sensitive set of factors, such as nearness to private schools with spaces for voucher students, allowing them to determine which public schools faced the most competition and would thus be more likely to feel the competitive effects of vouchers.[21] From their second, more original and nuanced analysis, Carnoy et al. find as follows:

> [T]est score gains are generally *not* significantly related to various indicators of direct competition … [not] the number of private schools within a mile of a public school, nor the relative number of voucher places nearby, nor the relative number of voucher applications from the public school.[22]

Curiously, the Friedman report notes—but never quotes—this second analysis, dismissing it as unnecessary in light of the first, less sophisticated, analysis.

This treatment is particularly important because the Carnoy study is one of the few independent studies among the 17, and it appears to have been misrepresented. In fact, only 2 of the 17 studies were published in independent peer-reviewed journals. Three were published by the pro-voucher Hoover Institution's journal *Education Next*. Seven were released by other school-choice advocacy organizations.

In fact, the majority of the studies were produced by a very small group of people largely associated with these same school-choice advocacy organizations. For instance, more than half of the 17 reports were authored or co-authored by either Forster (the author of the current report), his previous co-authors on the topic, or others who have published through the

Friedman Foundation. Further, all but three of the 17 reports were written either by this group of people or by authors affiliated with other pro-voucher organizations such as the Hoover Institute or Harvard's Program on Educational Policy and Governance. The three remaining studies, authored by scholars at Stanford, Princeton, and Wisconsin-Madison, are the most rigorous (that is, generally analyzing student-level data) and find the most modest effects for choice.

Also noteworthy is the inclusion of the centuries-old "tuitioning" programs in Vermont and Maine, which existed long before Milton Friedman conceived of voucher policies in the modern sense. The tuitioning programs were adopted not for competition, but for convenience, so that towns did not have to build new schools. But they were included in the new report, nonetheless, probably because a report on them (by the Friedman Foundation) produced results that supported the pro-voucher thesis.[23] The new report seems to assume that the magic of competition is both generic and universal, generalizing findings on demographic differences in Washington DC, to Florida schools, and imputing competitive effects of vouchers to a program that was created almost a century before anyone had actually thought of the modern concept of private school "vouchers."

REVIEW OF THE REPORT'S METHODS

Because the report is a review, it does not use a methodology per se, other than the unspecified selection process for the inclusion of reviewed studies. However, it is worth discussing the conclusions drawn by those studies in the context of the standards and limitations that typically guide this type of research review.

In the past, the author of this Friedman report has repeatedly held up randomized studies as the "gold standard" for "empirical" research.[24] Because the nature of the competition question effectively precludes the use of randomization—studying competitive effects by randomly assigning schools or students to be affected by, or shielded from, voucher competition—none of the 17 studies meets that purported highest standard.[25] (Indeed, the author even indicates that one of the studies he uses in support of his thesis had serious shortcomings.)

Consequently, the studies cited in the report necessarily use less rigorous methods to study voucher effects. These methods involve constructing an appropriate comparison group with which to contrast gains at public schools believed to be affected by vouchers, and controlling for demographic and other factors that might confound the results. As the report acknowledges:

Student outcomes are affected by so many different influences—including demographic factors (income, race, family structure, etc.), school factors (type of school, teacher quality, etc.) and intangibles such as the level of enthusiasm parents and teachers invest in a child's education (p. 13, parentheses in the original).

However, the studies do not account for all of these possible variables, so general claims about the effects of vouchers based on those analyses are tenuous, at best. Indeed, when comparing schools with markedly different populations, there are too many possible influences on a school's or a student's achievement to be certain which ones are the cause of a relative gain (or loss) for a student, much less a school. The research designs that can realistically be applied to this question of competitive effects can control only for observable factors, and not for other important influences such as motivation, perseverance, or commitment to education.

The report contends that it is "cumbersome" to collect demographic data on students, so we should "consider what the broader body of evidence indicates about this question" (p. 25). Oddly, though, it then cites only an unspecified subset of studies on Florida, arguing that scores improved in the public schools, although there was "no movement of students in these schools" (p. 25). This is an amazing claim—that student populations were completely stable in these schools—and no evidence or support is offered.

REVIEW OF THE VALIDITY OF THE FINDINGS AND CONCLUSIONS

In addition to the concerns already discussed about assumptions, use of literature, and methodological limitations, there exist good reasons to question the validity of the report's conclusion that competition from vouchers causes public schools to improve their academic achievement. It is worth noting that this finding comes from an organization that bills itself as "the nation's leading voucher advocates" (p. 4). Because of its announced agenda on this issue, publications such as this would benefit greatly from undergoing a blinded peer review prior to publication, to identify any problems with data, methods and interpretations. Such peer review is typical in university-based research in order to ensure some objective measure of quality. The arcane (but key) details in these types of research reports often require a fair degree of trust from readers who lack technical methodological expertise.

Moreover, the report makes an argument for the immediate effects of vouchers on the students who use them, contending that "[s]chool vouchers ... are among the most prominent and successful reforms in the education field" (p. 10). This is followed by the claim that there is "a substantial body of random-assignment research on the academic achievement of students who are offered vouchers, and it consistently finds that vouchers improve student achievement" (p. 13). Once again, on closer inspection, this "body of research" is not so "substantial," having been written mostly by the same group of advocates the report cites for its competition claims, and having been questioned and challenged by other scholars.[26]

Likewise, when discussing the impact of voucher programs, the report contends that "vouchers make public schools better off financially"—citing another report put out by the Friedman Foundation for Educational Choice.[27] I have reviewed the Foundation's prior work on this topic and found these conclusions to be more ideological than evidence-based.[28] In fact, the claim defies the basic logic advanced by the Friedman Foundation: if public schools are generally made better off financially when they lose students to vouchers, then they have a disincentive to improve performance in order to keep students, rather than the positive competitive effects described and endorsed in this and other Friedman reports.

Anticipating that the report's conclusions themselves might be in question, the author attempts to disprove three alternative explanations for improvements in public school achievement. For one of these, the statistical phenomenon called regression toward the mean, the author repeats a flawed argument he has made previously[29] and that I have discussed previously.[30]

The report also attacks the notion that the improved test scores in public schools, as found in the reviewed studies, might be due to choice selection effects. In particular, the report rejects the possibility that more advantaged students stay in public schools, while more difficult-to-educate students use vouchers to enroll in private schools[31]: "vouchers would have to be attracting participants disproportionately from among the lowest performing students. Instead of taking away the best students, as so many opponents of vouchers claim, on this theory vouchers would be taking away the worst students" (p. 24). However, the report names none of these "many opponents of vouchers" and the very theory that Forster now dismisses is one he himself made when he tried to explain away higher public school achievement in another study: "A much more likely explanation for [these] results is that when students enter private schools, they tend to have test scores a little lower than other students of their race and socioeconomic status."[32]

Readers should understand that the rules of any given voucher policy, combined with neighborhood demographics and other factors, are likely to affect the nature of the group receiving vouchers. So the voucher system in one district may draw disproportionately from lower-scoring students, while vouchers in another district may do the opposite. The "voucher effect" is not uniform. Each system should be empirically studied before drawing firm conclusions about its effects.

In rejecting the alternative explanation, the Friedman report includes no data on the demographic composition of the private schools accepting vouchers in these studies, but takes the position that the "best available analyses of this question have found voucher applicants to be very similar to the population of students eligible for vouchers in terms of demographics and educational background" (p. 11). To support this, the report cites studies of voucher programs in Washington, New York and Dayton—not Florida, Milwaukee or the vast majority of the other cases used in this report. Furthermore, the report does not address other direct evidence about voucher applicants indicating that there are differences from non-applicants in terms of parental education level, for instance,[33] not to mention "unobservable" factors such as motivation that distinguish applicants from non-applicants.

The report also questions the possibility that public schools improve not because of voucher competition, but because of the "stigma" of being labeled as a failing school (which, in some programs such as the Florida A-Plus program, make the school's students eligible to receive vouchers).[34] The report cites evidence from Florida, where a labeling device was in place both before and after the voucher program was introduced, to show that vouchers had an effect above and beyond the stigma effect. One problem with this approach is that it compares two time periods, so other factors besides vouchers might have had an impact on achievement. Furthermore, the most sophisticated examination of this question in Florida found the labeling device had a larger impact on achievement than did the competitive effect of vouchers, contrary to the Friedman report's contention.[35] Nevertheless, the report claims that "there do not seem to be reasonable grounds for attributing the positive results from the A+ program to a stigma effect" (p. 26).

Finally, the report notes the obvious response to its main contention: if vouchers are having such a beneficial impact, then why are the urban districts with voucher programs still performing at a low level? "Among those who wish to distract the public from this large body of high-quality scientific evidence, one of the most common strategies is to complain that public schools in places like Milwaukee are still failing to educate so many of their students" (p. 30). Although the report never says so, this complaint has come most prominently from notable voucher *supporters* who are starting to question their faith in vouchers in view of their less-than stellar track record.[36] The report ignores this—indeed, it includes no citations in support of this claim—and simply argues that there are too many variables to discern the impact of a voucher program on a district (an admonition the report otherwise disregards when making claims about voucher effects). Still, this is an interesting question, and the fact that it is a legitimate question strongly suggests that the competitive effects of vouchers are indeed quite modest and difficult to attribute to them with any certainty.

All this is not to say that vouchers have no effect on the performance of public schools threatened by vouchers. Indeed, some reputable scholars cited in the Friedman report have found a beneficial impact in some instances. But such findings suggest a much more mixed and modest impact than the new report would have us believe.

THE REPORT'S USEFULNESS FOR GUIDANCE OF POLICY AND PRACTICE

Ultimately, the Friedman report responds to the concern about voucher programs' failure to benefit urban districts in a very different way than have those voucher supporters who have come to conclude that the benefits of these programs have been much less than expected. Instead, this report recommends expanding voucher programs so that their purported effects may be increased.[37] In many ways, this logic is similar to that of market fundamentalists who, in the face of a global economic crisis widely considered to be caused by deregulated markets, argue that the remedy is further deregulation and more markets. The report also suggests that while expanding voucher programs, their focus on providing more equitable access for disadvantaged children should be removed, blaming the failure of voucher programs to have a larger impact on the means-tested criteria and "limits on families' ability to supplement" vouchers.[38] In doing so, the report does not directly address the fact that after the Florida and Milwaukee programs were expanded, evidence— including Forster's own data on Florida[39]—indicates that any positive effect of the programs on public school performance had diminished after that expansion.

This report begins—in its title—and ends with the notion that voucher programs do no harm, that these programs are a "win-win" in that they help students who use vouchers as well as the public schools those students leave. This claim is common in voucher advocacy,[40] often used as a defensive device when results are smaller than anticipated—"everyone wins, and even if they don't, nobody loses." Or, as expressed in this report: "No empirical study has ever found that vouchers had a negative impact on public schools" (p. 5; see also p. 34). In truth, the record is very thin. While many studies have examined the effects of vouchers on students who use them, few studies of any quality have been designed to measure the effects of vouchers on students who do not use them. We do not know how individual students, particularly non-choosers, are affected by voucher programs. And this new report does not help answer that question.

In the end, what this report offers is an overview of studies, the majority of which dealt with one state (Florida) where the voucher program has been terminated after being ruled unconstitutional.[41] However, the overview seems designed to build a pro-voucher argument rather than an even-handed presentation of research.

NOTES AND REFERENCES

1. Forster, G. (2009). *A win-win solution: The empirical evidence on how vouchers affect public schools.* Indianapolis, IN: Friedman Foundation for Educational Choice.

2. Friedman, M. (1995). *Public schools: Make them private* (Briefing Paper No. 23). Washington, DC: Cato Institute.

3. Greene, J. P., & Winters, M. A. (2006). *An evaluation of the effects of DC's voucher program on public school achievement and racial integration after one year.* New York, NY: Manhattan Institute.

4. Brown, D. J. (2002, May). *Competition for students: Spirals and school marketing.* Paper presented at the School Choice: Public Education at the Crossroads, University of Calgary, Calgary, AB. In the United Kingdom, these are known as "sink schools."

5. See, for example, Camilli, G., & Bulkley, K. (2001). Critique of "an evaluation of the Florida A-plus accountability and school choice program." *Education Policy Analysis Archives, 9*(7).

6. Lubienski, C. (2007). Marketing schools: Consumer goods and competitive incentives for consumer information. *Education and Urban Society, 40*(1), 118-141.

7. Braun, H. (2007, March/April). Are private schools better than public schools? *Principal, 86,* 22-25.
    Braun, H., Jenkins, F., & Grigg, W. (2006). *Comparing private schools and public schools using hierarchical linear modeling* (No. 2006-461). Washington, DC: National Center for Education Statistics.
    Carbonaro, W. (2006). Public-private differences in achievement among kindergarten students: Differences in learning opportunities and student outcomes. *American Journal of Education, 113*(1), 31-65.
    Lubienski, C., Lubienski, S. T., & Crane, C. (2008). What do we know about school effectiveness? Academic gains in public and private schools. *Phi Delta Kappan, 89*(9), 689-695.
    Lubienski, S. T., & Lubienski, C. (2006). School sector and academic achievement: A multi-level analysis of NAEP mathematics data. *American Educational Research Journal, 43*(4), 651-698.
    Reardon, S. F., Cheadle, J. E., & Robinson, J. P. (2009). The effects of Catholic school attendance on reading and math achievement in kindergarten

through fifth grade. *Journal of Research on Educational Effectiveness, 2*(1), 45-87.

Taningco, M. T. V. (2006). *Assessing the effects of parental decisions about school type and involvement on early elementary education.* Unpublished PhD dissertation, Pardee Rand Graduate School, Santa Monica, CA.

Wenglinsky, H. (2007). *Are private high schools better academically than public high schools?* Washington, DC: Center on Education Policy.

See also Forster, G. (2005, May 12). "F" for failure. *National Review Online.* Retrieved Dec. 22, 2005, from http://www.nationalreview.com/comment/forster200505120815.asp

8.   Chakrabarti, R. (2004). Closing the gap. *Education Next* (Summer).

Chakrabarti, R. (2006). Can increasing private school participation and monetary loss in a voucher program affect public school performance? Evidence from Milwaukee. *Journal of Public Economics, 92*(5-6), 1371-1393.

Chakrabarti, R. (2007). *Vouchers, public school response, and the role of incentives: Evidence from Florida* (Federal Reserve Bank of New York Staff Report No. 306). New York, NY: Federal Reserve Bank of New York.

Figlio, D. N., & Rouse, C. E. (2004). *Do accountability and voucher threats improve low-performing schools?* Cambridge, MA: National Bureau of Economic Research.

Forster, G. (2008a). *Lost opportunity: An empirical analysis of how vouchers affected Florida public schools.* Indianapolis, IN: Friedman Foundation for Educational Choice.

Greene, J. P., & Winters, M. A. (2004). Competition passes the test. *Education Next* (Summer).

Rouse, C. E., Hannaway, J., Goldhaber, D., & Figlio, D. N. (2007). *Feeling the Florida heat? How low-performing schools respond to voucher and accountability pressure* (Working Paper No. 13): National Center for Analysis of Longitudinal Data in Education Research. This report was reviewed by the Think Tank Review Project: Betebenner, D. (2008). *Review of "Feeling the Florida Heat? How Low-Performing Schools Respond to Voucher and Accountability Pressure."* Boulder and Tempe: Education and the Public Interest Center & Education Policy Research Unit.

West, M. R., & Peterson, P. E. (2006). The efficacy of choice threats within school accountability systems: Results from legislatively induced experiments. *Economic Journal, 116*(March), C46-C62.

9.   Greene, J. P., & Winters, M. A. (2008). *The effect of special-education vouchers on public school achievement: Evidence from Florida's McKay scholarship program.* New York, NY: Manhattan Institute. John Yun's review of this report for the Think Tank Review Project appears in Chapter Two of this Book.

10.   Carnoy, M., Adamson, F., Chudgar, A., Luschei, T. F., & Witte, J. F. (2007). *Vouchers and public school performance: A case study of the Milwaukee parental choice program.* Washington, DC: Economic Policy Institute.

Chakrabarti (2006); see note 8.

Chakrabarti, R. (2008). *Impact of voucher design on public school performance: Evidence from Florida and Milwaukee voucher programs* (Staff Report No. 315). New York, NY: Federal Reserve Bank of New York.

Greene, J. P., & Forster, G. (2002). *Rising to the challenge: The effect of school choice on public schools in Milwaukee and San Antonio* (Civic Bulletin No. 27). New York, NY: Manhattan Institute for Policy Research.

Hoxby, C. M. (2001). Rising tide. *Education Next, 1*(4).

11. Greene & Forster (2002).

12. Forster, G. (2008b). *Promising start: An empirical analysis of how EdChoice vouchers affect Ohio public schools.* Indianapolis, IN: Friedman Foundation for Educational Choice.

13. Greene & Winters (2006); see note 3.

14. Hammons, C. (2002). *The effects of town tuitioning in Vermont and Maine.* Indianapolis, IN: Friedman Foundation for Educational Choice.

15. Forster, G. (2009); see note 1; p. 17, quoting Carnoy et al; see note 10.

16. The quote is from page 2 of Carnoy et al.'s Executive Summary.

17. Caroline Hoxby conducted the initial study on this case, but some of her other work on school choice has been criticized when other researchers were unable to replicate her findings or uncovered errors in the data, methods or both; see

    Rothstein, J. (2007). Does competition among public schools benefit students and taxpayers? A comment on Hoxby (2000). *American Economic Review, 97*(5), 2026-2037.

    Roy, J., & Mishel, L. (2005). *Advantage none: Re-examining Hoxby's finding of charter school benefits* (Briefing Paper No. 158). Washington, DC: Economic Policy Institute.

18. Carnoy et al. (2007); see note 10; p. 2, emphases added.

19. Lubienski, C., Gulosino, C., & Weitzel, P. (2009). School choice and competitive incentives: Mapping the distribution of educational opportunities across local education markets. *American Journal of Education, 115*(4), 601-647.

    Sandström, F. M., & Bergström, F. (2002). *School vouchers in practice: Competition won't hurt you!* (Working Paper No. 578). Stockholm: Research Institute of Industrial Economics.

20. The voucher program was limited to Milwaukee. However, this is a questionable basis for comparison. Competition can be generated by other factors besides vouchers. For instance, private schools can attract students from more affluent families, and districts have been losing students to charter schools since the state passed authorizing legislation in 1993.

21. The Friedman report indirectly acknowledges this same point. In explaining why vouchers do not seem to have a discernible impact on districts, the report argues *against* using the whole district as a basis for gauging the impact of vouchers: "the overall performance of a school system can never by itself provide a reliable guide to whether any one factor (such as vouchers) is having a positive effect" (p. 30).

22. Carnoy, et al. (2007); see note 10; p. 2, emphases and parentheses in the original.

23. Hammons (2002); see note 14.

24. Forster, G. (2007). *Monopoly vs. markets: The empirical evidence on private schools and school choice.* Indianapolis, IN: Friedman Foundation. pp. 12, 16,

39, 43. The Think Tank Review Project's review of this report by Clive Belfield appears as Chapter Four. See also Forster, (2005); see note 7.

25. I would disagree that randomization is the sole type of methodology that meets the highest standards; see Lubienski, C., Weitzel, P., & Lubienski, S. T. (2009). Is there a "consensus" on school choice and achievement? Advocacy research and the emerging political economy of knowledge production. *Educational Policy, 23*(1), 161-193.

26. For example, see Krueger, A. B., & Zhu, P. (2004). Inefficiency, subsample selection bias, and nonrobustness: A response to Paul E. Peterson & William G. Howell. *American Behavioral Scientist, 47*(5), 718-728.
Metcalf, K. K. (1998, September 23). Commentary—advocacy in the guise of science: How preliminary research on the Cleveland voucher program was "reanalyzed" to fit a preconception. *Education Week, 18*, 34, 39.
Metcalf, K. K., & Tait, P. A. (1999, September). Free market policies and public education: What is the cost of choice? *Phi Delta Kappan, 81*, 65-75.
Witte, J. F. (1996). *Reply to Greene, Peterson and du: "The effectiveness of school choice in Milwaukee: A secondary analysis of data from the program's evaluation."* Madison, WI: Department of Political Science and The Robert La Follette Institute of Public Affairs, University of Wisconsin-Madison.

27. Forster, G. (2009); see note 1; citing: Aud, S. (2007). *Education by the numbers: The fiscal effect of school choice programs, 1990-2006.* Indianapolis, IN: Friedman Foundation for Educational Choice.
See the review in Chapter Eight of this Book: Baker, B. (2007). *Review of "School Choice by the Numbers: The Fiscal Effect of School Choice Programs 1990-2006."* Boulder and Tempe: Education and the Public Interest Center & Education Policy Research Unit.

28. See the review in Chapter 7 of this book: Lubienski, C. (2006). *Review of "Spreading freedom and saving money: The fiscal impact of the DC. Voucher program" from the Cato institute and Milton & Rose D. Friedman Foundation* (No. EPSL-0602-118-EPRU). Tempe, AZ: Educational Policy Research Unit, Education Policy Studies Laboratory, Arizona State University.

29. Forster, (2008b); see note 12; p. 26.

30. Lubienski, C. (2008). *Review of "Promising start: An empirical analysis of how EdChoice vouchers affect Ohio public schools" from the Milton & Rose D. Friedman Foundation.* Boulder, CO and Tempe, AZ: Education and the Public Interest Center & Education Policy Research Unit.

31. Recall, however, that no data on private school achievement or composition were included in the Friedman report.

32. Forster, G. (2005); see note 7.

33. Witte, J. F. (2000). *The market approach to education: An analysis of America's first voucher program.* Princeton, NJ: Princeton University Press.

34. Camilli & Bulkley (2001); see note 5.

35. Figlio & Rouse (2004); see note 8.

36. Dodenhoff, D. (2007). *Fixing the Milwaukee public schools: The limits of parent-driven reform* (WPRI Report). Thiensville, WI: Wisconsin Policy Research Institute.

Stern, S. (2008, Winter). School choice isn't enough. *City Journal, 18,* 1. Retrieved April 22, 2009, from http://www.city-journal.org/2008/18_1_instructional_reform.html

37.   One wonders if Forster would apply this same logic to other educational programs such as Head Start or class-size reductions.

38.   Forster (2009); see note 1; p. 31.

39.   Forster (2008a); see note 8.

40.   Greene, J. P. (2000). *A survey of results from voucher experiments: Where we are and what we know* (Civic Report No. 11). New York: Center for Civic Innovation, Manhattan Institute.

Greene, J. P. (2001). A survey of results from voucher experiments: Where we are and what we know. In C. R. Hepburn (Ed.), *Can the market save our schools?* (pp. 121-149). Vancouver, BC: The Fraser Institute.

Wolf, P. J. (2008). School voucher programs: What the research says about parental school choice. *Brigham Young University Law Review, 2008*(1), 415-446.

41.   As was Arizona's program in March 2009.

CHAPTER 2

THE EFFECT OF SPECIAL EDUCATION VOUCHERS ON PUBLIC SCHOOL ACHIEVEMENT

John T. Yun

Review of Jay P. Greene & Marcus Winters's "The Effect of Special Education Vouchers on Public School Achievement: Evidence from Florida's McKay Scholarship Program," published by the Manhattan Institute for Policy Research. This is a modified version of a review originally published on May 22, 2008.

INTRODUCTION

A new report released by the Manhattan Institute for Education Policy, *The Effect of Special Education Vouchers on Public School Achievement: Evidence from Florida's McKay Scholarship Program*, written by Jay P. Greene and Marcus Winters, attempts to examine how competition introduced through school vouchers affects student outcomes in public schools.[1] An important contribution of this report to the literature of voucher competition publications is its focus on students who are enrolled in special education

Think Tank Research Quality: Lessons for Policy Makers, the Media, and the Public, pp. 23–32

programs. However, this contribution is outweighed by errors in methods and analysis. In particular, the report does not include a clear explanation ("specification") of the statistical model chosen; the analysis fails to take into account alternative explanations; and it includes unsubstantiated assumptions about the direction of possible selection bias.[2]

Florida's McKay Scholarship Program is open to any student in the state who has been classified with a learning disability. These vouchers pay the full amount that the public school would have received had the student enrolled in it, or the lesser amount of full tuition at the chosen private school. Accordingly, for students who wish to enroll in high-tuition private schools, the difference in tuition would be the responsibility of the parents or guardians. Under Florida's normal funding system, public schools would receive different amounts of money depending on the nature of the disability. According to the report, in 2006-2007 McKay Scholarships ranged anywhere from $5,039 to $21,907, with an average of $7,206. This fact becomes important with regard to assumptions the authors make in their discussion of possible selection bias in their analysis.[3]

Given the special education focus of the McKay Program, the report addresses some important issues concerning voucher-based school choice programs involving this very important group of students. However, there are important weaknesses in the analysis and interpretations of the data that undermine any practical use of the results and conclusions.

Most troubling are fundamental problems with variable and model specifications (as explained below). In addition, the report includes critical unsubstantiated assumptions that lead to unwarranted weight given to estimates. The report does appropriately note the serious problems with selection bias in any analysis of this type, and it does acknowledge, in the technical version of the report, that the authors' methodology does not fully correct for it.[4] Yet, despite this disclaimer about the study's limitations, the report subsequently presents arguments suggesting that the authors can in fact anticipate the direction of possible bias in their analysis, an assertion that I challenge later in this review.

Without any tests or appropriate literature substantiating these assumptions, the report leads the reader down a path with a predetermined conclusion: that vouchers have a positive competition effect. Florida's McKay Scholarships, the report tells us, improve the educational outcomes of those special education students who stay in public schools, choosing not to use a voucher. The theory of action behind this conclusion is that increased competition leads public schools to improve their services or programs

If valid, such conclusions have key policy implications. However, the Manhattan report inadequately addresses several critically important issues, calling the report's conclusions into serious question.

FINDINGS AND CONCLUSIONS OF THE REPORT

The scope of the report is narrowly focused and is very brief given the complexity of the analysis attempted, leaving many questions unanswered and making it difficult to thoroughly examine the methods used or conclusions reached. The nation has seen a vigorous debate about whether private school vouchers promote competition between public and private schools, and more importantly whether that competition increases student outcomes for both groups of students (those who leave the public sector for private schools and those who remain).

The authors suggest that their analysis is designed to directly address this question by providing estimates of the effect on public school productivity of offering private school vouchers to students with disabilities. The authors contend that Florida's McKay Scholarship Program provides an excellent proving ground for this analysis because it is the largest private school voucher program in the nation and because it has seen a large increase in participation—rising to approximately 4.5% of eligible students (in the 2006-2007 school year, about 18,200 of nearly 400,000 students with disabilities in Florida).

The authors' main conclusion is that there is some evidence suggesting that outcomes for students in public school special education programs improve with increased exposure to voucher opportunities.[5] The authors estimated relatively small effect sizes of 0.05 and 0.07 standard deviation units in mathematics and reading scores (respectively) for students with specific learning disabilities and average exposure to voucher-accepting private schools. (Exposure to private school vouchers is defined at the number of schools that accept vouchers within a 5- or 10-mile radius). The authors assert that these results are likely lower-bounds and that the actual benefits are likely greater since any selection bias that may exist is likely to bias the estimates downward.

Yet, these estimates and this conclusion are based on poor model specifications, unclear analytic decisions, and questionable selection bias assumptions.

THE REPORT'S USE OF RESEARCH LITERATURE

In a very brief discussion, the authors characterize the findings in the research literature on competition in a relatively balanced way. They suggest that there is conflicting evidence on the question of whether public school outcomes improve when exposed to greater competition, either from the private sector or from public sector choice alternatives such as charter schools. In addition, they mention that several studies have found, using different methodologies, positive outcomes of Florida's accountability system, including its voucher provisions.[6]

However, in a different section of this report, where the authors discuss possible selection bias in their analysis, they use supporting literature that, while somewhat appropriate, does not fully characterize the unique issues faced by students with disabilities in this policy environment. This exclusive use of tangentially appropriate literature gives the superficial but incorrect impression that the explanations of possible bias raised in this literature are valid and complete.

In addition, the report completely omits any literature about the testing of students with disabilities and how accommodations may affect the results and outcomes of their study. The lack of substantive knowledge about the group examined may seriously compromise the validity of the report's findings.

REVIEW OF THE REPORT'S METHODS

The main text of the technical report describes the data used as the universe of public school data from Florida between the years of 2000-2001 and 2004-2005 (5 years of data), but some tables show data from fewer years.

In addition, the report's key exposure variable (number of private schools accepting vouchers within 5 and 10 miles of the school) is seriously flawed. In urban areas, multiple public schools likely share the same pool of voucher-accepting private schools. A private school "competing" with three public schools is likely to have a weaker effect (all other things being equal) on any given school than a private school competing with only one public school. The supply of voucher vacancies depends on both the number of spots available in the private schools and the pool of potential public school students near those schools. This suggests that the number of private schools willing to accept vouchers is less important than the number of available spots relative to the number of available public school students who could fill those spots. None of this is accounted for in any of the models estimated in this report.

Future researchers engaging in such analyses may want to use, as a measure, the number of spots available in the private sector relative to the number of public school special education students in similar grade levels within a chosen distance. Such a measure would be a much stronger indicator of the local supply of voucher spots available, since it would compare actual spots that could be taken by students in that particular school.

Another concern is that the exposure measure used in the report is actually measuring how urban the area surrounding the student is rather than the supply of voucher spots. This confounding of the two variables (urbanicity and exposure to vouchers) is due to the fact that urban schools would naturally have more public and private schools in close proximity to one another. Thus, any estimated effect attributed to the exposure variable would be partially due to the public school's location in an urban area, relative to a rural or suburban public school. This is particularly important because we know that special education students in urban schools are more likely to be in restricted environments and less likely to receive rigorous curricula. Such a modeling problem could be easily addressed by including appropriate geographical control variables (such as whether the area in which the student is attending school is urban, rural or suburban). This simple approach is not explored in the report, nor is any reason provided for this omission.[7]

Achievement Analysis

In the achievement regression models, the report uses student scores on state standardized reading and mathematics tests as the outcome in an individual level, fixed-effects analysis[8] to control for unobserved individual characteristics. It also includes a district fixed-effect variable, unspecified student characteristics, dummy variables indicating type of disability, the voucher exposure variable, and the interaction between disability type and exposure. The authors argue that the interaction between disability type and voucher exposure plus the main effect of voucher exposure represent the average effect of the McKay Program.

There are several problems with the model. The report never states which individual characteristics were included in the analysis. Perhaps more importantly, the choice of a district fixed effect is curious given the hypothesis that school rather than district changes were responsible for improvements in student test scores. The district variable, particularly in Florida (where countywide districts are the norm), simply does not make much sense as a control.

In addition, the authors never clarify what test-score metric they use for their outcome. Florida reports both a developmental scale for their examinations as well as a criterion-referenced scaled score. The developmental score is useful for measuring changes in an individual student year to year; the criterion-referenced score is useful for comparing cohorts of students in the same grade from year to year. The appropriate measure to use here would be the developmental score, but the report does not state which is used.[9]

Further, the sample in this analysis uses all grades (3-10) over all the years (presumably 2000-2004). This choice of analytical frameworks virtually assures that there will be serious issues of attrition, since 10th grade students in 2000 will only appear in the dataset one time, and 9th grade students in 2000 will appear only two times, and so on. This may account for the fact that the average number of observations for students is only about 2.5 years for each of the achievement regressions, even though the dataset covers 5 school years. This choice may again lead to biases in the estimates; however, it is unclear which direction this bias would lead.

Selection Bias

The report includes a useful outline of various types of selection bias that might be present in these estimates. However, the authors' assumptions about the directionality and mechanisms driving the bias are questionable, with many plausible mechanisms ignored and untested.

Attrition/Choice Bias

Non-random attrition from the sample is a critical problem for research such as this. The authors are attempting to determine whether the exit of students to private school and the threat of that exit affect the test scores of those who remain in public school. This begs the question of whether a subsequent increase in the scores of public school special education students is simply due to low-scoring students exiting the public system with vouchers, which would upwardly bias estimates of the effectiveness of the McKay program. Alternatively, it is possible that students of higher ability exit with vouchers, which would downwardly bias the estimated McKay program effect.

The authors suggest that Florida's private schools are "creaming" the best students from the public school systems. Accordingly, their estimates of the McKay program effect would likely be a lower bound (underestimated). Unfortunately, the authors fail to consider factors other than "creaming." For instance, the students who take the voucher are unlikely to be satisfied with the public system and may be performing below their potential. One could also argue that relatively high-performing special education students would be less likely to transfer out of the schools in which they were performing better than their peers. Also, the No Child Left Behind Act (NCLB) provides an incentive for public schools to encourage lower-performing special education students to take advantage of the voucher program and transfer out.[10] Such transfers would have two positive main effects under NCLB for the public school: they could lower the number of special education students sufficiently so as to take that subgroup below the reporting threshold for inclusion in NCLB calculations, and they could leave behind higher-performing special education students, helping the school's average subgroup score meet Adequate Yearly Progress targets.

Finally, since the severity of the disability is related to the size of the voucher, there is a potential incentive for new private schools to open (or existing private schools to broaden their scope) and admit students with more severe disabilities, likely lowering test scores.[11]

Each of these scenarios would result in an upward bias of the parameters estimated in the report (an overestimation of the voucher competition effect), rather than the downward bias that was conclusively set forth in the Manhattan report.

Assignment Bias

The authors also discuss the possibility of bias in assignment of students to special education by public schools. They suggest that these schools, fearful of competition, might classify fewer students as eligible for special education since that would qualify students for the voucher. This, they argue, would lead to fewer students with mild disabilities being placed in special education, leading to an attenuation of the voucher effect. An alternative scenario for this assignment bias could be that schools are more likely to assign students that they wanted to leave the school, such as those with behavior disorders. This may lead to the assignment of more students to special education, and those students may be relatively high-performing academically (relative to other special education students), thus biasing the effect upwards. Raising such additional possibilities is not intended as a criticism of those that the report includes. Rather, the criticism is that the possibilities treated seriously in the report are only those that support the conclusion that the results underestimate the competition effect.

Supply Bias

As the report explains, private schools could be choosing to accept vouchers based on the type of nearby public schools. One type of supply bias would occur if private schools were more likely to accept vouchers if located near public schools that are doing a relatively good job with their special education students. The private schools could more effectively skim the cream. Alternatively, if private schools located near low-performing public schools were more likely to accept vouchers, they may be able to attract dissatisfied students. Again, the authors argue that the transferring students would be high-performing relative to their peers.

Both of these alternatives, argue the authors, would bias their estimates downward since more academically able students would be leaving public schools, while less able students remained. This formulation of supply bias also relies on the premise that private schools skim the cream from the public system, but as we have discussed in previous sections, this contention is far from proven with regard to special education students. Private schools may have reasons for accepting lower-performing students, while the various motivations of those students and their families, as well as those of the public schools and their employees, also play a complicated role.

REVIEW OF THE VALIDITY OF THE FINDINGS AND CONCLUSIONS

The report is on its most solid ground when it describes the challenges in performing an analysis such as this—an analysis that uses general administrative data and does not include tracking information on the students who leave for the private system.

However, the report's findings rest on very weak foundations. The variables are vaguely defined and the models are poorly specified. The report also fails to take into account the possible effect of testing accommodations. The assumptions employed to explain the possible direction of selection bias is weak at best. And all of the conclusions rest on models that use a very weak measure of private school voucher supply. Moreover, consider the following two additional concerns.

First, the report does not sufficiently describe how such small numbers of students leaving public schools (an average of four per public school in Florida) would encourage such substantial changes in the behavior of public schools. Nor do the authors discuss how the mere presence of schools (absent large defections of special education students from the public schools) would trigger immediate changes in public school behavior that would be quickly reflected in student test scores. The report does not explain how public school officials would know how many private schools in the local area were accepting vouchers or the level of capacity in these private schools to enroll additional students with disabilities.

These issues of time lag and information gathering become important when one realizes that the number of voucher recipients was quite modest until nearly halfway through the sampled time period. In order for the hypothesized competitive effects to have caused improvements in nearby public schools, those schools would have had to almost immediately receive the signal that special education students were leaving their schools and then adjust their practices accordingly, with the effects of these changes then very quickly affecting test scores. Such a series of events seems unlikely given, for instance, the difficulty schools are having meeting even the general testing expectations of NCLB.

Second, the authors fail to account for the fact that special education students are exactly the group for which these standardized test scores have the least reliability given that, depending on the severity and type of disability, different accommodations are available to students. An important alternative explanation for the authors' findings could be that the longer special education students are in a school the better the school is at finding appropriate accommodations—which would allow them to score better on the state standardized test.

USEFULNESS OF THE REPORT FOR GUIDANCE OF POLICY AND PRACTICE

This report is a useful starting point for discussions and research around school vouchers for students with disabilities. However, the analyses are so vague and the approach so flawed that their only practical use is as an initial template for addressing the important issues of selection bias for studies such as this. Any attempt to use this report for decision-making or policy evaluation, prior to validation using different methods and more robust approaches, should be viewed with extreme skepticism.

NOTES AND REFERENCES

1. Green, J. P., & Winters, M. (2008). *The effect of special education vouchers on public school achievement: Evidence from Florida's McKay Scholarship Program.* Manhattan Institute, Retrieved May 18, 2008, from http://www .manhattan-institute.org/pdf/ Effect_of_Vouchers_for_SE_Students_on_Public_School_Achievement _2-19-08.pdf (Technical Version)
2. The Manhattan Institute released two versions of this report—a "general release" report and a more detailed version (hereinafter, the "technical version") made available on the Manhattan Institute website, also titled, "The Effect of Special Education Vouchers on Public School Achievement: Evidence from Florida's McKay Scholarship Program." Retrieved May 18, 2008, from http://www.manhattan-institute.org/pdf /Effect_of_Vouchers_for_SE_Students_on_Public_School_Achievement_2- 19-08.pdf. This review is based on the technical version of the report.
3. Selection bias is defined as bias in estimates due to how samples are selected and are unrelated to the actual underlying phenomenon that is being estimated. For instance, in the case of the McKay Scholarships, students who receive the vouchers and leave the system are only included in early years of the Manhattan analysis. If these students are different in some way from those who stay (which is quite likely), then estimates of special education students' progress are likely to be biased. The direction of that bias is unclear and there is no attempt in this analysis to determine it.

4. "Though our ability to evaluate the progress of individual students over time through the use of panel-data with individual fixed effects may help to mitigate those sample selection issues by accounting for unobserved student heterogeneity, these techniques do not account for non-random attrition entirely. Unfortunately there are no variables available in our dataset that could serve as a reasonable instrument to account for these sample selection problems, and thus we are unable to correct for this bias statistically" (p. 13 of the technical version).

5. The authors go further in their *Washington Times* editorial comments, writing, for example, "What we know from our study is that rather than harming public schools, vouchers improve the education that they provide to their disabled students." Retrieved May 20, 2008, from http://washingtontimes.com/article/20080429/EDITORIAL/399369326. This sort of causal statement cannot be supported by the analyses reported in the Manhattan study.

6. Damian Betebenner wrote a think tank review of one such study. See Betebenner, D. (2008, Jan. 15). *Review of "Feeling the Florida Heat? How Low-Performing Schools Respond to Voucher and Accountability Pressure."* Boulder, CO and Tempe, AZ: Education and the Public Interest Center & Education Policy Research Unit. Retrieved May 20, 2008, from http://epicpolicy.org/thinktank/review-feeling-florida-heat-how low-performing -schools-respond-voucher-and-accountability-

7. A possible reason for the choice of number of schools could have been an extension of a common approach used to determine probability of enrolling in private schools: distance to the nearest private school. Why this measure was not employed, but the density measure was employed, is unclear.

8. Fixed-effects analyses are used when there are multiple observations clustered in some way (such as multiple observations for a single individual, or many observations within a single school, which is the situation in this analysis). This clustering presents a problem since observations clustered in this way violate the assumption in ordinary linear regressions that all observations be independent of one another. Fixed-effects provide a way to take into account the clustering of observations by looking only at deviations within the clusters around the means of the clustered groups.

9. In subsequent contacts with the authors, they confirmed that they used the developmental scores in their analysis. However, failure to include such a critical piece of information in the text of the report is a critical oversight and contributes to the lack of clarity throughout the report.

10. Note that this is a discussion of incentives and of potential selection bias scenarios that should be considered; it is not an accusation that any public school educators are engaged in such "counseling out."

11. The nature and extent of this incentive would depend on the financial and other costs of educating a given student or category of students, in addition to the value of the voucher.

PART 2

Private School Supremacy and Voucher Achievement Gains

In arguments promoting vouchers, it is widely assumed that students will benefit from the ability to attend private rather than public schools. The studies reviewed in this section explore that assumption.

In Chapter 3, reviewer Jaekyung Lee compares two reports that use longitudinal data bases to investigate the question of whether private schools outperform public schools. The first is *Monopoly Versus Markets: The Empirical Evidence on Private Schools and School Choice* (2007), published by the Milton & Rose D. Friedman Foundation (MFF) and authored by MFF senior fellow Greg Forster. Using Educational Longitudinal Study data, Forster found that private schools significantly outperform public schools. The second, *Are Private High Schools Better Academically than Public High Schools?* (2007), was written by Harold Wenglinsky and released by the Center on Education Policy (CEP); it relied on data from the National Education Longitudinal Study. Wenglinsky found that low-income students from urban settings who attend private schools generally receive neither an immediate benefit in academics nor any long term advantage in the likelihood of attending college, experiencing job satisfaction, or engaging in civic life.

Think Tank Research Quality: Lessons for Policy Makers, the Media, and the Public, pp. 33–36

These discrepant findings from studies that share notable commonalities are a major reason Lee takes up the two studies in tandem. He determines the CEP study to be the more methodologically sound and therefore finds no reason to question the CEP report's finding that there is no appreciable difference between private and public school for low-income urban students. However, he also points out that the data and analyses in the MFF study provide little support for its conclusion of a private school benefit. This review includes Lee's independent cross-examination of the two data sources. His analysis of the CEP data indicates that the public-private high school gaps in math achievement gain scores were almost null; his analysis of the MFF data indicates results too small to be practically significant. Therefore, the seemingly divergent findings and conclusions at the first glance were largely due to different interpretations rather than real differences in the results.

Chapter 4 presents reviewer Clive Belfield's analysis of *Markets vs. Monopolies in Education: A Global Review of the Evidence* (2008), authored by Andrew Coulson and published by the Cato Institute. Coulson examined a collection of previously published research from a variety of countries (including the United States) comparing private and public school outcomes. He concluded that the literature demonstrated an advantage for private schools. Belfield finds multiple problems with the methodology in this study and concludes that "this report does little if anything" to help answer the question of whether international evidence indicates private school superiority. Among the most serious weaknesses in the Cato report is that, while it purported to present a global picture, the international studies included hardly offered a representative global picture. Of the 55 studies included in the analysis, for example, 23 examined market reforms in Chile. Moreover, many of the studies included were not peer-reviewed or even published, making their reliability questionable.

The weaknesses Lee and Belfield identify in the MFF and Cato studies are similar and substantive: gaps or quality concerns in the literature reviews, missing or limited definitions of such key concepts as *school success* or *educational monopoly*, and unwarranted policy recommendations. The reviews also illuminate several important questions for future researchers and policymakers.

For example, both reviewers point out that studies in this area tend to rely heavily on academic performance to determine whether private schools are "better" than public schools. Even when they do not, they tend to examine a range of outcomes too narrow to provide adequate support for policy decisions. Lee asks, "Better for whom, all students or specific subgroups, and for what purpose?" In considering this question, he also notes that comparison studies frequently ignore "equity as measured by narrowing test score gaps among different racial and social groups of students." He points out that parents may be concerned more about school makeup and climate than about achievement gains. Similarly, Belfield notes that society might hold broad and even conflicting views of important outcomes: "One of the reasons for having a public education system is the recognition that, beyond its private, individual benefits, education influences society, culture, and what it means to be a citizen. Societies do not only value higher test scores; they also care about social cohesion and social inequalities."

Such questions and observations make it evident that even if achievement gains were documented as being greater in private schools— a conclusion that the research base to date does not support—a policy recommendation would not be automatically forthcoming. Setting aside for a moment the diversity of desirable outcomes, Belfield notes that "very few studies accurately measure costs in public and private schools," making it impossible to evaluate cost efficiency of the options. Lee additionally points out that even when a difference in performance is identified as statistically significant, whether "the difference is large enough to be meaningful to policy and practice" is a separate question. Both reviewers suggest that the apparently simple question of whether private schools are better than public schools is far more complex than is often assumed, with relevant policy decisions requiring consideration of factors far beyond test score comparisons.

Two related reviews are available from the Think Tank Review Project (thinktankreview.org):

- We asked Martin Carnoy to review a study that found increased reading, but not math, gains for students who used vouchers to attend private schools in Washington, DC. Patrick Wolf, along with five of his colleagues, authored *Evaluation of the DC Opportunity Scholarship Program: Impacts After Three Years* (2009), which was published by School Choice Demonstration Project and the Institute of Educational Sciences, National Center for Educational Evaluation and Regional Assistance. Carnoy identified methodological weaknesses that raise questions about the robustness of the study's findings—but, perhaps more importantly, he makes clear that the study does not have national policy implications. Carnoy agrees with the *Wall Street Journal* and *Washington Post* that the study offers an argument for continuing the DC program because it seems to provide, at no increased cost, some positive and no adverse affects on students as well as greater parent satisfaction. However, he also explains why the study of a relatively small and limited system— methodological weaknesses aside—offers no definitive policy guidance: "After all, if the most we can hope for from an intervention is that students attending middle schools increase their reading score one-sixth of a standard deviation in three years, but their reading does not continue to get better in high school (and their math scores don't improve at all), that is not going to help very much.... [T]he DC results should not generate great expectations."

- An earlier version of a Think Tank Review focusing on studies with discrepant findings dates to a 2006 study from Harvard University's Program for Education Policy and Governance. In *On the Public-Private School Achievement Debate,* authors Paul Peterson and Elena Llaudet questioned the findings of two federally funded studies that found comparable academic achievement among students in private and public schools. In contrast, the Harvard authors' own analysis suggested a private school advantage. However, reviewers Christopher Lubienski and Sarah Theule Lubienski, authors of one of the federal studies, explained how the Harvard study "used inadequate and ill-suited variables, failed to account for missing data, and produced weaker estimates of student achievement," resulting in "critically flawed" evidence and claims.

CHAPTER 3

ARE PRIVATE HIGH SCHOOLS BETTER ACADEMICALLY THAN PUBLIC HIGH SCHOOLS?

Jaekyung Lee

Review of "Are Private High Schools Better Academically Than Public High Schools?" by Harold Wenglinsky, published by the Center on Education Policy, and of "Monopoly Versus Markets: The Empirical Evidence on Private Schools and School Choice," by Greg Forster, published by the Milton & Rose D. Friedman Foundation. This is a modified version of a review originally published on December 12, 2007.

INTRODUCTION

School choice remains one of the most controversial issues in educational policy. The original idea of school vouchers was proposed in 1955 by Milton Friedman as a solution to the public schools' perceived monopolistic control over schooling.[1] Debates over such vouchers often engage the question of whether private schools are more effective in educating students, a question which is the subject of two reports recently issued by think tanks.

The first report, *Monopoly Versus Markets: The Empirical Evidence on Private Schools and School Choice*,[2] was issued by the Milton & Rose D. Friedman

Foundation (MFF). This report was written by Greg Forster, a senior fellow of the foundation. It consists of a review of prior research on the effects of voucher programs and a new study presenting a public vs. private school comparison. My review will focus only on the latter. The second report, *Are Private High Schools Better Academically than Public High Schools?*,[3] was issued by the Center on Education Policy (CEP). It was authored by Harold Wenglinsky and focuses on a narrower public-private comparison than does the MFF study, providing an examination of the experiences of disadvantaged students in urban settings.

Both the MFF and the CEP studies attempt to add new empirical evidence to the existing literature on public-private gaps in academic outcomes. They share two notable commonalities: (1) each compares public and private schools in terms of students' learning outcomes as measured by standardized tests, and (2) each conducts secondary analysis of a nationally representative sample of high school students. While the MFF study broadly compares public and private schools in the Educational Longitudinal Study (ELS) data, the CEP study capitalizes on more detailed information on school subtypes available in the National Education Longitudinal Study (NELS) data. Specifically, the CEP study differentiates three subtypes of public schools (comprehensive public schools, magnet schools, public schools of choice) and five subtypes of private schools (Catholic diocesan, Catholic holy order, Catholic parish, non-Catholic religious, independent private). This differentiation acknowledges schools' different missions and organizations, which are often obscured by conventional, monolithic comparisons of public versus private schools.

Through its secondary analysis of the NELS data, the CEP report examines academic outcomes such as high school academic achievement (reading, math, science, social studies), educational attainment, civic-mindedness, and students' job satisfaction 8 years after high school. The MFF report begins with a literature review that discusses a broader set of outcomes, such as segregation, but limits its own study to two available measures—high school academic achievement (math only) and dropout rates. For other measures, it relies on its review of prior research.

Given the limitations of observational data and the two reports' uses of different data, this review takes the approach of cross-examining and cross-validating the research evidence in both studies.

FINDINGS AND CONCLUSIONS OF THE REPORTS

Despite their similar research problems and methods, the CEP report and the MFF report come to very different conclusions regarding the effects of public and private schools on academic outcomes. The CEP study finds that low-income students from urban public high schools generally did as well as their peers in private high schools on academic measures as well as on post-high school measures such as civic engagement and job satisfaction. Once key family background characteristics (such as socioeconomic status) and behaviors (such as parental involvement) were taken into account, CEP's findings were that: (1) public high school students performed equally well on achievement tests as their counterparts in private schools; (2) the chances of attending college was not different between public and private school students; and (3) young adults who had attended public high schools displayed the same levels of job satisfaction and civic engagement as those who had attended any type of private high school. The study also notes two exceptions to these general findings: (1) independent (nonreligious) private high school students obtained higher SAT scores than public school students and (2) Catholic schools run by holy orders such as the Jesuits had nominal positive academic effects. The CEP report concludes that, on average, students who attend private high schools receive neither immediate academic advantages nor longer-term advantages in the form of attending college, finding satisfaction in the job market, or participating in civic life.

The MFF report, however, finds that private school students achieved more academic gains than public school students even after taking into account race, income, parental education and family composition. The study claims that the private school effect is substantial. The report concludes that private schools in general, and school choice programs in particular, confer better academic and other benefits. But these conclusions about school choice are based primarily on the report's presentation and interpretation of prior research, not on the MFF's new analyses.

As discussed in the review of findings and conclusions below, the two reports' specific findings do not greatly differ. While it is true that the MFF study found a statistically significant benefit associated with private schooling and the CEP study did not, it is also true that the CEP study teased out some exceptions (for some independent schools and Catholic schools), while the benefit asserted in the MFF study is relatively small.

RATIONALES SUPPORTING THE FINDINGS AND CONCLUSIONS OF THE REPORTS

As both the CEP and the MFF reports claim, national longitudinal datasets (NELS and ELS data) are very useful in sorting out school effects because they track individual students' academic achievement over time.

The CEP study analysis of NELS data begins with a report of baseline-year differences in academic achievement between public and private school students in eighth grade. Private school students, particularly Catholic diocesan and independent private students, enter high school academically better prepared than their public school counterparts. Using national longitudinal data allows CEP to account for this difference in starting points and measure achievement gains made during high school. In contrast, and despite its use of baseline-year test scores for comparison, the MFF study does not report or explicitly account for the public-private school achievement gap in the 10th grade (note that the ELS database looks at public or private attendance in the 10th grade, not the 8th).

Even after considering the baseline difference, both studies still find that the initial achievement gap widened over time in some instances. CEP, for instance, finds that private school students, specifically independent private school groups, gained more than their public school counterparts during their 4 years of high school.[4]

Since these differences may be attributable to extraneous factors that are beyond the control of schools, such as family income and parents' expectations of their children, both studies attempt to capitalize on the readily available measures of student and family background variables in the national datasets. The CEP study notes significant differences between the two groups in terms of students' family socioeconomic status (SES), academic support and cultural capital, which could contribute to the widening of the preexisting achievement gap. After taking these differences into account through appropriate statistical procedures, the study finds that the private school advantages almost disappear. For example, the adjusted differences between independent private and comprehensive public schools in 12th grade achievement were too small to be statistically significant. What this means is that, while private schools appear at first glance to do better than public schools at educating students, most of the differences in scores can be accounted for by the fact that public and private schools have very different groups of students.

In contrast, the MFF study found that, even after taking into account selected student background factors, private schools outperform public schools in math achievement gains from 10th grade to 12th grade. However, while the difference in achievement gains reported by MFF was statistically significant, the difference was very small in absolute terms and its practical significance is questionable.[5]

The MFF report nonetheless states that the "private school effect is substantial in size" (p. 5), pointing to purported gains for 12 years of schooling. That is, the report extrapolates from the gains it finds for the last 2 years of high school. This assumes that changes in achievement in other grade levels would be the same in size (and would, in fact, be gains rather than losses). Without additional research, these assumptions cannot be reasonably made.

One can identify several reasons that the two reports may have come to such different conclusions. The two reports are based on different national datasets collected at different time periods during which other external factors may have influenced student achievement. They also varied in their target population. The MFF study used the entire group of students included in the ELS data set. The author argues that this unrestricted selection can produce insights on the effect of school choice on students who are not especially disadvantaged. In contrast, the CEP study restricted its analytical sample to those who: (1) attended urban high schools, and (2) had family income in the lowest quartile nationally. The CEP report justifies its more restrictive sample selection based on policy and methodological grounds (p. 26). With regard to policy relevance: "many policy discussions about private school choice, including voucher plans, are focused on creating alternatives for students in urban school systems." With regard to the elimination of confounding factors: "the comparison between public and private schools means something different in suburban areas, where suburban public schools have many of the advantages of private schools. Including suburban schools might bias models away from private school advantages." Despite these reasonable rationales, more descriptive information about the other characteristics of the subgroup CEP analyzed, in comparison with excluded ones, was not provided but would have been very helpful to readers. Without this information, it is not clear what unique and unreported aspects of this choice may have influenced the findings. Both studies should have discussed the implications of their analytical choice with full information on the students who were included and excluded in their studies.

THE REPORTS' USE OF RESEARCH LITERATURE

New empirical research should generally be guided by a comprehensive and balanced review of prior research. The two reports differ considerably in their reviews of the literature. The MFF report focuses on experimental studies, particularly randomized trials of voucher programs, while the CEP report focuses on secondary analysis of large-scale national data studies related to public-private school achievement gaps. The MFF report highlights studies and findings that support its overall recommendations and dismisses evidence that does not fit its thesis. For example, it colors the voucher-study findings by either inflating positive results or dismissing insignificant (neutral) results.[6] The conclusions reached by the

CEP review are less decisive about the possible achievement benefits of private school attendance.

In reviewing how educational outcomes could differ between public and private schools, the MFF report appears to be more comprehensive because of its broader touch on multiple educational outcomes. However, the MFF report is not balanced or thorough in synthesizing findings from prior research. First, it limits its review to studies that used random assignment for the evaluation of school voucher programs. It contends that random assignment is the gold standard for social science research, but nothing it presents justifies the wholesale exclusion of other types of studies, specifically quasi-experimental and correlational studies. In fact, randomized field trials are not always warranted, feasible, or ethical, and often lack external validity due to limited sample sizes. The selected studies were conducted exclusively in large cities (Charlotte, Milwaukee, New York, and Washington, DC); the generalizability of the findings to the broader national or state contexts or to suburban or rural settings is questionable. Further, there is a disconnect between the very limited literature review on voucher programs and the new empirical research the author then presents, which does not meet the "gold standard."

The CEP report's discussion of research focuses on earlier national high school longitudinal data, such as the studies by Coleman and his colleagues and by Bryk and his colleagues.[7] Both the CEP and the MFF studies claim that their use of longitudinal data allows them to cope with the limitations of some previous studies that used cross-sectional data, such as those that analyzed NAEP data.[8]

What is missing in both sets of reviews is the distinction between school subtypes within the public and private sector and a discussion of what accounted for the effects found in previous research. Such a discussion would be important to consider in understanding what a school effect means and where a private school effect, if any, exists.[9]

REVIEW OF THE REPORTS' METHODOLOGIES

Basic pieces of both reports' methodologies are appropriate for the data and their investigations, but there are several limitations not fully acknowledged in either report. Both studies use longitudinal data on student achievement to measure the value added from schooling, and use similar, appropriate statistical techniques to control for other factors. The MFF study's choice of control variables is consistent with conventional practice, controlling for race/ethnicity, family structure, family income, and parental education. The CEP study similarly controls for SES, parental involvement, and parental expectations. The CEP study not only includes SES, like the MFF study, but also takes an extra step to control for other aspects of parental influences (what parents do as opposed to who they are). Although this choice is theoretically justifiable, its actual contribution to the model fit appears to be marginal.

Neither the MFF report nor the CEP report provide descriptive statistics. Such reporting would have rendered more information, such as the percentages of students in each type of school or the central tendencies and spreads of the key variables for each type of school. This information would have helped readers better interpret the reports' findings. Neither report examines selection mechanisms—how public and private schools differ in terms of the student profiles and how students and their parents self-select into different types.[10]

The robustness of CEP report findings was verified through a propensity score matching analysis, presented in a companion study funded by CEP and written by a different researcher.[11] This procedure gives some assurance that the matching of public and private school students through the report's statistical modeling was successful. The MFF report findings were not confirmed but would have benefited from having been.

Both studies report that their findings meet certain levels of statistical significance. Knowing what these levels are is critical in gauging the likelihood that their sample results are not simply obtained by chance (and therefore can be generalized to the national population). While both studies follow conventional standards of .05, .01 and .001 for significance levels, they do not acknowledge that even a very small effects difference may turn out to be statistically significant since they use large-scale national sample datasets.[12] Despite the limitation of the statistical significance information, neither report fully interprets the *practical* significance of the public-private differences that they found. If an effect size is very small compared with the effects of other policies or factors, policy intervention may not be justified.

Furthermore, neither study examines whether certain groups of students seemed to benefit more by being at one school type rather than another. The CEP and MFF analyses both need further research in light of prior work such as Bryk and Lee's study of Catholic schools showing stronger positive school effects for disadvantaged students[13] and Howell and Peterson's studies of randomized school voucher trials in New York City, Dayton, and Washington, DC, which revealed positive effects only for Black students.[14]

Both studies use individual students as the unit of analysis. This approach cannot effectively differentiate school sector effects, if any, on within-school gaps from between-school gaps with regard to family background characteristics. In other words, questions remain as to whether private schools contribute to narrowing or widening the achievement gap for disadvantaged minority students. They may, for example, help narrow the gap within schools through curricular detracking, but widen the gap between schools through racial segregation. These school sector effects on academic equity could have been disentangled through multilevel analysis.

Finally, it is worth noting differences in how each report measures achievement. The MFF study uses T scores, an approach that shows how well students do in comparison to each other. T scores cannot, however, show how much student learning grows over time. A student may have learned a great deal over time, but it would not be reflected in her T score if everyone learned as much as she did. Her T score would stay the same. If she or her peers learned nothing, her T score would also stay the same over time. The CEP study uses IRT scale scores, which have the benefit of showing absolute growth (how much a student has learned over time) and is not affected by how others do. The choice of test score metrics may or may not make a difference in the studies' findings on the relative advantages of public versus private schools, but it makes a difference in our understanding of how much academic progress students make in each type of school.

REVIEW OF THE VALIDITY OF THE FINDINGS AND CONCLUSIONS

These two studies challenge readers to draw a distinction between scientific research and political propaganda. The question is where these reports fall on the continuum between the two. The MFF report's review of prior research and its interpretations of the results from its own empirical study reveals strong bias in favor of private schools and school choice. The MFF report provides vigorous arguments for school choice (including private schools) based largely on a selective literature review. In contrast, the CEP study is more balanced in its interpretations of its results.[15] An important difference in the studies is that MFF starts out trying to answer a policy question, while CEP is attempting to answer a research question with policy implications.

What are the threats to the internal and external validity of the two studies? Perhaps most importantly, researchers should not draw causal conclusions about whether public or private schools lead to better results for children based on observational studies, because of the many potential serious threats to internal validity. While neither report makes strong causal arguments, they do not fully explain the limitations of doing so, either. Indeed, there remain concerns with the validity of public and private school comparisons due to self-selection and creaming: the students in public and private schools may be different in fundamental ways. Private schools might have entrance criteria that public schools do not. Parents who are more engaged in their children's education might be more likely to use vouchers than parents who are not. Both reports' analyses may have failed to include important factors, which may have biased the results.

While the studies' use of large-scale national databases may contribute to their external validity, potential limitations still remain. Because they look at relatively short periods of time and only certain outcomes and subjects, the reports' findings cannot be generalized without concerns and limitations.

The small but notable differences in major findings between the two studies, along with mixed results from prior research, raise questions about the robustness of findings on public-private school gaps in terms of value-added student achievement gains. Beyond the methodological concerns above, one possible explanation is that public schools, private schools, or both may have changed over the past 3 decades so that what held true in the 1980s no longer does. Moreover, any changes in the differences between the subtypes of public and private schools may have been obscured in the aggregate comparisons. It should be noted that the results would differ depending on which group was used as a reference group for comparison: the MFF study uses all public schools as a reference group, while the CEP study uses only comprehensive public schools.[16]

Given the various design factors that may account for the differences between the two studies, it might be informative to compare the descriptive statistics of public and private high school gains in student achievement by applying common parameters to the two national datasets that these studies use. Table 1.3 offers such a comparison of NELS and ELS results on the 10th to 12th grade math achievement gain scores in public and private schools in T score and IRT-estimated number right metrics.

Although these direct comparisons do not make any adjustment for family background factors and the like, the patterns generally confirm what the two studies find: equivalent private school performance in the NELS data and higher performance of private schools in the ELS data.[17] However, a closer look at the effect sizes shows that the public-private high school gaps in math achievement gain scores are almost null (in the NELS), or too small (in the ELS), to be practically significant. Therefore, the reports' seemingly divergent findings and conclusions may be largely due to their different interpretations rather than real differences in the results.

The effect size appears in parentheses, showing standardized group mean difference in gain scores between public and private schools. By one conventional standard, any effect size of .5 or larger is deemed practically significant.

Table 3.1.   National Average Public and Private High School 10th to 12th Grade Math Achievement Gain Scores and the Private-Public School Gaps in NELS and ELS

Data	Outcome Metric	Public School	Private School	Gap (Effect Size)
NELS	T score	−.28	.04	.32 (.03)
	IRT-estimate	4.31	5.08	.77* (.06)
ELS	T score	−1.13	.00	1.13*** (.12)
	IRT-estimate	9.97	13.01	3.04*** (.26)

*Note: * $p < .05$, *** $p < .001$*

How likely is it that the above unadjusted public-private gaps simply reflect the effects of extraneous factors that are beyond the control of schools—such as SES and who decides to go to private rather than public schools? How much would the above results be changed by consideration of demographic differences (i.e., through statistical matching of students between the two sectors)? One may argue that leveling the playing field between school types based on SES, family support and parental involvement would make public school students show gains equivalent to their private school counterparts, which is what CEP reports for a limited subset of students and schools.

In contrast, one may make the *counterargument* that this statistical matching procedure may favor public schools and make the comparison unfair by taking away credit for any practices of school staff from affluent private schools that better mobilize parental engagement and support for children's education. This dispute cannot be easily resolved through secondary analysis of observational data. And neither of these reports really helps resolve the dispute. Rather, their different choices of control variables used for public-private school comparison just reinforce the lack of consensus on this issue.

Once the private school results in Table 3.1 from NELS and ELS data are further broken down between Catholic and other private school types, the results show that there are significant differences between public and Catholic schools but not necessarily between public and non-Catholic private schools: NELS shows only a Catholic-school advantage, whereas ELS shows both Catholic and independent private school advantages (statistically significant but very small gaps). Future studies need to take an in-depth look into differences between school subtypes within each sector as well as between public and private sectors.

USEFULNESS OF THE REPORTS FOR
GUIDANCE OF POLICY AND PRACTICE

Since the first modern-day school voucher law was passed by the state of Wisconsin in 1990 (targeting low-income families in Milwaukee), school choice programs have sprung up in several states and the District of Columbia. In light of the controversies over the effects of school choice, both the MFF and the CEP reports are timely and policy-relevant. While both reports address the common question, "Is private school better academically than public school?" this raises another question: "Better for whom, all students or specific subgroups, and for what purpose?"

There has been an evolution of school choice, including diversified goals and divergent forms.[18] While Milton Friedman's school voucher idea was originally intended to improve educational productivity in general, the contemporary argument for school choice appeals more to the goal of equalizing educational opportunities, especially for low-income, disadvantaged families in inner-cities. Therefore, student outcomes related to both "productivity" and "equity" goals deserve attention for the evaluation of current school choice policies and programs. The MFF and CEP studies tend to focus on productivity as measured by improving average test scores, while ignoring equity as measured by narrowing test score gaps among different racial and social groups of students.

Further, school choice programs differ in important respects, as do the various types of private and public schools, and research should do a better job of paying attention to these differences. The MFF study did not go the extra step and separate the issue of school choice within the public school sector from the issue of school choice across different sectors. The CEP study makes more of a contribution in this direction.

In tandem, the two reports offer contrasting views and results on public versus private school effects, which will promote further studies. The MFF study concludes that private schooling is more successful at increasing test scores, and it presents results that do show a small but statistically significant advantage for private schools in terms of increased test scores. The CEP study, however, reports nearly equal success in public and private schools. If private school students do make significantly greater gains than public schools students, the reason needs to be investigated and fully explained. Both studies examined here tend to take a purely outcome-driven approach, leaving the underlying student selection mechanism, school organization and schooling process hidden away in a black box. In this respect, the public versus private school comparisons in both the CEP and the MFF reports do not provide very useful guidelines for policy and practice, since these require nuance rather than global statements about performance.

In order to make their studies more accessible to lay people, the two reports focus a great deal on the substantive findings of their studies. In doing so, they minimize (or ignore) technical discussions and descriptions of statistical procedures and methodologies. The CEP report discusses methodological issues in the appendix and also explains some basic statistical terms (e.g., variable, correlation, and regression) for readers who do not have a background in statistical research. The MFF report does not include a technical appendix for explaining its data and methods in detail, which makes it harder to judge the quality of their work.

A major limitation of both studies is that their conclusions are based on the simple dichotomy of statistically significant or insignificant differences—whether there is in fact a difference—without considering if the difference is large enough to be meaningful to policy and practice. There is no one-size-fits-all criterion to evaluate the size of an effect or to judge the practical import of their findings about school effects. Nevertheless, both reports avoid this discussion as well as contextual information that would help readers come to their own conclusions about the importance of these effects.

In spite of these limitations, both studies provide food for thought. What counts as school success and whose values matter in school choice? What kind of student outcomes and school effects matter? For those concerned with school accountability, value-added achievement gains are generally seen as the most useful indicators of school effects. From this perspective, the findings of the CEP study indicate that public schools are doing just as good a job as private schools. The MFF study suggests slight private advantages, but the difference in value-added gains appears to be so small that public schools can compete well with private schools.

However, these two research reports may not give satisfactory answers to educational policymakers, practitioners, and parents, who may have different questions in their own minds. The current measures of school performance that matter under No Child Left Behind (NCLB)—the straightforward percentage of students meeting or exceeding state standards—are quite different from the researchers' value-added outcome measures. Likewise, parents may be more concerned about school make-up, climate and student performance at the time of their children's enrollment at school than about future value-added gains. These additional factors remain salient in the school choice discussion, particularly when information on academic progress is not readily available to parents and the current methodology of educational research cannot accurately disentangle the sources of contribution to academic progress.

Regardless of such divergent values and opinions among the different stakeholders (including think tanks) involved in the school choice policy debate, this synthetic review of the two reports suggests that students generally learn in public high schools about as well as in private high schools, but that there are still many unanswered questions about potential differences in the finer details.

NOTES AND REFERENCES

1. See Friedman, M. (1955). The role of government in education. In Solo, R. (Ed.). *Economics and the Public Interest.* Rutgers University Press.

2. Forster, G. (2007, Oct. 17). *Monopoly versus markets: The empirical evidence on private schools and school choice.* Indianapolis, IN: Milton & Rose D. Friedman Foundation. Retrieved Dec. 9, 2007, from http://www .friedmanfoundation.org/friedman/downloadFile.do?id=255

3. Wenglinsky, H. (2007, Oct. 10). *Are private high schools better academically than public high schools?* Washington, DC: Center for Education Policy. Retrieved Dec. 9, 2007, from http://www.cep-dc.org/document/docWindow.cfm? fuseaction=document.viewDocument&documentid=226&document FormatId=3665

4. Specifically, the gap in standardized test gain scores between independent private (IP) and comprehensive public (CP) school groups was 14 points in reading (20 points for IP vs. 6 for CP), 12 points in math (23 points for IP vs. 11 for CP), 9 points in science (13 points for IP vs. 4 for CP) and 5 points in history (10 points for IP vs. 5 for CP).

5. The adjusted difference in math gain score was a one-point margin and was statistically significant at the .001 level. However, the difference amounts to only 0.1 in standard deviation units (T score metric with mean of 50 and standard deviation of 10).

6. For example, in the result column of Table 2 (titled "Top-Quality Research Shows That Vouchers Improve Academic Outcomes"), the report provides annotated comments instead of simply describing the results. For its review of the study by Krueger and Zhu (2004), the report writes that "If legitimate methods are used, the positive results for vouchers becomes significant." The report also includes a prediction in reviewing the study of DC. Opportunity Scholarship Program by Wolf et al.: "This study is ongoing and the positive results for vouchers may achieve statistical significance in future years, as has always happened in previous studies using legitimate methods."

7. See Bryk, A. S., Lee, V. E., & Holland, P. (1993). *Catholic schools and the common good.* Cambridge, MA: Harvard University Press. See also Coleman, J. S., Hoffer, T., & Kilgore, S. (1982). *High school achievement.* New York, NY: Basic Books.

8. See Braun, H., Jenkins, F., & Grigg, W. (2006). *Comparing Private and Public Schools Using Hierarchical Linear Modeling.* Washington, DC: Government Printing Office. Lubienski, C., & Lubienski, T. (2006). *Charter, private, public schools and academic achievement: New evidence from the NAEP mathematics data.* New York, NY: National Center for the Study of Privatization in Education.

9. See Chubb, J. E., & Moe, T. M. (1990). *Politics, markets and America's schools.* Washington, DC: Brookings Institution; Bryk, A., & Lee, V. E. (1992). Is

politics the problem and markets the answer? An essay review of *Politics, Markets, and America's Schools. Economics of Education Review, 11*(4), 439-451. Chubb and Moe simply dichotomized public vs. private sectors for comparison and their study was instrumental in igniting the old debate on school choice through new empirical analysis of nationally representative sample data. Bryk and Lee reviewed their study, criticizing it on the grounds that the positive outcomes described in the research comparing public and private schools are actually more typical of Catholic schools, but do not generalize to the private sector as a whole. Bryk and Lee pointed out that the private school advantages in student learning gains arise from the social values and organizational forms associated with Catholic schools (strongly shared academic mission in communal and caring settings), rather than the general market-driven competition forces and entrepreneurial interests associated with independent private schools.

10. A major problem with conventional control function approach is lack of selection models that specifies and tests a mechanism by which subjects self-select into different groups (public vs. private schools in this case). For discussion of the issues, see Winship, C., & Morgan, S. L. (1999). The estimation of causal effects from observational data. *Annual Review of Sociology, 25,* 659–706. Control function estimators involve a control function entered into a regression equation in an attempt to eliminate the correlation between the treatment indicator variable and the error term. This approach is based on the assumption of ignorable treatment assignment that the probability of being assigned to the treatment condition is only a function of the observed variables (Rosenbaum & Rubin 1983). However, one problem with the regression approach is that it imposes a linearity constraint, and it is often difficult to know how the nonlinearity should be approximated. Matching solves this problem, although the average effect is not for the total population but only for that portion of the population where the treatment and control groups have common X values (Winship & Morgan, 1999).

11. For detailed statistics, see Jeong, D. W. (2007). "Do School Types Matter in Student Achievement in Urban High Schools?" The CEP companion study also reports more information on the demographic composition of its analytical sample between school types. Retrieved Dec. 10, 2007, from http://www.cep-dc.org/
index.cfm?fuseaction=document.showDocumentByID&nodeID
=1&DocumentID=226 (Sensitivity and Replication Report)

12. The CEP study uses a smaller sample than the MFF study, due to its selection of a subsample for urban disadvantaged students. While the insignificant results on public-private achievement gap in the CEP study are primarily due to truly small effect sizes, the results could have been influenced by other factors such as its smaller sample size and the adjustment of regression standard errors for design effect.

13. Bryk, A. S., Lee, V. E., & Holland, P. (1993). *Catholic schools and the common good.* Cambridge, MA: Harvard University Press.

14. At least in limited instances, and for certain model specifications. Howell, W. G., & Peterson, P. E. (2002). *The education gap: Vouchers and urban schools.* Washington, DC: Brookings Institution Press. See also Lubienski, C. (2007). *Review of "The ABC's of School Choice."* Tempe, AZ & Boulder, CO:

EPRU and EPIC. Retrieved November 24, 2007, from http://epsl.asu.edu/epru/ttreviews/EPSL-0709-241-EPRU.pdf.

15. The CEP report points out that findings about voucher program effects have been disputed and it refers to Belfield and Levin (2005) for a fuller review of the research on private school effects: Belfield, C. R., & Levin, H. M. (2005). *Privatizing educational choice: Consequences for parents, schools and public policy.* Boulder, CO: Paradigm.

16. The CEP report possibly misled readers by stating that "a positive number for any given school would indicate a private school effect pertaining to that school" (p. 14). Any positive number for the other two types of public schools (magnet schools and public schools of choice) would indicate the effect of "choice" schools within the public sector rather than the effect of private schools.

17. The data analyses were conducted using the AM program with use of sampling weights and strata and cluster variables for accurate estimation. The national average scores are shown for typical students who did not experience retention or dropout during the time period and also did not change schools. The T score gain is close to zero in private schools, whereas T score gain is slightly negative in public schools. The private-public gap in average math gains in the T score metric was negligible: .32 (.03 in SD unit) from NELS and 1.13 (.12 in SD unit) from ELS. The IRT-estimated number right gain score is positive in both public and private schools, which reflects absolute growth in math achievement. However, the gap between public and private schools in the IRT-estimated number right metric was significant and it tends to be relatively larger than the T score gap: .77 (.06 in SD unit) from NELS and 3.04 (.26 in SD unit) from ELS.

18. See Howell, W. G., & Peterson, P. E. (2002). *The education gap: Vouchers and urban schools.* Washington, DC: Brookings Institution Press.

CHAPTER 4

MARKETS VERSUS MONOPOLIES IN EDUCATION

Clive Belfield

Review of Andrew Coulson's "Markets vs. Monopolies in Education: A Global Review of the Evidence," published by the Cato Institute. This is a modified version of a review originally published September 30, 2008.

INTRODUCTION

The introduction of market reforms into education systems has been a popular policy over the last decade. Charter schools, voucher programs, and tax credits have all introduced greater competition and market forces into the American school system. At issue is whether these reforms have improved the quality of education.

Andrew Coulson's policy analysis report, *Markets vs. Monopolies in Education: A Global Review of the Evidence*,[1] endeavors to consider all the evidence on this important issue, domestic as well as international. The report attempts to answer a provocative question: "Would families and communities be better served by a free and competitive education marketplace than they are by our current system of state school monopolies?"[2]

Think Tank Research Quality: Lessons for Policy Makers, the Media, and the Public, pp. 53–63

The author claims that the evidence typically used to address this question is "inadequate or even irrelevant." Instead, he advocates the use of international evidence. The reasoning is this: if there is a large volume of international evidence and it all points to the same conclusion, then that conclusion should also apply to the United States.

The report collects evidence from 55 domestic and international studies from over 20 countries comparing public and private school performance. Eight dimensions of performance are covered: achievement, efficiency, parental satisfaction, classroom orderliness, condition of facilities, subsequent earnings, attainment (graduation rates of high schools, or highest average grade completed), and intelligence. Studies are then classified according to the freedom of the nation's educational system. The three criteria for a relatively free education system are: parents pay one-third or more of the cost of private school; private schools have managerial autonomy; and public schools receive at least 30% more government funding per pupil than most private schools.

This evidence is then used to answer two questions: *Across the globe, do private schools outperform public schools?* and *Is the private school advantage even greater in freer education systems?* If the answers to both questions are "yes," then the report admonishes policymakers to introduce as much market reform as possible.

FINDINGS AND CONCLUSIONS OF THE REPORT

Using an approach that tallies positive and negative conclusions, the report finds that the literature strongly supports the conclusion that private schools outperform public ones. Across all eight dimensions of performance, the number of studies finding an advantage for private schools exceeds the number finding the opposite. For example, of the 63 separate tests for achievement differences, 41 find a statistically significant private school advantage, while only 8 find an advantage in favor of public schools (with 14 reporting no difference). No study finds public schools to be better in terms of parental satisfaction, quality of facilities, or attainment. Based on a simple count of all 113 findings, nearly eight times as many favor private over public schools.

To identify public/private differences in systems with greater freedom, the report selects 26 of the 55 studies on the basis of meeting all three criteria of a free system. In this subset of studies, private schools are found to outperform public schools on all dimensions. For example, in comparisons of achievement, 15 studies favor private schools and only 2 favor public schools. Applying a simple count of all 38 tests in these 26 studies,

35 favor private schools compared with two that show a public school advantage.

The report draws on these tabulations of evidence to make several broad policy claims (p. 11):

- The content of schooling does not need to be overseen by the state.
- There should be universal access to minimally regulated education markets.
- Parents should directly pay at least some of the cost of their children's education.

THE REPORT'S RATIONALE FOR ITS FINDINGS AND CONCLUSIONS

The report's own rationale for its findings is uncomplicated and is based on three assertions.

- All the research evidence has been collected, correctly classified, and appropriately summarized.
- Overwhelmingly, private schools appear to outperform public ones.
- Moreover, given the magnitude of the difference in performance, no alternative way of summarizing the evidence is likely to overturn this result. However, this rationale is very much open to question.

THE REPORT'S USE OF RESEARCH LITERATURE

Although the report does include a substantial body of research literature, its use of that literature is problematic on several grounds.

First, although the stated goal of the report is to be comprehensive, it omits some relevant research. Surprisingly, some of that research might support the claims of the report. A series of research studies in England, for instance, examined how market forces might improve its "monopoly" system of education. In general, that research found market reforms to be beneficial.[3]

However, other research omitted from this review does not support the report's claims. These omitted studies raise serious questions about the report's methodological assumptions and about the usefulness of reviewing international evidence instead of relying on U.S. research.[4]

Specifically, in their review across ten Latin American countries, Somers et al. affirm that many earlier studies comparing public and private schools failed to properly control for correlated characteristics.[5] As an illustration, imagine a study comparing the performance of private school students to that of students at a nearby urban public school. A researcher should control for differences in family income across the schools; any observed test score difference may arise because of family income and not the quality of school. There are many such factors to control for, including family background, student ability, neighborhood resources. Based on more complete econometric models, Somers et al. find that:

> conditioning on a complete set of student, family and peer characteristics explains a large portion of the observed difference in achievement between public and private schools.... Across the 10 countries ... the mean private school effect is approximately zero.[6]

This omitted research study is significant for two reasons. First, it controls for characteristics that the new Cato report states are unlikely to influence the results, and it finds they do in fact matter. Second, the 10 countries are all in Latin America, which is represented heavily in the report's literature summary.

Another study not included casts more doubt on the applicability of the report's conclusions to the U.S. school system. In a paper released in August 2008 (probably too late to be found by Mr. Coulson's search), which was later published in the *Annual Review of Economics*, Cecilia Rouse and Lisa Barrow review the evidence on U.S. voucher programs. They conclude:

> The best research to date finds relatively small achievement gains for students offered education vouchers, most of which are not statistically different from zero. Further, what little evidence exists regarding the potential for public schools to respond to increased competitive pressure generated by vouchers suggests that one should remain wary that large improvements would result from a more comprehensive voucher system.[7]

This conclusion of Rouse and Barrow rests on a very sophisticated and detailed interpretation of all the U.S. evidence.

The very modest conclusions of these two, more careful studies are in sharp contrast to those in this report. Simply tallying results of unscreened studies is not a particularly useful way of summarizing research.

A second way in which the literature review is problematic is that it relies heavily on unpublished research. Of the 55 research papers cited in the literature summary, 32 are working papers or conference papers. Of those that were formally published, not all were published in peer-reviewed journals. Typically, literature reviews give more credence to published studies as one indicator of quality, while referring to unpublished studies in a supplementary way. This report makes no such distinction.

A third concern is that the included studies are not representative of the globe in any meaningful sense. Of the 55 studies, 23 refer to the market reforms in Chile. Another 16 studies refer to the U.S. education system and a full 5 of those U.S. studies test for public/private differences in one city: Milwaukee, Wisconsin.

Accordingly, almost half the report's international evidence of a private-school advantage is based on studies of the Chilean school system. Certainly, many economists and other researchers consider the Chilean experience to be the most expansive market reform of education. It is also the one that has received the most intensive research investigation (hence its prominence here). The research on Chile is far from conclusive in demonstrating private schools' superiority, however.[8] Another surprising finding is Chile's very weak relative standing on international tests.[9]

When the sample for analysis is reduced to include only those studies in systems with greater freedom, only a few countries are covered. Of the 26 studies, 6 refer to India and 4 refer to Tanzania. Another five refer to the U.S. Interestingly, Chile is not represented at all in the reduced sample.

Finally, even the cited research literature does not fully correspond with the author's argument. The report claims that "existing [U.S. school choice] programs are too small, too restriction laden, or both" and so we should survey education systems across the globe. But a number of the studies included in this review examine just such small programs; they are not system-wide comparisons. To take the U.S. examples: enrollments were 19,000 in the Milwaukee Parental Choice Program (2007-08), 5,700 in the Cleveland Scholarship and Tutoring Program (2004), 2,791 in the first year of the 3-city voucher experiment reported in Howell and Peterson (2002), and 1,400 in the DC Opportunity Scholarship program (2004). It is not clear why these studies of small-scale programs should be included in a review that purports to summarize international evidence across school systems.

REVIEW OF THE REPORT'S METHODS

A virtue of this report is that the method used is easy to understand. A simple distinction between public (monopoly) and private schools is set up. The evidence is tabulated and counted. Public and private schools are judged based on which have the most studies in their favor.

Unfortunately, the issue is more complex than this. Consequently, more detailed analysis is also required.

The report employs a rhetorical device to simplify what is actually a very complex issue. The public school system is stated to be a "monopoly," but the author never specifies which features make it so (both in absolute terms and relative to other countries). The standard textbook definition of a monopoly rests on "barriers to entry" exemplified by families who want different schools from the current offering(s) but are not allowed them. While we shouldn't minimize real economic, informational and logistic obstacles to school choice in the United States, there remains plenty of opportunity for American families to choose different schools: they can enroll in charter schools, home-school, move to a different school district, or pay extra for private school. Certainly, private schools compete at a disadvantage against subsidized public schools, but within the public system there is considerable heterogeneity. Moreover, other elements of "monopoly" exist elsewhere but not in the United States: countries such as the United Kingdom and France have a national curriculum that all schools—including private ones—must follow. Similarly, the Netherlands has public and privately owned schools, but both are heavily regulated. In short, the monopolistic nature of U.S. education, relative to other countries, is far from clear.

Similarly, the "market" concept used in the report is not straightforward. As the author notes, citing Merrifield, the market system includes "profit, price change, market entry, and product differentiation" (p. 2). But none of these elements are addressed here. There is, for instance, no investigation of the role of profit in education. In fact, most private schools, inside as well as outside the United States, are nonprofit enterprises. There is no treatment of prices, which might allow for cheap, low-quality private schools as well as expensive, high-quality ones. Finally, product differentiation is presumed away; in this report, schools are compared according to how their students perform according to a common metric.

In summary, when commentators style the public school system as a monopoly, it is important to ask: *In what sense?* Without specifics, it is not clear what to test for to see whether private schools are better. For example, do private schools have more efficient managers, motivated by profit? Do they have more flexibility over the curriculum or staffing? If private schools in the Netherlands offer an exemplar, might that mean that U.S. private schools should be more highly regulated rather than, as the Cato report argues, further deregulated?

A second way in which the method is overly simple is the method used to weigh the evidence: essentially a "vote count" of all studies. Each study is given a value of 1 if it finds private schools outperform public schools, 0 if no difference is found, and −1 if public schools are superior. These scores are then tabulated to see which type of school is superior. A second tabulation is then performed for the reduced sample, restricted to studies that meet all three market criteria and so have the most "market-like" features. Again, these studies are counted and tabulated to determine which school sector is superior.

The problem with using vote count methods is that not all votes—not all studies—are necessarily equal. There are two ways in which these "votes" are not equal.

First, some studies are better able to detect genuine differences in school quality than others. For example, it does not seem reasonable to equate a study based on random assignment of students to public and private schools with a correlational study that simply compares student outcomes following their independent choices of public or private school. The latter could easily confound preexisting student differences with differences caused by school quality.

It is possible for a random assignment study to be poorly implemented (or have low external validity). But scholars generally agree that there is a hierarchy of methods that allow for causal claims about outcome measures, with experimental methods at the top. Similarly, as noted above, some studies are published only after a rigorous peer review, while others are self-published or published in a non-peer-reviewed journal. The vote-count approach assumes that all studies are equally valid and useful.

Second, no account is taken of the power of each finding. For example, if two studies find a small positive impact from private schooling and one finds a large negative impact, the vote count method would find unambiguously in favor of private schools, but averaging the three studies might reverse the conclusion. Also, one study may be based on a small sample and another on population-wide data. Although this report catalogs sufficient studies in favor of private schools that this possibility is unlikely, the vote count procedure is still uninformative about the size of any advantage from attending a private school. It merely suggests (setting aside the other problems identified in this review) that private schools are probably better than public schools.

But even this conclusion is premature. Importantly, it is far from clear that any (or all) of these studies have properly identified a private school effect. Let us assume that private school students outperform public school students on raw achievement tests. This may be because private school students are from wealthier families, so studies must control for this. Most do, though some do not. More importantly, there may be other hard-to-observe characteristics that cause a private school advantage, such as parental engagement, the safety of the neighborhood or family religiosity.[10] Studies do not typically control for all these factors and often cannot. Moreover, it is necessary to control for the *decision* to choose a private school. That is, families choose private school because it is a better fit for them for many reasons; public school parents may or may not be doing the same. This selectivity bias may be substantial.

The report explicitly states that selectivity bias is not a concern. The author contends that either the bias is unimportant, or enough of the studies do control for it, or the bias is actually in favor of public schools. But each of these explanations is questionable. It is likely that the choice of school is motivated by the family's expectation about how well the child will do there. Simply put, these studies do not all include the controls they should. As noted above, Somers et al. illustrate how studies that fail to control for peer group characteristics can overstate the private school advantage.[11] Finally, the report never explains why families who enroll in private school might have characteristics associated with lower achievement.

REVIEW OF THE VALIDITY OF THE FINDINGS AND CONCLUSIONS

Even if we accept the report's conclusion that private schools outperform public ones, it is still not clear what policy reforms should be implemented.

For example, a market with more product differentiation might simply mean more charter schools. Yet, these schools are fully publicly funded and so fall afoul of the report's criterion that parents must pay directly. Even voucher programs include sizeable subsidies that families then turn over to their private schools.

Finally, the report does not explore or even mention any possible adverse consequences from a system of independent private schools. One of the reasons for having a public education system is the recognition that, beyond its private, individual benefits, education influences society, culture, and what it means to be a citizen. Societies do not only value higher test scores; they also care about social cohesion and societal inequalities. The report appears to implicitly assume that these public benefits of education are unimportant or that they are unaffected by the types of schools children attend.

USEFULNESS OF THE REPORT FOR
GUIDANCE OF POLICY AND PRACTICE

The report claims that its findings are of "profound" importance for U.S. education policy. At best this is an overstatement, for several reasons.

First, there is now a substantial evidence base on market reforms in the U.S. There have been many small-scale reforms, which have often been evaluated using high-quality research methods. These evaluations are included here. But there have also been large-scale reforms, such as charter schools and home-schooling, which arguably have radically changed the opportunities for parents wanting to choose a school outside of their public neighborhood school. Yet, the large body of literature on charter schools, much of which is high-quality and published in peer-reviewed journals, is not mentioned here.

Accordingly, and contrary to the basic assertion in the Cato report, there is little warrant for U.S. policymakers to draw policy conclusions from a tally of the results of a body of very uneven international evidence. The large and growing body of U.S. evidence about school choice and marketization is more accessible, applicable and useful than figuring out how international evidence applies to the United States.

Of course, it is hard to summarize all of the U.S. literature in a single conclusion. But as explained by Rouse and Barrow (quoted above), "The best research to date finds relatively small achievement gains for students offered education vouchers, most of which are not statistically different from zero."[12]

The author's argument that the report's findings have profound implications for U.S. policy is unconvincing for a second reason: some of the report's international evidence is from countries with education systems that are dramatically different from the American system. Aside from the five studies from the United States, more than half of the 21 studies included in the second (reduced) sample are from Pakistan, India, Tanzania, Ghana, and Nigeria. It is far from obvious what U.S. policymakers might infer from studies of these very different countries, which do not have universal secondary schooling (or, at least in the case of Pakistan, even universal elementary schooling), have public schooling often tied to religion, and have formal labor markets that cover only a small subset of the population. Indeed, in making any international comparison, scholars need to pay attention to substantial differences in such areas as curriculum, assessment, funding systems, political decentralization, religiosity, wealth, teacher labor markets, and, perhaps most importantly, the incentives to attend school. It is of course possible to learn from the experiences of other countries, but the lessons become harder to discern as countries are less and less similar.

Policymakers and practitioners rightly prefer localized evidence: the context of a reform matters. Further, education reforms often have diverse consequences that need to be accounted for. In rural areas, for example, private schools may not be able to operate on a scale sufficient to maximize profit or break even.

Finally, policymakers need to know not only whether a reform improves educational outcomes but also whether its costs outweigh the benefits. The

Cato report does not identify the size of any private school advantage, so it is not possible to assess the level of resources that would need to be spent to yield such an advantage. The report includes 26 tests that purport to assess efficiency; these ideally should provide an immediate economic answer. However, many of these 26 tests are far from compelling.[13] This is so for several reasons, but the primary one is that very few studies accurately measure costs in public and private schools. Further, these studies almost never consider the costs of implementing a reform. Conclusions about efficiency from this evidence base should therefore be made very cautiously.

In summary, it is possible that private schools are superior to public schools when all the international evidence is counted. However, we don't know, and this report does little if anything to help answer that question. What we do know is that the best studies in the United States and abroad control for many factors before drawing any conclusion, and, when these factors are accounted for, what is most surprising is how small the private school advantage is—where it even exists. As such, expanding market forces is unlikely to yield dramatic improvements in the quality of the U.S. education system.

NOTES AND REFERENCES

1. Coulson, A. (2008, Sept. 10). *Markets vs. monopolies in education: A global review of the evidence.* Washington, DC: Cato Institute. Retrieved September 12, 2008, from http://www.cato.org/pubs/pas/pa620.pdf

2. The question includes communities, but there is no discussion of community-specific effects of markets. For example, if a market allows families to segregate by race but all test scores go up, it is not clear whether communities are better served. Also, if private schools teach religious doctrine rather than math and science, it is not clear that communities are better served.

3. Gorard, S. (2003). What can we learn from school choice in England and Wales? *New Economy, 10,* 240-244.

4. The review also omits a separate study that confirms the findings of Braun et al. (2006). That study is Lubienski, C., &. Lubienski, S. T. (2004). Charter, private, public schools and academic achievement. New evidence from NAEP Mathematics data. Working paper. Retrieved Sept. 25, 2008, from http://www.ncspe.org/publications_files/OP111.pdf

5. Somers, M. A., McEwan, P. J., & Willms, J. D. (2004). How effective are private schools in Latin America? *Comparative Education Review, 48,* 48-69.

6. Somers, McEwan, & Willms. (2004).

7. Rouse, C., & Barrow, L. (2008). *School vouchers and student achievement: Recent evidence, remaining questions.* Retrieved Sept. 25, 2008, from http://ncspe.org/publications_files/OP163.pdf

8. See also Rouse, C., & Barrow, L. (2009). School vouchers and student achievement: Recent evidence, remaining questions. *Annual Review of Economics, 1,* 17-42.

9. This is evident from Table 1 of Coulson for achievement. McEwan (2002) has three tests: two show no difference and one favors private schools. McEwan and Carnoy (2000) have three tests: two favor private schools; the other favors public schools. Tokman (2001) has two tests: one favors private and the other public schools. Sapelli and Vial (2002, 2005) have two tests: one neutral and one favoring private schools. This suggests that—for Chile, at least—the type of private school and the method used to compare them will influence the comparison.

10. In the 2000 PISA, Chile is ranked 38th out of the 42 participating countries. In the 2003 TIMMS, Chile is ranked 39th out of 43 countries.

11. For example, religiosity may raise students' expectations of education success. See Regnerus, M. D. (2000). Shaping schooling success: Religious socialization and educational outcomes in metropolitan public schools. *Journal for the Scientific Study of Religion, 39,* 363-370.

12. Somers, McEwan, & Willms (2004); see note 5

13. Rouse & Barrow (2008); see note 7.

14. Generally, efficiency tests are problematic because few studies accurately measure full resource use in either the private or public sector. Notably, private schools are unwilling to declare budgetary information to researchers and fees are often an imprecise measure of resource use. Of the 26 tests, few are compelling. Three are attributed to Tooley et al. (2007), yet two cannot be found in the text and the third does not have a proper outcome measure. Three are from the same paper on Chile (McEwan, 2002) but the scores are 1, 0, and −1. Similarly, two are from the same paper on India (Bashir, 1997), but the scores are −1 and 1. This is also the case for the two tests for the Dominican Republic (Jimenez & Lockheed, 1995). The test by Howell and Peterson (2002) is not based on costs reported by the private schools but simply an inference based on the low cost of the voucher and simulated costs of education. Finally, five tests are from Jimenez and Lockheed (1995), whose costs analysis has been criticized as imprecise by Tsang, M. 1997. Cost analysis for improved educational policymaking and evaluation. *Educational Evaluation and Policy Analysis, 19,* 318-324.

PART 3

Contracting Out and Private Management

Several think tanks, reflecting the prevailing faith among free market advocates that the private sector can provide any service better than the public sector, have suggested that districts should hire outside vendors to provide ancillary services like transportation, or to take over poorly performing schools completely. The reports and reviews in this part of the book explore the assumption that such contractual arrangements result in reduced costs with no reduction—and possibly an improvement—in services or outcomes. Given that the No Child Left Behind law mandates restructuring for schools with several years of inadequate performance, it is especially important to consider whether private entities might more effectively and efficiently manage instructional services than public entities.

In Chapter 5, reviewer Clive Belfield examines a report offering guidance for stakeholders interested in contracting out arrangements for food, transportation and custodial services. That report, *A School Privatization Primer for Michigan School Officials, Media and Residents* (2007), was authored by Michael LaFaive and published by the Mackinac Center for Public Policy. The report focused on the prevalence of contracting out in Michigan, presenting a justification for privatizing services and examining factors influencing contracting decisions. It also provided an

Think Tank Research Quality: Lessons for Policy Makers, the Media, and the Public, pp. 65–67

extensive guide to contracting logistics. Belfield finds the document's pragmatic information to be useful, particularly to districts unhappy with in-house services. He concludes that it "may help districts avoid making costly mistakes or getting locked into unfavorable contracts."

Belfield also finds, however, an imbalance in the report's assumption "that the benefits of contracting out exceed those of public provision. It does not systematically itemize and compare the costs and benefits associated with each option." For instance, the report included advantages of privatizing services but not advantages of in-house services. It included potential savings of contracting out but not its less obvious costs. And it included a discussion of political mobilization against contracting out by unions but not business or ideological lobbying in favor of it. Most seriously, perhaps, many important claims in the report were presented with no supporting evidence. For example, while several officials reported saving money, no financial analyses demonstrating such savings and yielding dollar amounts were included.

In Chapter 6, reviewer Derek Briggs examines two conflicting reports on Philadelphia's recent strategy of contracting out management of some of its lowest performing schools to determine whether providers outside the district—some for-profit, others not—might demonstrate the ability to improve school performance. The first of these, *State Takeover, School Restructuring, Private Management, and Student Achievement in Philadelphia* (2007), was authored by Brian Gill and colleagues and published by the RAND Corporation and Research For Action (RAND-RFA). It found private management had no cumulative effect on math or reading achievement, while district management had a positive effect on math achievement but no impact on reading performance. The second, *School Reform in Philadelphia: A Comparison of Student Achievement at Privately Managed Schools with Student Achievement in Other District Schools* (2007), was authored by Paul Peterson and published by Harvard University's Program on Education Policy and Governance (PEPG). Largely a criticism and rejection of the RAND-RFA report, the Harvard study found that private management improved the percentage of students who attained "basic" levels of performance in math and reading and that district management generally had no effect on them. An important point to note in considering these reports, Briggs notes, is that Peterson had access to only school-level data, as compared to the student-level (and school-level) data used by the RAND-RFA researchers—making it not terribly surprising the analyses should reach different conclusions.

Much of Briggs' review considers and largely rejects Peterson's criticisms of the RAND-RFA report. In the end, he finds support only for an implied criticism—that the RAND-RFA report provides insufficient context to help the reader evaluate the use of the authors' fixed effects model. Briggs examines the other Peterson criticisms as well, but they come up empty. Briggs also presents his own analyses of each report and finds strengths and weaknesses in each, although he ultimately determines the RAND-RFA finding favoring district management more credible, in part because that study was based on better data. Still, the reviewer notes, "A clear strength of both reports is that they are each cognizant of the limitations of their analyses, and they are each relatively cautious in generalizing their findings." Such caution apparently did not to extend beyond the authors, however, because Briggs further notes, "The RAND-RFA report is currently being used by Philadelphia's Accountability Review Council as the justification for recommending the firing of under-performing private managers.... Meanwhile, the findings from the PEPG report have been reported in the *Wall Street Journal* and other media outlets." Like the authors, Briggs notes limitations in the analyses, and he notes especially that both studies lack important descriptive statistics. For example, no detail is given on the movement of students in and out of schools, so that it is unclear to what extent the cohorts being compared actually contain the same students. Similarly, neither report indicates how much test score gains varied within schools or across students.

While it is understandable for policymakers to want research studies to offer clear policy guidelines, like other reviews, these instead indicate the complexity of determining answers to policy questions. Both reviewers urge careful thought about study results rather than a rush to action. Belfield notes that contracting out *may* be desirable in some circumstances, but because circumstances vary so widely among school systems, "this change may not be financially or otherwise appropriate for any given district." And Briggs says of the Philadelphia studies, "Given NCLB's nod toward school restructuring, the outcomes in Philadelphia have national import. These two studies, read together, do contribute to our understanding of Philadelphia's experience. Yet ... neither study offers a complete picture, and more research is needed before drawing any definitive conclusions." We should not expect to find—or even look for—a one-size-fits-all answer to the question of whether or not to privatize educational services; local context and providers should shape local decisions.

CHAPTER 5

A SCHOOL PRIVATIZATION PRIMER FOR MICHIGAN SCHOOL OFFICIALS, MEDIA AND RESIDENTS

Clive Belfield

Review of Michael D. LaFaive's "A School Privatization Primer for Michigan School Officials, Media and Residents," published by the Mackinac Center for Public Policy. This is a modified version of a review originally published on February 19, 2008.

INTRODUCTION

"Contracting out" to private companies is an important issue in the provision of publicly funded services, including education.[1] If education or a service associated with education can be provided at a genuinely equivalent quality but at less expense by a private company than by a public enterprise, then a very compelling case can be made for hiring that company. With annual spending of over $440 billion on public education, any substantial cost savings would be economically important.

Think Tank Research Quality: Lessons for Policy Makers, the Media, and the Public, pp. 69–76

The decision to contract out educational services is ultimately a financial decision and a local one: it may generate cost savings in some cases but not in others, depending on the school district's circumstances. However, school district personnel need to know whether the option is worth investigating. It would be very valuable for decision makers to have information on topics such as how common contracting out is, what practical steps are necessary, what the important considerations are, and how to determine if a contract is successful in reducing expenditures while maintaining quality. *A School Privatization Primer for Michigan School Officials, Media and Residents*,[2] published by the Mackinac Center for Public Policy and authored by Michael LaFaive, is an advocacy document that addresses some of these issues. This review considers the merits and usefulness of the report, examining weaknesses associated with the report's presupposition that privatization will be beneficial.

FINDINGS AND CONCLUSIONS OF THE REPORT

The report examines the contracting out of three educational services: food, transportation, and custodial services. It addresses the prevalence of contracting out each service across states, with a focus on Michigan. According to the report, just under 40% of districts in Michigan had contracted out at least 1 of the 3 types of services. However, surveys and published reports show that the incidence of each service varies dramatically across states. Some states contract out these education-related services almost entirely, while others contract almost none. Surveys of district officials indicate that most districts that do so are pleased with their decision to contract out.

The report then presents a justification for privatization, along with a discussion of factors influencing contract decisions in Michigan. In addition, it contains a lengthy guide to the logistics of contracting out. It includes checklists for Requests for Proposals from potential contractors. It also recounts how agencies such as teachers' unions mobilize opposition to privatization. The report then outlines how districts might justify a decision to contract out services. It itemizes 10 rules of thumb about hiring a contractor and making sure that the terms of the contract are fulfilled. Finally, the appendices include a case study of a court challenge to privatization in Grand Rapids, Michigan, as well as a catalog of possible contractors in Michigan.

Overall, the report concludes that privatization is beneficial, although it also recommends that all contracts with private service providers be intensively monitored.

RATIONALES SUPPORTING FINDINGS AND
CONCLUSIONS OF THE REPORT

The report's suggested rationale for supporting privatization rests largely on the argument that if districts do it, it must be beneficial for them. Since almost 40% of districts in Michigan do contract out, the report assumes the practice must be beneficial in these districts.

In the case of food services, for example, contracting out is supposedly motivated by the savings accompanying economies of scale and by the desire to have another organization deal with the complex regulations associated with the task. It is implied that districts not contracting out are either unaware of the benefits or face too much opposition to privatization. The report does not seriously consider the possibility that the public provision of these services might be more beneficial in at least some instances. The decision either to provide a service in-house or to contract it out depends on many factors. The report focuses only on factors favoring contracting out and not on those that might lead a district to prefer public provision.

There are several key factors that might justify public provision. One is the size of "transaction costs," such as the costs of writing, administering, managing, and arbitrating the contract. None of these costs are considered in the report. For example, while the report does an effective job of itemizing the many steps needed to secure a contract, it neglects to address the resources and time district officials must devote to taking these steps. It is possible that the resources needed to secure a private contract exceed any potential cost-savings. Moreover, in the long run there may be a cost to being locked in to a single contractor for provision of a service. And if a private contractor anticipates that a contract might not be renewed, he or she may charge a "risk premium" to offset the loss of the contract. Again, none of these potential additional expenses is addressed in the report.

Another argument set forth in the report is that services such as food, transportation, or custodial services, while necessary, are not integral to the instructional goal of a school or district. One strand of this argument is that by divesting itself of the management and provision of these services, a district can focus on education. This focus, the argument continues, should help schools improve and raise achievement levels.

However, this claim—that contracting out allows a school district to focus on its core mission—is not substantiated. Anecdotally, testimony from the superintendent of the Houston Independent School District is cited as an example of how privatization is a "simplifier," but no research evidence is provided. I am not, in fact, aware of any research evidence on this point (i.e., research that considers the relationship between academic performance and the extent of private contracting). It is equally plausible that a contractor will be a distraction to a district if, for instance, it performs poorly.

The other line of reasoning in this argument is that education systems are too vast, employing too many workers not involved in the core mission of teaching children. However, no evidence is presented that these ancillary workers are unproductive or that education systems would be more efficient if their number were reduced. In applying this argument to Michigan, the report contends that contracting out becomes necessary because of deteriorating economic conditions. Yet, if contracting out is the better approach, it should be adopted regardless of whether the state is doing well or poorly.

The report also cites survey evidence of the opinions of officials of districts that contracted out services. The survey responses presented in the report show three-quarters claiming that the contract generated cost-savings, with one-fifth being unsure. In addition, district officials reported being highly satisfied with their decision to contract out.

However, these self-reports do not constitute adequate evidence either of benefits or of satisfaction. No comparison is made with the satisfaction levels of district officials who do not contract out services. Nor does the satisfaction felt by these district officials constitute evidence that the contract has yielded cost savings. No evidence on the dollar amounts of any such cost savings is reported.

The report also contends that private firms have the capacity and willingness to take over each of these services, so a lack of adequate providers should not hinder districts from contracting these services out:

> As with the transportation and food industries, the custodial services industry appears capable of meeting any increased demand from school districts for services. (p. 23)

However, this is simply asserted: no systematic information or data are presented on excess capacity. Instead, even as the report declares that such information would be very difficult to obtain, it nevertheless claims that:

> A Michigan school district that wishes to solicit bus service bids from private firms will probably find willing bidders even if no local firm seems likely to make an offer. (p. 21)

Basic economic theory would suggest otherwise: in order to draw forth an extra supply of bus fleets, higher salaries for bus drivers will be necessary. This would raise costs.

Contrary evidence is generally not considered. For example, no investigation is made either of the number of terminated contracts or of failed attempts to hire a contractor at lower cost than existing, public-sector provision of these services. Similarly, no mention is made of the likelihood that private contractors will "cherry-pick" the easiest, most profitable services and leave the public sector to provide the more expensive ones. For example, a private firm might provide transportation services in urban areas but not in rural ones.[3]

Finally, the only research that the report cites on cost savings is two studies on contracting out transportation services (see below), but no such studies for food services and custodial services are mentioned.

THE REPORT'S USE OF RESEARCH LITERATURE

The report's use of research literature is tendentious and limited. It cites very little published evidence on whether and how private businesses can be more efficient than public enterprises. The one legitimate citation (i.e., one that uses data to test its claims) is a study of the costs of transportation services in Tennessee. This study does show substantial cost-savings in the majority of school districts, but the sample is only 19 districts.

There is almost no published literature in academic journals on potential cost-savings from contracting out transportation, food, or custodial services by school districts.[4]

REVIEW OF THE VALIDITY OF THE FINDINGS AND CONCLUSIONS

The report argues that contracting out food, transportation, and custodial services is beneficial, with the single caveat that the contract must be effectively monitored. This is an overstatement, a somewhat misleading way to frame the decision over contracting out and an oversimplification of how education systems operate.

First, the report overstates the benefits of contracting out, not least by omitting a discussion of possible additional costs. It presupposes that districts without private contracts are not operating efficiently or are constrained by public-sector unions. As discussed earlier, the evidence presented to support this supposition is far from compelling.

Second, since the decision to contract out such services is largely a financial one, an accounting framework is necessary. The full costs of contracting out should be compared with the full costs of public sector provision, with a fundamental assumption that the quality of the service is the same. Instead, the report presumes that the benefits of contracting out exceed those of public provision. It does not systematically itemize and compare the costs and benefits associated with each option.

There is some literature on the benefits of private ownership, but none of it is cited in the report. One of the most widely cited papers in the general academic literature concludes that private enterprises are indeed more efficient than public ones.[5] Other published research concludes that private provision of public services such as sewers, roads, parks, mass transit, and refuse collection is more efficient.[6] Notably, studies of privatized public transit typically show either cost savings or lower prices for travelers; these results might be relevant for school transportation services.[7]

However, favorable results are not obtained from private companies in all sectors and critically depend on local economic conditions. Private sector enterprises have a larger cost advantage in noncare sectors (such as utilities). But where the service involves personal care, the results are less clear. For nursing homes, for example, the research suggests that while there is little difference between nonprofit and public homes, for-profit homes offer lower quality care.[8] Similarly, for-profit hospitals appear to be no more productive than public ones.[9] Moreover, this literature does not expressly deal with mixed enterprises, where part of the provision is public (instruction) and another part is private (food services). Rather, the literature directly pertains only to the transfer of ownership of an entire operation from public to private. Hence, it is debatable whether this work would strengthen the claims made in the report.

Finally, the report oversimplifies the education system. Schools are not simply "firms" producing students instead of cars or shoes. They are political and social entities and they are rooted in local communities, serving children whose parents need to feel that they are stake-holders in the school. If a district contracts out food services, for example, it is ceding control to an outside agency. Both the district and local families have only limited control over the quality of the service—limited to the initial negotiation of the contract. Yet, control is valuable: many schools now have school health councils to address issues related to food quality and nutrition.

The issue of job security and unionization, which is a running subtext of the report, also cuts both ways. It is true that contracting out decreases the job security for public sector workers. Some of the opposition to contracting out may be "ideological" in this respect, but some of it is a rational response to the loss of control associated with contracting out. If jobs are less secure, workers will require higher pay to perform them. This extra pay could easily approximate to the wages paid to current union workers. Also, regardless of the underlying motivations for opposition, a district may spend considerable time and resources responding to and mollifying it. In the end, and even assuming the validity of the report's claims of benefits, a district may find it more efficient to provide services directly.

Finally, the report only considers political mobilization against contracting out and not business or ideological lobbying in favor of it. Both occur and both may shape district officials' decisions.

USEFULNESS OF THE REPORT FOR
GUIDANCE OF POLICY AND PRACTICE

This report is useful. It presents credible surveys of current policies across states, showing that contracting out of food, transportation, and custodial services is widespread, although public provision is still more common. The report offers practical steps for issuing and monitoring contracts; these rules of thumb may help districts avoid making costly mistakes or getting locked into unfavorable contracts. Some districts may find useful the discussion of how unions sometimes oppose contracting out and the catalog of service providers in Michigan. These practicalities may have deterred some districts from investigating contracting out. Districts very dissatisfied with their in-house services may find this document helpful in moving forward with contracting out.

However, the report does not offer a balanced framework for assessing the costs and benefits of contracting out. It fails to consider transaction costs (e.g., the costs of writing Requests for Proposals, awarding contracts, and monitoring services). It relies on officials' assertions about the advantages of contracting out, yet does not fully consider the disadvantages. And it fails to make clear that the research evidence on contracting out in education is far from conclusive. As such, the report may be successful in persuading districts to consider contracting out, but this change may not be financially or otherwise appropriate for any given district.

NOTES AND REFERENCES

1. Contracting out is only one example of privatization in education: other prominent examples include the use of vouchers or tax credits for attendance at private schools. Only the contracting out of K-12 services is discussed here.
2. LaFaive, M. D. (2007). *a school privatization primer for michigan School Officials, Media and Residents*. Midland, MI: Mackinac Center for Public Policy. Retrieved Feb. 13, 2008, from http://www.mackinac.org/archives/2007/s2007-07.pdf

3.   Such "cherry-picking" by Education Management Organizations is noted by Miron, G. (2007). Educational management organizations. In Fiske, E. & Ladd, H. (Ed.), *Handbook of Research in Education and Policy*. New York, NY: Routledge

4.   This statement is based on a bibliographical literature review of the database of social science publications using combinations of: (1) privatization, contract, contracting out; (1) bus, transport, food, janitorial/custodial; and (3) schools, education, open.

5.   See Vining, A. R., & Boardman, A. E. (1992). Ownership versus competition—Efficiency in public enterprises. *Public Choice, 73*, 205-239.

6.   See Savas, E. S. (2000). *Privatization and public-private partnerships*. New York, NY: Chatham House; and Wolf, C. C. (1988). *Markets or governments: Choosing between imperfect alternatives*. Cambridge, MA: MIT Press.

7.   Karlaftis, M., & McCarthy, P. (1999). The effect of privatization on public transit costs. *Journal of Regulatory Economics, 16*, 27-43.

8.   See Chou, S-Y. (2002). Asymmetric information, ownership and quality of care: An empirical analysis of nursing homes. *Journal of Health Economics, 2*, 293-311.

9.   See Rosenau, P., & Linder, S. H. (2003). Two decades of research comparing for-profit and non-profit health provider performance in the United States. *Social Science Quarterly, 84*, 219-241.

CHAPTER 6

TWO PHILADELPHIA REPORTS

Derek C. Briggs

Review of "State Takeover, School Restructuring, Private Management, and Student Achievement in Philadelphia" by Brian Gill, Ron Zimmer, Jolley Christman and Suzanne Blanc, and published by RAND Corporation and Research For Action, and review of "School Reform in Philadelphia: A Comparison of Student Achievement at Privately-Managed Schools with Student Achievement in Other District Schools," by Paul Peterson, and published by Program on Education Policy and Governance at Harvard University. This is a modified version of a review originally published on May 7, 2007.

INTRODUCTION

When an American public school repeatedly fails to demonstrate progress in meeting the academic performance standards established by a state-wide accountability system, what should be done? According to the provisions of the No Child Left Behind (NCLB) Act:

If a school fails to make adequate yearly progress [in meeting proficiency standards] for a fifth year, the school district must initiate plans for *restructuring* the school. This may include reopening the school as a charter school, replacing all or most of the school staff, or turning over school operations

Think Tank Research Quality: Lessons for Policy Makers, the Media, and the Public, pp. 77–92

either to the state or to a private company with a demonstrated record of effectiveness.[1]

As of the summer of 2008, states began identifying schools that had failed to make adequate yearly progress under NCLB for 5 consecutive years. The number of schools identified as failing would be likely to grow with each subsequent year as the difficulty of meeting the requirements for adequate yearly progress increases.[2] One consequence of this is that states and school districts must come to grips with a difficult decision: what approach to restructuring schools is most likely to lead to improvements in academic achievement?

In 2002, just as the NCLB Act was going into effect, Philadelphia was already in the process of restructuring 86 chronically low-achieving elementary and middle schools located in the School District of Philadelphia (SDP). The schools were to be restructured according to what became known as the "diverse provider model." Under this model, school restructuring was to occur in four different ways:

1. Forty-five schools were to receive private management from one of seven for-profit, nonprofit, and university providers ("private management");
2. Twenty-one schools were to be managed by the SDP ("district management");
3. Sixteen schools were to continue to manage themselves (known as the "sweet-sixteen" schools); and
4. Four schools were to be transformed into charter schools.

All 86 schools were to be given additional financial resources. Four years after these changes were implemented, it became possible to compare changes in student achievement among the four types of restructured schools and with other schools in Philadelphia that were not restructured. Two reports that performed such comparisons arrived at seemingly opposite conclusions about the efficacy of private and district management.

The first report, *State Takeover, School Restructuring, Private Management, and Student Achievement in Philadelphia,* was written by Brian Gill, Ron Zimmer, Jolley Christman and Suzanne Blanc of the RAND Corporation and the organization Research For Action (RFA).[3] The second, *School Reform in Philadelphia: A Comparison of Student Achievement at Privately-Managed Schools with Student Achievement in Other District Schools,* was written by Paul Peterson, a faculty member at Harvard University's Kennedy School of Government and director of the Program on Education Policy and Governance (PEPG).[4] The PEPG published this second report. This review explores how the differing conclusions reached by the RAND-RFA and PEPG reports might be reconciled.

FINDINGS AND CONCLUSIONS OF THE TWO REPORTS

The RAND-RFA Report

The RAND-RFA report consists of two different analyses: a "district-wide analysis" and a "diverse-providers analysis." In the district-wide analysis, changes in aggregate student achievement for schools in the SDP from 2001 (preintervention) to 2006 (4 years after the restructuring intervention began) were compared with changes in similarly low-achieving schools across Pennsylvania. This analysis was conducted to test the hypothesis that the diverse-provider model might, by promoting internal competition, spur improvements in low-achieving schools across the SDP, including those schools that had not been restructured. In the diverse-providers analysis, the authors compare changes in student achievement for schools within the SDP as a function of whether and how the school was restructured as of 2002. Of primary interest was whether privately managed schools, district-managed schools, or the sweet-sixteen schools had larger gains than those found in schools that were not restructured or given any additional resources. (Students in the four schools that were being restructured into charter schools were excluded from all analyses.) Of secondary interest was whether the relative gains for privately managed schools varied among the seven for-profit, nonprofit and university management providers.

For its district-wide analysis, conducted with school-level data, the RAND-RFA team found that the percentage of elementary and middle-school students classified as "proficient" based on their performance in reading and math on the Pennsylvania State System of Assessment (PSSA) across the SDP had increased substantially (by about 10 percentage points in reading, and by a little over 20 percentage points in math) in the years since the state takeover. When these gains were compared with the gains of low-achieving schools in other parts of the state, statistically significant differences favoring SDP schools were found for Grade 5 and Grade 8 students after 3 years of the intervention. By the fourth year of the intervention, however, an SDP advantage could only be found for Grade 8 reading scores, which were five percentage points higher in SDP schools. On all other available measures of student proficiency, the 4-year proficiency gains of the SDP schools from preintervention baseline scores were "indistinguishable" from the gains of statewide comparison schools.[5]

While the SDP test scores during this period of time may have been affected by the restructuring policy, those scores may also have been affected by a number of other factors, including several additional district-wide initiatives enacted between 2002 and 2005, some of which were applied to all schools, some only to nonrestructured ones.[6] It is important to note that the key control group in both the RAND-RFA and PEPG reports—nonrestructured SDP schools—does not represent schools in which no other interventions were taking place.

The RAND-RFA team used student-level data for its diverse-provider analysis. Team members found that the cumulative 4-year achievement gains among privately managed schools and among sweet-sixteen schools were no different than the gains among nonrestructured schools in the SDP. In contrast, a positive and moderately sized effect[7] on math achievement was found for schools that had been restructured under district management. When privately managed schools were disaggregated by provider, few statistically significant effects were found—with the exception of large negative effects in reading and math for schools managed by Temple University, and in math for schools managed by the Victory organization. The RAND-RFA report concludes: "with four years of experience, we find no evidence of differential academic benefits that would support the additional expenditures on private managers."[8]

The PEPG Report

The PEPG report was written in response to the findings of the RAND-RFA report. In fact, much of the PEPG's report consists of criticisms of the findings and methods of the RAND-RFA report. But the PEPG report also includes an original analysis. Professor Peterson uses school-level data to compare the changes in the percentage of students classified at different performance levels on the PSSA math and reading tests. He compares data from two cohorts of students enrolled in restructured schools that were privately managed or district-managed to the change observed for all other SDP schools that had not been restructured.[9] The first cohort consisted of students who were in Grade 5 in 2002 and Grade 8 in 2005. The second cohort consisted of students who were in Grade 5 in 2003 and Grade 8 in 2006.

Peterson finds that for both cohorts the average increases in the percentage of students scoring at or above the "Basic" level on the PSSA in both reading and math for privately managed schools was between 4% and 13% larger than those found for schools that had not been restructured or had been district-managed. Similar effects were not found for privately managed schools when the outcome of interest was increases in the percentage of students scoring at or above the "Proficient" level. That is, findings of positive effects were limited to lower-scoring students. In neither case did Peterson find the positive effects for publicly managed schools that were indicated by the RAND-RFA report.

THE REPORTS' USE OF RESEARCH LITERATURE

The RAND-RFA report draws heavily from the work of Paul Hill[10] to establish a theoretical basis for the expectation that restructuring schools using a diverse-provider model should result in an increase student achievement. In principle, opening the management of schools to many possible providers is meant to create a

> competitive school marketplace in which districts manage a varied portfolio of schools, providers have wide rein to innovate, and both are held account-able for student outcomes by strong contracts and through the availability of meaningful choices for schools and parents.[11]

However, as the RAND-RFA report makes clear, the diverse provider model implemented in Philadelphia diverges from this principle, primar-ily because students and parents had not been given the option to choose their own schools. In addition, constraints were placed on the manage-ment options of external providers.

Neither report provides much of a conceptual framework for the theoretical efficacy of privately managed or district-managed schools. According to the RAND-RFA report, empirical findings on the effect of privately managed schools on student achievement have been mixed. The RAND-RFA team cites a prior large-scale evaluation of the Edison schools[12] in which it was found that while Edison-operated schools appear to have no effects on student achievement in the first 3 years of implementation, positive effects emerge in years 4 and 5.

REVIEW OF THE REPORTS' METHODS

Professor Peterson is justifiably critical of the approach taken in the first, district-wide analysis conducted by the RAND-RFA team. In that analysis, increases in the percentage of students scoring at the "Proficient" level of the PSSA among schools in the SDP were compared to schools in other Pennsylvania school districts. In the process, the RAND-RFA authors had restricted the schools in their "treatment" (SDP schools) and "control" (non-SDP schools) groups to these schools with aggregate student achievement in the lowest quartile of the statewide achievement distribution. This appears problematic for two reasons: First, from across grade levels it has the effect of eliminating between 17 and 35% of the SDP schools from the comparison (those above the lowest statewide quartile). This move raises questions about the generalizability of any results. Second, no descriptive statistics are provided by the RAND-RFA authors to make the case that the two groups selected on the basis of aggregate achievement are comparable demographically. This move raises some questions about the internal validity of any results.

Now we turn attention to the diverse-providers analysis. In order to explore why the RAND-RFA report and the PEPG report arrived at different conclusions about the effectiveness of privately managed and district-managed schools, we must first understand the differences in the data analyzed in each report. Figure 6.1 illustrates the general structure of the data made available to the RAND-RFA researchers by the SDP. Each cell in the figure represents the math and reading test scores for a cross-section of students in over 200 SDP schools for a particular grade and year. The letter in each cell indicates the type of test that was administered to students. For example, fifth grade students took PSSA tests in math and reading in 2002, but that cohort took the Terra Nova tests in math and reading as sixth grade students in 2003.[13] Test scores in 2001 can be considered baseline preintervention observations; test scores from 2002 forward represent postintervention observations. Each of the 12 diagonal lines in Figure 6.1 represents a distinct longitudinal cohort of students. All cohorts that included test scores in math and reading for at least two points in time were included in the RAND-RFA analysis (10 out of 12 cohorts). In contrast, the 4 shaded cells within 2 of these 10 cohorts represent the subset of data that was the basis for the findings in the PEPG report. These were the only data publicly available, and they were only available at the school level, not the student level.

There were two key decisions made by the RAND-RFA team in how they chose to analyze the data represented in Figure 6.1. First, the authors decided to specify a single statistical model—known as a fixed effects model—that incorporated information about test score changes from the 10 different student cohorts over the 2001 to 2006 time period. Second, the RAND-RFA team standardized test scores in each grade and year relative to all schools in the SDP as a means of establishing a common score scale out of the three different tests that were administered.[14]

In his report, Peterson criticizes the RAND-RFA methodological approach for the following reasons:

1.   Insufficient context is provided to help the reader evaluate the use of their fixed effects model.

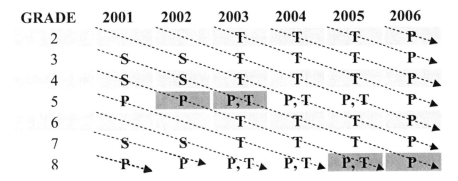

GRADE	2001	2002	2003	2004	2005	2006
2			T	T	T	P
3	S	S	T	T	T	P
4	S	S	T	T	T	P
5	P	P	P, T	P, T	P, T	P
6			T	T	T	P
7	S	S	T	T	T	P
8	P	P	P, T	P, T	P, T	P

Note: Structure of the Data Analyzed in RAND-RFA and PEPG Reports.

Figure 6.1.   *P* = PSSA Tests, *S* = Stanford 9 Tests, *T* = Terra Nova Tests.

2. Combining the results from different tests, some of which are high-stakes (PSSA) and some of which as low-stakes (Terra-Nova and Stanford 9), may lead to underestimating the effects of privately managed schools because students at these schools might take low-stakes tests less seriously.

3. The RAND-RFA analysis does not constitute a quasi-experimental analysis because "Instead of comparing gains during the pre-treatment with gains post-treatment, the researchers simply compared levels of achievement.... As a result, their study is seriously at risk of having under-estimated the impact of the privately-managed schools."[15]

Professor Peterson makes the first of these three criticisms only implicitly, but it is entirely on target. There are many different statistical models the RAND-RFA team could have specified to estimate the effects of different approaches to school reconstruction on student achievement, and the rationale for the one they chose to use is never entirely clear.[16] Even if one takes as a given the objective of applying a single model to the full set of longitudinal cohorts represented in Figure 6.1, one could just as readily specify a random effects model instead of a fixed effects model. Of course, different approaches have their advantages and disadvantages, but the RAND-RFA report never explains why the authors have rejected other modeling alternatives. A technical appendix with such information—with detail on any sensitivity analyses that were conducted—would have considerably strengthened the warrant for the report's conclusions.

Peterson's second criticism is less credible. To begin with, standardized tests in an accountability context are primarily high stakes for teachers and schools—not necessarily for the students who take them. As a threat to the validity of the RAND-RFA findings, problems induced through the use of different tests from year to year will mostly be mitigated by the fact that students in all schools under comparison also took these different tests. Hence, even if SDP students change their amount of effort when taking high-stakes instead of low-stakes tests, there is no reason to suspect that students in privately managed schools took these tests less seriously than students in any of the other SDP schools. The estimated effect of private management would only be underestimated if this differential effort were the case, and Peterson provides no evidence to support this supposition. It would be just as likely that the effect of private management was overestimated because students in the nonrestructured SDP schools took the tests less seriously than their privately managed counterparts.[17]

In Peterson's third criticism, he claims that the RAND-RFA team has—notwithstanding the authors' claims—failed to conduct what is known as a "quasi-experiment" to estimate the effects of private and district management. This claim appears to stem from a disagreement over what constitutes a quasi-experiment. After providing his own definition for the term, Peterson writes, "Had the RAND-RFA conducted such a quasi-experiment, its results would have considerable credibility. But the RAND-RFA did not conduct a quasi-experiment. Instead of comparing gains during pre-treatment with gains post-treatment, the researchers simply compared levels of achievement."[18] Here one must separate what appears to be a confusion over terminology from a critique of methods. The most widely cited and authoritative definition of a quasi-experiment has been provided by Shadish, Cook and Campbell as "an experiment in which units are not assigned to conditions randomly."[19] Clearly then, the RAND-RFP study represents a quasi-experiment—SDP schools and students were nonrandomly assigned to one of four interventions or to the control. Hence any subsequent analysis of this data represents a quasi-experimental analysis.

However, not all quasi-experimental analyses are equally strong as a basis for causal inferences. Peterson favors a particular methodological approach, and because this is not the approach taken by the RAND-RFA team, he implies that the study's fundamental conclusions about the ineffectiveness of private management and the effectiveness of district management are invalid. To illustrate the distinction between the approach Peterson prefers and the approach that the RAND-RFA team has taken, imagine that we have annual student test score data from two types of schools for the years 2000, 2001, and 2002. The "control" schools maintain the same management from 2000 to 2002; the "treatment" schools switch to private management as of 2002 (that is, for the final year). The cells in Table 6.1 indicate the test score averages that would be available in each year for the treatment and control schools.

Under Peterson's methodological approach, the effect of the treatment would be estimated as $[(\overline{Y}_{t02} - \overline{X}_{t01}) - (\overline{X}_{t01} - \overline{X}_{t00})] - [(\overline{Y}_{c02} - \overline{X}_{c01}) - (\overline{X}_{c01} - \overline{X}_{c00})]$. This mathematical expression communicates the idea that for both treatment and control schools, pre-treatment score gains are being compared to post-treatment score gains. Under the RAND-RFA approach (which would not use the available data for 2000, primarily because it would reduce their available sample size), the effect of the treatment would be estimated as $(\overline{Y}_{t02} - \overline{X}_{t01}) - (\overline{Y}_{c02} - \overline{X}_{c01})$. That is, for both treatment and control schools, pretreatment score *levels* (as opposed to gains) are being compared to post-treatment score *levels*. The two approaches will, in fact, produce the same results if the pretreatment score gains are the same for both treatment and control schools (i.e., when $(\overline{X}_{t01} - \overline{X}_{t00}) - (\overline{X}_{c01} - \overline{X}_{c00})$). The RAND-RFA team is able to present evidence that this equality holds for their data, which appears to refute this aspect of Peterson's criticism.[20]

Nonetheless, there are other assumptions of the RAND-RFA modeling approach that could be called into question. While some of these assumptions are briefly discussed in their report, few are given sufficient scrutiny. For example, the fixed effects model assumes that all unobserved variables that might confound the estimated effect of private management, such as student motivation and socioeconomic status, stay constant over time, so that when pre- to postintervention scores are computed for each school, the influence of these variables washes out. This seems somewhat implausible. It is an assumption that will be violated, for example, if students at privately managed schools become increasingly motivated to do well academically with each passing year. Yet if the intervention is working, one might expect to observe precisely those types of changes. This is the sort of issue that suggests a possible tension between the RAND-RFA team's statistical model and the actual situation in the schools. The authors are not entirely successful in reassuring the reader that these sorts of tensions do not compromise the validity of their findings.

While the methods employed in the RAND-RFA analysis place it on one end of a modeling complexity continuum, the methods employed by

Table 6.1. Illustration of Peterson's Critique of RAND-RFA Diverse Provider Analyses

	2000	2001	2002
Treatment Schools	$\overline{X}_{t00}$	$\overline{X}_{t01}$	$\overline{X}_{t02}$
Control Schools	$\overline{X}_{c00}$	$\overline{X}_{c01}$	$\overline{X}_{c02}$

the PEPG analysis are at the opposite end. On the one hand, it is a strength of Peterson's analysis that his approach for estimating the effects of private and district management is easy to follow. But the simplicity of Peterson's approach is also a weakness, because potential threats to the validity of his inferences are especially difficult to rule out. There are a number of potentially serious problems with the methodological approach in the PEPG report, and they are summarized below.

1. The baseline year for PEPG's comparisons of Grade 5 to Grade 8 growth in each of the two cohorts (2002, 2003) does not precede the restructuring interventions. This means that any initial effects of the reform are not captured by the PEPG analysis. Moreover, because the PEPG baseline year is different than the baseline year used in the RAND-RFA analysis (2001), the different effects estimated by the two reports are hard to compare.

2. The PEPG report only includes the privately managed and district-managed categories schools that include both Grade 5 and Grade 8. This is illustrated in Table 6.2. The two shaded (K-8 and 5-8) columns indicate the subset of schools that would be included in PEPG's analysis based on 2006-2007 data. However, Professor Peterson does not appear to impose the same restriction for the nonrestructured district schools used as his comparison group. As a result, the average gains for students who remain in privately managed schools over the 4-year period are compared to the average gains for two distinct groups of students: (a) those who stay in the same non-restructured school from Grade 5 to Grade 8, and (b) those who switch from an elementary to a middle school. If, for example, switching schools has a negative association with student achievement, this would lead to overestimating the effects Peterson has found for both privately managed and district-managed schools.

3. Based only on the school-level summaries of student achievement data available to Peterson, we have no way of knowing how many of the students represented in a given school's Grade 5 test scores are subsequently represented in the Grade 8 test scores for the same school. If the students with the highest test scores are more likely to stay in a given type of restructured school, while the students with the lowest scores are more likely to leave, any effect from restructuring would be overestimated. If the converse were true, any effect would be underestimated.

4. As noted above, Peterson's sample of schools is restricted because SDP schools vary in terms of the grade span they include. His

Table 6.2. Illustration of Subset of Private and District Providers Included in the PEPG Analysis Using 2006-07 Data

				Range of Grades in Restructured Philadelphia Schools							
Provider	K-5	K-6	K-7	K-8	5-8	6-8	7-8	8-9	7-12	9-12	TOTAL
Edison		4		8	4	2	2				20
Foundations		4		1			2			1	8
Temple				5				1			6
University of Penn		1		2							3
Victory		2			1				1		4
District	2	4	2	9			1		1	2	21
TOTAL	2	15	2	25	5	2	5	1	2	3	62
% of Column Total	3.2%	24.2%	3.2%	40.3%	8.1%	3.2%	8.1%	1.6%	3.2%	4.8%	100%

approach for comparing test-score change over time only works for schools that have students in both Grade 5 and Grade 8. Because he is only including data for about 40% of all privately managed schools, and between 20 and 40% of all district-managed schools in his two cohort analyses, it is unclear whether his estimated effects, even if he is accurately gauging them, generalize to the unrepresented schools.[21]

REVIEW OF THE VALIDITY OF THE FINDINGS AND CONCLUSIONS

Though the findings from these two reports appear contradictory, it is possible that both are correct. There are at least two reasons this might be so. One possibility Peterson puts forward is that private management may have a negative effect in elementary grades, but a positive effect in middle grades. When an overall effect across Grades 3 through 8 is estimated in the RAND-RFA report, the negative early grade effect may cancel the positive middle grade effect. Neither report, however, provides a cogent explanation for why this might be expected.

A second possibility concerns the PEPG analysis' use of only categorical test score information (i.e., the percentage of students in a school that fall into the "Basic" and "Proficient" performance levels on the PSSA). In fact, Peterson only found positive effects for privately managed schools when examining the change in the percentage of students at the "Basic" (but not the "Proficient") level. This outcome (improvement for students scoring at the Basic level) is a function of movement among students at the lowest end of the PSSA score scale. By contrast, the estimated effects summarized in the RAND-RFA analysis represent the average score gain across the full PSSA, Stanford 9, or Terra Nova standardized score scale for any given grade and year.[22] The take-home point is that while the PEPG analysis has found positive effects for private management, these effects are based upon both a very specific subgroup of schools (those containing Grades 5 through 8) and a very specific subgroup of students (those who have performed the worst on the PSSA test). The RAND-RFA analysis, on the other hand, found no overall effect for private management on the basis of all SDP schools and all SDP students. At issue is whether a single policy for all schools with all students is warranted, or whether that policy should vary by type of school and student.

It should be relatively straightforward to reconcile these differences empirically. If Peterson's school-level analysis were done with student-level test scores, using only students attending the same school in Grades 5 and 8, would the estimated effects for privately managed and district-managed schools more closely resemble those found by Peterson, or would they resemble the overall effects presented in the RAND-RFA analysis? This would be important to find out, because if private and district management have different effects on the achievement of elementary and middle-school students (as the PEPG analysis suggests), this finding would have clear policy ramifications.

Both reports are well-written, cognizant of the limitations of their analyses, and relatively cautious in generalizing their findings. A weakness of both reports—particularly the RAND-RFA report—is a lack of important descriptive statistics. A prime example of this is the failure to detail the movement of students in and out of the schools in the SDP during the time period being analyzed. Neither report gives the reader any sense of the variability of test score gains within schools or across students.

Of the two reports, the RAND-RFA report has the advantage of better and more comprehensive data during the 2001-06 time period in Philadelphia. Because of this, the report's conclusions about the efficacy of private and district management on student achievement are likely to carry more weight than those from the PEPG report, and this appears justifiable. There are threats to the validity of both reports, but because the PEPG report is only able to analyze a subset of the RAND-RFA data at the school rather than the student level, there are more reasons to doubt the PEPG findings.

USEFULNESS OF THE REPORTS FOR GUIDANCE OF POLICY AND PRACTICE

The results from the RAND-RFA report suggest that, on average, schools that were restructured though district management in Philadelphia were more effective at increasing math achievement than were comparable schools that were restructured with private managers. Also, none of the restructuring interventions had lasting and appreciable effects on reading achievement. In contrast, the PEPG report suggests that privately managed schools containing the Grades 5 and 8 are in fact having a positive effect on the reading and math achievement of students in the lowest part of the PSSA test score distribution.

Neither of these reports should be used as the primary basis for policy decisions until subsequent analyses have been performed to provide a more nuanced view of the effects of the restructuring interventions at different grade levels, and at different locations along the PSSA test score distribution.

Nevertheless, both of these reports appear to be having an immediate impact on policy and practice. The RAND-RFA report was, at the time this review was being written, being used by Philadelphia's Accountability

Review Council to justify the firing of underperforming private managers and as the basis for identifying the "schooling and organizational conditions that contributed to the success of the District restructured schools."[23] Meanwhile the findings from the PEPG report have been reported in the *Wall Street Journal* and other media outlets.[24]

Given NCLB's nod toward school restructuring, the outcomes in Philadelphia have national import. These two studies, read together, do contribute to our understanding of Philadelphia's experience. Yet, while the RAND-RFA study sheds more light on that experience than does the PEPG study, neither offers a complete picture, and more research is needed before drawing any definitive conclusions.

NOTES AND REFERENCES

1. U.S. Department of Education. (2003). *No Child Left Behind: A Parents Guide*. Washington, DC, p. 9.
2. Linn, R. L. (2003). Accountability: Responsibility and responsible expectations. *Educational Researcher, 32*(7), 3-13.
3. Gill, B., Zimmer, R., Christman, J. & Blanc, S. (2007). *State takeover, school restructuring, private management, and student achievement in Philadelphia*. Santa Monica, CA: The RAND Corporation.
4. Peterson, P. (2007). *School reform in Philadelphia: A comparison of student achievement at privately managed schools with student achievement in other district schools*. Kennedy School of Government, Harvard University, Program on Education Policy and Governance.
5. See p. xii in Gill, Zimmer, Christman, & Blanc, (2007); see note 3.
6. See Table 2.2, p. 10 in Gill, Zimmer, Christman, & Blanc, (2007); see note 3.
7. The actual magnitude of the effect, expressed as a proportion of the variability typical of math test scores (i.e., the standard deviation), was 0.2.
8. See p. 41 of Gill, Zimmer, Christman, & Blanc, (2007); see note 3.
9. Peterson does not distinguish the sweet-sixteen schools separately in his analysis. It appears that even though they received additional resources, they are grouped with all other nonrestructured schools.
10. Hill, P. T. (2006). *Put learning first: A portfolio approach to public schools*. Washington, DC: Progressive Policy Institute.
11. See pp. 8-9 of Gill, Zimmer, Christman, & Blanc, (2007); see note 3.
12. See Gill, B., Hamilton, L., Lockwood, J. R., Marsh, J., Zimmer, R., Hill, D., and Pribesh, S. (2005). *Inspiration, perspiration, and time: Operations and achievement in Edison schools*. Santa Monica, CA: RAND Corporation, MG-351-EDU, 2005. http://www.rand.org/pubs/monographs/MG351/ Note that this evaluation was also conducted by RAND and had the same lead author (Brian Gill) as the current RAND-RFA report.

13. Note that for the second grades and sixth grades, no tests were administered in 2002 and 2003. In the fifth and eighth grades two different tests were administered from 2003 through 2005.

14. Because SDP students did not take the same tests across grades, there is no criterion-referenced measure available to assess growth in scores over time. Test scores were standardized by the RAND-RFA team to get around this problem. For example, in 2001 test scores were available for Grade 4 students in the SDP that took the Stanford 9 math test. The RAND-RFA team took the score of each student in this sample, subtracted the average Stanford 9 math score for the SDP as a whole, and then divided by the standard deviation of the test scores. After doing this, all students had standardized scores that ranged between about three standard deviations above and below the district average. By the next year (2002), these same students were in Grade 5, but were administered the PSSA math test, which has a different score scale than the Stanford 9. Accordingly, the RAND-RFA team took the score of each student in this sample, subtracted the average PSSA math score for the SDP as a whole, and then divided by the standard deviation of the test scores. Because of this, all students once again had standardized scores that ranged between about three standard deviations above and below the district average. The upshot of this approach is that changes in test scores from Grade 4 to Grade 5 can only be given a relative interpretation in the RAND-RFA analysis: Has a student's achievement improved relative to his or her district peers?

15. See pp. 14-17 of Gill, Zimmer, Christman, & Blanc, (2007); see note 3.

16. For example, a more transparent approach might have been to specify separate statistical models for each of the four longitudinal cohorts of students that were tested in the baseline year of 2001.

17. An interesting supposition that might be more plausible is that some of the math and reading curricula associated with schools under different forms of management may be differentially aligned to the three tests being combined onto a common scale. If, for example, Edison's 'Success for All' curriculum is more aligned with the PSSA tests than the Terra Nova tests, while the curricula used by nonrestructured schools are more aligned to the Terra Nova tests, this might bias any estimated effect for an Edison school when test score changes are based on a transition from PSSA to Terra Nova.

18. See pp. 14-15 in Peterson (2007); see note 4.

19. See p. 12 in Shadish, W., Cook, T., & Campbell, D. (2002). *Experimental and Quasi-Experimental Designs for Generalized Causal Inference*.

20. See Table 4.1 on p. 31 of Gill, Zimmer, Christman, & Blanc, (2007); see note 3.

21. Peterson shows that the racial/ethnic mix and free- and reduced-lunch status of students in restructured schools included in the analysis is comparable to that of the restructured schools excluded in the analysis. However, there is little variability in these characteristics among the restructured schools, so this comes as little surprise. What would be more compelling

would be a comparison of the average Grade 5 or Grade 8 test scores for the included and excluded schools.

22.   It is entirely possible that the difference between the RAND-RFA findings and the PEPG findings might be captured by the inclusion of a series of dummy variables in the fixed effects model that represent the interaction between a given restructuring intervention and a student's location in the lowest achievement quartile in a prior year.

23.   Accountability Review Council. (2007). *Report to the School Reform Commission: The Status of 2005-2006 Academic Performance in the School District of Philadelphia*. February, 2007.

24.   See Peterson, P. (2007). The Philadelphia Story. *The Wall Street Journal*. February 23, 2007. Retrieved April 25, 2009, from http://www.ksg.harvard.edu/pepg/pr/WSJOPED_20070222.htm

PART 4

Vouchers Save Money

As is evident in earlier chapters of this book, free-market think tanks have promoted privatization on the assumption that private schools improve student achievement and provide ancillary benefits like increased parent satisfaction. The reports and reviews presented in Part 4 examine another common argument made to support private school choice mechanisms: If states provide conventional vouchers or tax-credit vouchers (neovouchers), the resulting migration of students to private schools will provide net savings to states and districts, meaning that government will have more money available to support students who remain in public schools. The three reviews that follow assess studies that purport to find support for this claim; all of these reports were published by the Milton and Rose D. Friedman Foundation, either alone or jointly.

In Chapter 7, reviewer Christopher Lubienski analyzes *Spreading Freedom and Saving Money: The Fiscal Impact of the D.C. Voucher Program* (2006), authored by Leon Michos and Susan Aud and published jointly by the Cato Institute and the Friedman Foundation. In Chapter 8, reviewer Bruce Baker looks at *School Choice by the Numbers: The Fiscal Effect of School Choice Programs 1990-2006* (2007), with Susan Aud as the sole author and Friedman as the sole publisher. In Chapter 9, reviewer Luis Huerta examines three Friedman reports, two of which were authored by Brian

Think Tank Research Quality: Lessons for Policy Makers, the Media, and the Public, pp. 93–95

Gottlob: *The Fiscal Impact of Tax-Credit Scholarships in Montana* (2009) and *The Fiscal Impact of Tax-Credit Scholarships in Georgia* (2008). The third, *The Fiscal Impact of a Corporate & Individual Tax-Credit Scholarship Program on the State of Indiana* (2009), was authored by David Stuit.

Despite the geographic and programmatic differences among the states examined, all of these studies found that vouchers and voucher-like programs produce net savings for states and districts. Reviewers found similarities among the reports beyond their findings. Generally, the reports' authors tended to ignore the same confounding factors. For example, Baker points out that Aud never defines "cost" and that her use of the term and idea is problematic. "Typically," he explains, "cost savings are defined in terms of achieving similar or better quality of outcome or output at lower investment. Cost necessarily assumes a level of product quality." Baker also notes that Aud's cost calculations focus only on direct government expenditures (the face value of the voucher); she does not account for additional resources, including indirect government subsidies. Lubienski adds that "the authors seem unaware that private school tuition is not necessarily an accurate reflection of private school costs, since tuition does not account for other inputs such as church support for schools, volunteer hours, or below-market salaries for religious workers." Further, Baker notes that "Increased migration of students to private schooling may increase the necessity for private philanthropic contributions to elementary and secondary education in the form of direct support to private independent and private religious schools," thereby simply shifting cost (including through tax deductions) rather than reducing it—even assuming such contributions would be forthcoming.

Other common weaknesses include authors' proclivity for making assumptions and claims without providing empirical support for them. Lubienski notes that the authors of the District of Columbia report "provide little or no empirical evidence to support their findings." For example, they "assert that the high spending in the District is a result of waste, but they fail to offer proof." Of the Aud study, Baker points out that the author simply assumed—with no supporting evidence—that governments will realize savings that might be available if student transfer patterns play out as she hopes. Huerta's reviews of the tax-credit voucher reports identify comparable assumptions underpinning the findings of positive fiscal impacts for states. For example, none of the three state reports seriously take into account the potential new cost of providing funding to students attending private schools who would have attended them even without a tax-credit voucher program in place.

Another pattern seen in these reports concerns the failure to employ or reference reputable and relevant earlier research. Lubienski terms the DC study "strangely divorced from the comprehensive research already published on this issue." Baker finds that the Aud report made "scant use of existing research literature on vouchers or tuition tax credits." He adds that "of the works cited that might be considered scholarly research all three were working papers or reports that were not yet published in scholarly journals." Huerta's appraisal is similar:

> The use of reliable research literature in the two Gottlob reports (Georgia and Montana) is very limited, and the validity of the literature that is used is highly suspect. They primarily rely on similar reports, most from the same author and from similar advocacy organizations (e.g., the Cato Institute and Goldwater Institute) to justify their methods and findings.

Overall, the five reports reviewed in the following chapters resemble one another in key ways. Each was supported by the Friedman Foundation, each reached the same conclusions, and each shared similar core weaknesses. All the reviewers conclude with a caution about using the reports for policy, as illustrated by Huerta's general assessment: "Policymakers should be cautioned to look beyond the seductive promises of increased fiscal savings and efficiency, which are unsubstantiated and inaccurately estimated in these reports."

A related report summarized below is available from www.thinktankreview.org.

- Reviewer Clive Belfield analyzed *The Fiscal Impact of the Milwaukee Parental Choice Program: 2009 Update*, authored by Robert Costrell and published by the School Choice Demonstration Project housed at the University of Arkansas. In this update of an earlier report, Costrell found that the program "saves Wisconsin [state-level] taxpayers a large amount ($37 million in FY2009)" but also that "property taxpayers in Milwaukee face a large fiscal burden ($45 million)." As opposed to the authors of the Friedman reports, Costrell recognized that the accuracy of cost estimates depends in part upon the number of students who use vouchers to attend private schools they would have attended even without a subsidy. However, lacking any certainty on this issue, Belfield found it possible that actual costs or savings of the program might easily range significantly upward or downward from the author's estimate. Although he considered the fiscal picture uncertain, Belfield found this study to be a useful guide to the financing of this particular system, one that offered a clear explanation of the city and state funding systems and of the way they interact to transfer resources from the city to the state. The report's "most fruitful policy contribution," according to the reviewer, was to raise questions in two important areas: "devising funding formulas for voucher programs, and debating the merits of voucher programs as public policy."

CHAPTER 7

FREEDOM AND SAVING MONEY

The Fiscal Impact of the DC Voucher Program

Christopher Lubienski

Review of "Spreading Freedom and Saving Money: The Fiscal Impact of the D.C. Voucher Program," by Leon Michos and Susan Aud and published by the Cato Institute and the Friedman Foundation for Educational Choice. This is a modified version of a review originally published on February 20, 2006.

INTRODUCTION

The nation's capital is a unique laboratory for studying the hotly contested issue of public funding for private schools. Washington, DC, has a rich tradition of private and religious schools, most of which have been inaccessible for impoverished families. The District of Columbia Public Schools (DCPS) have gained a reputation as a high-cost, low-quality education system, and residents have acquired experience with school choice through a substantial charter school sector. The District is self-contained, with its suburban neighborhoods located in Virginia and Maryland, and

Think Tank Research Quality: Lessons for Policy Makers, the Media, and the Public, pp. 97–107

Congress has the power to exercise its direct authority over the District without the obstacles presented by state law. In early 2004, a voucher program (called "opportunity scholarships") was launched to enable residents to attend private schools in the District at public expense—the "District of Columbia School Choice Incentive Act."

This law represents a major federal intervention into the issue of private school vouchers. Although there were already publicly and privately funded voucher programs in a number of cities (including a privately funded program in the District), voucher advocates wanted to increase the federal government's role in this arena. Congress overcame the traditional resistance to the idea of vouchers among local leaders by limiting the number of students who could enroll in the program, and by allocating $13 million to DCPS and another $13 million to the local charter schools for physical and programmatic improvements.

Spreading Freedom and Saving Money: The Fiscal Impact of the D.C. Voucher Program[1] attempts to evaluate the impact of the voucher program after its first year. Rather than examining the primary claim of voucher proponents—that students learn more in private schools—the authors instead look at the initial impact of the voucher program on educational spending, asking whether the plan has saved DC and its school district any money. The authors also examine some hypothetical scenarios, including the financial impact if program costs were carried locally instead of by the nation's taxpayers.

FINDINGS AND CONCLUSIONS OF THE REPORT

The report asserts four prominent findings:

1. The DC voucher program successfully responds to substantial demand on the part of parents to choose private schools for their children.

2. Principals do, in fact, exercise substantial control over variable costs, so that they may adjust school-level budgets to respond to the gain or loss of students.

3. The program currently saves the District money on education, with most of those savings coming from the additional grant from Congress.

4. Additional savings would accrue even if the program were fully funded through local sources, due to competitive incentives and efficiencies.

From these findings, the report describes a number of scenarios for possible reconfigurations of the program. Based on various assumptions of eligibility and participation for both students and schools, the report estimates potential savings to the taxpayers of up to $3 million.

The subsequent sections of this review will show how these findings are premised on questionable analyses and grounded in ideological assumptions about schooling and markets.

RATIONALES SUPPORTING THE FINDINGS AND CONCLUSIONS

The authors provide little or no empirical evidence to support their findings. Their use of the data tends to be decontextualized and simplistic, giving the misleading appearance that the data support their conclusions.

For example, to support the contention that public schools are failing, the report cites raw achievement scores from standardized tests such as the Stanford 9 and the percentage of District students (presumably those in public schools[2]) reaching "proficiency" levels in math on the National Assessment of Educational Progress, the "nation's report card." Yet the data, as presented in the authors' analysis, do not tell us anything about school effectiveness because they fail to control for student demographics, prior achievement, and other factors known to heavily influence student achievement. In order to suggest the lack of a causal link between inputs and outcomes, the report refers to spending data from the National Center for Education Statistics. According to the authors, these data report that DCPS has "nearly the highest per pupil spending of any district in the nation," but the analysis fails to consider student characteristics that might account for that level of spending, such as the greater need for services due to the high concentrations of students living in poverty, or students with limited English proficiency (p. 4). Furthermore, the report cites the concurrent decline in enrollment at DCPS and the emergence of charter schools in the District as proof of parents' preferences for options outside of DCPS, which it claims has caused the "downward spiral of DCPS" (p. 4). The authors fail to examine whether the decline of DCPS *causes* families to leave, or if families leaving DCPS causes the purported decline (or both).

Most of the report's fiscal conclusions are based on simple cost estimates of per-pupil funding and the amount allocated for vouchers. In making predictions about the fiscal impact of the program under different configurations, the authors introduce different assumptions into their calculations, some of which are indefensible. More importantly, however, the report only focuses on general costs and is unable to offer any insights into the much more important subject of cost-benefit analyses. (See discussion below.)

For the most methodologically sophisticated aspect of the study, the authors develop a regression model to test the supposition—which they see as key for competitive dynamics—that DCPS principals have a "high degree of flexibility in responding to student needs" (p. 6) and can therefore respond to the expressed preferences of consumers (i.e., the arrival or exit of students at their schools). Unfortunately, the authors provide only a few details about the model they used in making that determination; thus, it is impossible to assess the accuracy of the results.

THE REPORT'S METHODS AND USE OF RESEARCH LITERATURE

This failure to make clear the methods used in the analysis typifies the report's shortcomings for providing objective, grounded, or useful insights on the topic of vouchers. The limitations of the analysis are particularly evident in three areas: (1) the failure to truly examine the efficiency of the program; (2) the subsequent inability to consider nonrandom participation in the program, and the consequent likely detrimental impact to DCPS and its students beyond immediate fiscal considerations; and (3) the overreliance on hypothetical assumptions regarding market dynamics, rather than empirical evidence.

Missing Efficiency

The report argues for the efficiency of the voucher program: "If federal grant subsidies were withdrawn and the program were locally funded, the city would still save $258,402 due to the greater efficiency of school choice" (p. 2). However, efficiency can only be determined by looking at the ratio of inputs to outcomes; the analysis tells us nothing about the efficiency of the program (or its effectiveness) because it considers only the input side of the ratio in terms of spending. Thus, this "fiscal impact" study says nothing about value-for-money, efficacy, or results. This is problematic because it is possible that—as with other forms of privatization—these education reforms lead to a reduction in both costs *and* services.

Indeed, the report could have addressed this issue by acknowledging some of the work already done on school costs. The report consistently contrasts per-pupil spending in public schools to tuition in private schools, but this is not an accurate comparison of the resources devoted to schooling. The authors seem unaware that private school tuition is not necessarily an accurate reflection of private school costs, since tuition does not account for other inputs such as church support for schools, volunteer hours, and below-market salaries for religious workers.[3] Similarly, the analysis assumes that costs are inherently lower in private schools, but researchers have shown that higher costs in public schools are due largely to their having proportionately more special education students and higher salaries for a teaching force that is, on average, more qualified and experienced.[4] Yet the report simply maintains that higher public school costs are due to a bloated central office bureaucracy. While this may be true to some degree, the report fails to offer any evidence, even anecdotal, for this. Additionally, it does not consider that larger organizations, such as urban districts, can also *save* money by centralizing some functions, thereby accessing economies of scale.

More importantly, the report ignores the substantial literature on what is already known about the efficacy of vouchers. Again, the report looks only at inputs (costs), but, in considering the value of those costs, it needs to consider the results. On this issue, the previous work on academic achievement in voucher programs has been quite mixed. While some researchers have found modest gains for students using vouchers, others have not—which is a crucial consideration in weighing the value of a program.[5] The report's brief reference to other voucher programs focuses only on participation rates (not results) in other countries, where direct comparisons to the U.S. are difficult to sustain.

Missing Costs

Another limitation of the analysis is that the authors insist on considering costs only in terms of dollars immediately spent on schooling. The report notes at several points that the public schools are relieved of the burden of educating students using vouchers, but the students leaving DCPS are not a random sample. Rather, they tend to exhibit certain attributes associated with being easier, and cheaper, to educate—for instance, the report indicates that they are less likely to require special education services, and come primarily from the earlier grades, which are less costly to operate. By definition, these students are from families exhibiting (by the act of choosing) greater interest in their children's education. This is an important consideration because a large and established body of research demonstrates that students learn not only from a school's instructional program, but from the aggregate effect of the aspirations and attitudes of their cohort—the "peer effect."[6] Thus, when these students leave, they take with them attributes that would likely have boosted student achievement for the remaining students. Their more efficacious and involved parents also leave the public school community. As a result,

DCPS incurs the high cost of educating the majority of students—those who have chosen not to leave and, who (1) are likely (on average) to be more difficult and costly to educate, (2) will be subject to a less beneficial peer effect, and (3) will not have the benefit of the volunteering and fund-raising of departed parents. The report makes no attempt to account for these costs.

Instead, in the most sophisticated section of the analysis, the authors try to create a regression model to argue that "principals are able to reduce their costs by an amount similar to the reduction in [district-distributed] funding that they receive when a student leaves" (p. 10). That is, the authors contend that the departure of voucher students from public schools need not decrease the financial resources available to the public schools. This may or may not be the case. It is difficult to evaluate the details of their analysis because few details about their data or methods are explained. More importantly, the endeavor itself is not particularly useful. The problem with this analysis is that regression coefficients are *averages*, and in no way indicate that individual principals have the flexibility to reduce spending on a per-pupil basis. Most school-level costs are for teacher salaries, which can be adjusted only through hiring and firing. Most of the time, a one-student change in enrollment involves little change in substantive costs to the school. It only does so when the arrival or departure of that one student tips the scales to the extent that the class size in one grade grows or shrinks enough to justify the hiring or firing of an additional teacher. Thus, the only costs accounted for are rather marginal, at best.

Missing Research

Except for an unsupported foray into statistical models and a presentation of undigested descriptive statistics, the report contains a dearth of references to empirical evidence supporting its claims. For instance, the analysis is not grounded in the extensive research available on this topic. While just over a dozen reports are cited here, only one is from an arguably peer-reviewed publication.[7] Instead, the report relies on assumptions about how markets *should* work in public education according to an extreme laissez-faire perspective on markets. The report is preoccupied—as was the legislation—with creating new market-style incentives to guide the behavior of educators in the District. This comes from a theoretical perspective ("public choice theory") that denies non-market motivations, such as professionalism, as a factor influencing public employees. Thus, the report contends that "Competitive pressure to maintain enrollment should be a driving force that motivates principals to design programs that best meet the needs of their students" (p. 7)—making no mention of the possibility that principals might also be motivated by a desire to educate children. The report is fraught with such platitudes about the market. The problem is that many of them are presented as self-evident, not supported by any evidence. For example, the report notes that school problems "may be due to a lack of market pressure" (p. 7), but the authors never demonstrate that this is, in fact, the major problem (or even a substantial problem) facing schools. The authors claim that "external pressure [is] the only way to improve" schools (p. 4). To defend such a claim, the authors would have to disprove the efficacy of all other approaches to school improvement. The report makes no attempt to do this.

REVIEW OF THE VALIDITY OF THE FINDINGS AND CONCLUSIONS

The report's conclusions lack evidentiary support in four key areas. First, the report asserts that the voucher program responds to substantial demand on the part of parents to choose private schools for their children, but the low application rate for vouchers seriously challenges that conclusion. Indeed, the vast majority (over 95%) of parents with eligible children have chosen not to apply for vouchers.[8] This is problematic for the logic of this report: either most parents do not, in fact, exhibit a "strong desire...to exert control over their children's education" (p.4), or else these voucher advocates would have to claim that parents are generally poor judges of school quality (and, hence, should not be positioned as decision makers for their children's educational future).[9]

Second, the analysis finds that principals do, in fact, exercise substantial control over variable costs, so that they may adjust school-level budgets to respond to the gain or loss of students. As noted above, this finding—the most sophisticated in the report—is not particularly insightful or useful.

Third, the report concludes that the program currently saves the District money on education costs, with most of those savings coming from the additional grant from Congress. Yet, as the report acknowledges, "some of those students attended private or charter schools prior to the inception of the voucher program" (p. 8). This is a crucial bit of information, because it indicates that, in the case of those students already enrolled in private schools, the program is not saving taxpayers money, but instead costing them more money by shifting the burden from private to public coffers. Unfortunately, the study neglects to specify how many students were already enrolled in private schools.[10]

The report laments the additional grant from Congress to the DCPS (and charter schools) because it "essentially negates the oft-cited rationale for voucher programs—that creating competition will induce the public schools to operate more efficiently" (p. 9). This highlights the agenda at the center of the report, to financially punish "failing" schools (and, by extension, the students in them) to create a more perfect market, even though the report has not demonstrated that market-like conditions would necessarily benefit students.

Finally, the report concludes that additional savings would accrue even if the program were fully funded through local sources, due to competitive incentives and efficiencies. This claim is dubious because it relies on an incomplete accounting of costs, failing to account for the added public costs caused by the use of vouchers by families who would have opted for private schooling even without the voucher policy. Additionally, not only does the analysis fail to consider hidden costs imposed on others when a voucher is used, but it neglects to include the actual costs of the program when it estimates "savings" in a targeted program funded locally. The authors calculate savings by subtracting the amount of the voucher from the per-pupil cost of educating a typical student. However, when considering the cost of the program (something noted earlier in the report, but omitted later), the purported savings essentially balance out (the difference being less than 50 cents a student). Furthermore, the report neglects to explain where "savings" come from. The authors assume that they are "due to the greater efficiency of school choice," or the "economic benefits of school choice." Those "savings," however, have nothing to do with competitive "efficiency"—as the authors themselves note in their calculations of the current program. Instead, "savings" are simply (1) the lower amounts of money devoted to cheaper-to-educate children encouraged to flee public schools, and (2) lower teacher salaries.

THE REPORT'S USEFULNESS FOR
GUIDANCE OF POLICY AND PRACTICE

The District of Columbia is not a typical case, and, to the authors' credit, they do not explicitly argue for the generalizability of this analysis to other districts. However, the value even of lessons for education policy in the District is limited. The authors assert that the high spending in the District is a result of waste, but they fail to offer proof. Indeed, they generally ignore the relatively high degree of poverty in the District, a condition that often entails additional spending in order to obtain even modest gains in academic achievement.

Moreover, the analysis ignores the issue of ceding public accountability for education to private interests. Although there are many examples of fraud and waste in the public schools, abuses in the private realm are also well documented. In fact, voucher programs in places such as Milwaukee and Florida have led to criminal mischief and abuse. It is evident from the opening sentence that this report approaches this issue from a definite ideological perspective, preoccupied with applying market-oriented economic logic to public schools. The report begins by praising privatization in the telecom and airline industries, ignoring serious problems in those areas, such as the failure to lower cable rates and poor customer service from air carriers. A researcher should not prejudge privatization as inherently bad or good; rather, success should be determined empirically. Quite possibly, such success depends on the peculiarities of a given sector. While privatization might make sense with a private good such as information technologies, public goods such as public education may be a different story. Values such as equity, access, and diversity often resist private provision; forcing public goods into a business-style model can lead to unpredictable and often perverse outcomes.[11] Ironically, these advocates of purer markets for education are essentially asking for larger government subsidies for schools, and a greater government role in the private sector.

The Cato/Friedman report is useful mostly as a descriptive document on the DC voucher program, and as evidence of further market-based designs for public education. The analysis, however, is strangely divorced from the comprehensive research that has already been published on this issue. Perhaps most importantly, the report neglects not only the hidden costs, but even the actual costs of the program. Inexplicably, the analysis acknowledges, but fails to consider, that a substantial proportion of the program's costs are now devoted to paying for the private schooling of families that were not previously in the District's public schools. So not only does the program not "save" the District money, it actually adds to the taxpayer burden by subsidizing the private choices of families already paying for private school. The recommendation of the report that the voucher program be universally available and locally funded as a way to save money is simply not supported by the evidence presented in the report.

Finally, the analysis tells us nothing about the effectiveness or efficiency of the District's voucher program, even though that is a central claim made in the report. Although focused on "savings" in the form of reduced spending, the analysis begs the question of whether most citizens want to reduce educational costs without regard to the issues of efficiency and quality. Public opinion polls have repeatedly shown that people are willing to spend more money for quality schooling.[12] Because of its overwhelming focus on reducing costs—at any cost—and lack of empirical attention to issues of quality, the report contributes little to the productive deliberations of policy options.

NOTES AND REFERENCES

1. Michos, L., & Aud, S. (2006, January 31). *Spreading Freedom and Saving Money: The Fiscal Impact of the D.C. Voucher Program*. Washington DC: Cato Institute, p. 4. Retrieved February 1, 2006, from http://www.cato.org/pub_display.php?pub_id=5424

2. The authors give no indication of whether or not the NAEP sample for DC included the substantial proportion of DC students in charter public schools.

3. See: Levin, H. M. (1998). Educational vouchers: Effectiveness, choice, and costs. *Journal of Policy Analysis and Management, 17*(3), 373-392.

4. See: Rothstein, R. (1997). *Where's the money going? Changes in the level and composition of education spending, 1991-96*. Washington, DC: Economic Policy Institute.

5. See: Belfield, C. R. (2006). *The Evidence on Education Vouchers: An Application to the Cleveland Scholarship and Tutoring Program* (Occasional Paper No. 112). New York: National Center for the Study of Privatization in Education.

    Howell, W. G., & Peterson, P. E. (2004). Uses of Theory in randomized field trials: Lessons from school voucher research on disaggregation, missing data, and the generalization of findings. *American Behavioral Scientist, 47*(5), 634-657.

    Krueger, A. B., & Zhu, P. (2004). Another look at the New York City school voucher experiment. *American Behavioral Scientist, 47*(5), 658-698.

    Rouse, C. E. (1998). Private school vouchers and student achievement: An evaluation of the Milwaukee Parental Choice Program. *Quarterly Journal of Economics, 113*(2), 553-603.

    Witte, J. F. (2000). *The market approach to education: An analysis of America's First Voucher Program*. Princeton, NJ: Princeton University Press

6. See: Coleman, J. S. (1966). Equal schools or equal students? *The Public Interest, 4*, 70-75.

    Evans, W. N., Oates, W. E., & Schwab, R. M. (1992). Measuring peer group effects: A study of teenage behavior. *Journal of Political Economy, 100*(5), 966-991.

    Hoxby, C. M. (2000). *Peer effects in the classroom: Learning from gender and race variation* (Working Paper No. 7867). Cambridge, MA: National Bureau of Economic Research.

    Jencks, C. (1972). *Inequality: A reassessment of the effect of family and schooling in America*. New York, NY: Basic Books.

    Kahlenberg, R. D. (2000). *All together now: Creating middle-class schools through public school choice*. Washington, DC: Brookings Institution Press.

    Levin (1998); see note 3.

    Summers, A. A., & Wolfe, B. L. (1977). Do Schools Make a Difference? *American Economic Review, 67*(3), 639-652.

    Wenglinsky, H. (1997). How money matters: The effect of school district spending on academic achievement. *Sociology of Education, 70*(3), 221-237.

7. See note #9 in Michos & Aud (2006, January 31).

8. Wolf, P. J., Gutmann, B., Eissa, N., & Puma, M. (2005). *Evaluation of the DC Opportunity Scholarship Program: First Year Report On Participation*. Washington, DC: U.S. Department of Education/Institute of Education Sciences (p. xi).

9. Indeed, Kevin Chavous, mentioned in this report as a person committed to external pressure for school improvement, recently appeared on ABC's *20/20*, claiming that parents were a poor judge of school quality. According to John Stossel: "Even though people in the suburbs might think their schools are great, Chavous says, 'They're not. That's the thing and the test scores show that.' Chavous and many other education professionals say Americans don't know that their public schools, on the whole, just aren't that good." Retrieved January 28, 2006, from http://abcnews.go.com/2020/Stossel/story?id=1500338

10. Actually, the proportions are rather substantial. According to the official evaluation, over 40% of students in the program were previously in the independent sector (private or charter schools)—over 28% were already in private schools. The numbers might be deflated because we do not know what proportion of students entering school for the first time (in the early grades) with a voucher would have been enrolled in private schools anyway. See: Wolf, Gutmann, Eissa, and Puma (2005); see note 8.

11. Kuttner, R. (1999). *Everything for sale: The virtues and limits of markets*. New York, NY: University of Chicago Press.

12. Belsie, L. (1999, February 4). Spending on U.S. schools is more popular than ever. *The Christian Science Monitor Electronic Edition*. Retrieved February 5, 1999, from http://www.csmonitor.com/durable/1999/02/04/fp4s1-csm.shtml

    Henry, T. (2000, January 10). Poll: Better pay will alleviate school woes. *USA Today*, p. 8D.

    Rose, L. C., & Gallup, A. M. (2002, September). The 34th Annual Phi Delta Kappa/Gallup Poll of the Public's Attitudes toward the Public Schools. *Phi Delta Kappan, 84*, 41-56.

    Rose, L. C. & Gallup, A. M. (2003, September). The 35th annual Phi Delta Kappa/Gallup Poll of the public's attitudes toward the public schools. *Phi Delta Kappan, 85*, 41-56.

13. Rose, L. C., & Gallup, A. M. (2005, September). The 37th annual Phi Delta Kappa/Gallup Poll of the public's attitudes toward the public schools. *Phi Delta Kappan, 87*, 41-57.

CHAPTER 8

SCHOOL CHOICE
BY THE NUMBERS

Bruce Baker

Review of Susan Aud's "School Choice by the Numbers: The Fiscal Effect of School Choice Programs 1990 – 2006," published by the Friedman Foundation for Educational Choice. This is a modified version of a review originally published on May 24, 2007.

INTRODUCTION

Educational vouchers continue to stimulate political debate and spawn research and advocacy papers from think tanks, despite their limited nature in public elementary and secondary education in the United States. A recent report by Susan Aud, published by the Milton & Rose D. Friedman Foundation, indicates that since 1999-2000 there has been relatively large growth nationally in the use of publicly financed vouchers, with enrollments increasing from around 10,000 to more than 100,000 by 2005-06.[1] While this is a ten-fold increase, the overall number is very small; 100,000 students represents a paltry 0.2% of 2005 U.S. public school and enrollment (over 48 million) and just 1.58% of estimated private school enrollment.[2]

Think Tank Research Quality: Lessons for Policy Makers, the Media, and the Public, pp. 109–126
Copyright © 2010 by Information Age Publishing
All rights of reproduction in any form reserved.

That said, in a few circumstances where more aggressive and well-funded voucher programs have been implemented and have been in place for some time, substantial numbers of children have migrated into them. By 2004, voucher enrollment in the city of Milwaukee exceeded 13% of public school enrollment and has increased since. In Cleveland, the voucher share had reached just over 8% by 2004.[3]

Overall, these numbers paint a picture of a policy with only small import in terms of shares of children affected and dollars expended. Yet voucher policies nonetheless have potential importance on two other levels: the ideological level of individual liberty and opposition to government-run schools, and the financial level. The Aud report and this review expressly address only this last level.

FINDINGS AND CONCLUSIONS OF THE REPORT

The Friedman report summarizes and evaluates both voucher programs and individual and corporate tax credit programs across 11 different states. Table 8.1 provides a list of those states and programs.

Voucher programs—as the report implicitly defines them—are those where public tax dollars are made available to students and families to subsidize tuition at private schools. Only private school attendance qualifies under this definition; the report and the Friedman Foundation tend to dismiss those cases where parents choose to apply their vouchers to other public rather than private schools, on the implicit assumption that doing so would be inefficient.

Individual and corporate tax credit scholarship programs establish funds to provide voucher-like "scholarships" for defined groups of students. Individuals or corporations (depending on the state) may receive income tax credits for contributions to the scholarship fund. In effect, these programs enable taxpayers to divert their money to independent non-profit entities that provide scholarships rather than contributing that money to state government coffers.

The difference between traditional, government-funded vouchers and recently emerging tax credit policies is largely an operational one. Voucher policies use revenue collected by states through taxation to subsidize private schooling; by contrast, tax credit programs allow individuals and corporations to bypass government and send their money to scholarship-managing agencies. For simplicity's sake, in this review the two are treated the same and referred to collectively as "vouchers."

The report provides financial analyses of five states—Florida, Ohio (Cleveland), Wisconsin (Milwaukee), Arizona, Pennsylvania—plus Washington, DC.[5] The financial analyses set forth in this new report are relatively straightforward and transparent, but they are also significantly

**Table 8.1.   Voucher and Tax Credit Programs
Summarized by Aud (2007)**

States	Type of Program	Financial Analysis Provided
Vermont & Maine	Nonoperating districts with private school tuition option	N
Wisconsin	Milwaukee Vouchers (State/Local)	Y
Arizona	Individual and corporate tax credit, disabled student & foster child vouchers	Y
Florida	Corporate tax credit, A+ voucher, McKay voucher	Y
Pennsylvania	Corporate tax credit scholarships	Y
Washington, DC.	Vouchers	Y
Ohio	Cleveland vouchers, Autism vouchers, EdChoice vouchers	Y
Utah	Vouchers (Parent choice & Carson Smith)	N
Rhode Island	Corporate Tax Credit	N
Iowa	Individual Tax Credit	N

mischaracterized. In short, the report's approach is to compare the per-pupil cost of public financing (state and local) for a student attending a public school with the public financing of a student using a voucher to attend a private school. The author assumes that if the second is less than the first, then savings is achieved.

There is a superficial logic to this approach. It seems relatively straightforward that if government chooses to allocate a lower per-pupil subsidy for private schooling than for traditional public schooling, then for each child who takes the private school subsidy, government expenditures on school subsidies may decline, assuming that children currently opting out of the public system for private or home-schooling will either decline or be barred from access to the private school subsidy. As discussed below, however, this reduction in total government expenditures on elementary and secondary schooling does not guarantee that government—state or local—spends less overall, or that the actual cost of operating the system is less.

The report's conclusions are concisely summed up in the report's final paragraph on page 36:

> Overall, these twelve school choice programs have saved a total of *nearly half a billion dollars*. Because voucher and scholarship amounts are typically well below state formula funding per student in the public school system, state budgets have saved a total of $22 million. In addition, the migration of

students from public schools to private schools *has allowed districts to reduce their instructional spending levels*, spreading their local and federal revenue over fewer students. School choice allows students to attend the schools of their choice *at a lower cost* than they would incur in the public school system, contrary to the dire fiscal speculations of its critics. (Emphasis added)

The report suggests in a general way that savings are achieved, but it is short on the specifics of precisely who—government, taxpayers, students or teachers—are the beneficiaries of those savings. A general theme appears to be that everyone saves and everyone wins.

Regarding state governments, the report assumes that money not spent on elementary and secondary schooling because of the voucher differential it describes is money saved. Regarding local school districts, the report argues that public school districts are able to increase their per pupil instructional budgets while decreasing their total budgets. That is, children who remain in the districts are not harmed by reduction of funding but rather benefit from increased per-pupil funding. Further, state and local taxpayers may benefit from an overall reduction in district spending—a win-win scenario.

THE REPORT'S RATIONALE FOR ITS FINDINGS AND CONCLUSIONS

The concluding paragraph of the Friedman report quoted above includes several statements not supported by the analyses provided. As noted, the author simply evaluates the difference between state and local allotment for vouchers and for traditional public schools; she fails to develop this analysis in a way that would support the report's broader policy conclusions.

The report does acknowledge that differences in state funding approaches complicate whether and how potential savings are realized. For example, the report discusses the state funding systems in Pennsylvania and Milwaukee. She explains that because Pennsylvania's school finance system is not enrollment-sensitive, but rather is based on previous spending, school districts losing students to vouchers retain their revenues, leading to increased per-pupil spending on those students who remain. By contrast, the report shows that the Milwaukee voucher program in recent years has required the district to transfer local funding as well as state funding to private schools to finance vouchers. In Pennsylvania, school districts are basically held harmless with regard to state funding and thus seem to be in a position to increase their per-pupil spending even while reducing their local budgets. In Milwaukee, the current policy requires school district money to help pay for the vouchers, so these benefits would not accrue.

In short, one might expect contrary effects of the two plans. The Pennsylvania system would lead to steady increases in total funding for school districts as enrollments decline, or the funding would at least grow more slowly because of voucher attrition, thus leading to increased budgets per pupil for the remaining children. In Milwaukee, one might expect that if the total transfer via vouchers of state and local funding per pupil matched the district's current per-pupil spending, that per-pupil spending for children remaining in the district would remain constant.

But school finance and public budgeting rarely yield such transparent results. The report itself falls into this trap. It claims that districts have been "allowed" to reduce their instructional spending levels as a result of vouchers, but no actual analysis on this point is provided in the report. The report makes no effort to show that districts such as Milwaukee and those in Pennsylvania have realized savings for taxpayers by actually reducing their total budgets while holding harmless per-pupil spending on those who remain in the district.

Table 8.2 explores whether Milwaukee and Cleveland each did, in fact, accomplish the report's win-win scenario between 2000 and 2004, when voucher enrollments grew quite substantially and both districts experienced declining enrollment.

It shows that the regionally and inflation-adjusted instructional budget per enrolled pupil in Milwaukee was $4,797 in 2000, and the potential Milwaukee public schools budget if vouchered children came back (but their voucher funds did not) was $4,457 per pupil. That is, Milwaukee's instructional budget in 2000 was sufficient to provide $4,457 per pupil, including for those who were not enrolled in Milwaukee public schools. By 2004, Milwaukee public schools' enrollment had declined and voucher students increased, but the public school system budget had still increased sufficiently to reabsorb the vouchered students (without their vouchers) and suffer only a 1.3%, inflation-adjusted decline in instructional spending per pupil. Even with the state and local funds lost due to vouchers, the instructional budget per enrolled and non-enrolled (voucher) students did not decline substantially, but also did not grow. For pupils remaining enrolled in the district, Milwaukee did experience a 3.76% inflation-adjusted increase in per pupil instructional spending.

In Cleveland, where the city school system is not subject to per pupil budget growth caps as in Milwaukee (under Wisconsin state policies), budget growth (adjusted for inflation) was much greater, at 21% for those remaining in the district and still 16% if voucher recipients returned without their vouchers. Indeed, we do not know how much Cleveland or Milwaukee's budgets might have grown had they not been subject to voucher-related declining enrollment. The contrast between Cleveland and Milwaukee may be indicative of the requirement that Milwaukee pass along locally raised resources in addition to losing state aid. It is difficult to make much of that contrast at this point, however. A substantial portion of the difference is, in fact, likely associated with the larger decline in enroll-ment in Cleveland and the relatively slow pace at which school districts' budgets adjust to enrollment declines.

These two cases provide relatively strong support for the report's oth-erwise unsubstantiated conclusion that vouchers do not necessarily lead to a significant reduction of resources for children left behind. However, these cases do not support the win-win scenario that asserts that vouchers can increase per-pupil spending for those who remain in public schools while decreasing total school budgets. Neither Cleveland nor Milwaukee decreased their total budgets. The report's suggestion that they were "allowed" to do so may be correct. But savings were not in fact realized in the way that the report implies in its conclusions.

Notably, the analysis in Table 8.2 overlooks the distinct possibility that while exiting voucher students may be from relatively low-income fami-lies, they may also be from higher-income families than those left behind in a given district or given school. That is, the net effects to the school dis-tricts of out-migration may include increased poverty concentration. If this is the case, then the value of the education dollar in those districts—in terms of improving educational outcomes—could decline significantly.

As noted above, the report acknowledges that Pennsylvania's state school-finance system promotes similar budget growth regardless of enrollment. That is, school districts losing students to vouchers retain their state and local revenues.

The report argues that "school choice allows students to attend the schools of their choice *at a lower cost* than they would incur in the public school system" (emphasis added). Again, it may be reasonable to argue that increasing the government subsidy for private schooling to more than $0 but less than the subsidy rate for traditional public schooling can lead to a reduction of government expenditures.[7] But expenditures and costs are not the same thing. In fact, noticeably absent in the report is any definition of "cost." Typically, cost savings are defined in terms of achiev-ing a similar or better quality of outcome at lower investment. Cost neces-sarily assumes a level of product quality. Further, when one accounts for the cost of producing a product of specific quality, one must account for all the resources that went into the production of that product, not just the small portion that was government-subsidized.

Let us assume public school option A and private school option B pro-duce similar levels of student outcomes, after controlling for differences in student population. Assume the full public subsidy for the public school is $6,000 per pupil, but that the public subsidy for the private

**Table 8.2.   Changes in Total Budgets and
Per Pupil Budgets in Cleveland and Milwaukee**

Year		Milwaukee	Cleveland	
2000	Instructional Budget	$521,740,980	$340,406,992	
	Enrolled Pupils	99,729	76,559	
	Voucher Pupils	7,596	3,407	*
	Budget per Enrolled Pupil	$5,232	$4,446	
	Budget per All Pupils	$4,861	$4,257	
	NCES CWI	1.09	1.04	
	Adj. Budget per Enrolled Pupil	$4,797	$4,261	
	Adj. Budget per All Pupils	$4,457	$4,079	
2004	Instructional Budget	$609,401,019	$428,628,987	
	Enrolled Pupils	97,359	69,655	
	Voucher Pupils	12,778	5,887	*
	Budget per Enrolled Pupil	$6,259	$6,154	
	Budget per All Pupils	$5,533	$5,674	
	NCES CWI	1.26	1.20	
	Adj. Budget per Enrolled Pupil	$4,977	$5,138	
	Adj. Budget per All Pupils	$4,400	$4,737	
Change	% Increase per Enrolled Pupil	3.76%	20.59%	
	% Increase per All Pupils	−1.30%	16.14%	

*Includes both public and private school students who received vouchers, as listed by Aud.

1. Instructional spending data from the U.S. Census Bureau's *Fiscal Survey of Local Governments (F-33) Elementary and Secondary Education Finances*. Retrieved May 15, 2007, from http://www.census.gov/govs/www/school.html

Enrollment data from the National Center for Education Statistics, *Common Core of Data, Local Education Agency Universe Survey*. Retrieved May 15, 2007, from http://www.nces.ed.gov/ccd/pubagency.asp

National Center for Education Statistics, *Comparable Wage Index used for inflation and regional cost adjustment*. Retrieved May 15, 2007, from http://www.nces.ed.gov/edfin/prodsurv/data.asp

school is $3,000, perhaps just passing along to the private school the state share of public subsidy.

One might erroneously assume that option B was twice as cost-effective or efficient. In all likelihood, however, the private school in question actually spent more than $3,000 per pupil. One must make a full accounting of what was actually spent, from all revenue streams, to evaluate cost effectiveness. The report's concluding paragraph suggests that "School choice allows students to attend the schools of their choice *at a lower cost* than they would incur in the public school system." But the report's analysis can only be considered to address governmental contributions; it does not address cost in terms of maintaining current outcomes nor in terms of all the resources allocated to education in voucher-receiving institutions.

Private substitutes for public schooling in Vermont provide a useful example. Vermont's program allows towns not operating their own schools to make formal agreements with available local independent private schools as well as with other public school districts. Towns are then expected to raise sufficient property tax revenues that, coupled with state aid, will be used to pay full tuition for students.[8] If the private independent school wishes to charge more than the average for public unified high schools, the decision to accept or reject the higher tuition charge is put to town voters.

In Vermont, four private independent secondary schools serve students from several towns. Regarding the Vermont tuitioning model, the report notes:

> We could calculate the difference between the existing tuition rates at public schools and private schools if we had the necessary data, and call that the fiscal impact of the program. However, since we lack the necessary data for such an analysis, and the towns are paying tuition to schools of choice either way, it is appropriate to treat town tuitioning as revenue neutral. (p. 30)

In fact, a review of readily available data on 2007-08 tuition levels for Vermont secondary schools suggests otherwise. State average "Announced Tuition" (effectively, the payments for inter-district transfer of students, including students attending private and public schools) for 2007-08 was $10,394 at the secondary school level. Table 8.3 presents the rates for the independent schools receiving tuitioned secondary students from non-operating districts:

In each case, private independent providers of secondary education charge above the state average.[9] That said, the private schools may provide a superior product at that price, such that cost, per se, is neutral or even positive.[10]

Further, tuition alone does not reflect the full cost of operations in the private independent schools. For tax year 2006, Burr and Burton Academy

Table 8.3.   Announced Tuition at Private Providers of Secondary Education in Vermont 2007-08

Secondary School	Town	Tuition
Burr & Burton Academy	Manchester	$11,770
Lyndon Institute	Lyndon Center	$11,880
St. Johnsbury Academy	St. Johnsbury	$12,250
Thetford Academy	Thetford	$13,224

Source: http://education.vermont.gov/new/pdfdoc/data/announced/announced_08_030107.pdf

collected $8,583,696 in tuition and fees but had current expenditures of approximately $10,054,212 and total revenue of more than $14 million. That is, even at this predominantly tuition- (voucher-) funded institution, tuition covered about 85% of annual expense, leaving 15% to be covered by other sources of revenue. Notably, tuition made up only about 61% of total revenue.[11]

While public schools are also increasingly relying on private cash and in-kind contributions to support their operations,[12] private independent schools typically rely more heavily on such contributions. Catholic and other church-dependent schools rely on private contributions through the church or diocese to subsidize the cost of schooling. Increased migration of students to private schooling may increase the need for private philanthropic contributions to elementary and secondary education in the form of direct support to private independent and private religious schools. Contributions to tax-exempt scholarship programs may compete with direct contributions to churches and private schools. These issues get to the "cost" of the voucher systems, even though they are not included in the governmental expenditure calculations included in the report.

Also, the report's calculated Ohio savings are built on an assumption that low-income students who opted out of public school prior to voucher availability should have limited access to vouchers. The report does not clearly express an opinion on this matter, though full inclusion of those students would cut into its estimated total savings. Its calculations reflect current policy in Cleveland, which, if its findings are correctly understood, continues to only partially finance vouchers for students previously enrolled in private school. Fully financing these students would reduce its savings estimate.

Table 8.4 summarizes the total public and private school enrollments for each jurisdiction. It then presents private school enrollments of children below the poverty level and below the reduced-price lunch threshold (185% of poverty level). Data are from the American Community Survey of 2005, from the U.S. Census Bureau.[13] The children in poverty or below the 185% threshold who reported attending private schools in the Census are not necessarily the same children receiving scholarships.

In Cleveland, approximately 7,551 children between the ages of 5 and 17 who are enrolled in private schools are assumed to fall below 185% of poverty level. Currently, vouchers are awarded to 76% of them, 5,675 children. In Milwaukee the number of voucher recipients exceeds the estimated numbers of children below 185% of the poverty level.[14] The same is true in terms of raw numbers of voucher recipients in Arizona. But in Pennsylvania, Florida and the District of Columbia a smaller share is currently receiving vouchers. This suggests that there remains substantial capacity for increased voucher expenditures. Because these three voucher programs are generally open to people who already attend private school—not just those who transfer in from public schools—it would seem likely that the presence of low-income children currently attending private schools has little influence on the report's analysis. Such data might, however, be relevant for policymakers wishing to estimate the costs of implementing voucher programs.

The report's key point is that "Overall, these twelve school choice programs have saved a total of *nearly half a billion dollars*" (emphasis added). Calculated as a simple net difference between what state and local government might have spent on traditional public schools and what they supposedly spent on private school subsidies, and setting aside concerns about the report's assumptions and calculations, it is reasonable to draw such a conclusion. However, the conclusion should be rephrased to point out that state and local governments have had the opportunity to reduce their expenditures by this amount or improve their services. The report presents no evidence that they have done so.

Further, half-a-billion dollars in elementary and secondary education spending over a 15-year period amounts to a relatively small amount for any given state or district. American public schools serve 50 million children; spread over the 15 years, $444 million would be 60 cents per child per year. The report fails to put these dollars in context, leaving readers, intentionally or unintentionally, with the mistaken impression that it has discovered a major source of savings.

THE REPORT'S USE OF RESEARCH LITERATURE

The report makes scant use of existing research literature on vouchers or tuition tax credits, and the three works cited that might be considered

Table 8.4. Current (2005) Private School Enrollments by Poverty Group in Voucher Contexts

State/District	Total Public Enrolled	Total Private Enrolled
Pennsylvania	1,647,026	320,795
Florida	2,425,440	365,666
Arizona	980,472	74,279
District of Columbia	62,320	12,582
Cleveland	66,210	15,174
Milwaukee	95,019	22,326

	Private <100% Poverty	Private <185% Poverty	Currently Vouchered (2005)
Pennsylvania	26,622	62,048	27,261
Florida	24,567	64,165	27,146
Arizona	7,633	18,874	21,146
District of Columbia	1,410	2,939	1,027
Cleveland	3,794	7,511	5,675
Milwaukee	3,796	10,306	14,427

scholarly research are all working papers or reports that were not published in scholarly journals.[15] The report does not include a discussion of literature concerning educational quality; rather, it focuses exclusively on government expenditures regardless of quality.[16]

The report's presentation would have benefited from a more thorough review of the literature on public budgeting and finance, as well as on the spending behavior of state and local government in general and on public schooling in particular. Specifically, what is greatly needed in this new analysis is a more careful application of terminology, differentiating cost from expenditure, and an understanding of the relationship between tuition charges, costs and expenditures in public and not-for-profit finance.

The report makes direct use of only one specific source in its analyses. It relies on Brasington's *School Choice and the Flight to Private Schools*[17] as a basis for estimating the numbers of children who migrated from public to private schools *because of* an available subsidy in Pennsylvania and Arizona. Aud applies Brasington's price elasticity of demand for private schooling (0.32), which was derived using Ohio data. She uses the elasticity to estimate the number of children likely to migrate from public to private schooling as voucher levels increase. Aud notes:

We estimate the percentage of participants who would probably have attended a public school prior to receiving a scholarship using an estimate of the price elasticity of demand for a private school education. (p. 18)

There are a multitude of potential technical problems that arise from attempting to estimate choice behavior in Arizona or Pennsylvania based on a model of choice behavior derived from Ohio data. Perhaps most importantly, the location and supply of private schools are different (key variables in Brasington's models). If the report's use of Brasington's elasticity understates the numbers who would have stayed in public schools, its savings estimates will be overstated. Because recent (2005) private school enrollment rates in Ohio are double what they are in Arizona, it is reasonable to conclude that the supply density of private schooling in Ohio is greater than in Arizona.[18]

Brasington also finds a smaller price elasticity for poor than for wealthy households, a fact the report does not mention. In sorting out differences between rich and poor households under an assumption of vouchers being available to both, Brasington notes, "vouchers are often presumed to help poor students have better educational opportunities at private schools, but it is the rich who would most likely redeem school vouchers" (p. 28).

Finally, Brasington himself concludes that "a voucher system or a tuition tax credit that makes private schools more affordable will not cause a mass exodus from public schools, at least not immediately," because public and private schooling are not, for many families, the same product—they are only moderately weak substitutes for one another (p. 18).

REVIEW OF THE REPORT'S METHODS

There are few specifics to review in this report's relatively straightforward methodologies. Most concerns regarding the report's analyses are broad and conceptual. In fact, since the analyses are so limited, only one of the report's findings or conclusions can actually be supported by those analyses: that net state and local government spending might be less if state and local governments allocate less for vouchers than for traditional public schools. This is hardly a surprising finding. The remainder of the report's conjecture regarding this finding is simply not validated by its analyses.

Nonetheless a few seemingly trivial points are in order. First and foremost, it is relatively meaningless to discuss public expenditures, and education spending in particular, using only aggregate terms—millions and billions of dollars. Shares of total expenditures and total revenues, as well as amounts per capita or per pupil, are standard. That is, it would be useful to point out to the reader that $444 million is in fact 60 cents per child per year, or that $444 million is less than 0.1% of total education spending in a single year.

Second, as previously mentioned, the report's decision to apply Brasington's price elasticity (derived from Ohio data) to estimate private school migration in Arizona and Pennsylvania in isolation seems questionable at best, violating the principle of *ceteris paribus*—or "all else equal." It is standard in more rigorous peer-reviewed economic research to attempt to address important differences between the context that produced the original estimate and the context to which the author is applying that estimate.

Finally, the report made no attempt to adjust government expenditures for inflation.

REVIEW OF THE VALIDITY OF THE FINDINGS AND CONCLUSIONS

The report's conclusion of a potential net difference in government expenditures (if it had, in fact, characterized it as such) might be validly drawn from its analysis. The bigger question is whether this conclusion is in any way meaningful. Again, government can choose to spend less on product B than product A. And, if government buys more of product B in place of product A, government will have spent less. This analysis provides a very limited view; it tells us nothing about (1) whether product A and product B are perfect substitutes, or (2) if the reason that product B is cheaper is because someone else has paid part of the price—in this instance, church and private individual subsidies to private schools, which have their own tax benefits attached.

The following three issues are important to consider when evaluating the importance or relevance of the report's analyses.

1. Cost Savings Versus Government Expenditure Reduction

The relatively transparent analyses that the report puts forth as "cost savings" might be more appropriately reframed as offering something like *potential reductions to state and local government expenditures that might be realized by use of partial-cost tuition subsidies for private schooling*.

In short, the conclusions drawn from the analyses could be improved substantially by improving the precision with which certain terms are used. Most notably, it is entirely inappropriate to imply that *costs* have been reduced for anyone. The report provides no measure of schooling quality changes under the various programs evaluated. The report also makes the oversimplified assumption that the estimated net differences in formula appropriations will in fact be realized as savings. However, although the analyses suggest the possibility that state and local governments may find ways to reduce their obligation to spend on elementary and secondary schooling (potentially transferring a portion of that obligation to others), total public expenditures on elementary and secondary education may not be reduced, as discussed below.

The report should have used a cost-benefit framework, in which one takes full account of the costs—government-subsidized and privately subsidized—of providing education through traditional public schools or through vouchers to private schools. One must also consider the effects or benefits of policy alternatives. That is, are we getting equal or better quality at the same or lower cost? Are we getting better quality but at higher cost? Or, are we getting lower quality at higher total cost?

2. Is There a Net Change in Aggregate Public Expenditures on Elementary and Secondary Schooling?

Though not a central thesis, the report implies on several occasions the existence of a net cost reduction from providing a government subsidy for private schooling that is below the per-pupil revenue provided for public schooling. Yet it acknowledges the likelihood of an increased net expenditure under Pennsylvania's school finance system, and analyses in this review now indicate a net expenditure increase in Cleveland and Milwaukee, as well as higher average tuition rates for students tuitioned to private independent secondary schools compared with public secondary schools in Vermont.

Further, if we assume that (a) school districts do not reduce their budgets by the full amount that costs are reduced by exiting students, (b) states do not reduce their total spending by the full amount that costs are reduced by students subsidized at the lower rate, and (c) the increased migration of students to private schools necessitates an increase in philanthropic contributions to churches and private independent schools, then the net change in the total public contribution to elementary and secondary education will be positive and perhaps quite large. That is, the general public will be spending more to educate the same number of children. Assuming commensurate increases in quality, this option may be desirable. If not, however, this option is inefficient, although it might still be preferred by those who favor an individual liberty interest advanced by school choice over efficiency interests.

3. In Context, How Much Money Are We Really Talking About?

Finally, this review ends where it started, with the question of the overall importance of the issue at hand. The report boldly highlights the significance of its finding that educational vouchers have saved the American public $444 million over a period of about 15 years, $22 million of which was saved by states. However, in 2004-05 alone, current expenditures for elementary and secondary school in the United States were approximately $425 billion. Treport's $444 million is about one-tenth of one percent of the amount spent on direct allocations to elementary and secondary schools in 2004-05 alone. If this is divided by 15, it amounts to less than one-one hundredth of a percent—or 60 cents per child.

Even within the areas evaluated, the net-differenced hypothetical savings reported are very small. Table 8.5 summarizes the estimated 2004-05 voucher-related savings compared to total current state and local expenditures in those areas. Excluding the negative local impact, which eliminates entirely the potential positive spending effects of the Milwaukee voucher program in 2004-05, voucher savings would approach one-half of 1% for Wisconsin. No other program evaluated even approaches one-half of 1% for 2004-05. Ohio and Arizona programs "save" less than one-tenth of 1%.

USEFULNESS OF THE REPORT FOR GUIDANCE OF POLICY AND PRACTICE

It seems unlikely that the report will have much resonance with state policymakers, most of whom are familiar with their own state budget contexts.

Table 8.5.   Voucher Savings Relative to Direct Current Expenditures on K-12 Schools in 2004-05

State or Jurisdiction	Total Current Expenditures 2004-05	Estimated 2004-05 Voucher Savings	Voucher %
Arizona	6,451,870,327	$3,745,854	0.06%
District of Columbia	1,023,952,459	$2,203,942	0.22%
Florida	19,042,877,250	$52,255,112	0.27%
Ohio	17,167,865,841	$13,307,155	0.08%
Pennsylvania	18,711,099,728	$55,792,388	0.30%
Wisconsin*	8,435,358,679	$38,582,847	0.46%

* Assuming no change to local share (given the actual change to local share, the voucher percentage is zero).

These policymakers will realize that the figures of millions of dollars in savings accrued over 15 years actually amount, on average, to less than a rounding error in many states—a mere 0.1% of government expenditures on public schooling in a given year.

The evidence the report presents does not make a sufficient case to informed policymakers for the positive fiscal impact of vouchers and tuition tax credits. In fact, it suggests quite the opposite: that fiscal gains are trivial at best. Further, any reduction in government subsidy is not equivalent to an actual reduction in cost or even a reduction in total expenditures. Instead, it could fairly be characterized as amounting to a transfer of financial responsibility. Such transfers might reasonably be argued on philosophical grounds, rather than on economic ones. Accordingly, policymakers will still need to make decisions about whether or not to support vouchers and tax credits based on their ideological values.

NOTES AND REFERENCES

1.   Aud, S. (2007). *School Choice by the Numbers: The Fiscal Effect of School Choice Programs 1990-2006*. The Milton & Rose D. Friedman Foundation, p. 11.
2.   National Center for Education Statistics (2006, June). *Digest of Education Statistics: 2005*. (NCES 2006-030) Washington., DC: author. Retrieved May 15, 2007, from http://nces.ed.gov/programs/digest/d05/tables/dt05_002.asp
3.   This number includes voucher recipients from public schools and those previously attending private schools.
4.   Cost benefit analyses of these mechanisms are warranted—comparing the increased resources generated by states for these special revenue funds as a result of exempting only a portion of the contribution, and increased costs of managing the special revenue funds rather than collecting the additional general revenue. Such analyses may exist, but extensive review was beyond the scope of work here. Further, taxpayers already have the option of making tax-deductible charitable contributions directly to churches which subsidize religious private schools or directly to independent private schools.
5.   The report includes in its discussion, though not in its fiscal analysis, tuitioning programs that have existed in Vermont and Maine for well over a century. These programs exist where local jurisdictions have chosen not to invest in the infrastructure of their own public schools, usually secondary schools, and instead rely on tuitioning agreements, often with private independent schools as well as nearby public districts. Over time, in most of these cases, these private schools have effectively become the private providers of public schooling for a handful of communities. One might also classify these communities as nonoperating school districts for some grade levels. The communities collect tax revenue and use a portion of

that revenue for secondary school tuition which may be used at the assumed primary private provider or nearby public schools.

6.   A substantial body of recent research on marginal costs associated with poverty concentration shows that a 1% increase in subsidized lunch rates in an urban core school district may be associated with a .6% to 1% or greater increase in the costs of achieving constant outcomes. As such, if out-migration of voucher students led to a more than 4% increase in poverty rates among those left behind in Milwaukee, those left behind would in fact experience a net reduction in available resources. For summaries of estimates of these marginal costs, see Bruce D. Baker (2006). Evaluating the reliability, validity and usefulness of education cost studies. *Journal of Education Finance, 32*(2), 170-201.

7.   So too would choosing not to subsidize the education of those who would use private resources to gain access to private school education if subsidies did not exist.

8.   Title 16, Section 824 High School tuition (emphasis added): (a) Tuition for high school pupils shall be paid by the school district in which the pupil is a resident. (b) Except as otherwise provided for technical students, the district shall pay the full tuition charged its pupils attending a public high school in Vermont or an adjoining state, or a public or independent school in Vermont functioning as an approved area technical center, or an independent school meeting school quality standards. However, if a payment made to a public high school or an independent school meeting school quality standards is three percent more or less than the calculated net cost per secondary pupil in the receiving school district for the year of attendance then the district shall be reimbursed, credited, or refunded pursuant to section 836 of this title, unless otherwise agreed to by the boards of both the receiving and sending districts or independent schools. (c) For students in Grades 7 and 8, the district shall pay an amount not to exceed the average announced tuition of Vermont union high schools for students in Grades 7 and 8 for the year of attendance for its pupils enrolled in an approved independent school not functioning as a Vermont area technical center, or any higher amount approved by the electorate at an annual or special meeting warned for that purpose. For students in Grades 9-12, the district shall pay an amount not to exceed the average announced tuition of Vermont union high schools for students in Grades 9-12 for the year of attendance for its pupils enrolled in an approved independent school not functioning as a Vermont area technical center, or **any higher amount approved by the electorate at an annual or special meeting warned for that purpose.**

9.   A fairer approach might be to identify the nearest neighboring secondary schools to each of these schools and compare their tuition, perhaps integrating transportation cost changes into the analysis. Such detail was beyond the scope of this critique.

10.   Not surprisingly, Vermont independent schools have costs in excess of average comparable public school costs. More surprisingly, is data indicate that Catholic school per pupil costs (as opposed to Catholic school tuition)

may not be lower than public school costs. In a 2004 cost analysis of four Kansas City area Catholic high schools, Michael Sullivan found that average per pupil cost were just over $6,000, while the average operating expenditures for Kansas public schools in the Kansas City metro area were actually slightly lower. Sullivan. M. (2004). *Resource allocation in Catholic High Schools*. Doctoral Dissertation. University of Kansas.

11. IRS Form 990. Retrieved May 15, 2007, from www.guidestar.org

12. See in particular, Downes, T., & Steinman, J. (2006). *Alternative revenue generation in Vermont public schools*. Paper presented at the University of Kentucky symposium, "The Buck Starts Where? Paying for Public Services." Retrieved May 15, 2007, from http://www-martin.uky.edu/~web/buckstarts/papers/Downes.pdf

13. *Integrated Public Use Microdata Series*; Minnesota Population Center, University of Minnesota. Retrieved May 15, 2007, from www.ipums.org

14. It is important to understand that the U.S. Census, American Community Survey figures provided are estimates and not based on a universe population. Further, they are based on resident status within the city limits for Milwaukee and Cleveland, which may not be perfectly contiguous with school district boundaries. Finally, qualifying criteria for the various voucher programs are not necessarily associated with the poverty thresholds presented in the table and this discussion.

15. Brasington, D. M. (2004, Dec. 6). *School choice and the flight to private schools: To what extent are public and private schools substitutes?* Louisiana State University Economics Department, Working Paper 2005-02. Retrieved May 15, 2007 from http://www.bus.lsu.edu/economics/papers/pap06_04.pdf
    Greene, J. P., Howell, W. J., & Peterson, P. (1997, Sept.). *An evaluation of the Cleveland Scholarship Program*. Cambridge, MA: Harvard University, Program on Education Policy and Governance.
    Greene, J. P., & Forster, G. (2003, June). *Vouchers for Special Education Students: An evaluation of Florida's McKay Scholarship Program*. New York, NY: Manhattan Institute.

16. A brief review of the RAND report *What Do We Know About Vouchers and Charter Schools* might have provided a reasonable backdrop, at least where Washington, DC and Milwaukee were concerned. In addition, Levin (2002) discusses the importance of evaluating productive efficiency when evaluating vouchers. See Levin, H. M. (2002). A comprehensive framework for evaluating education vouchers. *Educational Evaluation and Policy Analysis*, *24*(3), 159-174.

17. Brasington, D. M. (2004, Dec. 6). *School choice and the flight to private schools: To what extent are public and private schools substitutes?* Louisiana State University Economics Department, Working Paper 2005-02. Retrieved May 15, 2007 from http://www.bus.lsu.edu/economics/papers/pap06_04.pdf

18. Based on the American Community Survey 2005 of the U.S. Census, 5- to 17-year-olds.

CHAPTER 9

SERIES OF REPORTS ON THE FISCAL IMPACT OF TAX-CREDIT SCHOLARSHIPS

Luis Huerta

Review of the series of reports from the Friedman Foundation for Educational Choice, "The Fiscal Impact of Tax-Credit Scholarships." This is a modified version of a review originally published on June 22, 2009.

INTRODUCTION

After the U.S. Supreme Court ruled that the Cleveland voucher program did not violate the First Amendment of the federal Constitution, many proponents of private school choice expected voucher programs to sprout throughout the country.[1] Seven years later, however, this has not happened.[2] Instead, the attention of many school choice advocates, and that of the legislators they hope to influence, has shifted to education tax credit programs, which have steadily expanded at the state level and been the focus of several federal bills.[3]

In particular, six states have adopted a type of tax credit policy recently labeled "neovouchers," which accomplish the main goals of conventional

Think Tank Research Quality: Lessons for Policy Makers, the Media, and the Public, pp. 127–140

vouchers but do so in a way that may have political and legal advantages.[4] These policies currently exist in Arizona, Pennsylvania, Florida, Rhode Island, Iowa, and Georgia. They provide a non-refundable tax credit to individuals or corporations contributing to non-profit "School Tuition Organizations" (STOs). The STOs then distribute the money in the form of vouchers—often called "scholarships" in the state laws.

A recent series of reports sponsored by the Friedman Foundation outlines proposals for education tax credit programs in Georgia,[5] Montana, and Indiana and are part of a wider series of reports that examine similar tax credit proposals in Kentucky, Florida, New Mexico and Utah. In *The Fiscal Impact of Tax-Credit Scholarships in Montana*[6] and *The Fiscal Impact of Tax-Credit Scholarships in Georgia,*[7] Brian Gottlob asserts that a tax credit policy will result in a more efficient and effective education system, both by saving taxpayer dollars when students transfer to private schools and by providing more students with the opportunity to enroll in presumably more effective private schools. David Stuit's *The Fiscal Impact of a Corporate & Individual Tax-Credit Scholarship Program on the State of Indiana* offers a similar analysis.[8]

This review describes and analyzes the methods and findings of the reports. Particular attention is focused on the claims made by the authors concerning the calculations of proposed savings in public expenditures due to tax credit programs and the assumptions linked to the projected response of the supply side of choice (the capacity of private schools) and the demand side of choice (parents seeking expanded school choice options).

FINDINGS AND CONCLUSIONS OF THE REPORTS

The two reports authored by Gottlob contend that proposed tax credit voucher programs in Montana and Georgia would result in a net revenue gain for local school districts for each student who exits public school ($2,759 for Montana; $6,600 for Georgia). Gottlob asserts that these savings would be realized because local and state per-pupil revenues vary in the degree of sensitivity to drops in enrollment (as explained later in this review). He also asserts that when a student exits a public school to enroll in a private school, although the district loses a portion of state and federal per-pupil revenues, it retains the full portion of local funding.

The reports then present some calculations for the cost of an STO tax credit program and describe how the total fiscal impact on the state depends largely on the number of students who choose to participate, the size of the voucher provided, whether the voucher will be means-tested with income eligibility, and the level of contributions that are made to STOs. For example, the Georgia report projects that a program providing

$50 million in voucher funding, with income eligibility levels set at 200 percent of the free and reduced-price lunch threshold, distributing vouchers of $3,500, would result in a net fiscal benefit of $94 million for local school districts and a savings of $6 million for the state.[9] Gottlob stresses that further fiscal benefits would be realized if income eligibility thresholds were increased and higher-income families (who, he claims, have a projected higher demand for private schools) were eligible to participate.[10] The report concludes that a tax credit voucher program is a more efficient method of distributing state and local education funding, compared to increasing state aid to public schools only. Specifically, he calculates that for every dollar of additional state aid, spending only increases by 44-64 cents in Montana and 53 cents in Georgia, based on his claim that local governments have a propensity to reduce local spending when state aid increases.

The third report, authored by David Stuit, analyzes a proposed STO tax credit program in Indiana that would provide $5 million in tax credits to businesses and individuals who contribute to the program.[11] Taxpayers would receive a credit of 50 cents for every dollar donated to Scholarship Granting Organizations (SGO). Eligibility for the program would be limited to students whose household income is at or below 200% of the federal free and reduced-price lunch program threshold and restrict students who are already enrolled in private schools, with the exceptions of students who enter private schools in Grade K.

The report concludes that Indiana could realize a net savings of up to $4.7 million in the first year of the program if vouchers in the amount of $500 were distributed to 19,000 eligible students. (As explained later in this review, that is a very unlikely scale of growth for private schools.) By year 5 of the program, the report estimates that savings could reach $17.6 million, based on a demand level the report calls moderate (with average vouchers of $1,500). Stuit explains that a larger voucher, in the amount of $5,000, would increase demand for private schooling for low-income public school families, but the program's $5 million overall tax credit cap would limit the number of vouchers (and recipient students) to only 1,900 students, and accordingly limit the savings he estimates for the state—which depends on a high number of transferring students. Stuit's estimates assume a minimal price elasticity for tuition, preserving the existing average private school tuition of $6,486.

THE REPORTS' RATIONALE FOR
THEIR FINDINGS AND CONCLUSIONS

The Gottlob and Stuit reports make three key claims to support the conclusion that tax credit voucher programs in Montana, Georgia and

Indiana will have positive fiscal impacts on state and local education budgets, while expanding school choice options to parents: (a) revenues have low sensitivity to enrollment declines, while expenditures have high sensitivity to enrollment declines; (b) there is a pent-up demand for publicly funded private school choice; and (c) the nature and degree of positive net effects on state and local revenues will depend on corporate and individual contributions to the tax credit voucher programs, the demand for vouchers, and the supply and amount of vouchers available. Each of these claims is explained below.

Enrollment, Revenues and Expenditures

The Georgia and Montana reports rely on the claim that education revenues sent from the state to local districts vary with enrollment, while local education revenue does not. For Montana, the report states that 83.3% of school revenues from state sources are calculated by enrollment, while 16.7% is not sensitive to enrollment changes.[12] Also, Montana schools receive state aid based on a 3-year average enrollment basis, which results in a buffer when enrollment drops occur. Thus, the report calculations assume that a per-pupil decline in local district enrollment eventually results in a loss of 83.3% of state revenues for that pupil, but an increase in per-pupil revenues available to students who remain enrolled in the district—though only on a short-run basis.

Similar calculations are presented for Georgia, where 90% of state revenues is stated to be based on enrollment.[13] The report calculates that when a student leaves a district, the loss in state revenues amounts to $3,931 (about 90% of the average state portion of funding), while the district retains $421 (the portion of state funding not dependent on enrollment), as well as $3,603 (the entire portion of local funding) and most of the $627 from federal sources. The report does acknowledge that the remaining local school revenues may be short-run and are dependent on local government decisions on how to allocate the residual revenues.

Importantly, the Montana report explains that increases in state education revenues do not necessarily result in a corresponding increase in school district expenditures. When the state increases revenues, local districts can respond by decreasing the local portion of education revenues by lowering taxes or redirecting local revenues to other public services. The report estimates that between 1996 and 2007, each additional dollar in state revenue for schools only resulted in 44 to 66 cents of expenditures by schools, a result of a decreased allocation of local revenues for schools. This calculation is central to the report's claim that the education financing system is inefficient and that a tax credit program funding private school tuition is a more efficient system. That is, state increases in funding are inefficient at channeling more money to education, since local decision-makers can subvert that aim by either lowering local taxes or moving that revenue to another need. The Georgia report makes a similar argument and estimates that between 1999 and 2007, schools only spent 53 cents of each additional dollar in state revenues they received.

The Indiana report explains that funding dependent on student enrollment is distributed in a Basic Grant appropriation, which makes up 94% of Indiana's total school funding (approximately $6,218 in state aid per pupil). In addition, the state employs a "declining enrollment adjustment" in the education funding formula that essentially buffers public schools from a drop in revenues due to declining enrollments. Specifically, the state calculates a 5-year rolling average of enrollment counts, compares this average to actual enrollment, and then provides districts with funding for whichever is larger, guaranteeing districts with large enrollment fluctuations a more consistent basic grant appropriation. The report's estimates of savings over a 5-year period under the proposed tax credit program are presented in scenarios that assume a moderate level of demand, both with and without the "declining enrollment adjustment." The scenario with that provision realizes a non-revenue-neutral program in the first 2 years that actually results in a significant cost to the state (estimated at $2.9 million) but then transforms into $17.6 million savings in the fifth year, assuming a transfer of at least 3,138 students with an average voucher amount of $1,500. Without the provision, the report's estimate yields a more inflated $29.5 million in savings to the state, with $1,000 vouchers. This savings is for the first year of the program but would level down to $16.6 million during the fifth year, when more students who entered private schools in Grade K would be accounted for in the program (an issue explained in greater depth below). Both of these scenarios assume a high number of transfers at a very modest voucher amount, less than 25% of the average private school tuition of $6,486.

Private School Choice Demand

The three reports all use varying voucher values to calculate estimates of the potential demand for private schooling under a tax credit voucher program that employs means testing. No effort is made to empirically survey how many families would actually transfer to private schools if a voucher were offered or to otherwise derive evidence-based estimates. The Stuit report on Indiana assumes that demand for private schooling will be high among eligible low-income families and that large savings to the state will be realized, even with modest voucher amounts. The two Gottlob

reports contend that expanding eligibility to higher-income families—
who presumably have a higher demand for private schooling based on
their ability to afford tuition—would increase the demand for vouchers.

Contributions, Voucher Supply and Voucher Demand

The calculations of estimated positive fiscal benefits in all three reports
are highly dependent on programs that would raise revenues through
corporate and individual contributions, which would then fund a large
enough supply of vouchers. In addition, the report reasons, a program
that expands the threshold of eligibility to higher-income families will
increase the demand for vouchers and result in greater savings for the
states.

THE REPORTS' USE OF RESEARCH LITERATURE

The use of reliable research literature in the two Gottlob reports (Georgia
and Montana) is very limited, and the validity of the literature that is used
is highly suspect. They rely primarily on similar reports, most from the
same author and from similar advocacy organizations (e.g., the Cato Institute and the Goldwater Institute), to justify their methods and findings.
This insular approach further calls into question the validity of the
reports' conclusions.

In several sections where research literature could have informed some
of the reports' estimates, the author states explicitly that key calculations
are based on assumptions and projections. Moreover, in the few instances
where reputable research is cited, it is not put to good use. The reports cite
research studies to support claims but make no effort to unpack the specific
elements from the literature that might bolster those claims. They also fail
to discuss or even acknowledge important questions that existing research
literature has raised that are relevant to the contents of the reports.
Specifically, school finance equity literature reports on how efforts to
equalize local tax burdens have resulted in state resources supplanting
local revenues. Other research examines the supply of vacant private
school seats that actually exist and the challenges of taking private school
choice policy to scale, and still other research examines the quality and
effectiveness of private schools in school choice programs and in general.[14]

The use of research in the Stuit report (Indiana) is more thoughtful
and does attempt to mobilize the literature and explain how it supports
claims made in the report. However, the research literature is not mobi-
lized methodically, and it is unclear whether existing research findings

can fairly be used to validate the report's estimates and conclusions. For example, while the report warns readers that findings from past studies that have calculated the elasticity of tuition prices should be "interpreted with caution" given their many shortcomings, it then relies on findings from those very studies to calculate an estimated tuition elasticity for Indiana in the context of the proposed tax credit program. An accurate estimate of tuition elasticity in the context of a program that might increase demand for private schooling demands a real assessment of private school operators. For example, such an assessment might include a survey of a random sample of operators focusing on how their schools would respond to an increase in demand for private schooling. Specifically, such research should directly investigate whether schools plan, or wish, to accommodate more students, whether current capacity could accommodate new students, and whether increased demand would require new capital construction and at what cost.

REVIEW OF THE REPORTS' METHODS AND VALIDITY OF THE FINDINGS

Measuring Equity of Resources and Calculating Expenditures

A large and growing research base explores disparities in school finance and analyzes new policies associated with inadequate finance. The two Gottlob reports neglect this literature, which could have helped explain the specific policy context in which finance equity formulas have evolved in both states. Consider, for example, the reports' claim that local expenditures for education decrease when the state increases its portion of revenues distributed to schools. Gottlob offers the rationale that local districts respond to increased state funding by reducing (supplanting) locally raised revenues. Both states, however, have finance formulas that employ a Guaranteed Tax Base (GTB) policy to reduce local tax efforts (that is, local taxes devoted to education) and increase equity and revenues for schools in lower-property-wealth districts as compared to those in higher-property-wealth districts.[15] A further disaggregation of these specific data by district type (rather then state averages) is important in order to fully understand whether the claimed difference in revenues compared to expenditures actually exists across all districts, or is a result of progressive tax-base equalization applied to low-property-wealth districts in Montana and Georgia. It is irresponsible to make sweeping claims about district response without first disaggregating to determine which districts did in fact supplant local revenues with the new state revenues.

Supply of Private School Seats and Demand for Private Schooling

The three Friedman Foundation reports fail to consider several key factors concerning supply and demand in the context of policies that expand publicly funded private school choice options. Specifically, the proposals do not account for whether a sufficient supply of vacant seats exists in the current private school stock and, if not, whether the tax credit voucher is sufficient to prompt private school suppliers to engage in capital improvement and build new schools to accommodate transferring students. The Gottlob reports completely neglect the available-seat issue, while the Stuit report offers only some loose calculations based on a pair of unsupported and very unlikely assumptions. Gottlob estimates that 3,188 new private school seats will be needed to meet the initial demand for private schooling. Then he accounts for the decline of enrollment in Indiana's private schools over the last decade (which he reports as an average loss of 14 students in each of the 588 operating private schools in the state) to calculate the existing supply of empty seats. He notes that an influx of 3,188 students would amount to only a 3% increase in school enrollment, an average of seven additional students per private school—only half of the recent loss—and he concludes that private schools have abundant seating capacity. In short, this loosely calculated figure assumes an even distribution of supply and, more importantly, an even distribution of demand across the diverse regions of the state. Both assumptions are highly improbable.

A review of existing research would have informed all three reports, allowing a useful and precise calculation of the supply of vacant private school seats. For example, in 1999 a ballot initiative known as Proposition 38 in California proposed a publicly funded voucher in the amount of $4,000 for all students in the state. Research on the potential effects of Proposition 38 revealed that only 32,000 vacant seats existed among 42,000 California private schools (limiting participation in the voucher program to only 0.5% of California's existing 6 million students).[16] In addition, the Catholic Diocese, which operates the majority of private schools in California, reported that "although it would be possible to shift current tuition subsidies toward new construction, a $4,000 voucher would still be insufficient to provide for both capital and educational costs."[17] Similarly, in Minnesota the Catholic Conference reported that Catholic schools could only begin to increase the supply of available seats through capital expansion if subsidy amounts were in the range of $12,000 to $14,000. Further, some private schools have restrictive growth policies in order to respect and preserve their mission.[18]

In calculating the demand for private schooling, none of the three reports relies on surveys that could gauge actual pent-up demand, nor do they use as reference points student take-up rates in recent tuition tax credit and voucher programs in other states. Instead, they assume that if a voucher for private school tuition is made available to low-income families, pent-up demand will lead to high take-up rates regardless of the voucher amount. For instance, the Georgia and Montana reports gauge demand by simply calculating the number of students who *must* transfer in order for the policy to have a positive fiscal impact on state revenues. They assume that specific policy and economic conditions would encourage student migration. First, the report concludes that a tax credit policy that limits eligibility to low-income students would be limited in its potential to yield positive fiscal effects. Second, he contends that an increase in positive effects would only be realized if higher-income families, who presumably have a higher demand for private school because of their increased ability to afford tuition, were eligible. Whatever readers may think of these broad assumptions, nothing in the reports allows for a true calculation or accurate prediction of the existing demand for private schooling.

Moreover, estimates of demand in all three reports are inconsistent with reliable research on tax credit policies, which has found that while substantial tax credits may increase demand for private schooling, schools would likely respond by raising tuition.[19] Instead, the Friedman Foundation reports seem to pay attention to only part of supply/demand pressure. Further, other research has shown that demand is dependent on the amount of the tax credit benefit and the elasticity of tuition, and both factors determine affordability. For example, research on the Minnesota tax credit program (which is different in form than the neovoucher approach but still informative in terms of supply and demand behavior) revealed that during a period of over 30 years, significant increases in the amount of a tax deduction benefit for private school tuition did not result in increased demand for private schooling. There were no significant spikes in enrollment in the years after the increases were implemented, and private school enrollment actually declined.[20] Such findings provide robust evidence calling into serious question the unsubstantiated method by which all three of the Friedman reports calculate projected demand.

Estimating Fiscal Impact and Beneficiaries

Claims that vouchers and tax credit policies produce savings of public revenues often rely on exaggerated estimates of the number of students who would transfer to private schools, allowing advocates to calculate a net savings.[21] The Montana report, for instance, estimates that 2,471 public school students would have to participate in the tax credit voucher program in order for the state to break even and offset the cost of the tax credit (an increase of more than 20% of the existing private school population[22]). In Georgia, the estimate would require that 12,778 public school students participate (a 9% increase in the existing private school population). These estimates are based on eligibility requirements that include both low-income and higher-income families, which according to the reports are necessary to ensure sufficient demand. As noted above, the calculations assume that a supply of empty seats is currently available in private schools, an important factor that the reports do not sufficiently assess.

It should be noted that this substantial (and unsupported) estimated growth in private school enrollment would still not yield the positive fiscal impact predicted by the reports without a real growth in supply in response to the estimated greater demand for private schools.

The Indiana report concludes that the program's target efficiency, linked to meeting the projected demand for private schooling among low-income parents, would require an average voucher of $5,000. However, this high amount would limit the overall savings. The report estimates that a program with $5,000 vouchers would result in a loss to the state of $2.9 million and $700,000, respectively, during the first 2 years of operation. By the fifth year of operation, however, when the costs of the "declining enrollment adjustment" begin to decrease, the report estimates that the program would yield a savings of $6.4 million, with vouchers distributed to fewer than 1,600 public school transfer students and an estimated 400 private school students who entered the program at Grade K. The author assumes that a $5,000 voucher would cover approximately 75% of the average private school tuition in Indiana ($6,350). Setting aside the possibility that tuition prices would increase as a result of the influx of new students, the report concludes that $5,000 is sufficient to entice low-income families to transfer to private schools. Furthermore, the highly inflated cost savings estimated at upwards of $17.6 million (taking into account the "declining enrollment adjustment") is based on a $1,500 voucher (equivalent to 24% of the average private school tuition) distributed to 3,138 public school transfer students plus 3,195 private school students who entered the program at Grade K.

This highlights an important oversight in the reports. Calculations of overall differences in public expenditures depend, in part, on two key terms: the number of students who switch from public to private schools in response to the availability of the neovouchers ("switchers"), and the number of families who receive neovouchers but would have attended private school even without the incentive ("non-switchers"). As mentioned earlier, the report says that Indiana's per-pupil state aid is $6,218. Assuming this is the full public expenditure, each switcher receiving a neo-voucher in the amount of $5,000 saves the state $1,218. But each non-switcher costs the state $5,000, since that student would not have attended public school even without the tax credit policy.

Even with a provision limiting eligibility to students who are switchers or are just starting schooling, the cohort of students entering kindergarten will include non-switchers who would have attended private school kindergarten even without the incentive. This cohort will move into first grade the next year, eventually (over a 12-year span) encompassing the entire private school population. Any calculation of effects on public expenditures must seriously address this fact.[23]

Unfortunately, the reports for Georgia and Montana make no mention whatsoever of the non-switcher costs; their estimates are apparently based only on switchers. The Indiana report, in the scenario without the "declining enrollment adjustment," does seem to consider the non-switcher costs but makes no effort to detail the implicitly presumed numbers of switchers and non-switchers used in its estimate of a $29.5 million savings in the first year and $16.6 million savings in the fifth year of operation. (The report does, however, state that these estimates are based on a $1,000 voucher, which amounts to less than 16% of the average private school tuition, meaning that there is less incentive for switchers, while non-switchers are simply receiving a $1,000 public subsidy for a decision they would have made anyway.) However, it is clear that a high number and a high percentage of public school students would need to transfer by year 5 in order to yield the inflated state expenditure savings number.

These calculations of positive fiscal impacts on the states are based on very questionable estimates of projected savings. The figures are dependent on the portion of revenues that the state would recapture or save when public school students exit and enroll in private schools, in addition to costs associated with providing vouchers to private school students—the non-switchers—including (in Indiana) those who entered the program at Grade K. They are also dependent on the unsubstantiated estimate that voluntary individual and corporate contributions to the tax credit voucher funds would reach $50 million (in Georgia) and $10 million (in Montana and Indiana). And, again, these factors depend heavily on poor estimates of demand for private schools and of the supply of private school spaces.

Last, the Georgia and Montana reports contend that the local portions of school revenues are not sensitive to enrollment drops and remain available to school districts even after enrollment declines. However, in most cases school districts and local school boards that govern districts do not have discretion over how local tax revenues are allocated. It is not clear whether local governments would choose to leave residual revenues in school district budgets or reallocate local revenues to other public services.

USEFULNESS OF THE REPORT FOR GUIDANCE OF POLICY AND PRACTICE

Expanding the quality and increasing the efficiency of schools for all families are important policy goals for legislatures, educators and parents. The three Friedman reports argue that tax credit voucher policies are an effective way to pursue these goals. But the reports do not adequately consider the short-term and long-term costs to the state.

Policymakers should be cautioned to look beyond the seductive promises of fiscal savings and efficiency, which are unsubstantiated and inaccurately estimated in these reports. Instead, policymakers should seek more balanced and empirically robust assessments that would allow them to make informed decisions about how to proceed with effective school reform polices.

NOTES AND REFERENCES

1. *Simmons-Harris v. Zelman*, 72 F. Supp.2d 834 (N. D. Ohio 1999), *aff'd*, 234 F.3d 945 (6 Cir. 2000), *reversed*, 536 U.S. 639 (2002).

2. Depending on whether one counts plans that have been declared in violation of state constitutions (in Florida, Colorado, and Arizona), six new voucher programs have been successfully implemented since Zelman: Washington D.C.'s Opportunity Scholarship Program (WOSP), Utah's Carson Smith Scholarships for Students with Special Needs (USSSN), Georgia's Special Needs Scholarships, Louisiana's Student Scholarships for Educational Excellence Program, Ohio's Autism Scholarship Program and the Educational Choice Scholarship Pilot Programs.

3. Welner, K. G. (2008). *NeoVouchers: The emergence of tuition tax credits for private schooling*. New York, NY: Rowman & Littlefield.
    Huerta, L. A., & d'Entremont, C. (2007, January/March). Education tax credits in a post-Zelman era: Legal, political and policy alternative to vouchers? *Educational Policy, 21*(1), 73-109

4. Welner (2008).

5. Tax credit legislation was proposed and enacted in Georgia in late 2008, following the publication of the Friedman report.

6. Gottlob, B. (2009, Feb. 5). *The Fiscal Impact of Tax-Credit Scholarships in Montana*. Indianapolis, IL: Friedman Foundation for Educational Choice.

7. Gottlob, B. (2008, Feb. 19). *The Fiscal Impact of Tax-Credit Scholarships in Georgia*. Indianapolis, IL: Friedman Foundation for Educational Choice.

8. Stuit, D. (2009, April 22). *The Fiscal Impact of a Corporate & Individual Tax Credit Scholarship Program on the State of Indiana*. Indianapolis, IL: Friedman Foundation for Educational Choice.

9. Gottlob projects that a program with similar factors in Montana would result in a net fiscal benefit of $7.5 million for local school districts and a savings of $1 million for the state, after year three of operation when the state would no longer provide a fiscal buffer to district's who lose enrollment.

10. The law that Georgia ultimately adopted does not, in fact, include a means-testing provision, meaning that higher-income families are eligible. See Welner (2008); see note 3.

11. Although that bill did not survive, Indiana's governor recently proposed a similar tax credit plan. See "Governor proposes new state scholarship tax credit," *Brazil Times* (June 4, 2009). Retrieved June 11, 2009, from http://www.thebraziltimes.com/story/1544996.html

12. The 16.7% is made up of state categorical aid and portions of the guaranteed tax base equalization revenues. The average pupil funding in Montana is calculated at $10,135 and is comprised of 47.9% state sources, 39.1% local sources and 13% federal sources.

13. The average pupil funding in Georgia is calculated at $8,582 and is comprised of 50.7% state sources, 42% local sources and 7.3% federal sources.

14. See Baker, B. D., & Green III, P. C. (2005). Tricks of the trade: State legislative actions in school finance policy that perpetuate racial disparities in the post-Brown era, *American Journal of Education, 111*(3), 372-413.

    Odden, A. R. and Picus, L. O. (2008). *School finance: A policy perspective* (4th ed.). New York, NY: McGraw Hill.

    Reschovsky, A. (1994, March). Fiscal equalization and school finance. *National Tax Journal, 47*(1), 185-197.

15. Also known as a "district power equalizing" program. A GTB program attempts to equalize the tax base per pupil across all districts and to guarantee the same level of tax base from which to draw local revenues. This approach is designed to provide tax relief for low-property-wealth districts.

16. Fuller, B., Huerta, L. A., & Ruenzel, D. (2000). *A costly gamble or serious reform? California's school voucher initiative—Proposition 38*. Berkeley, CA: Policy Analysis for California Education, University of California.

17. Huerta, L. A. (2000, October 19). Proposition 38 makes promises it cannot keep. *San Francisco Chronicle*, Opinion-Editorial, p. A3.

18. Huerta, L. A., & d'Entremont, C. (2007, January/March). Education tax credits in a post-Zelman era: Legal, political and policy alternative to vouchers? *Educational Policy, 21*(1), 73-109.

19. See Darling-Hammond, L., Kirby, S. N., & Schlegal, P. M. (1985.) *Tuition tax deductions and parent school choice: A case study of Minnesota*. Santa Monica, CA: The RAND Corporation.

    Wilson, G. Y. (2000). Effects on funding equity of the Arizona Tax Credit Law. *Education Policy Analysis Archives, 8*(38). Retrieved April 2, 2009, from http://epaa.asu.edu/epaa/v8n38.html

Malen, B. (1985). Enacting Tuition Tax Credit Deduction Statutes in Minnesota. *Journal of Education Finance, 11*(1), 1-28.

Jacobs, M. J. (1980). Tuition tax credits for elementary and secondary education: Some new evidence on who would benefit. *Journal of Education Finance, 5,* 233-245.

Longanecker, D. A. (1983). The public costs of tuition tax credits. In T. James & H. M. Levin (Eds.), *Public dollars for private schools: The case of tuition tax credits* (pp. 115-129). Philadelphia, PA: Temple University Press.

Augenblick, J. & McGuire. K (1982). *Tuition tax credits: Their impact on the states.* Denver, CO: Education Commission of the States.

Catterall, J. S., & Levin, H. M. (1982). *Public and private schools: Evidence on tuition tax credits.* Stanford, CA: Stanford University, Institute for Educational Research on Educational Finance and Governance.

Gemello, J. M. & Osman, J. W. (1982). *Analysis of the choice for public and private education.* Washington DC: Institute for Research on Educational Finance and Governance.

20. Huerta & d'Entremont (2007); see note 18.

21. See also Goldwater Institute (2003). *The Arizona scholarship tax credit: Providing choice for Arizona taxpayers and students*, Policy Report #186, Phoenix, AZ: The Goldwater Institute.

   Michos, L., & Aud, S. (2006). *Spreading freedom and saving money: The fiscal impact of the D.C. Voucher Program*, White Paper, Washington, DC: Cato Institute.

22. These estimates were calculated by the reviewer using NCES private school enrollment figures. See National Center for Education Statistics (2006). *Digest of education statistics*, Retrieved March 29, 2009 from http://nces.ed.gov/programs/coe/

23. See Welner (2008); see note 3.

PART 5

Charter Schools

Charter schools have become education's biggest political success story of the past decade. They are popular among a wide spectrum of politicians and appear headed for further growth. This growth and political success hasn't occurred in a vacuum. The charter movement has benefitted from a well-organized and well-funded campaign.[1] Think tank reports about charters have covered the gamut. Some are pure research and evaluation, some are pure advocacy, and some fall in between.

In Chapter 10, reviewer Derek Briggs examines a RAND Corporation report, *Charter Schools in Eight States: Effects on Achievement, Attainment, Integration and Competition* (2009), authored by Ron Zimmer and colleagues. This report falls into the pure research category, with the authors having no apparent ax to grind. Based on analyses of longitudinal data, the authors reached several findings: (a) charters and regular public schools generally showed comparable reading and math gains, (b) students who attend charter high schools in Florida and Chicago were significantly more likely to graduate and are more likely to attend a 2- or 4-year college than their peers in traditional public high schools, (c) charters were not skimming high-achieving students away from public schools, (d) charters were not affecting average student achievement in competing public schools, and (e) charters were generally not intensifying racial/ethnic

Think Tank Research Quality: Lessons for Policy Makers, the Media, and the Public, pp. 141–143

stratification. Because this stratification finding was based on highly aggregated data, however, Briggs finds it "equivocal." Overall, the reviewer finds the study's methods to be "sophisticated, thoughtful, and even-handed." He also points out that, as is typical of such analyses, inferences about cause and effect are open to some question.

The soundness Briggs finds in the RAND study contrasts with reviewers' assessments of reports from advocacy organizations presented in the following two chapters. Chapter 11 presents Ernest House's review of the Fordham Institute's *Trends in Charter School Authorizing* (2006), authored by Rebecca Gau. Chapter 12 presents Gary Miron's review of the Buckeye Institute's *Public Charter Schools: A Great Value for Ohio's Public School System* (2008), authored by Matthew Carr and Beth Lear. Both reviewers find serious flaws.

Gau analyzed a national survey to determine how charter schools were being authorized and by whom, an issue important to ensuring charter quality. The study concluded that authorizers based their decisions about renewing charters on student achievement and that they had become more cautious over time. It further concluded that nonprofit authorizers and independent chartering boards did a better job of authorizing than other organizations, including local education agencies, higher education institutions, and state education agencies. House finds these conclusions questionable on several grounds, noting in particular that the survey was not representative and that the author's judgments did not align with the data presented. Moreover, although the performance criteria upon which the survey was grounded are critical to the report's findings, they were drawn from only two teleconferenced focus groups involving 13 people, with no detail provided on the identity of the participants, how and why they were selected, and how the groups were conducted. Interested readers can also find, on the www.thinktankreview.org website, a response to this review from Chester Finn of the Fordham Foundation and a rejoinder from House, whose conclusions stand.

The Buckeye study examined the highly contentious issue of charter school financing. Miron notes that the issue is certainly worthy of empirical study. Public school advocates worry that charters are overfunded for the number of students served and services they provide, while charter school advocates believe it unfair that charters receive less per pupil and have fewer financing options for facilities. This study offered several findings supporting increased charter funding in Ohio, but the reviewer identifies major weaknesses. Miron criticizes the study's contention that charters in Ohio's "Big Eight" city systems operated with significantly less revenue per student than traditional public schools and produced a net gain in revenue for the systems. He also questions the claim that closing charter schools would produce a net loss for the public schools. Miron finds these conclusions based on "a false and misleading interpretation of the state mechanism for funding schools." He specifically points to a failure to consider several revenue sources. Miron's final assessment is that the report "is so misleading that it's tempting to see the distortions as intentional."

Together, these reviews illustrate characteristics typical of distinctions that can be drawn between the more and less credible studies reviewed throughout this book. For example, Briggs praises the RAND report for including significant detail concerning its methodology and assumptions, allowing readers to form their own opinion about the strength of findings. On the other hand, reviewers of the Fordham and Buckeye studies find inadequate methodological detail in those reports. Further, the Fordham study offered no justification for the criteria used to assess performance, and the Buckeye report did not provide support for assumptions guiding data selection. Although Briggs does not find the case made by the RAND authors to be fully convincing, that report properly used research literature to justify its methodology; authors of the other reports make little use of prior research. And, when the Buckeye authors did refer to a state study, they failed to mention that its findings contradicted their own.

A review of an earlier, and similar, Buckeye report is available from www.thinktankreview.org:

- *The Financial Impact of Ohio's Charter Schools* (2006), authored by Matthew Carr, found that charter schools in the "Big Eight" urban school districts produced greater achievement gains, increased revenues for traditional public schools, and operated at lower costs. Reviewer Gene Glass found these claims "without merit" and explored in some detail the weaknesses of each specific finding.

NOTES AND REFERENCES

1. See, for example, Scott, J. (2009). The politics of venture philanthropy in school choice policy and advocacy. *Educational Policy, 23*(1), 106-136.

CHAPTER 10

SCHOOLS IN EIGHT STATES

Effects on Achievement, Attainment, Integration, and Competition

Derek C. Briggs

Review of "Charter Schools in Eight States: Effects on Achievement, Attainment, Integration and Competition," by Ron Zimmer, Brian Gill, Kevin Booker, Stephane Lavertu, Tim Sass and John Witte and published by the RAND Corporation. This is a modified version of a review originally published on May 27, 2009.

INTRODUCTION

For some time now the effectiveness of charter schools has been a controversial topic. In theory, by "freeing" teachers and principals from many if not most of the constraints placed on traditional public schools by school districts, a learning environment can be fostered in which instructional innovations such as new curricula and new pedagogical strategies are encouraged and readily implemented. This would be matched by increased communication and involvement from parents and local communities. The appeal of this vision is considerable. If charter

Think Tank Research Quality: Lessons for Policy Makers, the Media, and the Public, pp. 145–158

145

school attendance leads to improvements in the way children are taught, it would seem hard to imagine a result that did not involve an effect on academic outcomes. In his first public address on the topic of education after taking office, President Obama expressed support for an expansion of charter schools as an alternative to traditional public schools, saying, "I call on states to reform their charter rules and lift caps on the number of allowable charter schools, wherever such caps are in place."[1]

Despite the political enthusiasm for charter schools, the empirical evidence of their effects on academic achievement has been mixed. In the cases where positive effects on achievement have been found,[2] these effects have tended to be relatively small and difficult to generalize. Given this backdrop, the RAND Corporation study, *Charter Schools in Eight States: Effects on Achievement, Attainment, Integration and Competition*, by Ron Zimmer, Brian Gill, Kevin Booker, Stephane Lavertu, Tim Sass and John Witte,[3] is very timely. The authors pose four primary research questions about charter schools:

1. What are the characteristics of students transferring to charter schools?
2. What effect do charter schools have on test-score gains for students who transfer between traditional public schools and charter schools?
3. What is the effect of attending a charter high school on the probability of graduating and of entering college?
4. What effect does the introduction of charter schools have on the test scores of students in nearby public schools?

The first of these questions is addressed through a descriptive analysis; the remaining three are addressed through the use of regression models.

FINDINGS AND CONCLUSIONS OF THE REPORT

The findings can be summarized as follows:

1. On average, students who transfer into charter schools have test scores similar to, or lower than, those of their peers in the public schools they previously attended. The authors conclude from this that charter schools are not "skimming" high-achieving students away from public schools. They also conclude that there is little evidence that students tend to transfer to charter schools with

considerably different racial/ethnic distributions of students. An important exception is African American students, who are most likely to attend charter schools with higher concentrations of African Americans than the public schools they leave.

2. In five jurisdictions, test score gains associated with charter schools in reading and math were about the same as those associated with traditional public schools. Only in Texas and Chicago were significant effects found for charter schools, and in those cases the effects were negative. In both cases the most defensible estimates generalize only to charter schools enrolling students in the secondary grades. In addition, the authors point to evidence that charter schools in their first year of operation and virtual charter schools (prevalent in Ohio) are most likely to have students who experience lower score gains than they experience in traditional public schools. Finally, there is limited evidence that charter school effects on student achievement are considerably more variable than public school effects. (Note that Florida was not included in this achievement analysis.)

3. Students who attend charter high schools in Florida and Chicago are significantly more likely to graduate and are more likely to attend a 2- or 4-year college than their peers in traditional public high schools. These results do not appear to be a function of school size or superior academic achievement. No graduation or college matriculation data were available for charter high schools in the other six geographic locations.

4. There is no evidence to support the hypothesis that the presence of charter schools affects the performance of nearby public schools, in either a positive direction (e.g., through competition) or a negative direction (e.g., by diverting financial resources).

In the report's final chapter the authors speculate about possible explanations for some of their more unusual findings, about broader implications for policymakers, and about methodological implications for future research on charter schools.

THE REPORT'S RATIONALE FOR ITS FINDINGS AND CONCLUSIONS

The report employs student-level panel data ranging from the 1994-95 through the 2007-08 school years across eight geographic locations. Three of these locations are entire states (Florida, Ohio and Texas), while five are large urban school districts (Chicago, Denver, Milwaukee, Philadelphia, and San Diego). The number of charter schools in each location ranges from a low of 21 in Denver to a high of 246 in Ohio. The number of years of available data ranges from a low of 4 in Ohio to a high of 9 in Chicago, San Diego and Texas. Information at the student level includes grade, race and ethnicity, and test scores in math and reading. In Chicago and Florida, information about high-school graduation and college attendance was also available. Within a given location, test scores used longitudinally were placed onto a common scale after standardizing each unique year and grade combination (using the district or state means and standard deviations). Some concerns with this approach are described below.

Relatively simple descriptive techniques involving the comparisons of means via cross-tabulations are used to describe the characteristics of students transferring into charter schools. Estimates of charter school effects on achievement, attainment and nearby public school performance are derived using statistical modeling.

The report's estimates of charter schools' effects on achievement are based on a linear regression model known as a "fixed-effects" regression, a method that allowed the researchers to compare the average test score gains of students over the years when they are enrolled in charter schools with the average gains when they are enrolled in public schools. Taking the difference of these gains (charter school gain minus public school gain) provides an estimate of the effect of a charter school on the academic achievement for each student; in other words, each student serves as his or her own control. In this sense, each student represents a fixed effect. The overall effect of charter schools is subsequently estimated as the average of these within-student effects across all students.

Estimates of charter effects on educational attainment in the RAND study are based on a probit analysis, in which the authors initially control for observable student-level variables that might confound the charter effect. To address the possibility of self-selection bias, they then control for unobservable factors that may contribute both to the decision to attend charters and to the likelihood of graduating from high school or matriculating to college by using a bivariate probit model. In this model two correlated equations are involved—one that predicts charter attendance and another that predicts either future high school graduation or college attendance. If the assumptions of the model are correct, this serves to purge the estimated charter effect of any bias due to student and family self-selection into charters.

Finally, the effects of charter school competition on nearby public school performance are estimated using another form of a fixed-effects regression. Competition is measured for each public school as either the distance to the nearest charter school or as the number of charter schools within 2.5 miles. The fixed effects of interest in this analysis consist of student-by-school interactions. As the authors write: "Competitive effects are, therefore, estimated by examining the growth of achievement of the same students in the same schools as the level of charter competition" (p. 80).

THE REPORT'S USE OF THE RESEARCH LITERATURE

The RAND study has a quasi-experimental design. Students and their families are not randomly assigned to charter or public schools, but self-select for reasons that may be observable (e.g., prior academic achievement, demographics) or unobservable (e.g., motivation, culture). The RAND authors use statistical models to adjust for selection bias. The extent to which such adjustments lead to valid inferences will always be open to debate, even when the approaches taken are defensible, as is typically the case in this report. The fact that most of the empirical research on charter school effects is based upon quasi-experimental designs is a primary reason that the results from this rapidly expanding literature are often taken with a grain of salt. The RAND authors demonstrate a solid appreciation for this through the research that they cite and in the approaches they take to estimate and interpret charter effects. Given their study design, they justify the use of fixed-effects regression models by noting that this approach has been endorsed in a methodological review by an organization known as the Charter School Achievement Panel.[3] However, the authors also clearly convey the potential problems with the fixed-effects regression model, problems recently elaborated upon by Caroline Hoxby and Sonali Murarka,[4] and by Dale Ballou, Bettie Teasley and Tim Zeidner,[5] in chapters in *Charter School Outcomes*.[6]

One conspicuous omission is any discussion of modeling approaches for estimating charter effects that involve the use of hierarchical linear modeling, also known as mixed-effects modeling. A high-profile and large-scale study of charters that applied a hierarchical linear model was conducted by Henry Braun and colleagues. The Braun study evaluated charter effects using NAEP data to resolve a preexisting dispute.[7] The implication of the RAND authors' choice of a fixed-effects model is that such an approach is superior to the one taken by Braun and colleagues—but they do not provide their rationale for this important methodological decision.

REVIEW OF THE REPORT'S METHODS

The Characteristics of Students Who Transfer to Charter Schools

The evidence that charter schools are not "skimming" high-achieving students or causing increases in racial/ethnic segregation would be more convincing if it were also examined at disaggregated levels. In a given geographic location, the RAND authors show that the average test scores of students transferring to charters tend to be lower than the average scores of students in the public schools they left. But no information is provided about the variability of this contrast across schools or school districts. This makes it difficult to rule out a competing hypothesis that within school districts, certain charter schools skim high-achieving students from traditional public schools while others focus specifically on low-achieving students. As illustrated later in this review, the approach used by the RAND authors does not allow such patterns to be detected.

By contrast, in their analysis of achievement effects (described below), the authors were very careful to present their results at both aggregate and disaggregated levels. An analysis that examined patterns in student-level transfer decisions over time using either a logistic or probit model might lead to more nuanced interpretations, along the lines of the approach taken by the authors in their Chapter 4 analysis.

The Effects of Charter Schools on Academic Achievement and Educational Attainment

A consistent theme in the analyses of achievement and attainment effects in Chapters 3-4 is the tradeoff between internal and external validity. These are issues that had been raised by Hoxby and Murarka and Ballou, Teasley, and Zeidner in the context of estimating achievement effects, and the authors are very attentive to them throughout their report. The key idea is that to make the case that an internally valid achievement effect has been estimated, the reader must be convinced that a reasonable proxy can be found for the key counterfactual outcome—the test score gain a charter school student would have experienced had he or she been enrolled in a public school. This counterfactual is identified under a fixed-effects regression as the observed gain of the same charter student when that student was (previously or subsequently) attending a public school. The upshot of this is that the RAND authors are restricting their sample of students used to estimate a charter effect to only those students who had been enrolled in both public and charter schools (e.g., "switchers") over a span of three or more years. To the extent that unobservable student-specific factors (e.g., motivation or family circumstances) do not change systematically over time, the resulting charter effect will be internally valid for charter switchers, but not externally valid (generalizable to charter stayers—those students enrolled only in charter schools). This limited generalizability is especially true if these stayers differ considerably from charter switchers.

The same issue arises in reverse when the study attempts to estimate internally valid charter effects on educational attainment (graduation and college matriculation) by restricting the sample to only those students who had attended a charter school prior to high school. The authors estimated the effects by comparing the probabilities of graduating high school or attending college for those students attending charter schools in both middle school and high school with those of students attending a charter in middle school and a traditional public school thereafter. As such, no charter effect on attainment is being estimated for students who switch from a public middle school to a charter high school. It would be possible to estimate effects of charter schools that apply to all enrolled students. Indeed, such an approach has been taken in other, previous studies.[8] But while such effects might be more externally valid, the authors of the RAND study appear to be unwilling to make this tradeoff at the perceived expense of internal validity.

A strength of the RAND study is that the authors consistently anticipate possible threats to validity, both internal and external, and bring them to the surface for objective consideration. When the estimates depend upon testable assumptions through choices made in the specification of their regression models, the authors test them against alternative specifications. For example, after estimating the effects of charter schools on math and reading test scores across seven geographic locations, the authors conduct a sensitivity analysis in which they restrict the sample of charter school students to those in secondary grades (middle and high school). The logic here is that students who switch from a public school to a charter school (or vice versa) "midstream" during the primary grades are different from those who switch at a structural transition point such as the completion of elementary school. (While the authors do not confirm this intuition empirically, they do show that across all charter schools, switchers tend to have lower test scores than stayers.) Interestingly, the results from this sensitivity analysis are largely consistent with those from their initial regression analysis: the effects of charter schools on reading and math scores are generally insignificant. Nonetheless they conclude that these are the most defensible estimates of charter effects. In only one location (Ohio) do the results change appreciably, moving from strongly negative to insignificant once the sample of students and schools is restricted.

As another example of a type of sensitivity analysis, the authors relax a constraint imposed by their initial regression model: that charter schools produce a single aggregate effect on achievement by test subject in each geographic location. First, the authors disaggregate charter effects in Ohio as a function of charter type (classroom-based or virtual/computer-based). Next, the authors differentiate their effect estimates by age of the charter schools (1, 2, or more than 2 years of operation). Finally, they disaggregate effects by the race/ethnicity of the student samples. These analyses provide insights about the conditions under which charter schools might be expected to be most effective or ineffective.

- The negative effects of charter schools in Ohio appear to be driven by a large presence of virtual charter schools in the primary grades. The authors note that this seems consistent with findings in an earlier analysis of virtual charter schools in California by the report's first author, Ron Zimmer, and his colleagues.[9]
- The authors find that in Chicago, Ohio and Texas, charter schools are most likely to have significant negative effects on achievement in their first year of operation. By contrast, in Denver, charter effects are large and positive for 12 schools in their first year of operation, but only with respect to test scores in math. In Milwaukee, Philadelphia, and San Diego there is no relationship between school age and the size of charter effects. Curiously, the authors conclude from these mixed results that "across locations, the performance of charter schools as measured by their achievement generally improves after their first year of operation" (p. 85). This statement does not seem consistent with the results they report.
- There are no clear patterns with respect to the differential effectiveness of charter schools by racial groupings. Most effect estimates are statistically insignificant. Unfortunately the authors provide no information about the sample sizes being used to estimate charter effects by race. If the number of switching students is small, the number of switching students of a particular race is even smaller. Hence it comes as little surprise that these estimates are noisy, given the low statistical power. One unexpected result to which the authors give little attention is the large positive effect of charter schools on the math scores of white students in Denver. One explanation for this might come from the authors' finding in Chapter 2 that white students who transfer to charter schools in Denver have slightly higher math scores than their public school peers. In contrast, African American and Hispanic students who transfer to Denver charters tend to have lower math scores than their public school peers.

In a related review, Robert Bifulco has pointed out three potential weaknesses in the achievement-oriented analyses in the RAND report.[10] The first is that the test scores used across grades, years and states may not be adequately comparable. The second is that no other models beyond a fixed-effects regression appear to have been considered or applied as a sensitivity check. The third is that the inclusion of a better set of mobility control variables could change the interpretation of charter effects—although in which direction is not entirely clear. For details on the second and third points, the reader is referred to Bifulco (2009, pp. 3-4). The first of these points merits a brief elaboration.

The longitudinal test score outcomes used in the RAND analyses appear entirely comparable at first glance, but this is an artifact of the choice made to standardize these scores by grade and year within each state or district under analysis. This approach, however, sweeps under the rug a number of important issues. To begin with, how well are the tests in a given state aligned with the curricula in public schools and charter schools? For example, if charter schools choose to implement innovative curricula, this content may not be captured on a traditional large-scale assessment. If true, this would bias the results against charter schools. Perhaps more importantly, when gain scores are used as the outcome in a fixed-effects regression, an implicit assumption is that these scores are continuous measures with interval properties. In other words, a 10-point score gain from, say, Grades 3 to 4 should have the same meaning regardless of the initial score in Grade 3. This assumption has been recently called into question in the context of psychometric approaches taken to scale tests such that score magnitudes are consistent within and across grades.[11] Even in an appendix section devoted specifically to their data sources, the authors of the RAND study provide minimal information that supports the validity of the tests used as outcome measures.

Finally, the RAND authors never mention one puzzling and potentially related finding from their analysis: the R^2 from the fixed-effects regressions varies quite dramatically by geographic location, from a low of 0.17 to a high of 0.46. Given that the variables included in the models are the same from location to location, this seems unexpected.

The Effect of Charter Competition on Nearby Public Schools

There are at least two principal reasons why estimating this sort of indirect effect using a fixed-effects regression (or for that matter, any statistical model) is especially difficult. First, under economic theory, the effect of competition occurs over the long term and would be unlikely to occur over the relatively short time span considered in the present study unless it were dramatic. The statistical power to pick up a small effect over a short time span is small. Second, any determination of when a charter school is "close enough" to put competitive pressure on a public school will be equivocal at best. Hence, beyond any issues that could be raised about the tenability of the assumptions of the specified fixed-effects regression, the construct validity of the "treatment" variable is very questionable, something that the RAND authors acknowledge.

REVIEW OF THE VALIDITY OF THE FINDINGS AND CONCLUSIONS

The Characteristics of Students who Transfer to Charter Schools

The RAND report indicates that charter schools do not appear to be skimming students by achievement or leading to the stratification of students by race. Aggregation bias is a plausible threat to this conclusion. One can imagine a hypothetical scenario of a school district with two public schools (A and B) and two charter schools (C and D). Imagine further that charter school C skims high-achieving students from school A, while charter school D attracts the low-achieving students from school B. Depending on the relative sample sizes of these schools and the students transferring between them, an aggregate finding consistent with those set forth by the RAND report would not be surprising, even though public school A may have lost a disproportionate number of its best students. A second level of potential aggregation bias comes from averaging over all years of available data. This may obscure important trends in the extent to which skimming by achievement may or may not be occurring. The same criticism applies to the RAND analysis of student sorting by race. The results found here seem to contradict the results found in studies by Bifulco and Ladd and Dee and Fu.[12]

The Effect of Charter Schools on Academic Achievement

The conclusions reached with respect to this research question tend to be carefully qualified and supported by defensible empirical analyses. The evidence about charter effects on student achievement also seems consistent with findings of previous quasi-experimental studies. At best, students in charter schools appear to show score improvements similar to the gains they demonstrated while in public schools. In two locations (Chicago and Texas) there is evidence they may do about a 10th of a standard deviation worse, and this would seem to be cause for concern.

The biggest threat to the internal validity of the report's estimates for charter effects on achievement is the largely untestable assumption that all confounding explanations for a difference in test score gains for a given student as that student shifts from a charter school to a public school (or vice-versa) stay constant over time. If this assumption is wrong, the estimated charter effects could also be wrong. For example, if students transfer to charter schools because of an increased motivation to do well in school, then the true effect of charters is probably lower than what has been found in this study; if students transfer because they have hit a rough patch and their parents are seeking a way to improve things, the true effect is probably higher than what has been found in this study. To their credit, the authors note this issue from the outset of the report. The best way to address it empirically would be to conduct a study under a randomized experimental design, estimate a "true" average effect, and then attempt to estimate the same effect using a fixed-effects regression with a nonexperimental control group. In fact, according to the authors, this approach is currently being taken in a federally funded study being conducted by Mathematica Inc.

The Effect of Charter Schools on Educational Attainment

The RAND report provides novel evidence that charter schools have a positive effect on educational attainment. The effect was estimated by comparing the probabilities of graduating high school or attending college for those students attending charter schools in both middle school and high school with those of students attending a charter in middle school and a traditional public school thereafter. As the authors note, the finding of positive attainment effects is based on a restricted sample of students in two locations (charter high schools in Chicago and Florida), so this limits the generalizability of the inference.

Some concerns about the internal validity of these results can be found by scrutinizing the parameter estimates from the underlying probit analyses. For example, the bivariate probit model suggests the presence of strongly *negative* selection bias. This implies that students who choose to attend charter high schools are those who are less likely to graduate or attend college than students who choose to attend traditional public schools. As the authors note, this finding seems counterintuitive. In addition, the results suggest that after controlling for prior test scores, demographic variables and self-selection, special education students attending charter schools are anywhere from 4% to 8% more likely to graduate from high school (whether the high school is a charter or traditional public) than their non-special education peers. (A similar result was found in the univariate probit specification.) This result is conceivable, but also seems counterintuitive. These sorts of unusual parameter estimates do not necessarily invalidate the estimate of charter effects on attainment, but they do hint at a possible mismatch between the data and the statistical model—a mismatch the authors may wish to explore should they seek to publish this study in a peer-reviewed journal.[13]

The Effect of Charter Competition on Nearby Public Schools

The RAND authors find no evidence of an indirect effect (negative or positive) on public schools through the competition engendered by their proximity to charter schools. This analysis comprises the shortest chapter in the RAND report (six pages)—and also the most equivocal. The authors note, "we regard the results in this chapter as suggestive but not definitive" (p. 80). Indeed, unlike the analyses in Chapters 3 and 4, the authors pay much less attention to checks on the sensitivity of their findings to alternate specifications of the statistical model. What can be concluded from these analyses is that there is no apparent evidence of short-term competition effects large enough to register as either statistically or practically significant.

USEFULNESS OF THE REPORT FOR POLICY AND PRACTICE

The RAND report represents one of the most extensive studies on charter school effectiveness across the United States to date and is sure to be influential as state policymakers decide whether or not to encourage an expansion in charter school availability. On the whole, the methodological approaches it takes are sophisticated, thoughtful, and even-handed. As with any analyses of this sort, the causal inferences that might be drawn are subject to threats against internal and (particularly with this study) external validity to varying degrees. Interestingly, this report will probably be used as empirical ammunition by both supporters and opponents of charter schools.

Supporters of charter schools are likely to emphasize the findings that charter schools do not appear to skim high-achieving students or increase racial or ethnic stratification, have positive effects on educational attainment (graduation and college matriculation), and do not appear to have negative impacts on nearby public schools. Opponents of charter schools are likely to emphasize the findings of insignificant charter effects on student achievement in five of seven locations, negative effects in two of seven locations, and the lack of evidence for positive competition effects on public schools.

While the findings related to skimming, sorting and competition are probably best classified as suggestive—since some very plausible alternative explanations can be advanced—the findings related to achievement and attainment effects rest on somewhat stronger methodological ground. In any case, it is important to note that these findings only generalize to (a) students who transfer from charter schools to public schools or vice versa, and (b) charter schools serving students in the secondary grades. The evidence on the effects of elementary charter schools on student outcomes to date is still unclear.

NOTES AND REFERENCES

1. Lehigh, S. (2009, March 13). Obama's challenge on charters. *The Boston Globe*.
2. Hoxby, C., & Rockoff, J. (2004). *The impact of charter schools on student achievement*. Harvard University manuscript.
3. Betts, J. R., & Hill, P. T. (2006). *Key issues in studying charter schools and achievement: A review and suggestions for national guidelines*. Seattle, WA: Center on Reinventing Public Education, Daniel J. Evans School of Public Affairs, University of Washington, National Charter School Research Project.
4. Hoxby, C. M., & Murarka. (2007). Methods of assessing the achievement of students in charter schools. In M. Berends, M. G. Springer, & H. J. Walberg (Eds.), *Charter School Outcomes* (pp. 221-241). New York, NY: Erlbaum.
5. Ballou, D., Teasley, B., & Zeidner, T. (2007). Charter schools in Idaho. In M. Berends, M. G. Springer, & H. J. Walberg (Eds.), *Charter school outcomes* (pp. 221-241). New York, NY: Erlbaum.
6. Berends, M., Springer, M. G., & Walberg, H. J. (Eds.). (2008). *Charter school outcomes*. New York, NY: Erlbaum.
7. Braun, H., Jenkins, F., & Grigg, W. (2006). *A closer look at charter schools using hierarchical linear Modeling*. National Center for Education Statistics, NCES 2006-460.
8. See for example Lubienski, C., & Lubienski, S. T. (2006). School sector and academic achievement: A multi-level analysis of NAEP mathematics data. *American Education Research Journal*, *43*(4), 651-698.
9. Zimmer, R., Buddin, R., Chau, D. Daley, G. A., Gill, B., Guarino, C., Hamilton, L. S., Krop, C., McCaffrey, D. F., Sandler, M., Brewer, D. J. (2003) *Charter school operations and performance: Evidence from California*. Santa Monica, CA: RAND Corporation, MR-1700-EDU.
10. Bifulco, R. (2009). *Review of "The Impact of Milwaukee Charter Schools on Student Achievement."* Boulder, CO and Tempe, AZ: Education and the Public Interest Center & Education Policy Research Unit. Retrieved May 16,

2009, from http://epicpolicy.org/thinktank/review-impact-Milwaukee-charter

11.   Ballou, D. (2009). Test scaling and value-added measurement. *Education Finance and Policy, 4*(4), 351–383.

12.   Briggs, D. C., & Betebenner, D. (2009, April 14). *Is growth in student achievement scale dependent?* Paper presented at the invited symposium "Measuring and Evaluating Changes in Student Achievement: A Conversation about Technical and Conceptual Issues" at the annual meeting of the National Council for Measurement in Education, San Diego, CA.

13.   Bifulco, R., & Ladd, H. F. (2007). School choice, racial segregation, and test-score gaps: Evidence from North Carolina's charter school program. *Journal of Policy Analysis and Management*, 26(1), 31-56.

14.   Dee, T. S., & Fu, H. (2004). Do charter schools skim students or drain resources? *Economics of Education Review, 23*(3), 259-271.

15.   For a cogent critique of the use of a bivariate probit model to adjust for selection bias, see Freedman, D. A. (2005). *Statistical models: Theory and practice*. Cambridge University Press, pp. 128-133.

CHAPTER 11

TRENDS IN CHARTER SCHOOL AUTHORIZING

Ernest R. House

Review of Rebecca Gau's "Trends in Charter School Authorizing," published by the Thomas B. Fordham Institute. This is a modified version of a review originally published on May 10, 2006.

INTRODUCTION

For the past decade charter schools have been one of the most popular educational reforms in the US. This study[1] of charter school "authorizing" was sponsored by the Fordham Institute, a nonprofit group that strongly supports charters. In the foreword to the study, Fordham's Michael Petrilli and Chester Finn say, "Charter school authorizing and the act of chartering schools are the most promising contemporary educational innovations ... the charter movement's credibility depends on bad schools being put out of business" (p. vii, viii). The mixed record compiled by charter schools has led to attempts to control their quality by authorizing good ones and eliminating bad ones. This study is a national

Think Tank Research Quality: Lessons for Policy Makers, the Media, and the Public, pp. 159–164

survey of the authorizers and was conducted by Rebecca Gau of Goal One Research in Arizona.

FINDINGS AND CONCLUSIONS OF THE REPORT

The study presents the following conclusions based on a national survey:

- The agencies that authorize charter schools often do not renew the schools because of poor academic performance.
- Authorizers have grown more careful over time about approving charter schools.
- Half of all authorizers exercise only limited oversight.
- Most authorizers are small-scale, school district sponsors.
- Most authorizers say they would use additional staff to monitor academics.
- Nonprofits and independent chartering boards do better authorizing than other authorizer types.

RATIONALES SUPPORTING THE FINDINGS AND CONCLUSIONS

Although the study is partly descriptive—who is doing the authorizing—it is also evaluative in seeking to discover which are the most effective types of authorizers. Or, in the words of Petrilli and Finn in the foreword to the study, "Are there organizations that should not be given the task of authorizing schools...? What types of sponsors do the best job...?" (p. viii).

The study introduces five practices "that we believe are hallmarks of effective charter school authorizing ... we suspect, but cannot yet prove, these practices lead to charter school quality and ultimately strong student achievement" (p. 1):

- Data-driven decision making and rigorous, objective, selection and renewal processes.
- Sound working relations between the authorizer and school.
- Skilled authorizer personnel.
- Adequate resources and autonomy.
- Parent and community input.

A national survey based on these criteria was sent to authorizers around the country.

REVIEW OF THE REPORT'S METHODS

The study is based on the five practices or criteria listed above, with emphasis on the criterion of data-driven rigor. The five criteria seem reasonable, but the researchers do not attempt to fully justify them. They were evidently derived from two teleconferenced focus groups consisting of 13 people, but it is not made clear how they were selected and how the focus groups were conducted.

The survey was sent to 561 authorizers the researchers identified. The survey return rate was 33% (184), a low return, especially since the responses were not representative across the primary categories of analysis. The researchers subdivided the sample into authorizer types: intermediate education agencies (14 responses, a 100% return); higher education institutions (20, a 100% return); independent chartering boards (3, a 75% return); local education agencies (LEA) (118, a 24% return); municipal offices (2, a 100% return); nonprofits (6, a 75% return); and state education agencies (SEA) (21, a 100% return). The low response and quite different numbers involved make comparative inferences somewhat problematic.

The authors construct two scales consisting of selected survey items—one for "quality" and one for "compliance." The quality scale crossed with the compliance scale yields a two-by-two table and four types of authorizing approaches:

- "hands on"—high attention to quality and compliance.
- "tight-loose"—strong attention to quality, but weak attention to compliance.
- "bureaucratic"—weak attention to quality, but strong attention to compliance.
- "limited"—weak attention to quality and compliance.

The best authorizing is from the "hands on" approach, though a case can be made for the tight-loose approach, according to the authors. Certainly, attention to quality is critical, meaning the first two approaches are best. Examining the authorizer percentages for these two approaches combined, higher education authorizers do best (60%), followed by nonprofits (50%), municipals (50%), SEA (50%), and LEA (42%). Independent boards (33%) and intermediate agencies (28%) do somewhat worse. However, these analyses seem contrary to a major finding of the study.

The executive summary says, "Some types seem more able to practice quality authorizing than others—the nonprofit organizations and the independent chartering boards ... tend to do well on both counts" (p. v). And Petrilli and Finn say in the foreword, "nonprofit organizations and

Independent Chartering Boards (ICB) show the greatest promise" (p. ix). In fact, the ICB rank poorly, and the nonprofits do about the same as SEA, LEA, and municipals, all of which come in behind the higher education authorizers on this data analysis, the most quantitatively rigorous in the study.

The report profiles each type of authorizer separately on each of the five criteria. The researcher(s) judged each type on each criterion and summarized their judgments about types in a final table. This is where the nonprofits and independent boards come out strongest. But again, some of these judgments seem contrary to the data. For example, throughout the study, "data-based decision making and objective rigor" is the dominant criterion. Two survey items closely associated with this criterion are "authorizers' use of data analysis models," and "sources of input for renewal decisions." Here are the "use of data analysis model" findings for three authorizer types (p. 34).

Importantly, the data models are ordinarily ranked with the "best" options first. That is, the author(s) consider fixed-effects models to be superior to value-added and both superior to longitudinal. (Some experts might dispute their ranking.) In the judgment of the author(s), the universities are downgraded on this criterion because they rate "scoring rubrics" only "somewhat important," and they "use the least sophisticated model to analyze student achievement data" (p. 21). The "verdict" is, "they get data directly from schools but don't use it in a sophisticated way." Accordingly, in the final summary, universities are rated only "moderate" on this criterion. However, as can be seen above, in the "data models" table, public universities ranked comparably: equal to nonprofits in the highest category, better than ICB in the top two combined, and better than nonprofits on the three combined.

The comparison between ICB and universities is particularly revealing concerning the author's or authors' use of judgment. Like the universities, the ICB are downgraded for rating the scoring rubric only "somewhat

Table 11.1.   Authorizer's Use of Data Models

	Public Universities	ICB	Nonprofits
Fixed/mixed effects	21%	33%	20%
Value added	29%	0%	40%
Longitudinal	29%	67%	0%
None	0%	0%	20%
Don't know	21%	0%	20%

Source: Gau, R. (2006) Trends in charter school authorizing. Fordham Foundation, p. 34.

important." But the researchers say, "they use a sophisticated model for data analysis." The verdict is, "they put a strong emphasis on the importance of data and data collection. They could update their models for data analysis" (p. 27). Universities are judged unsophisticated on data models, whereas independent boards are declared to need to simply "update" their data analysis. In the report summary ICB are judged "strong" on this criterion, universities moderate. However, as just noted, the public universities are superior to the ICB on the two best methods, 50% to 33%.

What about the nonprofits? The nonprofits rated the scoring rubric the same as universities and ICB, but the verdict is, "they collect a lot of data from their schools and appear to use it well." Nonprofits are awarded a "strong" rating on this criterion in the final summary. However, 20% of nonprofits state they have no method of data analysis at all. If one calculated a mean over categories (treating "don't know" as the lowest category), the nonprofits would come out worst of the three. How can they be judged stronger?

What about the other survey question on "sources of input for renewal?" If one averages across the 10 categories of response for this item, the universities have a mean score of 4.65, the ICB of 4.82, and the nonprofits 4.52 (calculated for purposes of this review; the means are not provided by the study). There is not much difference among them, it would seem, and no reason to declare the first one moderate and the last two strong. By selectively interpreting, the study arrives at conclusions contrary to some of its own data. In the summary table comparing types of authorizers, the author(s) award nonprofits and ICB four "strongs" and two "moderates," while universities receive no "strongs," five "moderates," and one "weak" rating overall.

Pertrilli and Finn, in the report's foreword, seem a bit uncomfortable with these conclusions, which elevate nonprofits above where the evidence seems to place them. "Yes, this could be our own bias—after all, Fordham is one the handful of nonprofits studied here. And we think highly of our hometown authorizer in Washington, D.C." (p. ix). It is unclear whether Fordham was one of the six nonprofits in the study, but if so that would seem an important consideration. Even if it was not included, the influence of the sponsor does loom over the report, calling its objectivity into question.

REVIEW OF THE VALIDITY OF THE FINDINGS AND CONCLUSIONS, AND USEFULNESS OF THE REPORT FOR POLICY AND PRACTICE

The credibility of the findings is weakened by the poor and differential return rate on the survey. How representative was the sample? If one accepts this limitation, the following conclusions seem reasonable: agencies often do not renew charter schools because of poor academic performance; authorizers have grown more careful over time; most authorizers exercise only limited oversight; most authorizers are small-scale; and, most say they would use additional staff to monitor academics. However, the conclusions comparing authorizer types are deeply flawed. The conclusion that nonprofits and independent boards are better able to handle the authorizing process seems to be contradicted by the data.

Given its flaws, this study is not conclusive enough to guide policy, though it might point to future directions for consideration.

NOTES AND REFERENCES

1.   Gau, R. (2006). *Trends in charter school authorizing*. Washington, DC: Thomas B. Fordham Institute.

CHAPTER 12

PUBLIC CHARTER SCHOOLS

A Great Value for
Ohio's Public Education System

Gary Miron

Review of "Public Charter Schools: A Great Value for Ohio's Public Education Sys-
tem," by Matthew Carr and Beth Lear and published by The Buckeye Institute for
Public Policy Solutions. This is a modified version of a review originally published on
December 10, 2008.

INTRODUCTION

The financing of charter schools is highly contentious. Traditional public
schools are concerned that charter schools receive too much money for the
students they educate and the range of services they provide. Charter
schools, on the other hand, are upset that they receive less per pupil and
have fewer options for facility finance. This issue remains controversial and
difficult to resolve due to a number of reasons, including the following:

Think Tank Research Quality: Lessons for Policy Makers, the Media, and
the Public, pp. 165–178
Copyright © 2010 by Information Age Publishing
All rights of reproduction in any form reserved.

- Funding formulas for public schools and charter schools alike tend to be complex and rely on many factors and variables. These complexities often play out differently for schools enrolling different types of students.
- Funding formulas for charter schools vary extensively from state to state.
- Multiple types and sources of revenues for charter schools are not easily captured and reported. In addition to public funding from local, state, or federal sources, many charter schools are effective in securing private sources of funding. Much of this funding can be outside the purview of analysts. Private funds are not incorporated into state purchasing and accounting systems or are held and spent on behalf of the charter school by a trust or foundation.

With each passing year, new analyses and position papers on charter school finance are released. Many of these further confuse charter school finance because they present only selective data or partial evidence that supports a particular position. A new Buckeye Institute report titled *Public Charter Schools: A Great Value for Ohio's Public Education System* falls into this group of papers that are intended to advocate, obscure, and redirect attention rather than deepen understanding and insight.[1]

FINDINGS AND CONCLUSIONS OF THE REPORT

Key findings from the report include the following:

- Ohio's public charter schools (referred to as "community schools" in Ohio) never receive funds raised by a school district's property tax.
- Charter schools operate with substantially less revenue per student, as compared to other public schools, in each of the so-called Big 8 city school systems (Akron, Canton, Cincinnati, Cleveland, Columbus, Dayton, Toledo, and Youngstown).
- Every Big 8 city school system receives a net gain in revenue, on average, for each student choosing to attend a charter school.
- The return of public charter students to each Big 8 city school district would result in a net per-pupil loss of revenues for the district. As a result, these districts would face either lower per-pupil spending levels or significant property tax increases to maintain current spending levels.

THE REPORT'S RATIONALE FOR ITS FINDINGS AND CONCLUSIONS

The findings and conclusions are largely based on a discussion of select aspects of the funding formula for public schools in Ohio. For instance, the finding that charter schools receive no funds raised by local property taxes is based on a superficial reading of the description of the funding formula for charter schools in the state's Foundation Funding Program.[2]

The finding that charter schools operated with less money than the Big 8 city school systems is based on a comparison of undated per-pupil revenue data, but (as discussed below) this analysis excludes several sources of revenues.

The findings that districts gain revenue for each student who attends a charter school and that there would be a net loss of revenues for districts if charter schools were closed are based on a false and misleading interpretation of the state mechanism for funding schools.

THE REPORT'S USE OF RESEARCH LITERATURE

The policy brief includes very few references to research literature. Only one research report is cited, an evaluation report prepared by the Legislative Office of Education Oversight.[3] Interestingly, this same report contains information suggesting that district school finance was negatively affected by charter schools—countering the claims in the brief—but such findings were not cited or considered in the Buckeye policy brief.

The absence of research literature is surprising for two reasons. First, extensive research on this topic exists,[4] and second, the lead author is a doctoral fellow at the University of Arkansas, a research university.[5]

REVIEW OF THE REPORT'S METHODS

The policy brief contains no specific methods section, although there are some references to methods used when these are not obvious to the reader.

The policy brief provides a partial description of the state funding formula for charter schools, although a more complete and accurate description of the funding mechanism for charter schools can be obtained from the Ohio Department of Education website[6] or from the state evaluation report of charter schools.[7]

With regard to the methods used to compare revenues, the authors create tables with undated information from select revenue sources. The data in the table are reported to be averages calculated for the charter schools in each of the eight large urban districts in the state. The authors then undertake summative analyses and compare charter schools with the Big 8 city school systems.

Assumptions underlying the data used for their analyses are not accurately spelled out and are misleading. For example, the policy brief assumes that all revenues are captured in the "FS-3" form that is used for calculating the school foundation formula. However, as described below, the FS-3 data exclude many sources of revenue. Furthermore, the authors have ignored important sources of finance data for charter schools in Ohio, namely, the audit reports from the Ohio Auditor of State Office[8] and the state's 5-year forecast reports.[9] The audit reports in particular provide a more comprehensive review of revenues and expenditures, and the data in these reports speak to the issue of financial viability and funding sufficiency.

When reading the new research literature as I prepared to write this review, I was struck by the fact that most analyses of charter school finance are riddled with explanatory notes. In fact, it would be difficult to provide a fair and balanced description of charter school finance without carefully stipulating all the exceptions to the rules and the limitations in the data. Nevertheless, the analysis from the Buckeye Institute does not list a single limitation in the data or provide a single cautionary note for readers.

REVIEW OF THE VALIDITY OF THE FINDINGS AND CONCLUSIONS

The Buckeye Institute policy brief claims that Ohio's public charter schools do not receive funds raised by a school district's property tax, but later qualifies this finding by stating that "public charter schools do not directly receive any locally raised property tax revenues." The key word is "directly."

It is true that state law prohibits charter schools from levying taxes and that the school district must levy a set property tax (minimum 30 mills) based on property values rather than the number of students that a district enrolls. It is also true that districts do not pay locally raised tax dollars directly to charter schools. However, these districts must deduct from their state funds an equivalent of a 32 mill tax regardless of the number of students enrolled in the district or in charter schools. If a district is affluent its 32 mill tax is large and offsets a considerable portion of state funds. If a district has a poor property base, it raises less with the millage tax and the state share is larger. In contrast, since charter schools are not required or permitted to levy taxes, they do not have to make deductions in the state funding they receive.

When a student moves from a district school to a charter school, state funding effectively follows. When state revenues are diverted to charter schools, less state revenues are provided to the local district, meaning that a greater proportion of locally raised money is needed to fund the education of district students. Accordingly, as described in greater detail later in this review, charter school enrollments do have an impact on locally raised taxes because those taxes are an inextricable part of the overall school funding mechanism in Ohio. Charter schools definitely benefit indirectly from locally raised taxes.

The authors clearly want to underline the point that public charter schools do not directly receive revenues from local property taxes.[10] This narrow interpretation, however, is misleading and the distinction has little relevance, especially since charter schools have caused there to be substantial increases in overall public spending on schools in Ohio.[11]

Charter School Finance in Ohio: A More Complete Description

The second key conclusion of the Buckeye Institute policy brief is that charter schools receive substantially less in revenues than do traditional public schools. This finding, to be meaningful, assumes that charter schools serve the same types of students and provide the same range of services, which is not the case. Furthermore, because this conclusion is based on only partial revenues, it is not possible to draw such a conclusion from the evidence presented in the report.

The intent of the Ohio funding formula is to provide equal funding for all public schools based on the types of students they serve and the range of services they provide. The statute *ORC 3314.08* provides the basis for how charter schools are funded in Ohio. Charter schools receive funding from the state through what is essentially the same per-pupil foundation allocation used for traditional public schools. Funding follows the student.

The foundation funding consists of a set formula amount, which for the 2008-09 school year is $5,732 for each student. On top of this base amount is added poverty-based assistance,[12] intervention aid, funding for limited-English-proficient students, professional development for teachers, all-day kindergarten, dropout prevention, class-size reduction, and community outreach. Schools that enroll children with special education needs receive additional funding that is based on a formula with six separate weights that reflect the differences in costs for typical remediation support, depending on the type of disability. Finally, charter schools also receive parity aid,[13] and they can receive support for gifted units, career-technical education, adult education services, and transportation, if they provide these services.

Cyber charter schools or e-schools also receive the formula amount and the special education weighted amounts, but they do not receive the other smaller categories or types of funding.

Relative to other states, Ohio's practices for funding charter schools are rather sophisticated and distinctive, making efforts to ensure equal funding to districts and charter schools based on the types of students they serve and the types of services they provide. The funding formula is exceptional in that it has a sensitive adjustment for children with special needs. Furthermore, the funding mechanism is sensitive to the movement of students during the school year.[14]

Cost Advantages and Disadvantages

While opponents of charter schools have argued those schools receive too much funding, advocates for charter schools claim that they are underfunded. Below, I have listed reasons or factors that suggest that charter schools might have cost advantages or disadvantages relative to traditional public schools.

Cost advantages for charter schools:

- Increased autonomy allows charter schools the flexibility needed to be more responsive and efficient.
- Charter schools are community-based and better able to solicit in-kind contributions from families, community partners, businesses, and private organizations.
- Charter schools are able to apply for additional federal grants and sometimes state grants for start-up and implementation of the school, as well as for the dissemination of ideas. Start-up grants are also available from private foundations and organizations.
- Charter school teachers typically receive lower salaries than traditional public school teachers.[15]
- Charter schools can limit enrollments to ensure an efficient match with existing facilities and instructors.[16]
- An increasing number of charter schools are cyber schools that require minimal infrastructure in terms of facilities.

Cost disadvantages for charter schools:

- Most charter schools are start-up schools that require a lot of initial funding, particularly for facilities, and federal start-up grants are insufficient, especially when the renovation or purchase of a facility is involved.

- Charter schools tend to be small, lacking districts' economies of scale.

Traditional public schools confront a few cost disadvantages when charter schools increase the movement of students across school types. The general unpredictability of enrollments creates both budgeting and planning problems for school districts that they did not have to deal with prior to the existence of charter schools.[17] Districts cannot cost-efficiently limit the number of students they enroll to match facilities and teaching staff. They must enroll all students who request a place and sometimes have to operate half-full classes. Also, district schools often find out about students leaving or returning too late to adjust staffing to efficiently accommodate the addition or removal of students.

Recognition of these particular cost advantages or disadvantages is important for understanding that both advocates and opponents of charter schools can present one-sided arguments that may not take into consideration the whole range factors that affect the equitable distribution of revenues.[18]

Serving Less-Costly-to-Educate Students and Providing Fewer Programs

The Buckeye Institute policy brief implicitly assumes that charter schools serve similar students and offer similar services and programs as traditional public schools. The evidence from the state evaluation of charter schools, however, concludes that, on the whole, charter schools are serving students who are less costly to educate.[19] The state evaluation report found that charter schools largely catered to elementary grades and were much less likely than traditional public schools to serve high school students. High schools tend to cost 20% to 30% more per pupil than elementary school students.[20] Further, traditional public schools enrolled almost twice the proportion of students with disabilities. To illustrate how important this factor can be, a few of Ohio's charter schools that serve a disproportionately *high* number of students with disabilities receive operating revenues close to $30,000 per pupil each year.

In summary, if a charter school provides a full range of services (e.g., vocational training, adult education, transportation, etc.) and serves the most-costly-to-educate students (e.g., students with severe disabilities and children in poverty), it can secure far more in revenues from the state.[21]

On average, however, this has not been the situation in Ohio, which explains why charters would tend to receive less funding through the state formula.

Considering All Sources of Revenue

The manner in which the evidence from the Buckeye Institute is presented also implicitly assumes that charter schools are not receiving federal grants or private sources of revenues. Yet as with all public schools, charter schools may seek additional funds through grants and other government and private sources. Other major grant opportunities are available only to the charter sector. Many—but certainly not all—charter schools are quite successful at attracting private sources of funding.

The Buckeye Institute policy brief attempts to portray the revenue situation for charter schools as unfair and inequitable. The brief makes its case by not reporting all revenues and by not acknowledging the large disparities in revenues among charter schools. A careful look at the complete set of revenues would reveal that—as is the case with public schools in general—some charter schools are clearly advantaged in terms of total revenues and some are clearly underfunded for the students they serve and the programs and services they deliver. On the whole, however, most charter schools in Ohio appear to be receiving fair and equitable amounts of total revenues.

A fair means of describing revenues requires a review of all sources. Sullins and Miron[22] thoroughly analyzed all sources of revenue for four charter schools in Cleveland and found that three of the four schools had substantial revenues from private sources. In fact, those three had total per-pupil revenues that exceeded the per-pupil revenues for the Cleveland Municipal School District in the same year.

The state evaluation of charter schools in Ohio contained the following findings that indicate that charter schools are receiving adequate revenues:

- Two-thirds of the charter schools that were audited had surpluses.
- Charter schools receive start-up grants from both the state ($50,000 for each of the first 4 generations of schools) and federal government (up to $450,000 over 3 years).[23]
- Charter schools were spending $224,232 (median value) a year beyond what they received in state aid, which strongly suggests they receive revenues from other sources.

While it is true that most—but not all—charter schools receive less per pupil in revenue than traditional public schools, it still is possible that charter schools have cost advantages if they serve less-costly-to-educate students and if they provide a narrower range of services.[24]

Charter schools are created based on a contractual relationship that is built on a transparent understanding of how they are funded. When charter schools sign the contract to begin operating, they do so with an understanding that they are willing to accept their responsibility to provide a quality public education based on the state funding formula. The fact that a larger number (approximately 315) of charter schools have opened in Ohio suggests that many operators are willing to accept the funding arrangements. Similarly, the fact that 10 for-profit education management organizations (EMOs) have chosen to operate charter schools in Ohio[25] also suggests that funding is sufficiently robust for even profit-oriented businesses to seize the opportunity.

Increased Charter School Enrollment Benefits Districts Financially—Really?

The last few conclusions in the policy brief are based on the premise that students who enroll in charter schools actually benefit districts financially. These claims are unfounded and outlandish.

The state evaluation of charter schools, led by the nonpartisan Legislative Office of Education Oversight (LOEO), closely studied the issue of financial impact of charter schools on districts. Contrary to the claims of the Buckeye Institute, the state evaluators concluded that charter schools were having a negative impact on the finances of school districts: "LOEO concludes that the greatest impact of community schools on school districts has been financial … [districts] are not able to reduce costs proportionately on a year-to-year basis."[26]

The Buckeye Institute policy brief was able to reach a different result by assuming that districts retain local tax revenues that were earmarked for charter school students. But local tax dollars are not raised on a per-pupil basis. The district collects the same amount of local tax dollars based on a 32 mill charge-off regardless of the number of students enrolled in the district or the number of students who leave for charter schools. In addition, the locally raised taxes offset state funding for district students. Therefore, as students leave for charter schools:

1. The overall costs go down for school districts;
2. The amount of locally raised taxes stays the same because it is based on a millage tax; and

3. As a result of this, the district receives fewer state dollars since the locally raised dollars cover a higher proportion of district costs.

The Buckeye Institute claims that districts receive as much as $4,030 extra for each student who enrolls in a charter school. The brief also contends that if charter schools were closed, local districts would have to reduce per-pupil expenditures or raise local taxes to accommodate students who would return to districts. Such claims are false, deceitful, and patently misrepresent how the funding of public schools works.

If charter schools closed and a large portion of students returned to district schools, this might present difficulties for the district, depending on the degree of advance notice.[27] However, the district would not have to alter its local taxes, and it would still receive the same amount of revenues per pupil. The only difference would be that the state share of the overall district costs would increase, with a shift in public funding from the charters to the school districts.

USEFULNESS OF THE REPORT FOR GUIDANCE OF POLICY AND PRACTICE

The report is so misleading that it's tempting to see its distortions as intentional. Policymaking needs to be based on valid and well-reasoned evaluations and research; for this reason, the Buckeye Institute policy brief has limited use.

NOTES AND REFERENCES

1. Carr, M., & Lear, B. (2008). *Public charter schools: A great value for Ohio's public education system*. Policy Brief dated November 14, 2008. Columbus, OH: The Buckeye Institute for Public Policy Solutions.
2. More about the state's school funding program is explained in a document available online from the Ohio Department of Education. Retrieved December 8, 2008, from http://www.ode.state.oh.us/GD /DocumentManagement/DocumentDownload.aspx?DocumentID=37836
3. Legislative Office of Education Oversight. (2003). *Community schools in Ohio: Implementation issues and impact on Ohio's education system* (Vol. 1). Columbus, OH: Author.
4. Here is a short list of some key research publications that are readily available that would assist the authors in preparing a research brief.
   Ascher, C., Cole, C., Harris, J., & Echazarreta, J. (2004). *The finance gap: Charter schools and their facilities*. Retrieved February 16, 2007, from the New York University Institute for Education and Social Policy: Retrieved

December 8, 2008, from http://steinhardt.nyu.edu/scmsAdmin/uploads/001/117/FinanceGap.pdf

Belfield, C. (2008). *Funding formulas, school choice, and inherent incentives.* Boulder, CO and Tempe, AZ: Education and the Public Interest Center & Education Policy Research Unit. Retrieved November 29, 2008, from http://epicpolicy.org/files/CHOICE-05-Belfield2.pdf

Duncombe, W. D., & Yinger, J. (2008). Measurement of cost differentials. In E. Fiske & H. Ladd (Eds.), *Handbook of research in education and policy.* New York, NY: Routledge.

Gill, B., Timpane, P. M., Ross, K. E., & Brewer, D. J. (2001). *Rhetoric versus reality: What we know and what we need to know about vouchers and charter schools.* Santa Monica, CA: RAND.

General Accounting Office [GAO]. (1998). *Charter schools: Federal funding available, but bar-riers exist.* Washington DC: Author.

Hansen, J. S. (2007). The role of nongovernmental organizations in financing public schools. In E. Fiske & H. Ladd (Eds.), *Handbook of research in education and policy.* New York, NY: Routledge.

Hassel, B. (1999). *Paying for the charter schoolhouse: Policy options for charter school facilities financing.* Washington, DC: Office of Educational Research and Improvement.

Krop, C., & Zimmer, R. (2005). Charter school type matters when examining funding and facili-ties: Evidence from California. *Education Policy Analysis Archives, 13*(50). Retrieved December 8, 2008, from http://epaa.asu.edu/epaa/v13n50/v13n50.pdf

Levin, H. M., & Belfield, C. R. (2005). *Privatizing educational choice.* Denver, CO: Paradigm.

Little, D., Roberts, G., Ward, D., Bianchi, A. B., & Metheny, M. (2003). *Charter schools: Investment in innovation or funding folly?* Latham, NY: New York State School Boards Association.

Nelson, H. F., Muir, E., & Drown, R. (2000). *Venturesome capital: State charter school finance systems.* Washington, DC: Office of Educational Research and Improvement, U.S. Department of Education.

Nelson, H. F., Muir, E., & Drown, R. (2003). *Paying for the vision: Charter school revenue and expenditures.* Washington, DC: Office of Educational Research and Improvement, U.S. Department of Education.

Picus, L. O., Goertz, M., & Odden, A. (2008). Intergovernment aid formulas and case studies. In E. Fiske & H. Ladd (Eds.), *Handbook of research in education and policy.* New York, NY: Routledge.

Prince, H. (1999). Follow the money: An initial review of elementary charter school spending in Michigan. *Journal of Education Finance, 25*(2), 175-94.

Osberg, E. (2006). Charter school funding. In P. Hill (Ed.), *Charter schools against the odds: An assessment of the Koret task force on K-12.* Stanford, CA: Hoover Institution.

Roza, M. (2005). Apples-to-apples fiscal comparisons. In R. Lake & P. Hill (Eds.), *Hopes, fears, & reality: A balanced look at American charter schools in 2005.* Seattle, WA: National Charter School Research Project, University of Washington.

Sugarman, S. (2002). Charter school funding issues. *Education Policy Analysis Archives, 10*(34).

5.   Two earlier reviews of reports by the first author of this new report also raised concerns about the poor use of prior research. See Glass, G. (2006). *Review of "The Financial Impact of Ohio's Charter Schools."* Boulder, CO and Tempe, AZ: Education and the Public Interest Center & Education Policy Research Unit. Retrieved December 8, 2008, from http://epicpolicy.org/thinktank/review-the-financial-impact-ohios-charter-schools
Baker, B. (2007). *Review of "Shortchanging Disadvantaged Students: An Analysis of Intra-district Spending Patterns in Ohio."* Boulder, CO and Tempe, AZ: Education and the Public Interest Center & Education Policy Research Unit. Retrieved December 8, 2008, from http://epicpolicy.org/thinktank/review-shortchanging-disadvantaged-students-an-analysis-intra-district-spending-patterns-o

6.   Ohio Department of Education (undated). *Funding for Community Schools.* Retrieved December 8, 2008, from http://education.ohio.gov/GD/Templates/Pages/ODE/ODEPrimary.aspx?Page=2&TopicID=662&TopicRelationID=878

7.   Legislative Office of Education Oversight. (2003). *Community schools in Ohio: Implementation issues and impact on Ohio's education system* (Vol. 1). Columbus, OH: Author.

8.   These reports can be downloaded from the Ohio Auditor of State web site. Retrieved December 8, 2008, from http://www.auditor.state.oh.us/AuditSearch, and from http://www.auditor.state.oh.us/LGS/CommunitySchools/Default.htm

9.   The 5-year forecast reports can be downloaded from the Ohio Department of Education's *Ohio Schools—Five Year Forecasts* web page. Retrieved December 8, 2008, from http://fyf.oecn.k12.oh.us/

10.   The LOEO (2003) state evaluation report (see Appendix K) notes that because state and local funds are combined to cover the costs for special education, schools that enroll students with disabilities are receiving a small portion of funds that were raised by local tax funds. This claim was also explained and supported by Barbara Shaner, Associate Executive Director of the Ohio Association of School Business Officials. Therefore, contrary to claims by the Buckeye Institute, a small portion of locally raised taxes are in fact diverted to charter schools.

11.   Legislative Office of Education Oversight. (2003). *Community schools in Ohio: Implementation issues and impact on Ohio's education system* (Vol. 1). Columbus, OH: Author.

12.   Poverty-Based Assistance (PBA) was formerly known as Disadvantaged Pupil Impact Aid (DPIA). For a number of years, DPIA and now PBA have served as a major source of state aid to school districts and charter schools with high percentages of economically disadvantaged students.

13.   The Ohio Department of Education is required to compute and pay parity aid to school districts and charter schools annually. Parity aid, like equity aid, provides funding beyond the formula aid although it is considered to be a part of the SF3 calculation and is distributed in converse relationship

to the local wealth of school districts. In terms of a local wealth measure, the lowest 80% of school districts and the charter schools within them received parity aid.

14. In many states, the funding for a specific year does not follow students that move after the official head count is taken in the early autumn. But Ohio has a separate head count later in the year.

15. While some point out that this is a result of insufficient funds, it is fair to say that this is a result of the lower level of experience or qualifications of the teachers (on average) that are recruited or that seek employment in charter schools. See Cannata, M. (2008). *Teacher qualifications and work environments across school types*. Boulder, CO and Tempe, AZ: Education and the Public Interest Center & Education Policy Research Unit. Retrieved November 27, 2008, from http://epicpolicy.org/files /CHOICE-06-Cannata2_0.pdf.

16. For example, a charter school with four teachers can choose to admit only 88 students to ensure that each class will have 22 students. A public school with four teachers may end up with 70 students or 95 students. Adjustments can be made and more staff hired, but the teacher-student ratio in traditional public schools often will not be the most cost-efficient.

17. Legislative Office of Education Oversight. (2003). *Community schools in Ohio: Implementation issues and impact on Ohio's education system* (Vol. 1). Columbus, OH: Author.

18. Roza (2005); see note 4.

19. Legislative Office of Education Oversight. (2003). *Community schools in Ohio: Implementation issues and impact on Ohio's education system* (Vol. 1). Columbus, OH: Author.

20. Miron, G. & Nelson, C. (2002). *What's public about charter schools? Lessons learned about choice and accountability*. Thousand Oaks, CA: Corwin Press. See Chapter 4.

Legislative Office of Education Oversight. (2003). *Community schools in Ohio: Implementation issues and impact on Ohio's education system* (Vol. 1). Columbus, OH: Author.

21. Transportation for charter schools has been provided by districts. Starting this year, charter schools can request to receive transportation funds that will be deducted from the revenues that were paid to districts. A small proportion of charter schools were providing vocational technical education.

22. Sullins, C., & Miron, G. (2005). *Challenges of starting and operating charter schools: A multicase study*. Cleveland: Report prepared for The Cleveland Foundation.

23. The Office of Community Schools at the Ohio Department of Education administers two federal grants funded through the Public Charter School Program (PCSP). The basic PCSP grant is for schools in their first 3 years of operation; the PCSP-Dissemination grant is for schools in successful operation more than 3 years and who have a promising practice to disseminate.

24. See Chapter 4 in Miron, G., & Nelson, C. (2002). *What's public about charter schools? Lessons learned about choice and accountability.* Thousand Oaks, CA: Corwin Press.

25. Molnar, A., Miron, G., & Urschel, J. (2008). *Profiles of for-profit education management organizations. Tenth annual report.* Boulder, CO and Tempe, AZ: Education and the Public Interest Center & Education Policy Research Unit. Retrieved November 27, 2008, from http://epicpolicy.org/files/EMO0708.pdf

26. Legislative Office of Education Oversight. (2003). *Community schools in Ohio: Implementation issues and impact on Ohio's education system* (Vol. 1, p. vii). Columbus: Author.

27. There is an assumption that all charter school students are coming from traditional public schools and that these students would return to a traditional public school if a charter school were closed. The state evaluation of charter schools notes, however, that only 79% of charter school students reported that they had come from district schools.

PART 6

School Funding

Many education reforms ultimately boil down to resources, and most resource issues boil down to funding. Are there sufficient resources, and are they distributed fairly? Is there enough money, and is it distributed fairly? Is the funding, and are the resources, at the level necessary to meet students' needs? The two reviews offered in the following chapters address reports that engage these issues.

Chapter 13 presents a review by education finance expert Bruce Baker addressing the Reason Foundation's *Weighted Student Formula Yearbook 2009*, authored by Lisa Snell. These Weighted Student Formula (WSF) reforms, also known as Weighted Student Funding, promote per-pupil funding adjusted for various student characteristics, with funds following students to specific locations. The Reason study outlined "key principles" and a set of benchmarks, examined funding systems in 14 cities and one state, and then offered a set of policy recommendations. The study's rationale stressed the importance of ensuring that district funds reach schools serving the neediest children and of enabling principals to use resources as they think best.

Baker's review finds the Reason report to be "a major step backwards" from the Fordham Foundation's 2008 *Fund the Child* study on WSF (one of two other WSF studies that Baker reviewed for us, as described briefly below). The review notes that, notwithstanding the study's equity ratio-nale, increased resource equity was not included in the report's bench-marks for assessing different funding systems. Nor did the study reference important parts of the existing research base, including studies that ques-tion the efficacy of school-site management (which the study promoted) and "the growing body of literature that questions whether WSF approaches actually achieve greater equity in resource distribution across schools within districts."

In addition, Baker finds that several strategies included in the Reason report were either unrelated to WSF or "substantively different from and conceptually antithetical to WSF reforms," making the set of strategies analyzed a "hodge-podge." He further criticizes as "unfounded" the report's recommendation that selected elements of WSF should be widely implemented. The report, he says, "haphazardly aggregates a multitude of discrete policy issues ... [and] irresponsibly recommends untested, cherry-picked policy elements, some of which may substantially under-mine equity for children in the highest-need schools in major urban dis-tricts." One such recommendation is that per-pupil formulas *not* weight for poverty.

In Chapter 14, reviewers Sean Corcoran and Lawrence Mishel examine a report on teacher pay with implications for teacher salary adjustments as a reform strategy. They assess the Manhattan Institute's *How Much Are Public School Teachers Paid?* (2007), authored by Jay Greene and Marcus Winters. The report attempts to refute suggestions that better pay might entice more qualified teachers to work with more challenging students. In fact, it claims that teachers are already better paid than the majority of other white-collar professional and technical workers. Working from annual salaries reported in the Bureau of Labor Statistics' National Com-pensation Survey, the study converted annual figures into weekly and then hourly averages. The resulting comparisons found teachers to be better paid than such other professionals as architects and mechanical engineers.

Corcoran and Mishel criticize the report on various grounds, but the most devastating condemnation is that the authors used the database in a way that that the Bureau of Labor Statistics (BLS) specifically warned against. That is, the BLS admonished that the National Compensation Survey annual figures should not be translated into hourly ones because of enormous differences in work schedules and entitlements among vari-ous professions. Why the report employs a method that the BLS specifi-cally warned against is unclear. As the reviewers point out, however, to believe the study's hourly estimates, "one would also have to believe that English professors (at $45.84 per hour) are better compensated than chemists ($32.23) and nuclear engineers ($39.92), and that airplane pilots (at \$97.51) are better paid than physicians (\$61.38) and make more than twice as much as aerospace engineers (\$42.27)." The reviewers endorse the need to better understand the impact of teacher salaries, but they find this report's insistence that it is offering factual information "disingenuous at best and blatantly dishonest at worst."

Although both of these reports included rhetoric about increasing equity, neither one offered policymakers credible information or useful advice. Similar problems were found for an Ohio report (published by the Buckeye Institute), but the above-mentioned Fordham report fared better. Those two WSF reports, reviewed by Bruce Baker and available at www.thinktankreview.org, are summarized below.

- In contrast to the *Yearbook* study, Baker found that a 2008 study, *Fund the Child: Bringing Equity, Autonomy and Portability to Ohio School Finance*, took "important steps forward from previous reports promoting large-scale implementation of weighted student funding coupled with decentralized governance and school choice." The study was both authored and published by the Fordham Institute along with Public Impact and a unit of the University of Dayton. Baker found notable its avoidance of "unfounded claims regarding the successes of decentralization in other, non-comparable settings." He further noted that the report acknowledged "the potential political influences that might compromise equity goals of weighted funding formulas."

- On the other hand, Baker criticized the Buckeye Institute's 2007 *Shortchanging Disadvantaged Students: An Analysis of Intra-district Spending Patterns in Ohio*. Authored by Matthew Carr and colleagues, the study concluded that the primary cause of disparate funding in high-poverty schools was due to district, rather than state, allocations—so that additional state funding was not necessary to remedy inequities. Baker states that the authors "failed to make their case," in part because they did not consider the margins of additional funding in higher-need districts. Whereas the Buckeye authors assigned responsibility for remedying inequitable funding to districts, Baker concluded that "between-district and within-district equity solutions must be implemented simultaneously."

CHAPTER 13

WEIGHTED STUDENT FORMULA YEARBOOK 2009

Bruce Baker

Review of Lisa Snell's "Weighted Student Formula Yearbook 2009," published by the Reason Foundation. This is a modified version of a review originally published on May 13, 2009.

INTRODUCTION

The *Weighted Student Formula Yearbook 2009* from the Reason Foundation, authored by Lisa Snell,[1] provides a simple framework for touting the successes of states and urban school districts that grant greater fiscal autonomy to schools. This framework is illustrated in Figure 13.1.

The report begins by laying out the key principles of Weighted Student Funding (WSF), with citations made primarily to the 2006 Fordham Institute Report, *Fund the Child* (FTC).[2]

Two main principles dominate the Reason Foundation rationale: (a) the importance of allocating budgets directly to schools within districts, based on the characteristics of children in those schools, with funding following the child and based on the needs of the child; and (b) the importance of allocating funding, as opposed to staff positions, to schools and then

Think Tank Research Quality: Lessons for Policy Makers, the Media, and the Public, pp. 183–195

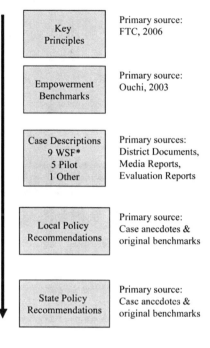

*3 new in 2008-09

Figure 13.1.   Framework of the *Weighted Student Formula Yearbook 2009*.

allowing school-level leaders (principals) latitude to use that funding as they see fit. Similar to a 2007 report published by Ohio's Buckeye Institute, which I also reviewed,[3] this report adds that the principles for allocating funding within districts should be replicated for all levels, including state and federal funding. The report also argues for simplicity and transparency.

The report next lays out a series of "empowerment benchmarks" from William Ouchi's *Making Schools Work* (2003).[4] These empowerment benchmarks provide the outline for the report's 14 city and 1 statewide (Hawaii) reform descriptions that make up the bulk of the yearbook. The report uses these case descriptions as a basis for identifying "best practices" for school districts implementing or considering WSF reforms.

Weighted Student Formula, also sometimes called Weighted Student Funding, is a fiscal resource allocation strategy to be used by states when allocating aid to school districts or by districts when allocating budgets to schools. Several previous reports have also attempted to cast WSF as an all-encompassing set of urban school reform strategies involving decentralized governance of schools and open-enrollment, school-choice programs.

The new Reason report's broad definition of WSF includes at least the following four distinguishable elements: (a) weighted student funding formulas; (b) site-based management; (c) site-based budgeting; and (d) school choice, including pilot, magnet or charter schools. Notably, this is a much broader net than cast in any previous report or analysis of which I am aware.

The report selects a hodge-podge of district reform strategies being implemented across 14 U.S. cities and one state. Nine of these reforms are district-wide reforms that include implementation of some form of weighted student formula—that is, a school-based budget allocation formula providing basic aid per pupil, with additional weightings, or multipliers, based on some committee- or administrator-determined set of "need" factors. Oakland, for instance, uses a variant of this approach, applying a flat foundation level per pupil but adding categorical grants in place of weights.

Other district reforms in the analysis have little to do with Weighted Student Funding at all, nor with whole-district reforms. Rather, the Boston, Chicago, Clark County, Los Angeles and St. Paul reforms set forth in the report involve designating a handful of schools within the district to receive lump-sum funding and granting them greater autonomy in management, contracting and hiring.

These reforms are substantively different from and conceptually antithetical to WSF reforms. While WSF reforms are designed to distribute fiscal and human resources more equitably *across all schools* within a district (or even a state), selective pilot school programs grant preferential autonomy to some schools with the intent of drawing resources and creative energy into those schools and away from others, generally without attention to the plight of those others. WSFs are intended, in part, to correct for the types of inequities that occur when elite magnet schools serving advantaged populations in urban districts draw resources away from disadvantaged students.[5]

The report's 10 empowerment benchmarks, which frame its analysis, also include limited emphasis on weighted student formulas, per se. The report's empowerment benchmarks may be categorized as shown in Table 13.1, with adjacent numbers reflecting the order in which the report presents the (uncategorized) benchmarks.

Notably absent in the report's Key Principles or empowerment benchmarks is the original objective of *Weighted Student Funding*: to increase resource equity across schools within districts.[6]

Table 13.1. Empowerment Benchmarks in Weighted Student Formula Yearbook 2009

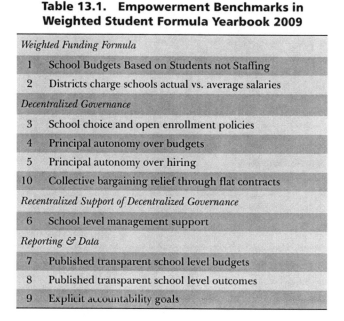

Weighted Funding Formula	
1	School Budgets Based on Students not Staffing
2	Districts charge schools actual vs. average salaries
Decentralized Governance	
3	School choice and open enrollment policies
4	Principal autonomy over budgets
5	Principal autonomy over hiring
10	Collective bargaining relief through flat contracts
Recentralized Support of Decentralized Governance	
6	School level management support
Reporting & Data	
7	Published transparent school level budgets
8	Published transparent school level outcomes
9	Explicit accountability goals

FINDINGS AND CONCLUSIONS OF THE REPORT

Applying these benchmarks, the report derives a set of policy recommendations, which include elements of current policies and practices found in 1 or more of the 15 included districts. Many of the selected practices remain either completely untested or are actually discredited in recent empirical studies. Most are simply references back to the benchmarks provided early in the report.

For example, the report argues that school districts should charge schools for the cost of teachers based on their actual salaries rather than average salaries. That is, school site budgets would be subject to deduction in the amount of either the average or actual teacher salaries. Oakland does; therefore it is recommended. These specific recommendations are discussed in greater detail later in this review.

THE REPORT'S RATIONALE FOR ITS FINDINGS AND CONCLUSIONS

In short, the report rationalizes that the 15 districts studied are all implementing their own brand of WSF; all are doing very well on one hand-picked outcome measure or another; and all are certainly much better than districts not implementing any brand of WSF. Therefore, one can look to these districts to identify best practices, which should be applied in all districts and eventually states.

THE REPORT'S USE OF RESEARCH LITERATURE

For Boston, one of the 15 cases presented, the report does reference, with reasonable accuracy, the findings of an external evaluation of the reform.[7] The report notes:

> A 2009 study by the Boston Foundation that more carefully controlled for student characteristics found that charter schools are outperforming both pilot schools and traditional schools. However, students in elementary and high school pilot schools outperform district schools, but middle school pilot students score slightly lower than middle school students in traditional district schools. (p. 31)

Findings were mixed for the pilot schools, and this is accurately conveyed in the report.[8]

However the report, by its own admission, does not rely heavily on recent empirical literature on the successes or failures of WSF reforms and relies only on "some" supporting studies. "This yearbook utilizes primarily district level documents including district budgets, policy manuals and Web site descriptions of school financing systems in addition to some supporting studies and newspaper accounts" (p. 5). Given this approach, readers should understand two major problems.

1. The Report Neglects Large Bodies of Relevant Literature

Because the report sidesteps entirely the issue of within-district equity, it ignores the growing body of literature that questions whether WSF approaches actually achieve greater equity in resource distribution across schools within districts.

For example, one study actually cited in the report, though for a different issue, that of Chambers and colleagues (2008), shows that between 2001-2002 and 2006-2007, implicit adjustment for poverty[9] across San Francisco schools has backslid, despite the implementation of weighted funding in 2002-03 (p. 74). The differences, whether improvements or backsliding, were statistically nonsignificant.[10] Further, Baker (2009) found that "widely reported WSF success stories provide no more predictable funding with respect to student needs than other large urban districts in the same state."[11]

The report also neglects existing literature that questions the efficacy of school-site management. In a comprehensive review of the literature on school-site management (SSM) and budgeting, Plank and Smith (2008), in the *Handbook of Education Finance and Policy*, present mixed findings at best, pointing out that while SSM may lead to a greater sense of involvement and efficacy, it seems to result in "little direct impact on teaching behaviors or student outcomes."[12]

The report also accepts the rhetoric of Ouchi (2003) and others (FTC, 2006) that "power to the principals"[13] (control over budgets and hiring) has only upsides and cannot possibly have any downside. Recent studies of principal labor markets and sorting indicated that the academic backgrounds of principals (whether they passed certification exams; the nature of their undergraduate and graduate training, etc.) are highly inequitably distributed across schools, both within and across districts.[14] Related research shows that principals with stronger academic backgrounds are more likely to recruit and retain teachers with stronger backgrounds when granted autonomy to do so. The inverse also holds true: weaker principals, weaker teachers. As such, the current inequitable distribution of leadership could be harmful for high-poverty, high-minority schools under highly decentralized systems. [15]

2. The Report Neglects Disagreeable Findings in the Literature it Does Cite

Most interestingly, the report fails to acknowledge findings in the studies it does cite when those findings disagree with the original benchmarks. For instance, one of the most intriguing findings of the recent American Institutes for Research[16] evaluation of the Oakland and San Francisco reforms is that Oakland's use of actual salary buy-back has not in fact resulted in improved distribution of teachers (as regards teaching qualifications). "Despite Oakland's additional incentive to retain newer teachers at higher-poverty schools, on average, San Francisco showed progress toward closing the experience gap whereas Oakland did not."[17]

REVIEW OF THE REPORT'S METHODS

While the yearbook does not present itself as a research study, it does present a framework, and that framework is deceptive. The reader is led to assume that these 15 districts are all implementing a similar strategy and that they are all showing better outcomes than they otherwise would have, had they not implemented this reform strategy.

As noted previously, however, no single reform strategy is addressed. No uniform measure or approach to measurement of outcomes is used. In many cases, no comparison groups are included, with or without controls for student population differences. Where convenient, the report uses average performance on state assessments, either compared to the district's own previous performance (Hawaii) or, in a handful of cases, compared to state averages or to other urban districts (Oakland). But convenience in other cases apparently led to the use of changes in performance instead, or changes in achievement gaps, depending on which shines the best light on the district being discussed. Honest research begins with a justified approach; it does not engage in an ad hoc search for ways to present results in the best light.

One noteworthy example is the report's choice to point out that Oakland has shown more improvement than all other large California cities. This comparison group includes San Francisco, which fell in the middle of the improvement pack in the graph in the Oakland section of the yearbook, but in the section on San Francisco, it is described as outperforming large urban districts for 7 years running—with no reference to the graph used to show Oakland's success.

Most problematic is the fact that in 5 of the 15 cases discussed, outcome successes actually occurred *prior to the implementation* of WSF or SBB/SBM (see Appendix). For example, the report commends New York City for winning the 2007 Broad prize—which it did the year before its Fair Student Funding policy was implemented. The report might arguably attribute this success to mayoral takeover, which began in 2002. But this is the WSF Yearbook, and even the expansive definition of WSF used in the report did not encompass mayoral takeovers.

Similarly, the report commends Hartford for raising its test scores in 2008, the year before implementing WSF, and it commends Denver for making strong improvements between 2005 and 2008, though WSF was implemented in 2008-09. These successes raise the question: why would these districts want to implement WSF and risk undoing their prior achievements?

The most egregious claim of retroactive causation appears in the press release for the report:

> The results from districts using student-based funding are promising. Prior to 2008, less than half of Hartford, Connecticut's education money made it to the classroom. Now, over 70 percent makes it there. *As a result*, the district's schools posted the largest gains, over three times the average increase, on the state's Mastery Tests in 2007-08 (emphasis added).[18]

Yet, the report itself states that Hartford only began implementing WSF in 2008-09, and only expected to achieve the 70% target of available resources allocated to schools and classrooms by 2009-2010 (p. 61). It is difficult to conceive of any defense for Reason's claims.

The Appendix to this review provides a tabular summary of the selected outcome evidence used in the report.

REVIEW OF THE VALIDITY OF THE FINDINGS AND CONCLUSIONS

The report's general conclusion is that WSF, however defined for any given district, is successful. This success is evidenced by invariably positive outcomes, albeit on widely varied measures. Therefore, the report concludes, selected elements of WSF should be implemented everywhere.

However, the initial benchmarks provided, as well as the "best practices" recommended, exist in a vacuum where critical inquiry, thought, or empirical analysis should be. When identifying best practices, the report reaches for a variety of potentially problematic and untested elements of policies adopted across the 14 cities and one state, without any critical analysis.

The report also seems enamored with the possibility of providing differential weights in the funding formula for high performance or giftedness, partially balanced by weights for low performance for incoming students, and elimination of weights for children from economically disadvantaged backgrounds. The presumption (based on Baltimore policies and anecdotal evidence) appears to be that policies that provide a "U" shaped weighting, high for both incoming low performers and high performers, will encourage schools to turn low performers into high performers. More likely, however, is the possibility that schools that serve clusters of the *most advantaged* children in larger urban districts will receive disproportionate resources, at the expense of schools with more "average" populations and higher-need populations. These systems may become more and more regressive (that is, reflecting a negative relationship between economic disadvantage and resources) over time.

While the new policies in Hartford and Baltimore warrant investigation, a substantial track record of inequities and gaming related to "gifted" child weights already exists. In a previous Think Tank Review, I found:

> One possible explanation for the lack of poverty-related support in Cincinnati is that the district includes a weight on gifted students (larger than the poverty weight), and across elementary schools in the district, the correlation between gifted identification rates and poverty is –.88.[19]

Further, in a series of state-level analyses of gifted-education funding, Baker and Reva Friedman-Nimz find that many states specifically politicize gifted-education funding, using it to drive more resources to otherwise less financially needy schools and districts.[20]

The report specifically advises against allocating weighting based on poverty, arguing instead in favor of weighting for low-scoring students (p. 18). However, allocating resources on the basis of low achievement itself may be far more problematic than using a reasonable proxy like poverty. Baltimore and Hartford appear to protect against the possibility of having to increase funding as a result of increasing failure. The report, though, fails to consider that if schools raise the achievement of incoming poor students or incoming low performers, those schools will lose the funding that enabled them to provide the programs, staff and opportunities that improved student performance. Yet, the underlying out-of-school factors that affect not only the child's starting point but also annual progress (through opportunities outside of school, including summer learning) will not have changed.[21]

As noted, a likely outcome of the report's recommendations for rewarding schools serving high performers and children identified as gifted, and for eliminating poverty weighting, would be the advent of more regressive within-district resource allocation formulas than have been seen to date. Baker and Green have shown that a handful of states have already mastered the tricks of the trade of inequitably distributing financial resources to school districts on a presumed basis of need.[22]

USEFULNESS OF THE REPORT FOR GUIDANCE OF POLICY AND PRACTICE

Unlike an earlier report from the Fordham Institute, which showed increased consideration for the complexities of WSF reforms and more thoughtful integration of state and district remedies,[23] the WSF Yearbook is a major step backwards. It haphazardly aggregates a multitude of discrete policy issues under an umbrella labeled as WSF and deceptively suggests that all related policies are necessarily good—even going so far as to credit those policies for improvements that took place before the policies were implemented. The report irresponsibly recommends untested, cherry-picked policy elements, some of which may substantially undermine equity for children in the highest-need schools in major urban districts. Additional "best practice" recommendations range from reasonable to innocuous, including greater transparency and clearer public reporting of school site budgets, improvements to state data systems for tracking school site expenditures, providing support to principals by moving toward site-based budgeting and management, and providing safeguards and mandatory intervention strategies for schools with continued lagging performance.[24] Sadly, those reasonable recommendations are overshadowed by others. Overall, the policy guidance provided by the Reason report is reckless and irresponsible.

NOTES AND REFERENCES

1. Snell, L. (2009, April 30). *Weighted Student Formula Yearbook 2009*. Los Angeles: Reason Foundation. Retrieved May 11, 2009, from http://reason.org/files/wsf/yearbook.pdf
2. Thomas B. Fordham Institute. (2006). *Fund the child: Tackling inequity and antiquity in school finance*. Retrieved May 11, 2009, from http://www.edexcellence.net/fundthechild/Manifesto%20Report.pdf
3. Baker, B. D. (2007). *Review of "Shortchanging Disadvantaged Student: An analysis of intra-district spending patterns in Ohio."* Boulder. CO and Tempe, AZ: Education and the Public Interest Center & Education Policy Research Unit. Retrieved May 6, 2009, from http://epicpolicy.org/thinktank/review-shortchanging-disadvantaged-students-an-analysis-intra-district-spending-patterns-o
4. Ouchi, W. G. (2003). *Making schools work: A revolutionary plan to get your children the education they need*. New York, NY: Simon & Schuster.
5. Even pundits favoring weighted student funding for many of the same reasons stated in the Reason Report acknowledge this point. For example, a column by Eric Osberg of the Fordham Institute quotes the Cincinnati school board president: "It was to help create an equitable system, because in the past, magnet programs got more money than neighborhood schools. This way, the dollars follow the student, not the program." http://www.edexcellence.net/flypaper/index.php/tag/weighted-student-funding/ Roza and Hawley-Miles (2004) also address this concern with specific regard to Cincinnati. Roza, M., & Hawley-Miles, K. (2004). *Understanding student-based budgeting as a means to greater school resource equity*. Seattle, WA: Center on Reinventing Public Education, University of Washington.
6. As noted previously, the Reason Report has cast WSF as something much broader than WSF itself. It therefore includes many more policy objectives and principles. However, Weighted Student Formulas themselves are intended by most accounts to improve equity in the distribution of resources across schools within districts in the same way that needs-based formulas, for decades, have been intended to improve equity in the distribution of resources across school districts in accordance with costs and needs. In fact, the equity objective even appears in the title of the Fordham Institute report *Fund the Child: Tackling Inequity and Antiquity in School Finance*. http://www.edexcellence.net/fundthechild/Manifesto%20Report.pdf

Others, including Baker and Thomas (2006) have more precisely articulated equity objectives of WSF. Baker, B. D., and Thomas, S. L. (2006) *Review of Hawaii's Weighted Student Formula*. Hawaii Board of Education.

7. *Informing the Debate: Comparing Boston's Charter, Pilot and Traditional Schools* (2009, January). The Boston Foundation. Retrieved December 29, 2009, from http://www.tbf.org/UploadedFiles/tbforg/Utility_Navigation /Multimedia_Library/Reports/InformingTheDebate_Final.pdf

8. The findings regarding charter schools are more problematic than that conveyed in the report, however, particularly since they were based a very select group of high-demand (waitlisted) charters.

9. This implicit adjustment is the average response of school site budgets to differences in poverty rates across schools.

10. Chambers, J. G., Shambaugh, L., Levin, J., Muraki, M., & Poland, L. (2008). *A Tale of Two Cities: A comparative study of student-based funding and school-based decision making in San Francisco and Oakland Unified School Districts*. Palo Alto, CA: American Institutes for Research.

11. Baker, B. D. (2009). Within-district resource allocation and the marginal costs of providing equal educational opportunity: Evidence from Texas and Ohio. *Education Policy Analysis Archives, 17*(3), 1. Retrieved May 6, 2009, from http://epaa.asu.edu/epaa/v17n3/

12. Plank, D., & Smith, B. (2008). Autonomous schools: Theory, evidence and policy. In H. F. Ladd & E. B Fiske (Eds.), *Handbook of Research in Education Finance and Policy* (p. 407, pp. 402-424). New York, NY: Routledge.

13. Ouchi, W. G. (2006) Power to the principals: Decentralization in three large school districts. *Organization Science, 17*(2) 298-307.

14. Baker, B. D., & Cooper, B. (2005). Do principals with stronger academic backgrounds hire better teachers? *Educational Administration Quarterly, 2005; 41,* 449.
Clotfelter, C., Ladd, H., Vigdor, J., & Wheeler, J. (2006). High poverty schools and distribution of teachers and principals. A paper presented at the UNC Conference on High Poverty Schooling in America. Chapel Hill, NC.
Fuller, E., Baker, B. D., & Young, M. D. (2007). *The relationship between principal characteristics, school-level teacher quality and turnover, and student achievement*. Working Paper.
Fuller, E., Young, M. D., & Orr, T. (2007). *Career pathways of principals in Texas*. Paper presented at the annual meeting of the American Educational Research Association. Chicago, IL.
Papa, Frank C. Jr., Lankford, H., & Wyckoff, J. (2002). *The attributes and Career Paths of Principals: Implications for improving policy*. University of Albany, SUNY.
Papa, F. (2004). *The career paths and retention of principals in New York state*. Submitted to the University of Albany, State University of New York in partial fulfillment of the requirements for the Degree of Doctor of Philosophy. Albany, NY.

15. At various points in the yearbook, Snell does recommend management support, training and intervention for principals operating under

decentralized system. While these may be reasonable strategies for partially offsetting potential inequities in leadership quality, they are largely untested and do not address the initial, underlying problem of inequitable distribution of principals.

16.   Chambers, et al (2008); see note 10.
17.   Chambers, et al (2008); see note 10; p. vii. Note that the logic of "actual salary" buyback makes sense as a strategy for improving equity in the distribution of teacher qualifications across schools within districts. If one assumes that higher-need, higher-poverty schools tend to have higher concentrations of inexperienced teachers, it is unfair for those schools to be required to buy teaching lines from the central office at the district average salary rather than the lower salaries of novices. Allowing them to buy back lines at actual salaries should provide greater financial flexibility, but apparently not enough (in this instance) to alter the district-wide experience distribution. The idea may be reasonable, but is oversold in this report and others.
18.   Reason Foundation. (2009, April 30). *Weighted student formula produces good results in some of the country's biggest cities* (press release). Retrieved May 11, 2009, from http://www.reason.org/news/show/1007460.html
19.   Baker, B. D. (2007). *Review of "Shortchanging Disadvantaged Student: An analysis of intra-district spending patterns in Ohio"* Boulder, CO and Tempe, AZ: Education and the Public Interest Center & Education Policy Research Unit, p. 14. Retrieved May 6, 2009, from http://epicpolicy.org/thinktank/review-shortchanging-disadvantaged-students-an-analysis-intra-district-spending-patterns-o
20.   Models of both aid distribution and opportunity distribution indicate a tendency of states more significantly involved in gifted education, as indicated by mandates and funding, to promote regressive distributions of opportunities (greater availability in schools with fewer low-income students) through regressive distributions of aid (higher levels of aid to districts with fewer children in poverty).
      Baker, B. D., & Friedman-Nimz, R. C. (2004). State policy influences and equal opportunity: The example of gifted education. *Educational Evaluation and Policy Analysis, 26*(1) 39-64.
      Baker, B. D., & McIntire, J. (2003). Evaluating state school funding for gifted education programs. *Roeper Review, 26*(3), 173-179.
      Baker, B. D., & Friedman-Nimz, R. C. (2003). Gifted children, vertical equity and state school finance policies and practices. *Journal of Education Finance, 28*(4), 523-556.
      Baker, B. D., & Friedman-Nimz, R. C. (2002). Determinants of the availability of opportunities for gifted children: Evidence from NELS '88. *Leadership and Policy in Schools, 1*(1), 52-71.
      Baker, B. D. (2001). Gifted Children In The Current Policy And Fiscal Context Of Public Education: A national snapshot & case analysis of the state of Texas. *Educational Evaluation and Policy Analysis, 23*(3), 229-250.
21.   Berliner, D. C. (2009). *Poverty and Potential: Out-of-School Factors and School Success.* Boulder, CO and Tempe, AZ: Education and the Public Interest

Center & Education Policy Research Unit. Retrieved May 11, 2009, from http://epicpolicy.org/publication/poverty-and-potential

Also, one real shortcoming of using school level rates of children qualifying for subsidized lunch as a basis for targeting funding to higher-need schools within large, poor urban districts is that in many large poor urban districts, there is little variation in rates of children qualifying for free lunch. Baker, 2009 and 2007, for example, explain that in Cleveland, all elementary schools reported 100% free lunch, yet there remain substantive differences in the degrees of economic disadvantage across Cleveland elementary schools. This measurement concern, however, is not a reason to disband use of economic disadvantage measures for redistributed resources across schools within districts, but rather, provides a reason to seek more fine grained measures of economic disadvantage.

22. Baker, B. D., & Green, P. C. (2005). Tricks of the trade: Legislative actions in school finance that disadvantage minorities in the post-Brown era. *American Journal of Education, 111*, 372–413.

23. Public Impact; The University of Dayton, School of Education and Allied Professions; and Thomas B. Fordham Institute. (2008, March). *Fund the child: Bringing equity, autonomy and portability to Ohio school finance how sound an investment?* Washington, DC: Thomas B. Fordham Institute.

Baker, B. D. (2008). *Review of "Fund the Child: Bringing Equity, Autonomy, and Portability to Ohio School Finance."* Boulder, CO and Tempe, AZ: Education and the Public Interest Center & Education Policy Research Unit. Retrieved May 7, 2009, from http://epicpolicy.org/thinktank/review-fund-child

24. I noted a total of about 27 district-level "best practices" and four state-level recommendations. Space prohibits thorough critique of each and every one. Many are similarly problematic to those critiqued here, including the assumption that losing incremental funding per student provides a more manageable buffer for enrollment decline than losing a staffing line when an additional section is no-longer needed. Arguably, it is no easier to cut one student's share of a teacher cost than it is to cut the whole teacher when the additional section is no longer needed.

Appendix: Reforms Investigated and Evidence of Success

City or State	Implemented	Retroactive Causation Effect[1]	Instantaneous/ Maintenance Effect[2]	Compared to Other Than Own Past Outcomes?[3]	External Cited Research[4]	Actual Statistical Controls[4]
Weighted Student Funding (9 districts)						
Baltimore	2008-09	Y				
Evidence of Success (select quotes and summaries)	"Baltimore's Maryland School Assessment Scores increased in 2008." (p. 16)					
Cincinnati	1999-2000*		Y	Y		
Evidence of Success	"Cincinnati continues to be one of the leaders among Ohio's urban school districts in performance. The district is tops among these urban city school systems in the number of report card indicators earned (nine versus the next highest urban school system, Columbus, with six) and is second only to Akron in its Performance Index Score." (p. 43)					
Denver	2008-09	Y	Y	Y		
Evidence of Success	"From 2005 to 2008, Denver students made strong improvements in reading, math, writing and science." (p. 56)					
Hartford	Phase in began in 2008-09	Y				
Evidence of Success	"Hartford schools significantly raised scores on both the 2008 Connecticut Mastery Test and the 2008 Connecticut Academic Performance Test this year—the first increase since 2001, according to preliminary results released to the district by the State Department of Education." (p. 66)					
Hawaii	2004-05					

Evidence of Success	Report compares Hawaii against prior performance in Hawaii on NAEP. (p. 74)			
Houston	2000-2001 (2001-2002 WSF phase in. See Baker and Thomas, 2006)			
Evidence of Success	Varied anecdotal evidence on numbers of schools meeting standards, numbers of schools improving passing rates, advanced placement courses offered and participation rates. (p. 82)			
New York City	Mayoral control in 2002. Phase in of WSF began in 2007-08.	Y	Y	Y
Evidence of Success	• NYC won the 2007 Broad prize (p. 96) for most improved. • In 2008, NYC elementary and middle school students made substantial progress at every grade level in English language arts and math since 2007, outpacing statewide gains. • Performance significantly up since 2002. Achievement gap narrowing since 2002. (p.97) • Impressive gains on 2007 NAEP, compared to 2005. (p. 97) • Numerous additional comparisons of gains from 2002, or 2003 to 2007.			
Poudre School District, Ft. Collins, CO	2007-08	Y	Y	Y

Appendix continues on next page.

City or State	Implemented	Retroactive Causation Effect[1]	Instantaneou/ Maintenance Effect[2]	Compared to Other Than Own Past Outcomes?[3]	External Cited Research	Actual Statistical Controls[4]
Evidence of Success	• "On 2008 Colorado Student Assessment Program students continued to perform higher than students state-wide in all 27 areas." • "district-wide averages remain well ahead of state averages ..." • "Proficiency scores improved or remained the same ..." (p. 121)					
Mixed/Undefined Approach (one district)						
Oakland	2004 expanded to all schools			Y		
Evidence of Success	Oakland demonstrates the largest 4 year API gains among large CA Urban Unified Districts (from 2004-2007, 2008).					
Pilot Autonomy Programs (5 districts)						
LA Belmont Pilot	Phase in beginning 2007-08					
Evidence of Success	Report provides anecdotal discussion of High School for the Arts					
Boston Pilot	1995-96			Y	Y	Y
Evidence of Success	Report cites: Informing the Debate: Comparing Boston's Charter, Pilot and Traditional Schools, The Boston Foundation, January 2009: http://www.tbf.org/UploadedFiles/tbforg/Utility_Navigation/Multimedia_Library/Reports/InformingTheDebate_Final.pdf					
Chicago Renaissance Schools	2005-06			Y		

Evidence of Success	Report cites: Charter Schools Performance Report 2007-2008, Chicago Public Schools, http://www.ren2010.cps.k12.il.us/docs/ONS%20report%202-25_FINAL.pdf			
Clark County Empowerment Schools	2006-07 (17 schools in 2009-10) **	–		
Evidence of Success	Report notes average test scores of 4 schools higher than in previous year -(p. 48)			
St. Paul, MN	2002-03		Y	
Evidence of Success	"Overall Saint Paul public school students made gains across the board on state-wide tests in 2008. Yet, the district still scores lower than state averages and struggles with large achievement gaps between subgroups." (pp. 128-129)			

*Temporarily suspended in 2009

**NCES CCD2006 includes 325 CCSD Schools

1. In other words, cases where the report credits WSF for successful outcomes that occurred before WSF was implemented.
2. Does the outcome evidence include claims of improved outcome that occurred concurrent with implementation—before implementation was completed and could have had any measurable effects (Instantaneous)? Maintenance effect refers to those cases where the report explains that the district continued to improve, in many cases at a rate of improvement similar to improvement at the beginning of, or prior to the reform.
3. Many cases address performance outcomes only with respect to the district's own past performance but do not explain, for example, whether the district's own performance gains are better or worse than those of other districts.
4. This column addresses whether any attempts were made to compare effects of the reforms on otherwise similar (randomly selected or with statistical controls) students, in any of the analyses, internal to the report or externally cited evidence.

CHAPTER 14

HOW MUCH ARE PUBLIC SCHOOL TEACHERS PAID?

Sean P. Corcoran and Lawrence Mishel

Review of "How Much Are Public School Teachers Paid?" by Jay P. Greene and Marcus A. Winters and published by the Manhattan Institute. This is a modified version of a review originally published on February 19, 2007.

INTRODUCTION

A new report from the Manhattan Institute purports to show that teachers are better compensated than editors, reporters, architects, psychologists, chemists, economists, and mechanical engineers. Moreover, the report contends that teachers are better paid than the vast majority of white-collar, professional, and technical workers. In *How Much Are Public School Teachers Paid?*[1] Jay P. Greene and Marcus A. Winters make this surprising argument using a national survey of employers from the Bureau of Labor Statistics (BLS). Their findings will likely find receptive readers among those hoping to resist calls for higher teacher pay, but the measures used by these authors are considerably flawed. In fact, the BLS itself has explicitly advised against the exact approach they chose to use.

Think Tank Research Quality: Lessons for Policy Makers, the Media, and the Public, pp. 201–211

How teachers are compensated is an important issue. By some measures, teacher quality has been on a long, slow decline for decades,[2] and there is evidence to suggest that at least some of this trend can be explained by relative declines in teacher pay.[3] As higher-paying job opportunities have opened up for women, teaching has become less attractive. At the same time, mounting evidence has pointed to the significance of teacher quality in promoting student achievement, and the nation has seen many policy innovations related to teacher compensation, such as merit pay. These changes have increased the importance of research on teacher labor markets.

Unfortunately, this 6-page report (and its 17 pages of tables) covers no new ground[4] and contributes almost nothing to the policy discussion surrounding teacher compensation. We certainly see value in the premise of the report: an apples-to-apples comparison of pay for a unit of work. But the authors ultimately rely on an hourly pay measure from the National Compensation Survey (NCS) that is fundamentally flawed for these purposes.

The authors might be excused for their choice of measure if the same government agency that published these statistics hadn't explicitly advised against such uses of the data. Further, a report we published with Sylvia Allegretto in 2004[5] demonstrated plainly how the NCS does not measure hourly rates of pay for teachers in the same way as they do for other professionals. The authors did read our report (it is the only authority they cite on this matter that they themselves did not author), but they do not address this measurement issue nor do they explain or justify their omission.

The end result is a missed opportunity to shed light on some of the more pressing and complex issues related to the measurement and structure of teacher compensation. The matter of relative teacher pay has recently been a subject of substantial interest in the economics of education literature,[6] yet Greene and Winters elect to ignore these writings in their entirety. Instead, readers are left with an unproductive and irresponsible statistical sleight-of-hand.

THE REPORT'S FINDINGS AND CONCLUSIONS

Greene and Winters use hourly earnings data from the BLS to compare the pay of public elementary and secondary teachers with that of various comparison groups (white-collar, professional specialty and technical, and certain professional occupations). National averages as well as averages within metropolitan areas are presented. From these, they draw the following conclusions:

- "The average public school teacher in the United States earned $34.06 per hour in 2005 ... 36% more per hour than the average non-sales white-collar worker and 11% more than the average professional specialty and technical worker" (p. 2 and Table 1).

- Comparing teachers to professional workers, "teachers have higher earnings than 61 of these 85 occupations. For example, editors and reporters earn 24% less than public school teachers; architects, 11% less; psychologists, 9% less; chemists, 5% less; mechanical engineers, 6% less; and economists, 1% less" (p. 3 and Table 2). Public school teachers earn 61% more than private school teachers (p. 4 and Table 3).

- "Full-time public school teachers work on average 36.5 hours per week during weeks they are working," compared with white-collar workers' 39.4 hours, professional specialty and technical workers' 39 hours, and private school teachers' 38.3 average hours per week (p. 4 and Table 4).

- Teacher earnings vary considerably across the 60 metropolitan areas for which data are available. For example, "the Detroit metropolitan area has the highest average public school teacher pay among metropolitan areas ... at $47.28 per hour" (p. 2) and Greensboro the lowest, at $22.38. Elkhart, Indiana has the highest compensation relative to white-collar workers (at 87% more); Detroit has the eighth highest (61% more). In only 11 metropolitan areas do public school teachers earn less than professional specialty and technical workers, and teachers earn 20%, 23% and 12% more than professionals in New York, Los Angeles, and Chicago, respectively (pp. 2-3 and Tables 1A-1C).

- Similarly, teachers' weekly hours worked varied across metropolitan areas, ranging from a low of 32.6 in Grand Rapids to a high of 40 hours per week in Milwaukee and Amarillo.

Finally, the authors use regression analysis to explore the relationship between relative teacher compensation—measured using the hourly pay figures discussed above—and high school graduation rates in a cross-section of metropolitan areas. Controlling for various student and metropolitan area characteristics, they find no statistically significant relationship between relative teacher pay and student outcomes.

REPORT'S RATIONALES FOR ITS FINDINGS AND CONCLUSIONS

For this report, Greene and Winters rely on publicly available data from the 2005 National Compensation Survey conducted by the Bureau of

Labor Statistics (BLS).[7] The NCS is a survey responded to by employers (e.g., school districts) for which the BLS randomly selects employers and occupations within selected firms.[8] Although the NCS (and this new report) state earnings on an *hourly* basis, *the data are not necessarily collected in this way*. Employers are asked to report occupational earnings on an annual, weekly, or hourly basis, as appropriate, together with scheduled hours worked per day or per week, and weeks worked per year.[9] For salaried workers not on a rigid work schedule, the "typical number of hours actually worked [is] collected."[10]

For full-time, professional salaried workers (the class of workers the Manhattan Institute report is primarily concerned with), hourly earnings would be calculated by the BLS as the annual salary divided by weeks worked per year, divided again by the number of hours worked per week. This hourly rate of pay constitutes the basis for all of Greene and Winters' earnings comparisons.

Comparing the compensation of teachers with that of other professionals on a basis other than annual earnings does make a certain amount of sense. After all, schoolteachers are not paid for the same length work year as full-year workers, making annual earnings problematic (particularly when comparing earnings at a single point in time).

Accordingly, the problem lies not in the concept but in the improper use of these data. On an hourly basis and using the Manhattan Institute figures, teachers could not justifiably be considered the underpaid candidates for sainthood, as they are often portrayed. Yet if one were to believe these figures, one would also have to believe that English professors (at $45.84 per hour) are better compensated than chemists ($32.23) and nuclear engineers ($39.92), and that airplane pilots (at $97.51 an hour) are better paid than physicians ($61.38) and make more than twice as much as aerospace engineers ($42.27).[11]

REVIEW OF THE REPORT'S USE OF RESEARCH LITERATURE

Teacher labor markets have been an intensely studied topic in recent years. These authors, however, cite only two publications on the subject—the first being their own 2005 book with Greg Forster, *Education Myths*. The other is our 2004 paper with Sylvia Allegretto, *How Does Teacher Pay Compare? Methodological Challenges and Answers*.[12] The fact that Greene and Winters reference our work is puzzling—it is cited only as "previous research [that] has used BLS data to draw conclusions about the proper level of teacher pay" (p. 2). Nothing in that description informs the reader that a large portion of our 2004 paper was devoted to explaining the methodological problems surrounding the use of the NCS for these very same purposes.

While one hesitates to harshly criticize a six-page policy report for its lack of a literature review, a recurring frustration here—as we also found to be the case with *Education Myths*—is that these authors could make a considerably stronger argument for their thesis, if only they had been more thorough in their research. For example, they are correct in pointing out the difficulties inherent in comparing teacher compensation with that of other workers, but they ignore a growing literature that has explored these issues in some depth, literature that has rejected their hourly pay measure.[13] Likewise, there is a sizable body of research that investigates the relationship between teacher pay and student outcomes as Greene and Winters do here. But a cursory read of this literature reveals that simple cross-sectional regression estimates of this kind are almost nonsensical. While teacher pay might affect student outcomes (through better teacher quality), student outcomes as well as school context also affect teacher pay. In general, teachers are paid more to work in the lowest performing schools. As economists Susanna Loeb and Marianne Page have demonstrated, once these factors are controlled for, conclusions regarding teacher pay are quite different.[14] This new report addresses none of these nuances.

REVIEW OF THE REPORT'S METHODS

Because the NCS hourly rate of pay calculation hinges on the measurement of weeks and hours worked, Greene and Winters defend the validity of this measure in some detail. This part of the report is highly misleading. Both weeks worked per year and hours worked per week are measured in different ways for teachers from other professionals.

Citing the BLS policy of collecting the "typical number of hours actually worked" for salaried workers, the authors argue that the reported 30- to 40-hour teacher work week includes time devoted to grading papers, preparing for class, and the like, as well as paid lunch and rest periods. They quote the following from a 1994 BLS bulletin (which we must assume was still applicable in 2005):

> Virtually all teachers worked from 30 to 40 hours per week, which included paid lunch and rest periods, as well as preparation and grading time if such activities were considered by the school to be a part of the teacher's workday. Additional hours for extracurricular activities were included only if considered part of the regular work schedule.[15]

The same bulletin, however, later reveals important details relevant to the NCS annual weeks worked measure: "Teachers are typically employed for a fixed number of days—for example, 180—over a 9- or 10-month contract. For many teachers, school holidays are not included in the days contracted for and are therefore not designated as paid holidays."[16] For example, during Thanksgiving an architect and a teacher might both not work on Thursday and Friday, but the NCS data would show the architect as having worked 5 days, while the teacher is shown to have only worked for 3.

Determining the number of weeks worked per year is critical for weekly and hourly earnings calculations for workers paid annually, yet nowhere in this report do Greene and Winters report these statistics. One can, however, readily calculate these numbers using published NCS tables.[17] For professional occupations broadly defined, this yields (1,829/39.0) = 46.9 weeks of work; for architects (2,155/41.4) = 52.0; for mechanical engineers (2,122/40.8) = 52.0; and for lawyers (2,157/41.5) = 52.0. In other words, according to NCS data the typical professional is considered to have worked about 52 weeks per year (including paid holidays). This constitutes the denominator in the calculation of weekly (and by extension, hourly) pay for these groups. Public school teachers, on the other hand, are calculated to work an average of (1,403/36.5) = 38.4 weeks per year (38.0 weeks per year for elementary teachers).

Why should these denominators matter if indeed teachers work a shorter work year than other professionals? The answer is that weeks worked for professionals *includes* time off, while the same statistic for teachers *excludes* days not spent working. When calculating hourly pay, an inflated number of weeks worked will considerably *deflate* compensation for a week (or hour) of work.

Greene and Winters also contend that preparation and grading—and work completed at home if the job requires it—are all somehow included in the reported average of 32.6 to 40 hours of work per week:

> If any of this work at home, either by teachers or other professionals, is considered by the employer to be part of the *actual* hours worked, it is included in the BLS figures. It is possible that teachers, as well as other professionals, put in some hours at home that are not captured in these numbers, but those hours would not be considered part of their jobs and thus are not part of paid employment. (p. 4)

There was no need for the authors to speculate about this. Other published data document the activities that constitute these 30 to 40 hours of work.[18] The U.S. Department of Education, for example, periodically surveys teachers as part of its Schools and Staffing Survey (SASS) program, asking very specific questions regarding time use.[19] In the 2003 wave of the SASS, public school teachers reported that they were required to work an average of 37.7 hours per week to receive base pay, with approximately 27 to 29 of these hours devoted to direct instruction.[20] These hours correspond closely to those negotiated in the typical union contract. Accordingly, these are the logical figures that a principal would provide in response to a survey question about teachers' contracted work hours. When asked to include other school-related activities (including grading), teachers in the SASS reported an average of 52.4 hours of work per week. This is consistent with a basic understanding of teacher work-load; it is difficult to believe that the 30- to 40-hour work week includes all activities realistically required of the job. If indeed it does, teachers should be able to reduce their workload up to 15-hours per week with no harm done, as these extra hours are, according to Greene and Winters, "not considered part of their jobs and thus are not part of paid employment."

The authors go on to argue that teachers' hours of work may be further overestimated in the NCS data because their stated hours include lunch and "rest periods." They quote again from the BLS: "[T]eachers, more than the other groups, were the most likely to have paid lunch as well as paid rest periods."[21]

What they do not point out is that the measure of weekly hours includes paid lunch and rest time for only a small minority of teachers. The very same BLS bulletin states that only "14 percent of teachers received paid lunch time, and just 20 percent received paid rest time."[22] This is not surprising—employers are asked to include paid lunches and breaks only if the worker's contract *formally includes* these periods. This is rarely the case for most professional occupations, and the comparatively higher fraction of teachers with paid breaks surely stems from instances where collective-bargaining agreements specifically delineate these periods.[23]

Perhaps what is most frustrating about this report's use of hourly compensation is that the agency that collects and publishes this data has explicitly advised users *not* to compare hourly rates of pay. Prominently displayed on the National Compensation Survey's earnings website is the *frequently asked question*: "When compared with other occupations, the hourly earnings for some occupations, such as teachers and airline pilots, seem higher than expected. Why is this?"[24] The BLS responds:

> Unfortunately, this method may not work well for certain occupations with unusual hours. Teachers who only work only 9 or 10 months per year are an example of this problem. Another example is the airline pilot occupation ... Because of these issues, comparisons of annual salaries published by the National Compensation Survey (NCS) might be more appropriate when considering certain occupations.[25]

Our published 2004 correspondence with a BLS chief on this matter confirms the agency's reservations:

> because the published NCS wage estimates do not reflect leave entitlements and the work years of teachers are so dissimilar from most other professional occupations, I would only use the annual salary estimates from NCS to compare teacher pay with the pay of other professionals.[26]

REVIEW OF THE VALIDITY OF THE FINDINGS AND CONCLUSIONS

As shown above, the earnings measures reported by the NCS (and relayed by the Manhattan Institute) are constructed using annual salary data and concepts of "weeks worked" that differ markedly between teachers and other professionals. Further, it is clear from publicly available data that the hours-per-week measure used by the NCS for teachers almost certainly does not, as Greene and Winters incorrectly suggest, include all the activities expected for employment. Each of these measurement issues is serious, though the latter concern may cause less of a bias in the numbers because, as Greene and Winters point out, reported hours for other professionals may also understate the number of hours they spend in work required for employment, although without better data, it is unclear for which class of workers the understatement of required work hours is greater.

In the end, Greene and Winters rely on a fundamentally flawed measure of relative teacher compensation, and this defect prevents their study from providing any usefulness. It can add little if anything to the public discussion of teacher pay and school policy. The report's repeated insistence that it is "facilitating a fact-based approach" (p. 1) and "simply offering facts" (p. 6) is disingenuous at best and blatantly dishonest at worst, given that the report ignores existing research and measurement concerns directly related to these "facts." Tacking on a regression analysis purporting to show no association between teacher pay and student outcomes only adds insult to injury. This regression analysis would not pass muster even if the relative pay measures were valid.

REPORT'S USEFULNESS FOR GUIDANCE OF POLICY AND PRACTICE

The Manhattan Institute report misses an opportunity to shed light on some of the complexities and policy considerations related to the measurement and structure of teacher compensation. Rather than leading us down an unproductive path of counting contracted weeks, hours of work, paid lunches, and breaks, analysts should focus on identifying the most efficient policies for attracting high-quality graduates into the teaching profession. While the authors are correct in pointing out the fundamental differences between a teacher's work schedule and that of other professionals, new graduates view potential occupations in terms of "bundles" of amenities that include pay, time off, and working conditions. Policymakers might ask whether the once-attractive 9-month work year (with its correspondingly lower annual pay) has the same appeal to the workforce—in particular, working women—that it once did.

As stated in the introduction to the report, "the policy debate on education reform has proceeded without a clear understanding of these issues" (p. 1). Unfortunately, Greene and Winters have done little to promote such an understanding.

NOTES AND REFERENCES

1. Greene, J. & Winters, M. (2007). *How much are public school teachers paid?* New York, NY: Manhattan Institute for Policy Research. Retrieved January 26, 2010, from http://www.manhattan-institute.org/html/cr_50.htm

2. Corcoran, S. P., Evans, W. N., & Schwab, R. M. (2004). Changing labor market opportunities for women and the quality of teachers, 1957-2000. *American Economic Review, 94*(2).

3. See for example, Bacolod, M. P. (2007). Do alternative opportunities matter? The role of female labor markets in the decline of teacher quality. *Review of Economics and Statistics, 89*(4), 737-751.

4. Richard Vedder, for example, also used hourly earnings from the National Compensation Survey to contrast teacher pay with that of other professions. Vedder, R. (2003, Summer). Comparable worth. *Education Next, 3*(3).

5. Allegretto, S. A., Corcoran, S. P., & Mishel, L. (2004). *How does teacher pay compare? Methodological challenges and answers.* Economic Policy Institute.

6. For examples, see: Allegretto, Corcoran & Mishel (2004).
   Podgursky, M., & Tongrut, R. (2006, Fall). (Mis-)Measuring the Relative pay of public school teachers. *Education Finance and Policy, 1*(4).
   Taylor, L. L. (Summer 2006). Comparable Wages, Inflation, and School Finance Equity. *Education Finance and Policy, 1*(3).

7. Despite the authors' claim that "no one has organized and reproduced [BLS earnings] data so that others can easily observe the information and form their own interpretations" regarding teacher pay (p. 2), all of the National Compensation Survey data used in their report are taken directly from published BLS reports. The data can also be quickly and easily downloaded from the Bureau of Labor Statistics website (http://www.bls.gov/ncs/ocs/home.htm). Greene and Winters use data primarily from the 2005 wave of this survey, and report wages (excluding benefits) for full-time workers only.

8. That is, in the first stage of the sample selection employers are chosen at random. Then, in a second stage employees (or more precisely, occupations or jobs) are selected for the collection of detailed wage data.

9. Appendix A ("Technical Note") (2006, August). *National Compensation Survey: Occupational wages in the United States, June 2005*. U.S. Bureau of Labor Statistics. Retrieved Feb. 11, 2007, from http://www.bls.gov/ncs/ocs/sp/ncbl0832.pdf.

10. Appendix A ("Technical Note") (2006, August).

11. U.S. Bureau of Labor Statistics (2006, July). *National Compensation Survey: Occupational Wages in the United States, June 2005 Supplementary Tables*. Retrieved Feb. 11, 2007, from http://www.bls.gov/ncs/ocs/sp/ncbl0831.pdf Authors' calculations, using data from the above and from Greene and Winters' Table 2 (p. 15).

12. Allegretto, Corcoran & Mishel (2004); see note 4.

13. Podgursky, M., and Tongrut, R. (2006, Fall). (Mis-)Measuring the Relative Pay of Public School Teachers. *Education Finance and Policy, 1*(4).
     Taylor, L. L. (2006, Summer). Comparable wages, inflation, and school finance equity. *Education Finance and Policy, 1*(3).

14. Loeb, S. and Page, M. E. (2000). Examining the link between teacher wages and student outcomes: The importance of alternative labor market opportunities and non-pecuniary variation. *Review of Economics and Statistics, 82*, 393-408.

15. U.S. Bureau of Labor Statistics (1994, Aug. 24). *BLS Bulletin 2444*. Retrieved Feb. 11, 2007, from http://www.bls.gov/ebs/sp/chp2sl.txt. Quoted on page 4 of Greene and Winters.

16. U.S. Bureau of Labor Statistics (1994).

17. U.S. Bureau of Labor Statistics (2006, July); see note 10.
     All of the following calculations use mean annual hours from Supplementary Table 4.2 and mean weekly hours from Supplementary Table 4.1. We perform similar calculations in Allegretto, Corcoran, & Mishel (2004).

18. See also the survey results in Drago, R., et al (1999, April). New estimates of working time for elementary school teachers. *Monthly Labor Review*, pp. 31-40.

19. See National Center for Education Statistics (undated). Overview, *Schools and Staffing Survey*. Retrieved Feb. 11, 2007, from http://nces.ed.gov/surveys/sass/

20. National Center for Education Statistics (2006, April). *Characteristics of schools, districts, teachers, principals, and school libraries in the United States: 2003-04 Schools and Staffing Survey*. Retrieved Feb. 11, 2007, from http://nces.ed.gov/pubs2006/2006313.pdf
     An earlier wave of this survey (1999-00) asked the time-use questions somewhat differently; in that year teachers reported that they were required to spend an average of 37.9 hours per week in school, 3.2 additional hours per week working with students, and another 8.7 hours per week in grading and preparation activities.

21. National Center for Education Statistics (2006, April).

22. National Center for Education Statistics (2006, April); see note 19.

23. Thus, if anything, it is surprising that a *higher* fraction of school employers do not report that their teachers receive paid breaks.
24. U.S. Bureau of Labor Statistics (2005, Oct. 21). *People are asking...* Retrieved Feb. 12, 2007, from http://www.bls.gov/ncs/ocs/peoplebox.htm
25. U.S. Bureau of Labor Statistics (2005, Oct. 21).
26. Allegretto, Corcoran & Mishel (2004); see note 4.

PART 7

No Child Left Behind and Standards-Based Accountability

The title of the first report reviewed in Part Seven accurately captures the focus of this section—*Answering the Question That Matters Most: Has Student Achievement Increased Since No Child Left Behind*. That 2007 report, authored and published by the Center on Education Policy (CEP), found positive effects on achievement. A second 2007 report reviewed in this segment, authored by Neal McCluskey and Andrew J. Coulson and published by the Cato Institute, came to the opposite conclusion, again evident from the title—*End It, Don't Mend It: What to Do with No Child Left Behind*. A related 2008 report, published by the Fordham Institute and authored by Tom Loveless, Steve Farkas and Ann Duffett, investigated the performance of *High-Achieving Students in the Era of NCLB*. It found that the achievement gap had narrowed, but that high achievers had shown too little improvement. The review of this third report is not included here in order to minimize repetition. However, authors of all three reviews—John T. Yun (the CEP report), Bruce Fuller (the Cato report) and Gregory Camilli (the Fordham Institute report)—find similar strengths and weaknesses.

Think Tank Research Quality: Lessons for Policy Makers, the Media, and the Public, pp. 213–216
Copyright © 2010 by Information Age Publishing

Taken together, our reviewers' assessments of the reports' findings point to the methodological difficulty of assessing any change (or lack of change) in student performance as well as to the difficulty of establishing a causal link between achievement results and NCLB. Although Yun, for instance, compliments the CEP report as a thoughtful analysis that takes into account various factors rarely considered, he identifies several methodological issues inherent in the data, despite the researchers' efforts to use state-level data carefully. Different conclusions, he notes, were necessarily based on non-uniform data from different states. In some cases, it is not even possible to say definitively what year a state effectively implemented NCLB strategies, making it "impossible to draw reliable conclusions relating the implementation of NCLB to state test score changes."

Similarly, in critiquing the Cato report's glum assessment of achievement gains, Fuller points out that recent results from the National Assessment of Educational Progress (NAEP) are more encouraging—but he also notes that "whether these can be attributed to federal action, as opposed to long-running state efforts, remains a pivotal question." And, in discussing the findings of the Fordham report, Camilli makes the important general point that "Correlation does not imply causation.... The problem here is that effects can have multiple causes."

Two themes are evident in such criticisms: there are challenges inherent in analyses making use of any available achievement data, and not every dataset or analytic approach warrants causal claims. Researchers who want to assess achievement must first decide which instrument provides the data most useful for their purposes. Some choose the state standards-based tests taken by most students. Others choose the National Assessment of Educational Progress (NAEP), which is administered randomly to a selected nationwide sample of students. State assessments, which are used in the CEP report, are better aligned with a state's specific standards and instructional objectives; however, the fact that state standards vary greatly makes reliable national comparisons of state results exceedingly difficult. Compounding this difficulty is the fact that state-level data are not uniform, with available information varying not only from state to state but also sometimes from year to year. Moreover, the results of state assessments are likely to be affected by the common practice of "teaching to the test."

Other studies, including the Cato and Fordham reports, attempt to avoid such problems by using NAEP datasets, which, because of uniformity and a nationally representative sampling approach, allow for a wider variety of detailed comparisons. However, the NAEP is likely somewhat inexact in that it may target instructional objectives that states may not have included or emphasized in their standards. That is, states may be requiring students to learn about apples while NAEP may test their knowledge of oranges. Although some would argue that such a mismatch is a good thing because it reveals gaps in state expectations, it nevertheless undermines the reliability of comparisons about student achievement. An additional limitation of the NAEP is that its particular sampling approach undermines researchers' capacity to tease out many subgroup trends.

An even greater difficulty in assessing achievement is that even if data were comparable and reliable, the analyses in these reports were able to reach only correlational conclusions. Indeed, the reports themselves included such acknowledgements. The CEP study, for example, noted that "It is very difficult if not impossible, to determine the extent to which these trends and test results have occurred *because* of NCLB" (p. 1). Similarly, the Fordham report's Executive Summary said that "We cannot say that NCLB 'caused' the performance of the nation's top students to stagnate any more than it 'caused' the achievement of our lowest-performing students to rise dramatically." In each school and state, a variety of other factors can affect student performance. These may include changes in instructional objectives, staff, materials and procedures, which may or may not be related to NCLB and which may or may not have pre-dated it; significant changes in school demographics; and, even changes in the economy, which can result in housing instability and food insecurity. The influences on the achievement of any student or school are numerous, complex, and not easily or reliably disentangled.

Despite their disclaimers, two of the three NCLB reports, however, slipped into causal language and attributed results to NCLB. Reviewing the CEP report, for example, Yun notes that its very title promises to answer the question of whether NCLB has increased student achievement, and he concludes that "the wording of the numerous findings and key conclusions . . . implies a much stronger connection between the implementation of NCLB and the outcomes measured than can be substantiated by the data." Camilli finds a like problem in the Fordham report when the authors of the Foreword said, one page after the disclaimer, "The major finding of this dual study is that, in one respect at least, [NCLB] is working precisely as designed."

Ironically, one real contribution of these achievement studies is that their methodological limitations cumulatively demonstrate the complexity of the challenge to reach definitive findings about the relationship of national accountability policies to student performance. This, in itself, is an important policy conclusion.

Reviewers also identify some issues with literature reviews. Yun notes that the CEP report fails to consider research on NAEP scores with contradictory findings about achievement gains, or research suggesting that test score inflation might have influenced state results. Fuller finds some of the research cited in the Cato report reputable and relevant, but also that "the authors use older, empirical work in highly selective, even misleading ways." Camilli notes that in the Fordham report, the literature review is "cursory," with no literature review at all provided for one of the two research topics addressed in the report.

More positively, another contribution that these reports make, and that reviewers commend them for, is their fine-grained look at various parts of the overall puzzle of student achievement. They turn readers' attention now here and now there, contributing to an understanding of multiple factors that must be considered in any composite picture. The CEP study examined not only whether student proficiency changed but also the extent of that change. These factors are important to consider in tandem, because finding a positive trend has less policy import than the question of whether the trend is negligible or large. The Cato report detailed the several studies that find no achievement gain, but it also raised the question of whether the federal government has overstepped its constitutional boundaries. And, it highlighted unintended negative effects of NCLB, including some lowered state standards and excessive narrowing of the curriculum. The review of the Fordham study similarly commends that work for focusing attention on Black, Hispanic and poor high-achieving students, which Camilli terms "long overdue."

Overall, however, the reviewers temper their compliments with cautions about the use of all three reports to inform policy. Yun finds the thoughtful methods of the CEP report "instructive," and he encourages policymakers to use the report to help "understand what types of supports would help states implement NCLB." However, he also suggests that the report's findings should be used cautiously and "should not overshadow the more important and concrete findings regarding data difficulties." Of the Cato report, Fuller warns that the report's authors jumped from a reasonable analysis of NCLB to an unsupported advocacy of school-choice policies: "Critical analysis of policy strategies is sorely needed . . . [and this report] offers such a critical analysis, but only when considering NCLB. When attention is turned to market proposals for replacing NCLB, the report offers only the party line." Camilli notes that an "empirical synthesis" of studies on NCLB effectiveness would be useful, and he finds that the Fordham report "would make a contribution to this synthesis, but does not stand on its own as a document for informing instructional policies."

CHAPTER 15

END IT, DON'T MEND IT

What to Do With No Child Left Behind

Bruce Fuller

Review of "End It, Don't Mend It: What to Do with No Child Left Behind," by Neal McCluskey and Andrew J. Coulson, published by the Cato Institute. This is a modified version of a review originally published on October 8, 2007.

INTRODUCTION

The authors of the Cato Institute's policy analysis *End It, Don't Mend It: What to Do With No Child Left Behind*[1] lead with the radical conclusion that Washington should fully abdicate its role in the perennial struggle to improve the nation's schools. Instead, full authority should be held by the states and tax dollars should go back to parents (or at least to those parents who earn enough to benefit from tuition tax credits).

This conclusion proceeds via a dramatic inferential leap from a more tightly reasoned examination of No Child Left Behind (NCLB). In all, the Cato authors do the following: (1) usefully review evidence on whether students are doing better under NCLB; (2) examine what the authors

Think Tank Research Quality: Lessons for Policy Makers, the Media, and the Public, pp. 217–226

believe are self-serving political interests that led to NCLB's initial enact-
ment and continue to shape the widening debate on Capitol Hill over
reauthorization; (3) review the Congress' constitutionally bounded role in
education; and (4) conclude that after scrapping the federal government's
role, the nation should organize school finance solely through tax credits
or vouchers, shifting to a market system.

Cato's entry into the debate over what to do with No Child Left Behind
comes as congressional Democrats begin to float compromise proposals
aimed at striking a balance between supporters and critics of the current
NCLB regime. To editorialize briefly, the rising clamor inside the Washington Beltway over how to fix NCLB is reminiscent of the dysfunctional
family portrayed in *The Royal Tannenbaums*. Surface-level symptoms drive
heated debates that ignore underlying dynamics while family members,
somehow drawn to shared commitments, keep talking past each other.

Rep. George Miller of California, the principal House architect of
NCLB in 2001, has advanced alternative forms of student assessment, a
shift to tracking children's growth rather than relying exclusively on static
benchmarks, and basing teacher pay in part on the pressing needs of
inner-city schools or on the performance of their charges.[2]

Miller and his coauthors, including liberal House Speaker Nancy
Pelosi, are facing sharp resistance from the teacher unions and others who
see leading Democrats as largely staying the course on NCLB, siding with
the Bush White House. At the same time, odd bedfellows—civil rights
groups and conservative organizations—are blasting Miller for trying to
allow alternative forms of testing and perhaps consequently identifying
fewer perennially low-performing schools.[3]

"We are ready in California to go to war," declared Dean Vogel, vice
president of the California Teachers Association, outside the Capitol Hill
conference room where Miller's bill was getting its inaugural hearing.[4] By
mid-September 2007, Vogel's group was mailing colorful posters throughout California featuring photos of the Democratic leaders and reading,
"Pelosi and Miller are getting it wrong."[5] So, at the very moment Democratic leaders are trying to rally middle-class voters around their policy
agenda, labor is countering with pointed, quite public criticism.

FINDINGS, CONCLUSIONS, AND RATIONALES OF THE REPORT

It is against this stormy backdrop that the conservative Cato Institute
weighs in with *End It, Don't Mend It*, by Neal McCluskey and Andrew J.
Coulson. It offers a refreshingly blunt assessment of NCLB's weaknesses,
leading to radical recommendations. The authors begin with negative
answers to the questions of whether the law has worked (an empirical

issue) and whether Washington should be aggressively engaged in school reform (a matter of political philosophy). From these two starting points, they arrive at a crisp recommendation: Congress should simply kill NCLB. The authors would return us to the states' rights era of the early 1950s, limiting the federal government's role "to its constitutional bounds by ending its involvement in elementary and secondary education" (p. 1). In addition, they argue, a universal system of tax credits or school vouchers should replace the current system of public funding and governmental oversight of schools.

The Cato authors start with a pivotal question: has NCLB made any difference on the ground, raising students' test scores? Without much in the way of evidence, President Bush began declaring that the federal reform strategy was "working" in January 2004, just 2 years after signing "No Child."[6] The Bush administration's optimistic drumbeat has quickened in recent months as the White House pushes Congress to renew No Child Left Behind.[7]

The Cato authors detail how the evidence remains uneven at best for the claim that NCLB has, since it was enacted in 2002, raised achievement beyond the effects stemming from states' own accountability programs. The National Assessment of Educational Progress (NAEP) tracks student performance in reading and mathematics among fourth-, eighth-, and 12th graders. Just one of these six barometers showed continued growth over the first 4 years of NCLB implementation: fourth-grade students continued to progress in math, a trend that had begun in the late 1980s (pp. 3-5).

Soon after the Cato brief appeared, encouraging news did arrive, based on the spring 2007 NAEP assessments. Progress in math was sustained at the fourth-grade level, and eighth-graders showed signs of progress along with stronger math performance. The magnitude of gain equaled up to two scale-score points between 2005 and 2007 (one point equals about one-tenth of a grade level, 3 weeks of instructional time).

But eighth-graders showed no gains in reading, and the fourth-grade reading uptick centered largely in southern states and the Midwest, where state accountability programs have been historically weaker and where larger concentrations of poor children reside. Therefore, it remains difficult to attribute these uneven gains to No Child Left Behind—after 5 years of implementation and over $90 billion in Title I spending. It is doubtful that these results would have led the Cato authors to rethink their critique or conclusions.[8]

Given NCLB's mandate that all children be grade-level proficient by 2014, the report describes how governors and state school chiefs have found inventive ways to show progress. Many states have lowered the definition of "proficient" achievement, the exact opposite intent of NCLB's promise of high standards, as the Cato authors point out (pp. 6, 7). This is the so-called "race to the bottom."[9] The Cato authors detail how officials in several states have admitted to simply making their assessments easier, or re-weighting item scores to artificially inflate total test scores.

Another consequence of NCLB, say the Cato authors, is a narrowing of what is taught (p. 7). Proponents of improved science and social studies instruction complain that these subjects have shrunk in many schools, along with music and the arts.[10] Health officials worry that the rise of childhood obesity might stem from reduction in time spent in physical education. As an empirical matter, this narrowing of the curriculum may have stemmed from NCLB or it may have resulted from states' own accountability programs, but this historical perspective is lacking throughout the Cato brief. From these authors' perspective, states are almost always to be trusted but Washington's actions are presumptively harmful.

In sum, the authors offer three conclusions regarding the effects of NCLB: (1) it has failed to raise performance standards, instead encouraging states to lower the proficiency bar, (2) evidence that "No Child" has boosted achievement remains weak at best, and (3) unintended effects may not be healthy for the enterprise of liberal education. This may help to explain uneven support for NCLB among suburban parents.

The authors then examine current efforts to simply tinker with the legislation, essentially placing Cato alongside the teacher unions in rejecting the Pelosi-Miller attempts at incremental fixes. They recount education secretary Margaret Spelling's comparison of NCLB to Ivory Soap: "It's 99.9 percent pure … there's not much needed in the way of change" (p. 7). The Bush White House, like the House Democrats to a great extent, has tried to postulate that NCLB is working and has argued against fixing something that is not broken. The new NAEP results—5 years and $90 billion into NCLB implementation—do show a smattering of progress. But whether these can be attributed to federal action, as opposed to long-running state efforts, remains a pivotal question. This wider recognition of state and federal reform efforts would better inform Cato's readers.

The Cato report then dissects the modest changes proposed by Spellings, House Democrats, and the Aspen Institute's bipartisan study group. Such proposals include narrowing confidence intervals around mean test scores to make it tougher for schools to make growth targets; raising licensing requirements for school principals; and requiring states to test students in the 12th grade. The authors ask whether such tweaks would do anything beyond adding more rules and sanctioning additional schools (pp. 7-10).

The Cato authors go after other proposed fixes, such as Democratic Senator Chris Dodd's proposal to set national curricular standards and a common definition of what proficient achievement means at each grade level. This idea strikes them as too centralized and likely to open the door to various education groups that would have little interest in maintaining the NAEP's higher performance standards (pp. 9, 10).

Instead, the authors conclude that a radical market model of school finance should take the place of federal involvement in education. They endorse a Republican bill that would take all federal education dollars and dole them back to IRS-filers through tax credits. How the millions of Americans who earn too little to pay federal income taxes would be served remains unclear. The authors also support the nation's smattering of publicly and privately funded voucher programs, drawing selectively on evaluation studies while failing to mention others that show no achievement effects (pp. 12-15). This point is further discussed below.

THE REPORT'S USE OF RESEARCH LITERATURE

To back their contentions regarding NCLB's limited benefits, the Cato authors draw heavily on analyses conducted by Harvard and Berkeley scholars, which they accurately detail. Jaekyung Lee, working with Gary Orfield's Civil Rights Project, has conducted the most sophisticated analysis thus far into the question of whether NAEP achievement trends, going back to the early 1990s, were bumped upward on a new trajectory in the wake of NCLB. Lee's statistical analysis concluded that they have not, that NCLB is associated with no such positive trends.[11]

My Berkeley research group came to similar conclusions after tracking changes in both state and federal NAEP scores for 12 states from 1992 forward, as the Cato authors summarize.[12] On the other hand, the Center on Education Policy in Washington tracked state test score trends from 1999 forward and found that in 9 of 12 states that could provide time series data, growth in state scores had accelerated slightly under NCLB.[13] But the pre-NCLB period only included 2 years of data for some states, and the CEP report has been criticized for additional flaws.[14]

As they move deeper into their argument, the authors use older empirical work in highly selective, even misleading ways. They fail to mention the work of Hoover Institution Fellow Eric Hanushek, which has shown that NAEP scores rose more steeply in the 1990s in states that mounted aggressive accountability programs, while progress was slower or absent in states with weak accountability regimes.[15] When the authors conclude with their pitch for a market model of school finance, they lean heavily on a single study of Chile's nationwide voucher program conducted by a pro-school-choice economist, Caroline Minter Hoxby (pp. 12-13), ignoring the considerable additional research on that program that has shown much more troubling results.[16]

They also ignore the large body of work studying domestic programs, including that conducted by provoucher researcher Paul Peterson and his colleagues—studies that have yielded mixed findings, conditioned by local situations, the supply of private and Catholic schools, and the ethnicity and grade level of students receiving vouchers.[17]

REVIEW OF THE REPORT'S METHODS AND OF THE VALIDITY OF ITS FINDINGS AND CONCLUSIONS

Notwithstanding their review of evidence of NCLB's lack of success, the Cato authors are skeptical that a serious recrafting of the federal role is in the cards, given the unflagging optimism about NCLB inside the Washington Beltway. Even if the teacher unions, state leaders, and local school boards are fed up, congressional leaders and the White House will, the Cato authors believe, hold together the odd coalition of civil rights groups (focused on such elements as disaggregated results and an increased federal role in funding and in regulating local decision making) and moderate business groups (who are invested in stiff accountability measures).

This result, though, is far from their ideal. The Cato authors conclude that NCLB should be thrown on the rising heap of discarded school reforms and replaced by a national voucher or tax credit system. Since Cato has long advocated a provoucher position, this report's preference for that alternative is not a surprise, but neither does it necessarily follow from the authors' critique of NCLB. Left out are other policy options, such as thoroughly rethinking the federal role or devising better ways for Washington to strengthen the states' ability to hold schools accountable.

Instead of NCLB, the authors praise vouchers and a Republican proposal to convert federal spending into tax credits, and they urge "more effective structural [i.e., choice and market-based] reforms" (p. 12). They argue that NCLB is a naïve attempt at centralized control, implicitly representative of all collective forms of action aimed at improving the schools—approaches that should be abandoned. Yet the report's inferential leap toward its blanket support of market remedies ignores the inconclusive evidence on school choice. The critical eye that the Cato authors have successfully brought to their analysis of NCLB is quickly lost when they turn to vouchers.

Logical and Methodological Gaps

Authors McCluskey and Coulson squarely confront the tightly constrained debate over No Child Left Behind currently unfolding on Capitol Hill. Three of the Act's key original authors—Bush, Kennedy, and Miller—define the task of salvaging core elements. Their shrinking count of allies wants to mend it. A rising count of conservatives and others want to end it.[18]

Yet the authors ignore key empirical facts and prematurely set aside the question of whether a more effective federal role might be crafted. Both federal and state test scores rose rather dramatically during much of the 1990s, and racial gaps in achievement narrowed markedly. After dipping in the early 1990s, the mean NAEP score for blacks rose more than one grade level between 1994 and 2002 before leveling off. The average performance of Latinos rose at a similar clip. The performance of whites also grew, but at a slower rate, equaling about half a grade level.[19]

Given the authors' lack of interest in historical dynamics, we learn nothing about the policy mixes or demographic shifts that could inform a stronger federal role. Instead, the Cato authors generalize from the NCLB era to claim that Washington is ill-equipped to devise a more efficacious presence in school reform. This is like arguing that government should never have intervened in the public health field in the nineteenth century because early collective efforts had not worked.

Some readers might credit Cato's McCluskey and Coulson for breaking with other conservative positions. For example, they criticize the narrowing of school curricula which they believe stems from NCLB (p. 7). Nor do the authors hold any faith in state governments' ability to boost the public schools, inadvertently discarding Jeffersonian political theory.

The authors more typically reflect the ideological right's views on education when they fail to mention the vast inequalities that continue to mark our public schools, from gross interstate disparities in spending per pupil to the abominable conditions of many urban schools. These scholars—reminiscent of Ronald Reagan—see government excess as the problem. That is, they cast the naiveté of NCLB's architects and their penchant to regulate and sanction behavior as a major distraction from other policy remedies.

In doing so, they fail to question or investigate the political economies of metropolitan areas and the grossly unequal forms of schooling that still persist. Their report does not consider how market remedies would address the structural stratification that marks schooling in America. And with their affection for school choice, they fail to mention that even pro-voucher scholars like Harvard's Paul Peterson have found quite uneven benefits for children of color.[20]

USEFULNESS OF THE REPORT FOR
GUIDANCE OF POLICY AND PRACTICE

The first two-thirds of the Cato brief provides a revealing analysis of how NCLB has failed to deliver on its promise of raising student achievement while yielding inadvertent effects inside states and schools. It offers a classic case study of how well-intentioned policy, built on a simple, rather mechanical theory of how to motivate new behavior locally, can backfire. This part of the brief also illustrates how some libertarian-conservatives are trying to make sense of Washington's unprecedented entanglement with local schools.

But this analysis of NCLB's shortcomings fails to advance careful thinking about a range of alternative strategies. Market approaches are presented as an almost magical solution—a more resourceful and surgical way of helping states achieve accountability. Over the past generation, Washington has seriously reshaped how collective action delivers welfare and family support for poor households, as well as how public health care is provided through local organizations, and how voucher-like Pell Grants can support college students. In each case, Washington did not abandon its commitment to the sector simply because prior policy or institutions were proving inadequate. Instead, new policy tools were invented or new forms of local institution-building were created. These policies include market elements, thus illustrating the value of conservative scholars who think inventively and who honestly confront the persistent disparities that characterize American society and the poor quality of some mass institutions that reproduce class inequalities. Critical analysis of policy strategies is sorely needed, including studies that build on principles of local empowerment and market relations. This Cato report offers such a critical analysis, but only when considering NCLB. When attention is turned to market proposals for replacing NCLB, the report offers only the party line.

NOTES AND REFERENCES

1. McCluskey, N., & Coulson, A. (2007, Sept. 5). *End It, don't mend it: What to do with No Child Left Behind*. Policy Analysis No. 599. Washington, DC: Cato Institute. Retrieved Sept. 28, 2007, from http://www.cato.org/pubs/pas/Pa599.pdf

2. U.S. Congress. (2007). Miller-McKeon discussion draft, Title I: Amendments to Title 1. Washington, DC.

3. Schemo, D. (2007a, Sept. 11). Teachers and rights groups oppose education measure. *New York Times*. Retrieved Sept. 28 from http://www.nytimes.com/2007/09/11/education/11child.html

Schemo, D. (2007b, Sept. 6). Secretary of Education criticizes proposal. *New York Times*. Retrieved Oct. 1, 2007, from http://www.nytimes.com/2007/09/06/education/06child.html

Holland, R. (2007, Sept.) *Portfolios: A backward step in school accountability.* Arlington, VA: Lexington Institute. Retrieved Oct. 2, 2007, from http://lexingtoninstitute.org/docs/holland_portfolio_assessment_8_29_07.pdf

4. Hoff, D. (2007, Sept. 10). NCLB: Act II; California teachers oppose 'Miller/Pelosi' bill. *Education Week* (online weblog entry). Retrieved Oct. 1, 2007, from http://blogs.edweek.org/edweek/NCLB-ActII/2007/09/california_teachers_oppose_pel.html

5. Cheever, J. (2007, Sept. 10). Teachers bring giant postcard protest to Pelosi. *FogCityJournal.com*. Retrieved Oct. 1, 2007, from http://www.fogcityjournal.com/news_in_brief/bcn_no_child_left_behind_070920.shtml

6. Bush, G. W. (2004, Jan. 3). President's weekly radio address. Washington DC: The White House. Retrieved Oct. 1, 2007, from http://www.whitehouse.gov/news/releases/2004/01/20040103.html

7. Schemo (2007b); see note 3.

8. Cavanagh, S., & Manzo, K. K. (2007a, October 3). NAEP Gains: Experts Mull Significance. *Education Week*, *27*(6), pp. 1,16-17.
    Cavanagh, S., & Manzo, K. K. (2007b, September 25). NAEP Reading and Math Scores Rise. *Education Week* (online), *27*. Retrieved Oct. 1, 2007, from http://www.edweek.org/ew/articles/2007/09/25/05naep_web.h27.html?print=1

9. Linn, R. (2000). Assessments and accountability. *Educational Researcher, 29*, 4-16.

10. Manzo, K. K. (2005, March 16). Social studies losing out to reading, math. *Education Week*, *24*(27), 1, 16-17.

11. Lee, J. (2006, June). *Tracking achievement gaps and assessing the impact of NCLB on the gaps.* Harvard University, Civil Rights Project.

12. Fuller, B., Wright, J., Gesicki, K., & Kang, E. (2007). Gauging growth: How to judge No Child Left Behind? *Educational Researcher, 36*, 268-278.

13. Center for Education Policy (2007). *Answering the question that matters most: Has student achievement increased since No Child Left Behind?* Washington, DC. This CEP report was the subject of a Think Tank Review by John T. Yun. See Chapter 16 of this volume.

14. Dillon, S. (2007, June 6). New study finds gains since No Child Left Behind. *New York Times*. Retrieved Oct. 1, 2007, from http://www.nytimes.com/2007/06/06/education/06report.html

15. Hanushek, E., & Raymond, M. (2006). School accountability and student performance. *Regional Economic Development*, *2*, 51-61 (Federal Reserve Bank of St. Louis).
    Carnoy, M., & Loeb, S. (2002). Does external accountability affect student outcomes? *Educational Evaluation & Policy Analysis*, *24*, 305-331.

16. See McEwan, P. J., & Carnoy, M. (2000). The effectiveness and efficiency of private schools in Chile's voucher system. *Educational Evaluation and Policy Analysis*, *22*, 213-239.

Hsieh, C., & Urquiola, M. (2003). *When schools compete, how do they compete? An assessment of Chile's nationwide school voucher program*. NBER Working Paper No. 10008.

17. Howell, W., & Peterson, P. (2006). *The education gap: Vouchers and urban schools*. Washington, DC: Brookings Institution Press.

18. See pp. 7-10 in Cato brief, and Zuckerbrod, N. (2007). Education panel chairman spars with union over merit pay for teachers. *Education Week*, September 11, on the web: www.edweek.org/ew/articles/2007/09

19. Time-series trends are reviewed, for NAEP and state test scores, in Fuller et al (2007); see note 12.

20. Howel & Peterson (2006); see note 17.

CHAPTER 16

ANSWERING THE QUESTION THAT MATTERS MOST

Has Student Achievement Increased Since No Child Left Behind?

John T. Yun

Review of "Answering the Question That Matters Most: Has Student Achievement Increased Since No Child Left Behind?" published by the Center on Education Policy. This is a modified version of a review originally published on June 26, 2007.

INTRODUCTION

The report released by the Center on Education Policy, "Answering the Question That Matters Most: Has Student Achievement Increased Since No Child Left Behind?"[1] has received a great deal of attention in the press and is likely to be cited often in the debate on the reauthorization of the No Child Left Behind Act (NCLB). The report analyzes the complex issue of test score improvement before and after the implementation of NCLB in 2002. There are some important weaknesses in the analysis,

Think Tank Research Quality: Lessons for Policy Makers, the Media, and the Public, pp. 227–236
Copyright © 2010 by Information Age Publishing
All rights of reproduction in any form reserved.

however, that may have resulted in the report presenting a much more optimistic picture of the impact of the legislation than the data warrant.

In addition to these methodological issues, which bring into question the robustness of some of the results, some results are overstated. The title of the report sets the stage for an examination of the direct impact of NCLB on student achievement as measured by state-level test scores. The report does not do this, however, and was never designed to do this. As the authors explain concerning one of their main conclusions,

> It is very difficult if not impossible, to determine the extent to which these trends and test results have occurred *because* of NCLB. Since 2002, states, school districts and schools have simultaneously implemented many different but interconnected policies to raise achievement. (p. 1)[2]

Given this appropriate disclaimer (and many similar disclaimers throughout the report), it is unclear why the Center chose to release the report under a title that blurs the line between causal and descriptive analyses. The report's title is not the only source of confusion. The wording of the numerous findings and key conclusions in the report implies a much stronger connection between the implementation of NCLB and the outcomes measured than can be substantiated by the data, resulting in a possible overestimate of the impact of the legislation on the actual changes in test scores.

This new report does offer some thoughtful analyses that take into account some important issues that have not been often addressed in the past. For instance, the authors use multiple measures of growth (change in percent proficient and effect sizes), acknowledge the problem of changes in the testing systems across years and states, describe the weakness of using cut scores to determine proficiency levels, and identify and correct errors in the data-reporting systems state by state. Yet these positive steps are undermined by several issues not adequately addressed in the report, which weaken the overall approach and make the findings far less compelling. Methodological problems with this report include issues of scope, measurement, and selection bias,[3] which ultimately call into question the robustness of the findings, rendering the report's conclusions far from definitive.

In general, while this report represents progress toward a more comprehensive way to examine the results of a complex and wide-ranging federal policy like NCLB, the main emphasis of the report probably should not have been the tenuous connection between the date on which NCLB was implemented and subsequent achievement changes. In fact, the report makes a second, much stronger point, which is largely hidden behind the causal headline: the lack of coordination and support for comprehensive, state-by-state data reporting and analysis. Such improved data would likely assist states, districts and schools in their decision-making—which is arguably the ultimate goal of all good data analysis.

FINDINGS AND CONCLUSIONS OF THE REPORT

The scope of the report is extremely wide-ranging and ambitious. Though relatively short (approximately 100 pages), the report discusses the issue of data collection and analysis across all 50 states and then examines achievement at multiple grade levels using multiple tests across every state over multiple years. In addition, the authors use two different measures of achievement and growth (change in percent proficient and change in effect sizes[4]) across all available states, years, and grade levels, and then try to expand their analysis to determine how achievement gaps have changed among various ethnic/racial groups.

Such a complex analysis is difficult under the best of circumstances, as suggested by this report's many conflicting findings. The key summary conclusions (those that are most likely to be used in ongoing policy debates) cannot capture the reasons for these conflicts, but can only provide a summary picture over multiple, noncomparable and occasionally conflicting measures.

One of the main problems is quickly evident: each main conclusion in the report is based on analysis from a greatly differing number of states, since the authors chose to include or exclude states in their analyses based on the amount and type of available data. While this choice improves the comparability of test data from year to year, it also introduces the possibility of selection bias and artificial test score gains. These dangers will be explored later in this review.

The report's five main conclusions are as follows:

1. In most states with three or more years of comparable test data, student achievement in reading and math has gone up since 2002, the year NCLB was enacted.
2. There is more evidence of the narrowing of achievement gaps between groups of students since 2002 than of gaps widening. Sill the magnitude of the gaps is often substantial.
3. In 9 of the 13 states with sufficient data to determine pre- and post-NCLB trends, average yearly gains in test scores were greater after NCLB took effect than before.

4. It is very difficult if not impossible, to determine the extent to which these trends and test results have occurred *because* of NCLB. Since 2002, states, school districts and schools have simultaneously implemented many different but interconnected policies to raise achievement

5. Although NCLB emphasizes public reporting of state test data, the data necessary to reach definitive conclusions about achievement were sometimes hard to find or unavailable, or had holes or discrepancies. More attention should be given to issues of the quality and transparency of state test data. (p. 1)

If supported by the data and analyses, the first three of these conclusions would seem to provide substantial support for the position that NCLB has indeed contributed a great deal to improving average achievement on state examinations. The final two conclusions suggest that a degree of caution and care should be taken in pursuit of the answers to the research questions, and they suggest an important focus on the future availability and use of data in state testing systems.

It is also important to take note, however, of a key finding that the CEP authors report but do not list as one of their main conclusions. The authors state that there is almost no correlation between the findings of the study, which are based on various state assessments, and scores reported by the National Assessment of Educational Progress (NAEP). This is troubling, since one would expect true achievement gains not to be test-specific. The authors suggest that this lack of consistency may be due to a lack of alignment of NAEP with the state standards, a lack of motivation among students on the NAEP as opposed to the state examinations, different inclusion criteria, score inflation, or differences in the grades analyzed (pp. 71-72). These are all legitimate possibilities that should be considered and explored. Some of these explanations are more damaging for the CEP report than others, however. In fact, as discussed below, the possibility of score inflation on state examinations may be the most likely explanation, which throws into question the robustness of the report's overall conclusions.

THE REPORT'S USE OF RESEARCH LITERATURE

The format of the report is not designed around an examination of the research literature; instead it is focused on an analysis of the new datasets the authors created. The literature they cite is therefore largely in support of their methodological choices or rival explanations for the results they find. For instance, the report invokes previous research[5] to support explanations for the NAEP test scores not matching the analyses performed in the report and to support the possibility that test score inflation is a factor in their state test results. There is no examination, however, of past research on the topic of how test scores have changed over time on state examinations.[6]

A 2002 paper by Linn found that average yearly changes in percent proficient on the NAEP were modest in the 1990s (well before NCLB was implemented). For instance, between 1992 and 1998, only 3 of the 33 states administering the assessment showed 1% or more yearly gains in scores in fourth grade reading. Similarly, only 17 of 34 states showed such gains in mathematics from 1992 to 2000. In addition, Linn found that very few states showed any decreases (7 of 33 states in reading and 1 of 34 states in mathematics in 1992-200).[7] These earlier findings, had they been included and discussed in the report, could have helped place several of the report's findings in context, since the numbers of states showing increases and declines on their own state examinations were very similar to these NAEP results prior to NCLB—particularly the relatively small numbers of states showing declines during this period.

In addition, there exists a very rich literature utilizing the NAEP to examine trends in achievement gaps between racial and ethnic groups.[8] Yet no literature of this type was cited or used. In fact, NAEP data on the widening or narrowing of the achievement gap was not used at all, even as a comparison for the gap findings in this report. Such context could have helped readers understand whether the changes before and after NCLB reported in this report are large or small compared to other authors' estimates. Thus, readers would be able to better determine whether these changes are part of a consensus overall trend toward narrowing gaps, or a change from a static or increasing situation. Given the care used by the authors in designing their trend studies, this omission is somewhat puzzling.

REVIEW OF THE REPORT'S METHODOLOGIES

The report makes good use of the data that the authors collected within the states. The approach used in this report illustrates, in a very clear way, the problems inherent in creating strong inter- and intrastate comparisons, particularly given the lack of transparency of many state data systems and the rapid changes in state testing systems. Some critical problems remain, however. I will discuss three of the most serious, concerning the report's trend, gap, and pre/post analyses.

Trend Analysis

Trend analysis was used to support conclusion No. 1: "In most states with three or more years of comparable test data, student achievement in reading and math has gone up since 2002, the year NCLB was enacted." But this analysis suffers from fundamental problems with measurement, selection and robustness brought about by analytic design decisions.

Trends were defined by the average change in test scores across a minimum of 2 to 3 years, depending on the state. Moderate-to-large changes were defined as changes larger than one percentage point per year, slight changes as less than one percentage point per year (p. 2). In effect, this means that the actual average yearly increase relies on the selection of the first year of data and the last year; the years in between do not play any role in the overall change. If either the first or last year is lower or higher than the "true" score (a hypothetical perfect measurement), either through some random process like measurement error or through non-random process like score inflation, the estimates of growth will be biased. As explained below, this is in fact very likely, given how the states were selected into the various samples.

Data were included in the "trend" analysis if they met particular criteria. Among these criteria is the condition that the state data set must have no "breaks" in the data, that is, changes in the state testing system that have the effect of making consecutive years noncomparable (pp. 78-79). In any states with these breaks, only data that were comparable—that is, data subsequent to the breaks—were analyzed. This inclusion criterion, while intended to ensure comparability, resulted in the exclusion of some or all data from 39 states.[9]

This approach, however, simply trades one problem for another, biasing the sample toward states more likely to have inflated test scores. A 2002 analysis by Koretz provides strong evidence that new tests result in a depression of the initial scores, followed by rapid increases in subsequent years.[10]

Had the NAEP data shown independent confirmation of the changes observed in the state tests, there would be more evidence that the changes were real and not a function of test-score inflation. But given the weak to nonexistent correlation between the NAEP and state test results, these questions about the validity of the reported improvements on the state examinations should have been more fully addressed.

In addition, state graphs of percent proficient provided on the CEP website show a great deal of variability, which suggests that if different endpoints were selected, the results of the analysis could radically change—particularly given the small-to-average changes (1% per year) that define slight or moderate increases. This is important for two reasons.

First, for states with breaks in the data, the initial score point is defined as the first year of the new testing regime, not necessarily 2002, the NCLB implementation year. Second, for those states without breaks, the first year (2002) may not be the year the state actually responded to the implementation of NCLB. According to *Education Week*, by the 2004-2005 school year only 23 of the 50 states and the District of Columbia were testing students in math and reading in Grades 3 through 8, and even fewer were also implementing other aspects of NCLB.[11] Thus, the problem of random variability is compounded by the fact that the state's actual implementation date for NCLB is unknown, making it impossible to draw reliable conclusions relating the implementation of NCLB to state test score changes.

Gap Analysis

Gap analysis was used to support conclusion No. 2: "There is more evidence of the narrowing of achievement gaps between groups of students since 2002 than of gaps widening. Still, the magnitude of the gaps is often substantial."

All of the methodological concerns discussed above regarding trends analysis also apply to the gap analysis. Further, the gap analysis is complicated by small sample sizes for some of the included racial and ethnic groups, which are therefore more likely to show greater variability in their estimates of percent proficient. This variability may well render the gap measures even less robust than the trend measures because unreliability is built into each of the percent-proficient estimates.

Pre- and Post-NCLB Analysis

The pre- and post-NCLB analysis is used to support conclusion No. 3: "In nine of the 13 states with sufficient data to determine pre- and post-NCLB trends, average yearly gains in test scores were greater after NCLB took effect than before."

The value of this analysis is seriously damaged by issues of selection. Only 13 states had sufficient data pre- and post-NCLB to allow for this analysis—a very small sample size. Moreover, these 13 were not randomly selected. The states included are those that had not changed any key elements of their testing policies from 1999 to 2006, the span of this study.

These states all had accountability systems designed well before NCLB, some of which met the NCLB guidelines closely enough not to be changed.

With the others, the states either decided that the current system served them well under the NCLB regime or that they would not alter the current system even though it might result in considerable sanctions under NCLB.

Either way, it is exactly the wrong group of states to be examining in order to determine whether or not NCLB had an impact on student achievement, since any comprehensive investigation of the impacts of a policy intervention should consider whether the intervention induces changes in the behavior of the state. This report, in contrast, excludes very important information about such state policy changes. It includes those states that had instituted a testing program and set of standards well prior to NCLB, so any change before and after the NCLB implementation date cannot reliably be attributed to NCLB's testing or standards requirements.

Robustness

The report should be praised for several cautionary notes that help readers understand some of its limitations. The three serious limitations described above were not among those discussed in the report, however. Moreover, the report's authors could have addressed some of these concerns by, for instance, using slightly different criteria for the start- and end-dates to see if the results changed due to random variation. In addition, the authors might have attempted to equate tests across breaks, as an alternative approach for maintaining comparability.

Without such explorations and without a rationale for dismissing or minimizing these problems, the data cannot be seen to convincingly support the report's conclusions.

REVIEW OF THE VALIDITY OF THE FINDINGS AND CONCLUSIONS

The report is on its most solid ground in its more cautionary conclusions: conclusion No. 4 concerning the causal warrant to suggest that NCLB is improving test scores, and conclusion No. 5 concerning the difficulty in obtaining data. In particular, the difficulty that the CEP authors describe in obtaining and analyzing their data is well documented and supported, and it points to an important need for the future.

The report's analytical findings rest on very weak foundations, however. The approaches employed to fix data problems may well have created other problems that were not addressed in the report and that ultimately undercut their substantive conclusions.

USEFULNESS OF THE REPORT FOR
GUIDANCE OF POLICY AND PRACTICE

The description of the difficulty the Center on Educational Policy researchers encountered in simply trying to gather what should be publicly available data is instructive and should be noted by policymakers trying to understand what types of supports would help states implement NCLB.

The substantive data analysis provided on the potential impact of NCLB on students' achievement is suspect, however. While the conclusions of this study are sure to be cited in the debate around reauthorization, the data and analyses should be viewed with great caution, and should not overshadow the more important and concrete findings regarding data difficulties.

NOTES AND REFERENCES

1. Center on Education Policy. (2006, June 5). *Answering the question that matters most: Has student achievement increased since No Child Left Behind?* Washington, DC: Author. (No individual author is listed for the report.)
2. Center on Education Policy (2006).
3. Selection bias is defined as bias in estimates due to how samples are selected and which are unrelated to the actual underlying phenomenon that is being estimated. For instance, a survey of parents conducted only at university daycare centers would be biased toward parents with more formal education and could not justifiably be generalized to the entire population of parents.
4. NCLB requires states to move all students to full proficiency on their state language arts and mathematics examinations by 2014 with the definition of proficiency to be determined by each state. Effect sizes are measures of how large a change in scores is, relative to a given state's distribution of the scores. A full definition of these terms and a description of the authors' approaches is provided in the CEP report on pages 21-26.
5. For examples of such literature cited see: Hamilton, L. (2003). Assessment as a policy tool. In Flooden, R. E. (Ed.), *Review of Research in Education, 27,* 25-68.
    Linn, R. L., Graue, M. E., & Sanders, N. M. (1990). Comparing states and district test results to national norms. *Journal of Educational measurement: Issues and Practice, 9,* 5-14.
    Koretz, D. (2005). *Alignment, high stakes, and the inflation of test scores.* Los Angeles:, CA: National Center For Research and Evaluation, Standards, and Student Testing.
6. For a description of one such study see Fuller, B., Gesicki, K., Kang, E., & Wright, J. (2006). *Is the No Child Left Behind Act working? The reliability of how*

states track achievement. Policy Analysis for California Education, Working paper 06-1.

7. Linn, R. L., Baker, E. L., & Betebenner, D. W. (2002). Accountability systems: Implications of requirements of the No Child Left Behind Act of 2001, *Educational Researcher, 31*(6), 3-16.

8. See examples: Lee, J. (2002). Racial and ethnic achievement gap trends: Reversing the progress toward equity? *Educational Researcher, 31*(1), 3-12.
    Hedges, L., & Nowell, A. (1999). Changes in the Black-White gap in achievement test scores. *Sociology of Education, 72*(2), 111-135.
    Jenks, C., & Phillips, M. (1999). *The Black-White test score gap*. Washington, DC: Brookings Institution Press

9. See report Table 22, p. 80.

10. Koretz, D. (2002). Limitations in the use of achievement tests as measures of educators' productivity. *Journal of Human Resources, 37*(4), 752-777.

11. Olsen, L. (2004, Dec. 8). Taking root. *Education Week*. Retrieved June 15, 2007, from http://www.edweek.org/ew/articles/2004/12/08/15nclb-1.h24.html?print=1

PART 8

Report Cards: Bad Grades Make Headlines

Given the complexity of educational issues, various types of report cards have widespread appeal in that they purport to deliver an easily understood "bottom line" for school performance. As our reviewers in Part Eight detail, however, the apparent simplicity of such reports depends upon simplistic manipulations of data in support of a predetermined agenda. Both of the reports reviewed in the following chapters exemplify that trend and constitute mere advocacy, not inquiry.

Chapter 17 offers Kenneth Howe's review of the Fordham Institute's *The State of State Standards 2006*, authored by Chester Finn, Liam Julian, and Michael Petrilli. After assigning grades to each state's standards and comparing them to various state test scores, the study found that states with better content standards did better on performance standards. The study was accompanied by an ancillary document, *It Takes a Vision: How Three States Created Great Academic Standards*, authored by freelance writer and blogger Joanne Jacobs. The *Vision* document offered case studies of three states where superior standards were linked to improved achievement.

Howe finds the report's conclusions unsupported and *Vision* to be empty rhetoric. The report first assigned grades to state standards, then compared these grades to state scores on various tests to determine alignment.

Think Tank Research Quality: Lessons for Policy Makers, the Media, and the Public, pp. 237–239

The report assumed there *would* be a correlation between standards and achievement, failing to address a significant body of research literature that casts doubt on the premise. In addition, the report did not specify the criteria used to assess standards or how they were applied. Howe notes that perhaps criteria can be inferred from Fordham's 2000 report. But that would be troubling as well, since an expert used for that earlier report applied personal criteria at odds with the standards issued by an authoritative national disciplinary group. Howe finds the study's grades and findings further weakened by the report's failure to specify how many raters were involved or what their qualifications were. In a nutshell, Howe highlights the subjective and advocacy nature of the grading criteria.

Of Jacobs' case studies, Howe critiques the selection of cases in detail and then concludes that "post-hoc massaging of the data reach[ed] the point of absurdity," and that the *Vision* document read "like a morality tale, in which sensible, hard-headed, altruistic 'reformers' who support rigorous, precise, and clear standards are 'tough, hand-to-hand combatants' engaging in the 'good fight' against muddled, soft-headed, self-serving 'progressives.' " In general, Howe finds not a shred of credibility in either document.

The report critiqued in Chapter 18 is no better. In his review of the 2007 *Report Card on American Education*, authored by Andrew LeFevre and published by the American Legislative Exchange Council, Gene Glass finds an even wider range and number of problems. The report presented five findings: (a) that significant increases in education funding did not yield significant gains in achievement; (b) that no correlation existed between pupil-to-teacher ratios and achievement, or (c) between teachers' salaries and achievement; (d) that strong accountability measures helped ensure resources flow where they were most needed; and (e) that parental choice enhanced children's educational future. Glass notes that these wide ranging findings were presented in a "scant" 11+ pages—accompanied by 132 pages containing "literally tens of thousands of bits of undigested data." However impressive the data may have appeared, little of it was analyzed for the report.

In instances where analysis did appear, Glass notes that the methodology was extraordinarily simplistic—"a century out of date." Moreover, measures of student achievement were inappropriate. Among Glass' criticisms of achievement data is that some of the tests included were never intended to measure achievement. For example, he observes that the SAT and ACT "are measures of aptitude specifically designed not to be greatly influenced by schooling experience." Of the report's use of prior research literature, Glass finds that the study "ignores, intentionally or unintentionally, the many studies that flatly contradict its findings and conclusions" and that it includes no research studies at all in its bibliography, an "oversight" that he finds "indefensible." Glass' final assessment is that "In spite of being clad with myriad numbers and statistics, the *Report Card on American Education* is rhetoric, not research."

The primary value of these reports to policymakers is to demonstrate how completely devoid of credible content advocacy documents masquerading as research can be.

CHAPTER 17

THE STATE OF STATE STANDARDS 2006

Kenneth R. Howe

Review of "The State of State Standards 2006," by Chester E. Finn, Jr., Liam Julian, and Michael J. Petrilli, and published by the Fordham Institute. This is a modified version of a review originally published on September 11, 2006.

INTRODUCTION

Educational standards have become a central issue in educational policy over the last several decades and have assumed particular importance with the passage and implementation of the No Child Left Behind Act of 2001 (NCLB). Standards are divided into two types: *content* and *performance*. Content standards specify the knowledge and skills to be learned in a given subject area; performance standards specify the level of learning deemed sufficient, typically labeled as "proficient."

Content and performance standards work in tandem in test-based accountability systems like NCLB. In theory, such systems "incentivize" educators to produce improved student learning by holding them accountable for improvement on performance standards, as measured by standardized tests. Performance standards must be "aligned" with content

Think Tank Research Quality: Lessons for Policy Makers, the Media, and the Public, pp. 241–248
Copyright © 2010 by Information Age Publishing
241

standards; content standards drive improvement in performance if they are sufficiently rigorous and provide guidance to educators by being clear, precise, and manageable in number.

The report under review, *The State of State Standards 2006*, rates each state's "subject" (i.e., "content") standards in U.S. history, English/language arts, mathematics, science, and world history, using an A-F scale.[1] The report then compares those grades to earlier ratings from 2000. An accompanying document, *It Takes a Vision: How Three States Created Great Academic Standards*,[2] provides a separate account of the development of the three state standards judged best: those of California, Massachusetts, and Indiana.

The report was produced by the Thomas B. Fordham Institute, which has "raising standards" and "strengthening accountability" at the forefront of its stated mission.[3] The authors of the report are Chester Finn, President of the Fordham Institute and Assistant Secretary of Education in the Reagan administration; Michael J. Petrilli, Vice President for National Programs & Policy of the Fordham Institute; and Liam Julian, Associate Writer and Editor, also of the Fordham Institute. Joanne Jacobs, author of the accompanying document ("It Takes a Vision"), is a freelance writer and blogger.

FINDINGS AND CONCLUSIONS OF THE REPORT

The main report reaches two primary conclusions, while the *It Takes a Vision* document offers a third:

1. Between 2000 (pre-NCLB) and 2006 there has been no overall progress in raising the quality of state content standards. While some have gotten better, this is offset by others getting worse. The average grade in 2000, C–, remained the average grade in 2006.
2. Students in states with better content standards do better on performance standards.
3. Effective leadership on the part of office holders, representatives of business, and academic experts, against often significant resistance, is required for states to develop good content standards.

RATIONALES SUPPORTING THE FINDINGS AND CONCLUSIONS

To support the first conclusion—that there has been no progress overall in raising the quality of content standards between 2000 and 2006—the report compares the average letter grade Fordham Institute experts gave in 2000 with the average letter grade its experts gave in subsequent years, ending in 2006.

To support the second conclusion—that students in states with better content standards do better on performance standards—the report identifies states that had made statistically significant gains in the percentage of students who attained proficiency in certain subject areas of National Assessment of Educational Progress (NAEP) and then relates this to the states' grades on the corresponding standards. Three examples are provided, one each from English/language arts, science, and mathematics.

To support the third conclusion—that effective leadership is required for states to develop good content standards—case studies are provided documenting the development of content standards in the three states that Fordham judges to have the best standards: California, Massachusetts, and Indiana.

THE REPORT'S USE OF RESEARCH LITERATURE

The Fordham Institute exhibits a strong commitment to the centrality of education standards, both in its mission statement and in the report under consideration (e.g., subject matter standards "are the foundation of standards-based reform, the dominant education policy strategy in America today"… and …"exert enormous influence over what actually happens inside the classroom" p. 6). By not including a meaningful discussion of the research literature, the report is able to simply assume that the "dominant education policy" is unproblematic. Research-based arguments on both sides question whether standards-based accountability regimes like NCLB improve student performance.[4] A rating or grading system like the one used in the report is necessarily based on a belief in a strong connection between the policy and an outcome goal that is believed to be beneficial.

REVIEW OF THE REPORT'S METHODS

The accompanying document by Joanne Jacobs employs a case-study methodology—an approach that, generally speaking, is both useful and defensible. However, the methodology that the report itself uses to support its conclusions is highly problematic.

States' grades were determined by raters who were deemed experts by the report's authors. How many raters were used and what their qualifications might be are not addressed in the report.

State standards are judged based on whether they are "clear, rigorous, and right-headed about content" (p. 6). A few slightly more specific subject area examples are provided from English, science, and history. The report does not specify the criteria that are employed, nor does it tell the reader what the various grades mean in terms of such criteria. The reader is instead referred to the individual evaluations for each state for more specificity. But the individual state reports don't offer much more information. Instead, they give the reader short descriptions of Fordham's summary judgments, but fail to provide specific criteria or even the state standards to which Fordham's judgments are applied.

A much more detailed description of the grading criteria—which presumably remained the same—can be found in *The State of State Standards 2000*.[5] Still, this earlier document provides little description or defense of the procedure by which the criteria were developed and validated. In the case of English grading criteria, for example, the reader is referred to a 1997 one-page document by Sandra Stotsky, which vaguely describes a procedure that makes unspecified use of outside reviewers (neglecting to mention who, how many, what they attended to, etc.) and which depends heavily on her individual judgments. The resulting standards.[6] include criteria such as English-only instruction in English/language arts and also "anti criteria," that is, things to be avoided, such as relating lived experiences to literature and addressing contemporary social issues. This means that Fordham's standards are quite at odds with those of authoritative groups such as the National Council of Teachers of English.[7] Although the value judgments embedded in standards like Stotsky's may accurately reflect the beliefs of Fordham's leadership, readers are ill-served when important information about the nature of its standards is hidden from view, as is the case with the report under review here.

In general, the report provides no evidence for the reliability of the grades—either that grades assigned by the same expert are consistent over time (test-retest reliability) or that different raters agree on grades assigned (inter-rater reliability). The grading process also apparently had no control for rater bias by insuring that raters were blind to information that might distort their judgments, for example, that a given state had done well or poorly on NAEP or that "progressives" or "postmodernists" were influential in determining the standards. In sum, no evidence is offered that the grades are valid measures of the quality of state content standards. Readers are asked simply to place blind trust in the overall conclusions reached by Fordham and its graders, supplemented by a few cursory statements in the state documents regarding strengths or weaknesses.

REVIEW OF THE VALIDITY OF THE FINDINGS AND CONCLUSIONS

Because of its methodological shortcomings regarding reliability and rater bias, the report's first conclusion, about how states' content standards have or have not changed, is poorly supported. Worse, there is no indication that the grades were in any way validated.

The report's second conclusion, that students in states with better content standards do better on performance standards, is even more poorly supported. The report acknowledges that "there is no simple relationship" between Fordham's grades and student performance. Indeed, the figure presented in the report, plotting fourth grade NAEP proficiency percentages against Fordham grades (p. 13), suggests not only that there is no "simple relationship" but that no relationship exists at all.

Yet the authors of the report find the evidence inconclusive and decide to keep looking for a relationship. They argue, in effect, that the straightforward comparison is wanting because it is based on only one moment in time. They thus offer an alternative: "what matters is whether any reform, including adoption of rigorous standards, leads to progress over time" (p. 13). Using this approach, the report presents three analyses of the data, based on states whose NAEP scores have improved over time. These alternative analyses aim to establish a positive relationship between Fordham's grades and state-level student performance. Below is a brief description and critique of each of these analyses.

Analysis 1, English/language Arts

Of 10 states that made statistically significant progress for at least one group in fourth-grade reading on NAEP between 1998 and 2005, 9 received at least a C from Fordham for their English/language arts standards.

Inspection of the data for the analysis (provided in the Table on p. 14) raises a number of questions. Of the 40 states (39 plus the District of Columbia; Iowa is not included) that failed to produce statistically significant gains, 33 had a grade of C or above; their average grade was 2.25. This compares with 9 of the 10 states that did make significant gains, which were given an average grade of 2.4. Any conclusion about a positive relationship between Fordham's grades and student performance drawn on the basis of these small quantitative differences is exceedingly dubious, particularly because the small number of states (only 10) that produced significant gains decreases the stability of the summary statistics associated with them.

Other observations further weaken Fordham's analysis. For example, California and Massachusetts, the two states with A grades among the 10 that produced significant gains in fourth-grade reading on NAEP, did so for only one of four relevant groups, the same number produced by Wyoming, with a grade of F. Of the four states that produced gains for the most student groups, three had C grades and one had a B grade.

Another—and better—way to compare Fordham's grades and student performance is to do so in terms of changes in each, that is, determine how improvements in Fordham grades between 2000 and 2006 are related to improvements in performance.[8] Indeed, this is more faithful to their own view, quoted above, that "what matters is whether any reform ... leads to progress over time" (p. 13). If content standards drive performance, then improvements in performance should reflect improvements in content standards. Although still burdened by all the validity questions concerning the assignment of state grades, this approach more directly addresses the key question and also uses data from all the states rather than those with significant gains in NAEP. The results of this form of analysis further diminish Fordham's case. Gains in Fordham grades do not correlate with gains in student performance. The 10 states that produced significant gains in fourth-grade reading on NAEP had a mean improvement in their Fordham English grade of 0.2; 3 of these states improved their grade, 2 got worse, and 5 stayed the same. The remaining 39 (Idaho and Iowa are excluded) that failed to produce significant gains on NAEP had a mean improvement in their Fordham English grade of 0.62 (over three times the improvement of the states that produced significant gains on CSAP); 20 states (51%) improved, eight (21%) got worse, and 10 (26%) stayed the same. States with lower grades showed greater improvement.

Analysis 2, Science

Of the five states that made statistically significant gains on the science NAEP between 2000 and 2005 in both fourth and eighth grade, three had A grades.

Less impressive is the fact that the two other states that made significant gains received a D and an F. Fordham's rating system seems to have "worked" for three out of five states—a little better than the 50% mark one would expect from random guessing.

Analysis 3, Mathematics

Four of six states that received "honors" grades from Fordham produced statistically significant gains in the percent of students proficient on the eighth-grade NAEP mathematics test between 2000 and 2005.

Why the reversal in the analysis strategy here? Why not an analysis parallel to examples 1 and 2 in which the starting point for the analysis is the identification of states that produced a statistically significant improvement on NAEP proficiency percentages? The apparent answer is that 23 states produced significant gains yet did not have content standards that were praised by Fordham. Using a consistent approach would have yielded answers inconsistent with the report's conclusions.

In summary, these three analyses were selectively mined from data gathered by Fordham—data which themselves are flawed and for which there is no evidence of validity. No rationale for Fordham's unorthodox and ad hoc analyses is provided, and those analyses are sorely lacking in methodological rigor. Indeed, the post-hoc massaging of the data reaches the point of absurdity, as the authors search for some approach to the data that might lend support to Fordham's conclusion that content standards of the kind it rates highly do in fact lead to improved student performance.

The case studies of California, Massachusetts, and Indiana provided by Jacobs are less problematic, but there is good reason to be cautious. While readers should not demand that Jacobs live up to an unattainable ideal of perfect objectivity, it is possible to go too far in the direction of subjectivity, which Jacobs does. The account she produces exhibits a marked bias in favor of Fordham's position on standards. It reads like a morality tale, in which sensible, hard-headed, altruistic "reformers" who support rigorous, precise, and clear standards are "tough, hand-to-hand combatants" engaging in the "good fight" against muddled, soft-headed, self-serving "progressives."

THE REPORT'S USEFULNESS FOR
GUIDANCE OF POLICY AND PRACTICE

Because there is no evidence supporting the validity of Fordham's grades, it would be unwise to base any decisions about policy or practice on them. It may very well be true that higher-quality content standards improve results on performance assessments. But the Fordham report fails to offer a valid and reliable grading system to judge content standards. It also fails to establish that its grades are associated with improved student performance.

Jacob's case studies have some potential utility for understanding the various dimensions of standard setting. But those case studies pale in comparison to the kind of understanding provided by more rigorous and scholarly treatments of the subject.[9]

NOTES AND REFERENCES

1.   Finn, C. D., Julian, L., & Petrilli, M. J. (2006) *The State of State Standards 2006*. Washington, DC: Thomas B. Fordham Institute. Retrieved January

26, 2010, from http://www.edexcellence.net
/doc/State%20of%20State%20Standards2006FINAL.pdf

2. Jacobs, J. (2006). *It takes a vision: How three states created great academic standards*. Washington, DC: Thomas B. Fordham Institute. Retrieved January 26, 2010, from http://www.edexcellence.net
/doc/It%20Takes%20a%20Vision.pdf

3. "Fordham Mission" (n.d.). Thomas B. Fordham Institute. Retrieved January 26, 2010, from http://www.edexcellence.net/index.cfm/fordham
-mission. Previously retrieved August 31, 2006, from http://www
.edexcellence.net/foundation/global/page.cfm?id=6

4. See, for example, Amrein, A. L. & Berliner, D. C. (2002, March 28). High-stakes testing, uncertainty, and student learning. *Education Policy Analysis Archives*, *10*(18). Retrieved August 30, 2006, from http://epaa.asu.edu/epaa/
v10n18/
Carnoy, M., & Loeb, S (2002). Does external accountability affect student outcomes: A cross-state analysis. *Educational Evaluation and Policy Analysis*, *24*(4), 305-331
Lee, J. (2006). *Tracking achievement gaps and assessing the impact of NCLB on the gaps: An in-depth look into national and state reading and math outcome trends*. Cambridge, MA: The Civil Rights Project at Harvard University;
Center on Education Policy (2006). *From the capital to the classroom: Year 4 of the No Child Left Behind Act*. Retrieved September 2, 2006, from http://
www.cep-dc.org/nclb/Year4/Press/

5. *The State of State Standards 2000*. Retrieved September 1, 2006, from http://
www.edexcellence.net/foundation/publication/publication.cfm?id=24

6. *The State of State Standards 2000*, pp. 129-130.

7. See *NCTE Standards*. Retrieved September 1, 2006, from http://
www.ncte.org/about/over/standards/110846.htm
Number 10 states: "Students whose first language is not English make use of their first language to develop competency in the English language arts and to develop understanding of content across the curriculum." Number 3 states: "Students apply a wide range of strategies to comprehend, interpret, evaluate, and appreciate texts. They draw on their prior experience...."

8. The 2000 English grades upon which this analysis depends are reported in *The State of State Standards*, p. 136. Retrieved September, 1 2006, from http://www.edexcellence.net/foundation/publication/
publication.cfm?id=24

9. See, for example, McDonnell, L. (2004). *Politics, persuasion, and educational testing*. Cambridge, MA: Harvard University Press.

CHAPTER 18

REPORT CARD ON AMERICAN EDUCATION

Gene V Glass

Review of Andrew T. LeFevre's "Report Card on American Education," published by the American Legislative Exchange Council. This is a modified version of a review originally published on January 8, 2007.

INTRODUCTION

The *Report Card on American Education,* published by the American Legislative Exchange Council,[1] attempts to touch all the bases in contemporary education policy: education finance, teacher preparation and compensation, tuition tax credits, charter schools, and vouchers. Little of importance escapes author Andrew T. LeFevre in this wide-ranging assessment of the nation's K-12 public education system. If the quality of the recommendations matched the report's ambitions, then policymakers might be wise to embark on the complete revolution in public education that would result from following them. Budgets would be slashed; public monies for educating children would go directly from the government to children's parents; private profit-making companies would provide the

Think Tank Research Quality: Lessons for Policy Makers, the Media, and the Public, pp. 249–259
Copyright © 2010 by Information Age Publishing

bulk of the nation's teaching; and the training, licensing, and pay of teachers would be revamped from top to bottom.

FINDINGS AND CONCLUSIONS OF THE REPORT

The findings are reported in the scant 11½ pages of text that are contained in this 143-page document; the other 132 pages list literally tens of thousands of bits of undigested data, mostly organized by state, all of which could be downloaded from the internet.

The *Report Card on American Education* makes the following five assertions (p. 3):

- In spite of increases in per-pupil expenditures greatly exceeding (by 77%) the rate of inflation since 1983, 71% of U.S. eighth graders "are still performing below proficiency" in mathematics, according to the National Assessment of Education Progress (NAEP); the report's author sees a "growing consensus that simply increasing spending on education is not enough to improve student performance;"

- There is no correlation—therefore presumably no causal link— between pupil-to-teacher ratios (commonly discussed in terms of class size) and educational achievement;

- There is no correlation between teachers' salaries and educational achievement;

- "Strong accountability measures" will help focus resources where they are most needed; and

- Parental choice—as evidenced in the charter school system—will benefit a child's educational future.

RATIONALES SUPPORTING THE FINDINGS AND CONCLUSIONS

LeFevre presents a great deal of data, but the vast majority of these data are not analyzed. He bases his findings and conclusions loosely on the more than 50 tables and figures containing tens of thousands of pieces of raw data. More than 100 measures of educational "inputs" and "outputs" are arrayed in dozens and dozens of tables. Fifty pages are devoted to profiles of individual states, with each state described in terms of "outputs" (SAT, ACT, and NAEP averages), "inputs" (per-pupil spending, pupil-teacher ratio, average teacher salary), and student demographics (White, Black, Hispanic, etc.).

The report's analysis leans heavily on an examination of the relationship of inputs and outputs in a composite measure of the author's own devising. To create a measure of educational achievement comparable across the 50 states and the District of Columbia, LeFevre formed an arithmetic composite based on NAEP (eighth grade math), SAT, and ACT test score averages for each state. A state's ranking on NAEP (1 highest, 51 lowest) was divided by 51 to produce a scaled score ranging from .02 to 1.00. For 26 states reporting SAT scores, the average scores were similarly scaled (the state that ranks #10, for instance, would receive a scaled score of 10/26 = .38). A similar calculation was made for the 25 states reporting ACT averages. The three constituents were summed and ranked to determine a final achievement ranking for each state. Massachusetts ranked highest; the District of Columbia ranked lowest.

Having arrayed these data points across all 51 states, the author proceeds to examine the "vital question" (p. 102) of the relationship between inputs and outputs by placing them

> side-by-side on four different tables. Looking at these tables gives an idea of possible correlations between educational inputs and outputs. For example, if a state spends a relatively large amount of money per pupil and has a relatively high average SAT score, then it may be the case that spending large amounts of money leads to higher SAT scores. (p. 102)

These data displays cry out for formal, precise statistical analyses of the co-relationships between the scores and the expenditures, rather than just an eye-balling of 51 separate pairs of numbers. Such statistical analyses would also allow researchers who are familiar with these relationships to compare these findings with existing research findings. The report's author, a recipient of a BA in political science from Temple University with apparently no formal training in statistics, is using methodology that is a century out of date. It is as if Karl Pearson (1857-1936) had never lived to invent the correlation coefficient.

As discussed below, the author also reports "two standard regression tests" in an appendix to "account for the possibility that several educational inputs are important to student achievement" (pp. 102-3). These models, too, have serious flaws.

THE REPORT'S USE OF RESEARCH LITERATURE

The *Report Card on American Education* fails to take advantage of the voluminous research literature on precisely the topics it regards as most important. In fact, it ignores, intentionally or unintentionally, the many studies that flatly contradict its findings and conclusions. Its bibliography lists only the sources of the myriad tabulations of raw data; no research studies are cited. Particularly for a report with such sweeping, far-reaching recommendations, this oversight is indefensible.

Relationship between Spending and Student Performance

Research on the relationship between education expenditures and achievement is decades old. Although truly experimental research is lacking, sophisticated statistical analytic methods have superseded the type of simple correlation studies presented in this report. Moreover, aggregation of study findings by meta-analysis has moved the debate off of simplistic questions such as "Are expenditures related to student achievement?" Those researchers without a rigid agenda have formed a consensus around the work of Greenwald, Hedges, and Laine,[2] who concluded that "a broad range of resources were positively related to student outcomes, with effect sizes large enough to suggest that moderate increases in spending may be associated with significant increases in achievement" (p. 361).

As discussed below, Greenwald and his colleagues also stressed the importance of limiting analyses of these relationships to the school-district level, arguing that aggregating data at higher levels can lead to inaccurate conclusions. The *Report Card on American Education*, by using state-level analyses, runs afoul of this advice.

Class Size

LeFevre examines the class size issue by reporting pupil-to-teacher ratios in apparent innocence of nearly a century of experimental and quasi-experimental research on class size and achievement,[3] as well as the exemplary and widely heralded Tennessee STAR experiment that conclusively demonstrated the benefit of reducing class size.[4]

Teacher Quality and Salary

The report ventures into the domain of teacher quality when it claims that teacher salaries are unrelated to educational "outputs," and ipso facto that such markers of higher salaries as certification and experience have no benefits in terms of achievement. Were this the case, it would be some comfort to charter school operators who typically hire uncertified and inexperienced personnel and pay them at lower rates than traditional public school teachers. But the report's claim lacks support and is inconsistent with other research.[5]

Any policy analyst who writes for a lay audience appreciates the need to hold in check the scholarly enthusiasm for citations to the research literature. But to ignore widely accepted findings from peer-reviewed literature marks a work as political polemic rather than a policy analysis.

REVIEW OF THE REPORT'S METHODS

Measurement Methods

LeFevre's devising of a measure of educational "output" represents the only derived measure in the report. Essentially, the author calculated an arithmetic average of each state's percentile rank on average NAEP eighth grade math, SAT, and ACT scores. The resulting measure of achievement bears only a very weak relationship to the results of school teaching and learning. It essentially gives equal weight to the NAEP, which is a legitimate measure of achievement, and the SAT and ACT, which are measures of aptitude specifically designed not to be greatly influenced by schooling experience.[6] Varying participation rates make state-level SAT and ACT averages virtually useless even as measures of scholastic aptitude—and certainly as measures of achievement levels.[7] Test validity aside, the transformation of state averages into percentile ranks induces curvilinearity into any possible relationships among variables, rendering them inappropriate for correlation and regression analysis.

The other, nonderived measures are merely data downloaded from various government websites. Per-pupil expenditure data are taken from the U.S. Department of Education, National Center for Education Statistics, and Common Core of Data Surveys. As such, they reflect all expenditures in a state, including administrative and support personnel, and are poor proxies for the resources spent on classroom instruction. More careful research shows that only a small portion of increased spending has gone to regular education—to the sorts of programs that are likely to show up in test scores. For example, Rothstein and Miles (1995) studied expenditures in nine typical U.S. school districts and found that

> the share of expenditures going to regular education dropped from 80% to 59% between 1967 and 1991, while the share going to special education climbed from 4% to 17%.... Per pupil expenditures for regular education grew by only 28% during this quarter century—an average annual rate of about 1%.[8]

In addition to special education, the new money has been focused on such items as dropout prevention, transportation, health insurance, school lunch programs, and security.

Since one of the *Report Card*'s main contentions is that expenditures have risen historically while achievement "outputs" have not—a contention like others in the report that is unsupported by the report's own data and proven false by other sources of information—it would have been advisable for the author to at least attempt to determine the portion of expenditures spent on teaching.

Analysis Methods

Granted, many members of a lay audience might have some difficulty with even middle-level statistical analyses, but the *Report Card on American Education* eschews even the simplest displays and calculations that would support or fail to support its points. Indeed, the predominant method of analysis might be called "juxtaposition," where numbers coming from variables purportedly related are listed side-by-side. Are expenditures and achievement correlated? Well, look at the numbers side-by-side, the report invites the reader. Of course, correlations often cannot be seen even by experienced researchers scanning columns of side-by-side numbers. So LeFevre extracts a couple of examples: "Of the ten states that increased their per pupil expenditures the most over the past two decades, ... only New Hampshire (3rd) and Vermont (5th) ranked in the top ten in academic achievement" (p. 4). Such examples are offered to demonstrate a missing correlation, but in truth these facts are not inconsistent with a positive relationship between per-pupil expenditures and achievement.

REVIEW OF THE VALIDITY OF THE FINDINGS AND CONCLUSIONS

Relationship Between Spending and Student Performance

The *Report Card* states that in spite of increases in per-pupil expenditures exceeding the rate of inflation by 77% since 1983, 71% of U.S. eighth graders "are still performing below proficiency" (p. 3) in mathematics, according to the National Assessment of Education Progress (NAEP). The report thus concludes that increasing costs of education are somehow associated with poor performance, or that increases over the past two decades should have produced a greater percentage of "proficient" students. This correlation rests on a single data point that is itself an impossibility, since we have no data on the math proficiency rate in 1983 and thus no knowledge of the level of improvement. Moreover, the statement relies heavily on the validity of the NAEP performance levels, which label students as "proficient," "advanced," or "basic." Unfortunately for this report's conclusions, the validity of the NAEP performance levels has been authoritatively condemned, both by scholars and by the federal General Accounting Office.[9] (NAEP has resisted to this day any fundamental changes in its flawed methods of establishing performance levels.) It is therefore impossible to attach any significance at all to the juxtaposition of NAEP levels and spending.

The Report Card's author assumes that increasing per-pupil expenditures should produce greater academic achievement. As noted earlier, no attempt was made by this same author to track whether those increasing dollars are actually spent on regular instruction of students. In fact, past studies that have gone to the trouble of tracing these dollars have reached very different conclusions. With the federal and state governments imposing increasingly onerous unfunded burdens over the last 2 decades—including recent requirements concerning student tracking and reporting—most of the increase in expenditures appears to never reach the classroom, certainly not in ways likely to directly increase a school's average test scores. This does not mean that expenses for dropout prevention, special education, or health insurance are unnecessary or not useful—only that a simple comparison of average spending with average test scores is not well-designed to detect such usefulness.

The Report Card's most important conclusion concerns dollar "inputs" and achievement "outputs":

> The first conclusion of these [regression analyses] is that differences in educational inputs ... (students per school, schools per district, student to teacher ratios, per-pupil expenditures, teacher salaries, and funds received from the federal government) taken together do not explain differences in student achievement. (p. 103)

This conclusion is based on two regression analyses. In the first, LeFevre's measure of educational achievement (a conglomerate of NAEP and aptitude scores) is predicted from per-pupil expenditures, among other things. The second analysis regressed changes in SAT state averages between two dates 1983-84 and 2003-04 onto changes in per-pupil expenditures between those same dates, plus other variables. (As a side note, it appears that a log transformation was applied to some of these variables before analysis, but no rationale is given. Readers are expected to trust, but not verify, the author's modeling and conclusions.) Of all the possible analyses that could have been performed, only these two have been reported. No rationale is given for selecting only these to report. Yet one can hardly accuse the author of "cherry-picking" favorable results since his results bear no apparent relationship to any conclusion.

The second regression analysis is particularly egregious. Not only are SAT averages scarcely reflective of educational attainment, they are seriously confounded by self-selection. Most of the variability in state SAT averages is due to the percentages of students electing to take the SAT exam instead of the ACT test or no test at all. Further, as a larger portion of the U.S. population considers attending college, the tests are taken by an increasingly nonelite slice of the high school population. What might be considered a success by public school educators (pushing more students to consider college) is transformed by this analysis into something that looks like a failure (lower average test scores). This analysis is largely meaningless, and even its meaningless results seem to bear no direct link to any of LeFevre's conclusions.

Not reported among the results—which led LeFevre to conclude that these inputs "do not explain differences in student achievement"—is the fact that his "per pupil expenditures" do in fact correlate at +.41 with NAEP eighth grade math state averages.[10] Correlations of this magnitude generally constitute substantial evidence of a relationship between inputs and outputs.

Teacher Quality and Salary

The *Report Card* concludes that there is no correlation between teachers' salaries and educational achievement (p. 3). Yet the data presented in the report itself could have been used to show a +.20 correlation between average teacher salary (by state) with NAEP eighth grade math average score.[11]

State-Level NAEP Data

But set aside for a moment the fact that the conclusions of the report are inconsistent with its own data. Even the use of such data is ill-advised. Ironically, the *Report Card* appeared within days of the call for a moratorium on the use of state-level aggregate NAEP data by the editor of *Education Policy Analysis Archives*, a leading, peer-reviewed scholarly journal.[12] Editor Sherman Dorn noted that NAEP data have been publicly available for some time at the level of individuals. Analyzing NAEP data aggregated to the level of states is to commit what is known in research methodology as the "ecological correlation" fallacy.[13]

For instance, imagine that Wyoming experiences an increase of $X per pupil while achievement averages a decline of Y points. From this small amount of information, it cannot be concluded that those students whose scores declined were the recipients of the increased funding. It is entirely possible that those particular schools receiving the increased funding showed gains in achievement while their influence on the state average was offset by decreases in the other schools for different reasons. Negative correlations of aggregate data points are not inconsistent with positive causal relationships at the level of the constituent data. Greenwald, Hedges and Laine made this point in their 1996 review of research on school resources and achievement.[14]

Parental Choice

LeFevre concludes that parental choice—such as that seen in the charter school system—will benefit a child's educational future (p. 3). In Chapter Four of the *Report Card*, data on charter school enrollments are tabulated, documenting a rapid increase in the numbers of schools and students. No attempt is made to relate charter school attendance to achievement or even to cite collateral research that might support a claim of superiority for charter schools. In language that would be appropriate if uttered from a politician's soapbox but not in legitimate reports of research, author LeFevre concludes:

> As more and more parents see that they can—and should—have a choice in their child's education, it causes more and more leaks in the dam that has been holding back real educational reform. And soon, the educational establishment will run out of fingers to plug those leaks and then the flood of educational reform and school choice will finally be free to flow all across this great nation—bringing liberation to many that have struggled far too long to escape from an educational system that has failed them all too often. (p. 131)

Choice and a glorious new day for American education become linked again by the mere fact of being juxtaposed in the same paragraph.

THE REPORT'S USEFULNESS FOR GUIDANCE OF POLICY AND PRACTICE

In spite of being clad with myriad numbers and statistics, the *Report Card on American Education* is rhetoric, not research. Legislators may find value in looking up education statistics for their own state and comparing them with other states. But they will find neither credible findings nor any firmly established facts on which to base policy decisions.

NOTES AND REFERENCES

1. LeFevre, A. T. (2006, November). *Report card on American education: A state-by-state analysis, 1982-1983 to 2004-2005*. Washington, DC: American Legislative Exchange Council.
2. Greenwald, R., Hedges, L. V., & Laine, R. D. (1996). The effect of school resources on student achievement. *Review of Educational Research, 66*(3), 361-96.
3. Among others see Glass, G. V, Cahen, L. S., Smith, M. L., & Filby, N. N. (1982). *School class size: Research and policy*. Beverly Hills, CA: SAGE.
    Finn, J. D. (2002). Class size reduction in Grades K-3. In A. Molnar (Ed.), *School reform proposals: The research evidence* (pp. 27-48). Greenwich, CT: Information Age Publishing.
4. Mosteller, F. (1995). The Tennessee study of class size in the early school grades. *The Future of Children 5*(2), 113-127.
5. Darling-Hammond, L. (2000). Teacher quality and student achievement: A review of state policy evidence. *Education Policy Analysis Archives, 8*(1). Retrieved January 2, 2007 from http://epaa.asu.edu/epaa/v8n1/. Darling-Hammond writes: "Quantitative analyses indicate that measures of teacher preparation and certification are by far the strongest correlates of student achievement in reading and mathematics, both before and after controlling for student poverty and language status."
6. The SAT acronym originally stood for Scholastic Aptitude Test, but aptitude having fallen out of favor in the last several decades, the College Board now gives no explanation of the acronym at all. Since 1995, the College Board refers to the old aptitude section as a "reasoning test."
7. See Wainer, H. (1986). Five pitfalls encountered while trying to compare states on their SAT scores. *Journal of Educational Measurement, 23*(1), 69-81. Fetler, M. E. (1991). Pitfalls of using SAT results to compare schools. *American Educational Research Journal, 28*(2), 481-491.
8. Richard R., & Miles, K. H. (1995). *Where's the money gone?* Washington, DC: Economic Policy Institute, p. 1.
9. A General Accounting Office review of the NAEP proficiency levels was prompted by a report of a small group of scholars who labeled the National Assessment Governing Board (NAGB)—the body that sets the proficiency levels—as "incompetent" and the levels themselves as "ridiculous." The GAO review concluded: "NAGB's ... approach was inherently flawed, both conceptually and procedurally, ... the approach [should] not be used further until a thorough review could be completed.... These weaknesses are not trivial; reliance on NAGB's results could have serious consequences" (p. 38, U.S. General Accounting Office [GAO]. (1993). *Educational Achievement*

Standards. NAGB's Approach Yields Misleading Interpretations. GAO/PEMD 93-12. Washington, DC: Author.

10.   From this reviewer's own calculations extracting data from the report's Table 1.7, p. 72 and Table 2.1A, p. 88; District of Columbia was eliminated from the calculations because it is a 3.7 standard deviation outlier on the NAEP variable.

11.   From this reviewer's own calculations extracting data from the report's Table 1.10A, p. 76 and Table 2.1A, p. 88. Again District of Columbia data are eliminated because it is a 3.7 standard deviation outlier on the NAEP variable.

12.   Dorn, S. (2006). No more aggregate NAEP studies? *Education Policy Analysis Archives, 14*(31). Retrieved January 2, 2007 from http://epaa.asu.edu/epaa/v14n31/

13.   Robinson, W. S. (1950). Ecological correlations and the behavior of individuals. *American Sociological Review, 15*, 351-57.

14.   Greenwald, Hedges & Laine (1996); see note No. 2.

PART 9

Preschool

As research literature demonstrating individual and social benefits of early childhood education has grown, so has national interest in expanding early learning opportunities for children. Such an expansion has been supported by President Obama.[1] In addition, several states have taken steps in this direction.[2] But efforts vary widely. Approximately 90% of Oklahoma 4-year-olds receive a free public education; other states have rates near 10%.[3] Some spend as much as $10,000 per child, others spend less than $2,500 or have essentially no program at all. In the face of such disparity, there has been growing interest in formulating federal policy to support early childhood education. What that policy should look like has been the source of much debate, especially concerning whether pre-K programs should be universal (UPK) or targeted only to disadvantaged children.

In Chapter 19, Steven Barnett reviews a report that weighed in on this issue: the Lexington Institute's *How Sound an Investment? An Analysis of Federal Prekindergarten Proposals* (2008), authored by Robert Holland and Don Soifer. The report asserted that UPK proponents have ignored research indicating that pre-K education can have negative effects on behavior and that it does not benefit all children. It also concluded that a universal program would be unnecessarily expensive, would drive private

Think Tank Research Quality: Lessons for Policy Makers, the Media, and the Public, pp. 261–263
Copyright © 2010 by Information Age Publishing
All rights of reproduction in any form reserved.

child care providers out of business, would limit parents' options, and would likely harm the social development of many children. Further, the study challenged the need for pre-K teachers to hold bachelor's degrees, as some suggested policies have proposed. The report recommended instead that federal policy target children in poverty and either offer their families vouchers to purchase private early childhood services or offer businesses tax credits.

Barnett's review states that the report "sets up a false dichotomy [between private and public] for policymakers and voters" and "presents inaccurate information about current pre-K programs and the research into their effects." While the report suggested that existing proposals would exclude private providers, Barnett points out that all four bills included in the report's own Appendix either allowed or encouraged them to participate in expanded programs—and two mandated that 25% of funding go to private providers. Rather than limiting parental choice, the reviewer finds that expanding pre-K opportunities would likely to increase it. Barnett also criticizes the report's assumptions that universal proposals preclude a focus on poor children or require 100% funding for all children. In fact, most proposals include an emphasis on disadvantaged populations, and they could include a sliding fee scale.

Most significantly, Barnett identifies important information that was omitted from the report but that would have refuted the report's assertions. He finds that the Lexington report ignored research on how UPK impacts children's learning and how its benefits compare to those of targeted programs. As a result, Barnett finds that the report's finding in favor of targeted programs "is not supported by the evidence presented." The reviewer's overall assessment is that rather than clarifying issues in an important policy area "ripe for change," the report instead "manages to muddy the waters and obstruct reasoned discussion."

Barnett's review of a related proposal, available from www.thinktankreview.org, is summarized below.

- The Reason Foundation's 2006 *Assessing Proposals for Preschool and Kindergarten: Essential Information for Parents, Taxpayers and Policymakers*, authored by Darcy Olsen and Lisa Snell, used a selective review of early childhood studies to argue against both UPK and all-day kindergarten. Asserting that such programs have no lasting educational effects, the report found public investment in them unnecessary and recommended vouchers instead. Barnett found that the report employed inconsistent use of standards for research quality and selective citation of research. The reviewer concluded that the report's policy recommendations did "not relate well to the literature reviewed or to the authors' findings."

NOTES AND REFERENCES

1. E.g., "We will invest in early childhood education, by dramatically expanding Head Start and other programs to ensure that all of our young children are ready to enter kindergarten" (http://www.barackobama.com/issues/education/)
2. Barnett, W. S., Epstein, D. J., Friedman, A. H., Boyd, J. S., & Hustedt, J. T. (2008). *The state of preschool: 2008 State Preschool Yearbook*. New Brunswick, NJ: National Institute for Early Education Research, Rutgers University.
3. Barnett, Epstein, Friedman, Boyd, & Hustedt (2008).

CHAPTER 19

SOUND AN INVESTMENT

An Analysis of
Federal Prekindergarten Proposals

W. Steven Barnett

*Review of "How Sound an Investment? An Analysis of Federal Prekindergarten Pro-
posals," by Robert Holland and Don Soifer, and published by the Lexington Institute.
This is a modified version of a review originally published on March 24, 2008.*

INTRODUCTION

There is a growing national movement to provide more early learning
opportunities for children. State investments in the education of young
children have increased rapidly in recent years, coinciding with increasing
evidence of the broad individual and societal benefits of early childhood
education.[1] However, substantial disparities have emerged among states
in enrollment rates, program standards, and funding levels. For example,
three states serve more than 40% of their 4-year-olds, while 12 have no
pre-K program at all. Spending varies from more than $10,000 per child
to less than $2,500. Some states have no class size or ratio limits at all.[2]

*Think Tank Research Quality: Lessons for Policy Makers, the Media, and
the Public,* pp. 265–275
Copyright © 2010 by Information Age Publishing

These disparities have spurred proposals for a federal role in preschool education beyond Head Start, particularly support for universal prekindergarten (UPK), to ensure adequate funding, higher standards, and wider access. The issue of what the federal government might do to improve matters has been taken up by presidential candidates and among members of Congress. The new Lexington Institute report, *How Sound an Investment? Analysis of Federal Prekindergarten Proposals*,"[3] seeks to inform public debate regarding proposals. However, its data and analysis are incomplete and biased.

FINDINGS AND CONCLUSIONS OF THE REPORT

The report suggests that proponents of universal preschool education fail to consider all of the relevant evidence, particularly research indicating negative effects on behavior and that all children do not benefit from pre-K. It also raises questions about the cost and educational effectiveness of requiring a bachelor's degree to teach pre K.

It concludes that a government-run preschool program for all children would be unnecessarily expensive and would provide little benefit to most children. In addition, such a program "would drive many private child care providers out of business, drastically decrease options for parents, and, ultimately, likely impair the social development of many children" (p. 14). The report instead urges policymakers to consider either giving tax credits to businesses or giving vouchers to low-income families to purchase private early childhood care and education.

RATIONALES SUPPORTING FINDINGS AND CONCLUSIONS OF THE REPORT

In its overview of the national context and support for preschool programs, the Lexington Institute report cites position statements from the National Education Association (NEA), a Congressional Joint Economic Committee report, and statements from Democratic and Republican presidential candidates. Except for the Republican candidates, all of these groups and individuals express support for ensuring that all children have access to quality preschool education. The Republican candidates are instead described as advocating parental choice in schooling. Four current legislative initiatives for new federal early childhood policies are summarized in the report's appendix. However, as discussed below, careful scrutiny of these proposals suggests a disconnect between the Lexington Institute's characterization of policy proposals and what is actually being proposed.

The report briefly discusses research on four issues: the costs and benefits of universal versus targeted programs; negative effects from pre-K on behavior; pre-K teacher qualifications and classroom quality; and public support for private preschool education programs rather than ones in the public schools.

The Lexington Institute report cites two studies that find a negative association between participation in preschool programs and later classroom behavior.[4] In addition, it cites a study that finds expulsion rates for preschoolers in state pre-K programs to be several times higher than expulsion rates in K-12.[5] The report uses these findings to raise questions about whether preschool education pressures young children excessively. The report relies on the expulsion rate study to suggest that preschool programs may cause the behavior problems that result in expulsions from pre-K.

The report attempts to make its case for not requiring pre-K teachers to have a college degree by pointing to two additional studies. The first did not find an association between children's academic gains in state pre-K classrooms and the quality of teachers and classrooms.[6] Holland and Soifer report that that study concludes that a bachelor's degree "may not be sufficient to ensure quality in every classroom" (p. 8). The other study found that the quality of parenting was more strongly associated with children's development through Grade 6 than was the quality of child care, thus suggesting (in the view of the Lexington authors) that additional requirements for pre-K teachers would be of limited benefit.[7] The Lexington report then criticizes several current proposals that would require that increased qualification requirements be phased in over time in order to receive federal funding for preschool education. The authors dismiss these requirements as unnecessary.

The writings of the economist James Heckman are cited in support of the view that preschool should be subsidized only for poor and at-risk children—rather than for all children—and that vouchers are the best means of providing this subsidy. Heckman indicates that the largest economic benefits accrue from serving children in poverty because they have the worst developmental outcomes and their families have the least capacity to invest in their development.[8] In addition, the Perry Preschool study[9] is identified as a "prime basis for assertions of enormous social and economic benefits" from preschool (p. 10). The report points out that the Perry Preschool sample was highly disadvantaged and that it would be inappropriate to assume from this study that preschool benefits all children.

A Reason Foundation report is then cited as evidence that public preschool education for all would not produce the educational and economic benefits that advocates promise.[10] The Reason report speculates that benefits of the Perry Preschool program were primarily due to its home-visitation component. This speculation is linked to the finding that parenting has stronger impacts on child development than do preschool programs. The Reason Foundation report also finds that Oklahoma and Georgia (2 states with UPK) were among the bottom 10 states for percentage-point changes in fourth-grade reading scores between 1992 and 2005 on the National Assessment of Educational Progress (NAEP). This is presented as evidence that UPK did not improve elementary school education outcomes.

The Lexington report's concluding argument, in favor of "choice," emphasizes the size of the existing private child care sector and that sector's advantages to parents. The private sector is said to have excess capacity that could offer access at lower cost, and it is stated that universal preschool education would displace private providers. Choice also is advocated on the grounds that parents' needs and wants vary depending on length of day (part- or full-day), schedule (some parents work night or swing shifts), and preference for religious providers.

Exercising choice through vouchers, the report argues, would increase parents' engagement in general, which has other positive benefits for children's learning. The report cites a study that describes Georgia pre-K as voucher-like and as offering parents more choices than if pre-K were available only in public schools.[11] This study found Georgia pre-K to produce the same educational results as Head Start but at a lower cost. The report also cites a newspaper article that describes the success of New Jersey's "targeted pre-K voucher program" in improving children's learning (p. 13).

THE REPORT'S USE OF RESEARCH LITERATURE

The report cites two longitudinal studies as evidence that pre-K increases behavior problems. These studies, however, concerned children who primarily attended private programs with minimal standards and public oversight. As correlational studies, the authors could not rule out the plausible alternative hypothesis that children more prone to behavior problems are more often enrolled in the preschool programs—something not mentioned in the Lexington report. The report also fails to indicate that the observed negative effects are modest (effect size less than .20), which limits their value in making policy decisions.[12] More importantly, the report fails to mention national randomized trials of Head Start and

Early Head Start which found that these programs *reduced* behavior problems.[13] This flatly contradicts the findings of one of the correlational
studies that Head Start produced negative effects on behavior, and it casts
doubt on the validity of the nonexperimental approach to estimating
these effects.[14] Finally, the report neglects the randomized trials and
other rigorous studies that have found that high-quality preschool education reduced later delinquency and crime.[15]

The Lexington report does, however, acknowledge that the study the
authors cite for the lack of a link between a bachelor's degree and preschool teacher "credentials" and education quality is contradicted by
much of the other research on this topic. What the report does not mention are the limitations of this and other education "production" studies,
and it omits findings that counter the authors' views. For example, the
study that they cite as evidence of their assertion also found that the bachelor's degree was associated with higher achievement in math and further
found education and credentials to be associated with several other measures of teaching quality and children's test scores.[16] Another important
omission that detracts from their argument is that only programs with
highly educated teachers who are paid public school salaries and benefits
have been found to produce the large gains in achievement and school
success cited by the proponents of UPK.[17]

Also troubling is the authors' overreliance on James Heckman's view
that new investments in early education should focus on disadvantaged
children—a view based on his belief that impacts and rates of return are
highest for these children. However, Heckman acknowledges that he lacks
hard evidence to support his view. Other economists do agree that the
rate of return is higher for disadvantaged children, but they argue that
the larger total net benefits from including all children in public early
education initiatives favor universal programs over targeted programs.[18]
The analyses of these other economists, which demonstrate that a universal program can be a more economically efficient policy, are not acknowledged.

The report's conclusion that preschool programs should focus
exclusively on disadvantaged children is also grounded in the contention
that the research support for preschool is dependent upon one particular
study: the Perry Preschool study. However, that study is not the only
research on the effects and economic benefits of preschool education that
informs pre-K policy proposals. This other research, including studies of
the effects of UPK, is essentially ignored by the report, and the citations
pulled from the Reason Foundation report are misleading at best.[19]
(Again, the Reason report speculates that the positive effects should be
primarily attributed to the home visitation component of the Perry
program.) The Perry Preschool program did include a home visiting

component, but since the Perry study found no effect on parenting practices, changes in parent education as a result of home visits is not a plausible mechanism for program effects.[20]

The finding derived from the Reason Foundation report on poor NAEP scores in states with UPK is similarly flawed. Reason's choice of 1992 as a starting point (many years prior to UPK), its use of aggregate NAEP scores, and its focus on reading scores appear to be careful choices made to support a desired conclusion.[21] In contrast, a comparison of scores for Whites, Blacks, and Hispanics separately (because the population's ethnic composition changes over time) a few years before UPK and in 2005 reveals that NAEP scores rose in Georgia for reading and math, as they did in Oklahoma, with the exception of reading for Whites.[22]

Finally, the evidence provided about choice in pre-K is incomplete and inaccurate. The report describes Georgia's pre-K policy as voucher-like and as offering parents more choices than if pre-K was only offered in public schools. This is true, but it does not mean that Georgia parents would not want more public school pre-K programs than they have access to currently.[23] The report does not present any rigorous evidence on the quality and effectiveness of actual voucher or voucher-like programs. Florida's UPK program is a true voucher program with minimal standards, but it is not discussed in the report with respect to either its effects on parent choice or its educational quality and effectiveness.

The report suggests that New Jersey has a targeted pre-K voucher program that has led to improved student learning. However, New Jersey's program is not a targeted voucher program. It is universal in the 31 school districts with high percentages of children from low-income families. Although most providers are private, school districts deliver the program through contracts with private providers as well as through public school programs. Both the public schools and the private providers are responsible for program quality and effectiveness.[24]

The report also incorrectly suggests that Head Start providers are public programs; in fact, most are private.[25]

REVIEW OF THE VALIDITY OF THE FINDINGS AND CONCLUSIONS

The Lexington Institute report describes a dichotomous policy debate between proponents of UPK offered through public schools and supporters of targeted programs that would provide children in poverty increased access to private programs. This oversimplifies the debate and does not accurately represent most policy proposals, which stress serving the most disadvantaged children first and include the participation of private programs. In addition, the report uses language to introduce subtle biases.

For example, the report contrasts "government day care" with "vouchers that they can redeem for early childhood education services from the private or public provider of their choice" (pp. 10, 13)

The report frames the issue by leading with the NEA position statement, which is the only proposal this author is aware of that would in fact limit public funding for pre-K to the public schools. It is also the only one to suggest mandatory kindergarten, which is not a feature of any of the proposed pre-K plans. By contrast, all four bills in the report's Appendix permit or encourage private providers to participate. Two, including Sen. Hillary Clinton's bill, specify that at least 25% of the funds must go to private providers[26] (a feature the report omits from its description of the bill). Similarly, the Early Childhood Investment Act sponsored by Sen. Chris Dodd and Rep. Rose DeLauro would provide funds through the Department of Health and Human Services to state public-private partnerships that would help finance a broad array of public and private programs.

Two key assertions in the report—that UPK proposals fail to consider all the evidence on impacts and that UPK is ineffective—are not adequately supported and are contradicted by information omitted from the report, which ignores rigorous studies of the impacts of UPK on children's learning and analyses that compare projected benefits for universal programs and targeted ones. The report's conclusion that targeted programs should be preferred over universal programs is not supported by the evidence presented. Moreover, the debate is more complex than the report indicates, and much of the rationale for UPK is unexamined, including three crucial claims: that parents are reluctant to participate in a program restricted to the poor; that positive peer effects have been found for at-risk children in UPK; and that a program that is offered for all children will have greater public support for quality.[27]

The reality is that most proposals are more nuanced than the report suggests. Prominent legislative proposals and those of the 2008 Democratic presidential candidates include private providers and could expand parental choice. The report's conclusion that private providers will be driven out of business is not based on data or on proposed legislation; rather, it appears to be based only on the unwarranted premise that public UPK would exclusively be in the public schools. Also, most of the proposals emphasize serving disadvantaged populations first and foremost, as James Heckman recommends. The proposals do not expressly call for 100% public funding for all children regardless of income. Ensuring all children access to quality early education might be done with sliding fee scales that might provide no subsidy at some income levels.

The report's discussion of presidential candidates' proposals is also somewhat misleading. The focus is on choice, with Republican proposals getting higher marks. But the Republican proposals entail an increase in parental choice for pre-K only in so far as their proposals for increased choice in the public schools would apply to existing pre-K. None of the major Republican candidates proposed expanded access to pre-K, either public or private. The Democratic candidates' proposals to expand choice through public funding include public and private organizations, with minimum levels of participation by the private sector. Moreover, when states have implemented similar proposals, actual levels of private provision have been higher. Accordingly, even by the standards set up by the Lexington report, the Democratic proposals may result in more choice.

In addition to potentially providing more choice, UPK proposals might be more effective and economically efficient. New Jersey's program—which is favorably cited in the report—has been found to produce strong positive effects using mostly private providers in a system that combines elements of parental choice with high standards and oversight by the public schools.[28]

Effective choice requires that vouchers provide enough funds that low-income families can purchase a quality education. The report does not discuss this concern or mention that Florida's pre-K voucher was less than $2,200 per child in 2005-06, which limited choice substantially.[29] It also does not fully discuss the research indicating that vouchers would not lead to large gains in children's achievement, though vouchers might better accommodate child care needs and preferences for provider religious affiliation.[30]

USEFULNESS OF THE REPORT FOR GUIDANCE OF POLICY AND PRACTICE

The report presents itself as a fair and balanced analysis of the potential value of federal involvement in pre-K, but it is misleading with respect to both the content and the likely consequences of the proposals currently being debated in Congress and among presidential candidates. The report presents inaccurate information about current public pre-K programs and the research into their effects. Although it provides some useful cautions to policymakers, it exaggerates risks in comparison to the potential benefits of pre-K.

The report also sets up a false dichotomy for policymakers and voters: UPK exclusively in public schools *or* targeted programs that provide increased access to private pre-K programs for children in poverty. The report's discussion omits much of the relevant research and many of the analyses on program effectiveness and the relative merits of targeted and universal approaches to preschool education—information that could have provided for a much more nuanced and thoughtful policy discussion. Rather than capitalizing on an opportunity to clarify an area of policy that is ripe for change, the report manages to muddy the waters and obstruct reasoned discussion of approaches for improving opportunities for many of the nation's children.

NOTES AND REFERENCES

1. Barnett, W. S., Hustedt, J. T., Friedman, A., Boyd, J., & Ainsworth, P. (2007). *The state of preschool 2007*. New Brunswick, NJ: National Institute for Early Education Research, Rutgers University.
2. Barnett, Hustedt, Friedman, Boyd, & Ainsworth (2007).
3. Holland, R., & Soifer, D. (2008, March). *How sound an investment? An analysis of federal prekindergarten proposals*. Arlington, VA: Lexington Institute
4. Magnuson, K. A., Ruhm, C., & Waldfogel, J. (2007). Does prekindegarten improve school preparation and performance? *Economics of Education Review, 26*(1), 33-51.
    Holland and Soifer cite an earlier draft working paper of Belsky, J., Vandell, D., Burchinal, M., Clarke-Stewart, A., McCartney, K., Owen, M., & the NICHD ECCRN. (2007). Are there long-term effects of early child care? *Child Development, 78*(2), 681-701.
5. Gilliam, W. (2005, May). Prekindergarteners left behind: Expulsion rates in state prekindergarten programs. *FCD Policy Brief Series, 3*. New York, NY: Foundation for Child Development.
6. Early, D. M., Bryant, D. M., Pianta, R. C., Clifford, R. M., Burchinal, M. R., Ritchie, S., Howes, C., & Barbarin, O. (2007). Are teachers' education, major, and credentials related to classroom quality and children's academic gains in preKindergarten? *Early Childhood Research Quarterly, 21*(2), 174-195.
7. Belsky, Vandell, Burchinal, Clarke-Stewart, McCartney, Owen, & the NICHD ECCRN (2007); see note 4.
8. Heckman, J. (2005, June). Interview with James J. Heckman. *The Region*. Minneapolis: Federal Reserve Bank of Minneapolis. Retrieved March 16, 2008, from http://www.minneapolisfed.org/pubs/region /05-06/heckman.cfm#
9. Schweinhart, L. J., Montie, J., Xiang, Z., Barnett, W. S., Belfield, C. R., & Nores, M. (2005). *Lifetime effects: The High/Scope Perry Preschool study through age 40* (Monographs of the High/Scope Educational Research Foundation, 14). Ypsilanti, MI: High/Scope Educational Research Foundation.
10. Olsen, D., & Snell, L. (2006, May). *Assessing proposals for preschool and kindergarten: Essential information for parents, taxpayers, and policymakers*. Los Angeles, CA: Reason Foundation. For a full critique of this report see:
    Barnett, W. (2006). *Review of "Assessing Proposals for Preschool and Kindergarten: Essential Information for Parents, Taxpayers, and Policymakers."* Boulder, CO and Tempe, AZ: Education and the Public Interest Center &

Education Policy Research Unit. Retrieved January 7, 2010, from http://epicpolicy.org/thinktank/review-assessing-proposals-preschool-and-kindergarten-essential-information-parents-taxpay

11. Levin, H. M., & Schwartz, H. L. (2007). Educational vouchers for universal pre-schools. *Economics of Education Review, 26*(1), 3-16.

12. Belsky, Vandell, Burchinal, Clarke-Stewart, McCartney, Owen, & the NICHD ECCRN (2007); see note 4.

13. Puma, M., Bell, S., Cook, R., Heid, C., Lopez, M., Zill, N., Shapiro, G., Broene, P., Mekos, D., Rohacek, M., Quinn, L., Adams, G., Freidman, J., & Bernstein, H. (2005). *Head Start impact study: First year findings.* Washington, DC: U.S. Dept. of Health and Human Services, Administration for Children and Families.

    Love, J. M., Kisker, E. E., Ross, C. M., Schochet, P. Z., Brooks-Gunn, J., Paulsell, D., Boller, K., Constantine, J., Vogel, C., Fuligni, A. S., & Brady-Smith, C. (2002/2004). *Making a difference in the lives of infants and toddlers and their families: The impacts of Early Head Start. Volume I: Final technical report.* Princeton, NJ: Mathematica Policy Research.

14. Magnuson, Ruhm, & Waldfogel (2007); see note 4.

15. Schweinhart, L. J. & Weikart, D. P. (1997). The High/Scope preschool curriculum comparison study through age 23. *Early Childhood Research Quarterly, 12*(2), 117-143.

    Schweinhart, Montie, Xiang, Barnett, Belfield, & Nores, (2005); see note 9.

    Raine, A., Mellingen, K., Liu, J., Venables, P., & Mednick, S. A. (2003). Effects of environmental enrichment at ages 3-5 years on schizotypal personality and antisocial behavior at ages 17 and 23 years. *American Journal of Psychiatry, 160*(9), 1627-1635.

    Reynolds, A. J., et al. (2007). Effects of a school-based, early childhood intervention on adult health and well-being: A 19 year follow-up of low-income families. *Archives of Pediatrics and Adolescent Medicine, 161*(8), 730-739.

16. Early, Bryant, Pianta, Clifford, Burchinal, Ritchie, Howes, & Barbarin (2007); see note 6.

17. Barnett, W. S. (2007). Benefits and costs of quality early childhood education. *The Children's Legal Rights Journal (CLRJ), 27*, 7-23.

18. Barnett (2007).

    Bartik, T. J. (2008). *The economic development effects of early childhood programs.* Kalamazoo, MI: Upjohn Institute for Employment Research.

    Lynch, R. G. (2007). *Enriching children, enriching the nation: Public investment in high-quality prekindergarten.* Washington, DC: Economic Policy Institute.

19. Barnett, W. S., & Belfield, C. (2006). Early childhood development and social mobility. *Future of Children, 16*(2), 73-98.

    Gormley, W. T., Gayer, T., Phillips, D. & Dawson, B. (2005). The effects of universal pre-k on cognitive development. *Developmental Psychology, 41*(6), 872-884.

    Barnett, W. S., Jung, K., Wong, V, Cook, T., & Lamy, C. (2007). *The effects of state prekindergarten programs on young children's school readiness in five states.*

New Brunswick, NJ: National Institute for Early Education Research, Rutgers University.

Frede, E., Jung, K., Barnett, W. S., Lamy, C., & Figueras, A. (2007). *The Abbott preschool program longitudinal effects study (APPLES)*. New Brunswick, NJ: National Institute for Early Education Research, Rutgers University.

20.   Weikart, D. P., Bond, J. T., & McNeil, J. T. (1978). *The Ypsilanti Perry Preschool Project: Preschool years and Longitudinal results*. (Monographs of the High/Scope Educational Research Foundation, 4). Ypsilanti, MI: High/Scope Educational Research Foundation.

21.   Olsen & Snell (2006, May); see note 10.

22.   Barnett, W. S. (2008). Analysis available from the author.

23.   There is evidence of waiting lists at public and private centers, and it is difficult to know where demand most exceeds the available slots. Public schools do seek to place excess demand in the private sector, see for example, http://www.athensparent.com/articles/featuregen/prek4.html

24.   Education Law Center. (2007). *Abbott pre-K is not an unregulated private school "voucher" program*. Newark, NJ: ELC. Retrieved March 15, 2008, from: http://www.edlawcenter.org/ELCPublic/
elcnews_070509_AbbottPreKInvestment.htm

25.   Head Start Bureau. (2005). *Biennial report to Congress: The status of children in Head Start programs 2005*. Washington, DC: U.S. Department of Health and Human Services, Administration for Children and Families, Head Start Bureau.

26.   Ready to Learn Act of 2007, S. 1823, 110th Cong., 1st Session (2007).

27.   Barnett, W. S., Brown, K., & Shore, R. (April, 2004). The universal v. targeted debate: Should the United States have preschool for all? *Preschool Policy Matters, 6*. New Brunwick, NJ: National Institute for Early Education Research.

Barnett, W. S. (2004). Maximizing returns from prekindergarten education. In *Federal Reserve Bank of Cleveland Research Conference: Education and economic development* (pp. 5-18). Cleveland, OH: Federal Reserve Bank of Cleveland.

28.   Barnett, Jung, Wong, Cook & Lamy (2007); see note 19.

Frede, Jung, Barnett, Lamy, & Figueras (2007); see note 19.

29.   Barnett, W. S., Hustedt, J. T., Hawkinson, L. E., & Robin, K. B. (2006). *The state of preschool 2006*. New Brunswick, NJ: National Institute for Early Education Research, Rutgers University.

30.   Levin & Schwartz (2007); see note 11.

Belfield, C. R. (2006). *The evidence on education vouchers: An application to the Cleveland Scholarship and Tutoring Program*. New York, NY: National Center for the Study of Privatization in Education, Teachers College, Columbia University.

PART 10

Teacher Quality

A substantive body of research literature confirms a positive relationship between teacher quality and student achievement. Less clear is how to objectively identify high-quality teachers or would-be teachers and exactly which characteristics of high-quality teachers influence achievement. It is also unclear which strategies might help enlarge the pool of high-quality teachers, especially for high-needs schools that have difficulty attracting and retaining them.

A growing movement supports expanding alternative routes to certification, which frequently have lesser requirements than traditional certification programs. Proponents argue that these requirements serve only as needless obstacles, preventing or discouraging potentially valuable teacher prospects, and that they do nothing to improve the likelihood of classroom success. Opponents argue that evading rigorous teacher training will undermine teacher quality and professionalism and will negatively affect student achievement.

In addition to these alternative route strategies—easing hiring restrictions as well as certification requirements—market-oriented reformers have suggested providing financial incentives. Other reformers have suggested that improving working conditions will help recruit and retain

Think Tank Research Quality: Lessons for Policy Makers, the Media, and the Public, pp. 277–280

better teachers in schools serving disadvantages students. The following two chapters address several aspects of these teacher quality debates.

In Chapter 20, Sean Corcoran and Jennifer Jennings review a 2009 report from Mathematica Policy Research, *An Evaluation of Teachers Trained Through Different Routes to Certification: Final Report*, authored by Jill Constantine and colleagues. The study found no difference in student achievement for elementary students taught by traditionally certified (TC) or alternatively certified (AC) teachers, suggesting that traditional teacher certification programs have little effect on student outcomes. The study was based on a comparison of test scores from students in the same school and grade who had been randomly assigned to TC or AC teachers, with a total of 174 elementary teachers participating. Of the study's methodology, however, Corcoran and Jennings say that "if one set out to design a study that would find no statistically significant differences between the achievement of students taught by traditionally and alternatively certified teachers, this is precisely the study one would design."

They offer several specific criticisms. First, the particular population of teachers, schools and students sampled is not only small but highly specific, precluding generalization to a wider population. The issue here is in large part one of whom the AC teachers are being compared with. The study needed to identify schools that routinely employed AC teachers, which are most often found in disadvantaged neighborhoods. As a result, sites for the study were disproportionately affected by issues of concentrated poverty, distinct even from other schools in the same districts. The teachers compared also disproportionately represented K-2 classrooms, where schools tend to place weaker teachers, saving their strongest for grades subjected to NCLB testing requirements. Another confounding factor is that while some highly qualified teachers do choose to work in such schools, there is evidence to suggest that in general, TC teachers in such schools are less competitive and less qualified than their counterparts in more advantaged schools.

The reviewers further point out that the categories of TC and AC are not as distinct as one might initially think. The AC teachers took varying amounts of coursework—sometimes the same coursework as some TC teachers. The specific differences in their preparation were unclear. Moreover, they note that AC teachers often receive support unavailable to their TC counterparts, including mentoring, professional development and administrative support, which may have affected their performance. The reviewers find that such factors make it difficult, if not impossible, to define exactly what treatment was applied in the study and what other factors might have influenced outcomes.

Among other weaknesses that Corcoran and Jennings point to is that the study paid little or no attention to relevant findings that undermined its claim that TC and AC teachers are equally effective. For example, the reviewers note that the study found no difference in math performance, but that finding was based on an analysis that excluded scores from half of the math tests administered to students in grades 2-5. The reviewers call this omission "a surprising design choice," and note that one of the report's exhibits showed that "the students of alternatively certified teachers from low coursework programs scored *significantly lower on math computation*," with the difference being substantial (emphasis in original). Corcoran and Jennings find that, over all, the study could make "no claims about the long-term effects of a wholesale movement away from traditional teacher certification." Instead, the study should be understood to have indicated only that "a small number of AC teachers in a select population of schools, grades, and states performed only somewhat worse than TC teachers in the same schools."

Chapter 21 features Raymond Pecheone and Ash Vasudeva's review of the Cato Institute's 2006 report *Giving Students the Chaff: How to Find and Keep the Teachers We Need*, authored by Marie Gryphon. This study examined what the reviewers term "a narrow band of research literature"—a subset of research that supported several conclusions offered in the report. Among these conclusions were the following: that high-quality teachers leave because bureaucratic school systems undermine hiring practices, that private and charter schools are able to hire high-quality teachers, and that increased school choice and competition will improve teacher quality.

The reviewers find that the study relied heavily on literature that defined teacher quality only in terms of standardized test scores, and that it excluded evidence suggesting that quality has been—and should be—measured by such other characteristics as teacher preparation, certification, professional development and mentoring. They note, for example, that "Numerous studies conducted at the individual classroom, school, district, and state levels have found that students' achievement is significantly related to whether their teachers are fully prepared or certified in the field they teach." Pecheone and Vasudeva also question the report's assumption and claims that private and charter schools outperform public schools. The reviewers do agree that in some cases bureaucratic tangles may impede hiring practices, but they find untenable the claim that revised hiring practices will inevitably alleviate shortages of quality teachers in hard-to-serve schools. They note that the study ignores "a simple and arguably more compelling explanation for any variation in teacher quality in these districts: teachers' self-selection into schools with better working conditions." Overall, Pecheone and Vasudeva find that while the report's emphasis on teachers and teacher quality is sound, its "other elements are undermined by a propensity to filter the evidence base in favor of a particular point of view."

CHAPTER 20

EVALUATION OF TEACHERS TRAINED THROUGH DIFFERENT ROUTES TO CERTIFICATION

Sean P. Corcoran and Jennifer L. Jennings

Review of "An Evaluation of Teachers Trained Through Different Routes to Certification: Final Report," by Jill Constantine, Daniel Player, Tim Silva, Kristin Hallgren, Mary Grider, John Deke, and published by Mathematica Policy Research. This is a modified version of a review originally published on March 10, 2009.

INTRODUCTION

A new study by Mathematica Policy Research finds that students randomly assigned an alternatively certified teacher did no worse on achievement tests than students whose teacher came through the traditional teacher-education route. Moreover, the report, titled *An Evaluation of Teachers Trained through Different Routes to Certification* and funded by the Institute of Education Sciences,[1] concludes that there is no association between greater amounts of teacher training coursework and effectiveness in the

Think Tank Research Quality: Lessons for Policy Makers, the Media, and the Public, pp. 281–300
Copyright © 2010 by Information Age Publishing
All rights of reproduction in any form reserved.

classroom. These findings are likely to be warmly received by commentators calling for the scaling-up of alternatives to traditional teacher certification. For example, Malcolm Gladwell advocates that "Teaching should be open to anyone with a pulse and a college degree—and teachers should be judged after they have started their jobs, not before."[2] Yet such a reception is not warranted in this case, because few if any valid conclusions about teacher certification policy can be drawn from the Mathematica study, and those conclusions that can be drawn tend to favor traditional routes.

Later in this review we outline the results that we think should have been given greater attention in the report. But we want to be careful here not to overstate the findings—because in reality the findings are minimal and few results meet the standard of both practical and statistical significance. This is for good reason: if one set out to design a study that would find no statistically significant differences between the achievement of students taught by traditionally and alternatively certified teachers, this is precisely the study one would design.

The study utilizes only a moderately small sample of 174 elementary teachers, with an average of 3 years experience, and is heavily weighted towards teachers in Grades K-2, who comprise 71% of the study's teachers. Because the authors intentionally sampled from schools that routinely hire alternatively certified teachers, the average school in the study is located in a central city, is highly disadvantaged, and is demographically distinct even from other schools in the same district. Many of these schools have high turnover among their teachers and draw heavily on alternatively certified teachers. These characteristics are important in part because the traditionally certified teachers who are the comparison group in the study are only those employed by these disadvantaged schools. While many of these teachers are highly qualified individuals who choose to serve the most needy students, it is very likely, based on the evidence provided here and in other studies, that the teachers at these schools are, on average, the least competitive, and least qualified among traditionally certified teachers.

Yet despite this and other aspects of a study design that favor finding no differences even where differences exist, the report does find negative and statistically significant outcomes associated with alternatively certified teachers in a number of settings. For example, students in Grades 2-5 with alternatively certified teachers who had taken relatively low amounts of teacher-education coursework did substantially worse on a test of math computation. Students of alternatively certified teachers who were concurrently enrolled in coursework (43% of these teachers) also performed worse than students of their traditionally certified peers.

The main concerns we have with the Mathematica report fall into three categories:

1. The study's design makes it difficult to discern what, exactly, constitutes the "treatment" in this experiment, thus limiting its internal validity.

2. The report's findings cannot be generalized beyond a highly specific population of high-needs, high-turnover classrooms of early grade students, thus limiting its capacity to address questions about the relative success of traditional and alternatively certified teachers, and policy questions about teacher preparation.

3. The limited attention to findings of negative outcomes associated with alternatively certified teachers distorts the study's policy implications.

THE REPORT'S FINDINGS AND CONCLUSIONS

The Mathematica team compared the math and reading test scores of students taught by teachers certified through alternative routes (AC) to those of students taught by traditionally certified teachers (TC). Classroom practices of AC and TC teachers were also observed and compared. (Details on the study design are provided in the next section.) From this, they draw the following conclusions:

> There was no statistically significant difference in performance between students of AC teachers and those of TC teachers.... Therefore, the route to certification selected by a prospective teacher is unlikely to provide information, on average, about the expected quality of that teacher in terms of student achievement. (p. xviii)

> There is no evidence from this study that greater levels of teacher training coursework were associated with the effectiveness of AC teachers in the classroom ... Therefore, there is no evidence that AC programs with greater coursework requirements produce more effective teachers. (pp. xviii-xix)

> There is no evidence that the content of coursework [including required hours of pedagogy instruction, or fieldwork] is correlated with teacher effectiveness. (p. xix)

These are strong statements about the relative effectiveness of traditional and non-traditional teacher training programs, and the policy community and news media have naturally been quick to take note. For example, *New York Times* columnist Nicholas Kristof summarized the implications of the study this way:

> The latest Department of Education study, published this month, showed again that there is no correlation between teacher certification and teacher effectiveness.... The implication is that throwing money at a broken system won't fix it, but that resources are necessary as part of a package that involves scrapping certification."[3]

Indeed, the Mathematica report's authors do not shy away from drawing broad implications from their findings. They suggest, for example, that their findings on relative student achievement will be "relevant to principals faced with a choice between hiring an AC or a TC teacher" (p. xvi). Likewise, their findings on the impact of teacher training coursework will provide guidance "to policymakers and designers and administrators of teacher training programs in their efforts to identify the training characteristics and certification requirements that are related most positively to student achievement" (pp. xvi–xvii).

Mathematica's own press release presents its findings as having broad and unqualified generalizability:

> In one of the largest and most rigorous studies of alternatively certified teachers ever conducted, researchers found that students with an alternatively certified teacher did no worse on achievement tests than students whose teacher came through the traditional route.[4]

The report's lead author adds: "Our study reveals that alternatively certified teachers do not produce harmful consequences for students."[5] As we explain below, such broad statements are not warranted from the study design, or from its own findings.

REPORT'S RATIONALES FOR ITS FINDINGS AND CONCLUSIONS

As many of Mathematica's large-scale evaluations do—and often do well— this study relies on random assignment of subjects to "treatment" and "control" conditions. In this setting, the subjects are students, while the treatment and control conditions are the classrooms of teachers certified through AC and TC routes, respectively. As in pharmaceutical research, randomized control trials (RCTs) are commonly viewed as the "gold standard" for evaluating the effects of interventions and of social and educational programs.[6] Since 2002, the U.S. Institute of Education Sciences, which funded this study, has explicitly worked to promote RCTs in education. In principle, the RCT is a straightforward, clean, and powerful design for making causal inferences about interventions and programs.[7] In practice, though, RCTs often have limited applicability outside their study sample.[8]

Mathematica designed its RCT as follows. First, a sample of 63 AC programs was selected from a total of 165 nonselective AC programs operating in 12 states.[9] Second, schools that hired from these 63 programs were recruited to participate. Only schools where AC and TC teachers taught the same grade were eligible to participate, and all participating teachers had to be "relative novices" (initially defined as three or fewer years of experience, and later redefined as five or fewer years). A total of 87 AC teachers and 87 TC teachers in 63 schools made the cut. Third, students within the same school and grade were randomly assigned to an AC or TC teacher. Finally, outcomes in AC-led classrooms were compared with those of (matched) TC-led classrooms. The average difference in outcomes is interpreted as the average "treatment effect" of AC teacher instruction.

For the purposes of this study, AC teachers were not considered to provide a uniform "treatment." Rather, they were differentiated into two subgroups based on the amount of class instruction and fieldwork required by the AC programs the teachers had chosen. "Low coursework" teachers were in programs requiring relatively little prior training, while "high coursework" teachers were in programs requiring relatively more instruction and fieldwork (47 AC teachers fell into the first category and 40 were in the latter). Drawing an analogy to medical RCTs, students were instructed by teachers who received different "dosages" of teacher instruction.

The authors also perform non-experimental analyses, using multiple regression models to examine the effects of other observable differences between AC and TC teachers and classrooms. Characteristics they control for include student pre-test scores, teacher and student demographics, teacher education, and teacher experience. Due to random assignment, student characteristics should not vary systematically between AC and TC classrooms in the same school. But AC teacher characteristics vary according to state and program training requirements, and differential selection into the AC route. It is these AC teacher characteristics that together constitute the study's "treatment."

REVIEW OF THE REPORT'S USE OF THE RESEARCH LITERATURE

The report provides an ample literature review of current studies of AC. But the report's authors do not adequately address a large literature on teacher labor markets—in particular, the process by which teachers are sorted among and within schools—that informs the context and generalizability of their study.[10] The report's literature review would also have benefited from attention to the following three issues that are ultimately raised by the sample participating in the study.

The interaction between certification type and years of experience: The authors cite a number of studies on the effectiveness of AC.[11] To the extent these studies find negative effects of AC on student achievement, the authors correctly note that those effects are limited to the first 2 years of teaching. The debate about AC teachers appears to be entirely about what happens to students exposed to these teachers in their first 2 years. But there is a major disconnect here between the findings of this cited research and the sample utilized by the Mathematica study: 57% of the Mathematica sample has three or more years of teaching experience. What is missing from the review, then, is an express discussion of this issue. Given its sample, the Mathematica study's findings shed little light on the question of what happens to students who are exposed to less experienced AC teachers in their initial years.

The effects of teacher certification and the size of teacher effects in the early grades: A large and growing literature on teacher effects in the grades tested under No Child Left Behind (in particular, Grades 3-8) has inspired a fruitful debate over the role of certification in teacher quality, but no such studies exist for the lower grades (K-2), which comprise 71% of the Mathematica study's teachers. The only study of which we are aware that examines the magnitude of teacher effects across the early grades, that of Nye, Konstantopoulos, and Hedges, finds that teacher effects on reading are somewhat smaller for the earlier grades than for higher grades, though teacher effects on math are not dissimilar from those reported in Grades 3-8.[12] However, without the benefit of observing teachers multiple times (as most teacher effects studies do), Nye et al. potentially overstate the size of teacher effects due to sampling variation. In short, whether teacher effects in K-2 are of similar size to those in Grades 3-8—whether because there is less variation in teacher quality among early grades teachers or because there are fewer reliable measures of skills in the early grades—remains an open question.

The sorting of teachers within schools: The Mathematica study assumes that there is no systematic relationship between teacher quality and the grade levels to which teachers are assigned. However, in the current accountability climate, there are good reasons to believe that principals strategically deploy their most effective teachers to the tested Grades (3-8). Previous research on the implementation of high-stakes testing in New York State found support for this idea.[13] If this is the case, then one might expect the least effective teachers in the earlier grades. Since the report's sample is comprised largely of K-2 teachers, the possibility of teacher sorting within schools should have been given substantially more attention.

REVIEW OF THE REPORT'S METHODS

Our concerns with the Mathematica report's methods fall into three categories. The first addresses the report's internal validity—its ability to accurately draw inferences about the effects of a treatment on an outcome. The study's design makes it difficult to discern what, exactly, constitutes the "treatment" in this experiment. The second concern relates to the report's external validity—its ability to generalize beyond the unique and idiosyncratic settings of the study to other populations. We show that the findings of the Mathematica report cannot be generalized beyond a highly specific population of high-needs, high-turnover classrooms of early grade students. Our third concern relates to the authors' selective emphasis of their findings. The authors find numerous cases of negative outcomes associated with AC teachers, but more often than not choose to deemphasize these findings.

Internal Validity: What Is the Nature of the Treatment?

Mathematica's experimental analysis randomly assigned students attending the same grade in the same school to either an AC teacher or a TC teacher. Because most American students are taught by a traditionally certified teacher, one can think of assignment to a TC teacher as the control state and assignment to an AC teacher as the treatment. So how do the study's authors operationalize this notion of "treatment?" That is, what is it that students assigned to AC teachers are "getting" that differs from what students assigned to TC teachers receive? And how confident should readers be that this study identifies the effects of this treatment?

In this study, TC teachers are defined as those who began teaching only after completing their certification requirements, while AC teachers are defined as those placed in a classroom prior to completing these requirements. Accordingly, the key distinguishing feature of TC and AC teachers is not the actual amount of "traditional" coursework and experience they had at the time of the study but rather the point at which they began classroom teaching.

AC teachers are further subdivided into low- and high-coursework teachers, depending on how much instruction and fieldwork their programs required. These teachers were not randomly assigned, but were determined mostly by geography and state requirements. Two-thirds of the low-coursework teachers were in Texas, while half of the high-coursework teachers were in California (pp. 29-30).

While there is no commonly accepted definition of an alternate certification teacher (or a low- or high-coursework AC program), this report's definition results in a very broad range of "treatments." For instance, while timing of entry into the classroom differs for these teachers, the instructional training required of AC and TC teachers overlapped considerably. The Mathematica report's executive summary states,

> the total hours required by AC programs ranged from 75 to 795, and by TC programs, from 240 to 1,380. Thus, not all AC programs require fewer hours of coursework than all TC programs... in California, the range of coursework hours required was similar for AC and TC teachers. (pp. xvii-xviii)[14]

Moreover, some AC and TC teachers in the study were trained in the same institutions, and may have taken the same courses (pp. 25-27).[15]

Further muddying the waters, teachers are also categorized into low- or high-coursework programs based on "the requirements of the programs they attended and the amount of coursework required for certification, *not the amount actually completed at the time of the study*" (p. xxiii, emphasis added). So very little is known about how much training the teachers in the study actually received by the time they were observed. Given the report's description of the categorization of AC and TC teachers and of the experiences and training they brought to the classroom, there does not seem to be a unique "treatment" that students assigned to AC teachers were really receiving.[16]

Interestingly, one dimension on which the AC teachers did differ markedly from TC teachers was the availability of a mentor, master teacher, or supervisor during their first year of teaching. According to the report, 93.5% of low-coursework AC teachers worked with a mentor during their first year, compared with 78.3% of their TC counterparts (pp. 47-49). The difference between high-coursework AC teachers and their TC counterparts was even larger. AC teachers also reported more professional development and administrative support than TC teachers (pp. 48-50). None of these differences are unexpected, as some AC programs involve these supplemental services. But they do illustrate another component of the "treatment" that students assigned to AC teachers receive—additional classroom support during the school year—that TC counterparts did not. Measured outcomes therefore might reflect the effects of mentoring, professional development, or administrative support, rather than (or in addition to) other aspects of alternative certification.

Internal Validity: Cooperation and Interference

A central assumption of randomized controlled trials is that there is no interference between units in the experiment. In other words, a subject's outcome must depend only on the subject's own treatment assignment, not the treatment assignments of other subjects.[17] In settings like elementary schools where teachers often work together in grade-level teams, this assumption is often violated. Strictly speaking, in the Mathematica study *students* are the subjects randomly assigned to treatment and control states, not teachers. However, to the extent TC and AC teachers interact with each other, support each other, and plan together, we would expect their students' outcomes to look more similar to each other than they would in the absence of such cooperation, thus increasing the likelihood that the study would show—as it mainly did—no significant effects. Nowhere in the study do the authors discuss the incidence or likelihood of these interactions.

Internal Validity: The Effects of Teacher-Student Race Matching

A number of studies have found that African American students perform better academically when they are taught by African American teachers,[18] which is relevant to the Mathematica study because AC teachers are 2.7 times more likely to be African American (36.1% versus 13.6%), and the teachers in this study are predominately in schools with high proportions of African American students. Recognizing this issue, the Mathematica authors test for an interaction effect of teacher and student race, and indeed find that African American students perform better when they are matched to African American teachers. These effects are substantial in size,[19] but the authors dismiss this issue as not relevant to their estimates of the effects of AC teachers because these effects are not statistically significant at the .05 level. Considering the substantial size of these race matching effects, the Mathematica study would have been strengthened if the authors reported the effects of AC and TC teachers (net of teacher race) and of the interaction between teacher and student race. By failing to do so, the report only raises additional questions about the nature of the AC "treatment."

EXTERNAL VALIDITY: TO WHAT POPULATIONS DO THESE RESULTS APPLY?

By design, the Mathematica report restricted its analysis to AC and TC teachers in schools that (a) regularly hired a large number of AC teachers, and (b) had "relatively novice" AC and TC teachers providing instruction to the same grade level. From a design point of view these choices were practical, for two reasons. First, the authors were limited to schools that already hire from this pool of teachers. Second, in a desire to compare "apples to apples," the authors justifiably sought to compare teachers instructing the same grade in the same school. But such decisions strictly limit the schools, grades, and teachers for which this study has relevance.

Selection of Schools and Districts

Schools and districts that hire AC teachers—especially teachers from the kinds of non-selective training programs studied here—look markedly different from the general population of schools and districts in the United States. Alternative certification programs emerged in large part in response to staffing shortages, particularly in hard-to-staff schools and localities. In particular, urban schools serving high concentrations of poor and minority students historically have found it difficult to recruit and retain certified teachers. The report fails to discuss how closely the schools and districts in its study resemble the general population of schools and districts, or how these choices should inform inferences drawn from the study.

Fourteen of 20 districts and the vast majority of schools in the study are in central cities of urban areas.[20] The study's schools have an average of 79% eligibility for free and reduced-price lunch, and an average of 93% non-White enrollment. By contrast, 38% of students in the nation at large are eligible for free or reduced-price lunch, and 45% are non-White.[21]

Striking dissimilarities exist even when comparing participant and nonparticipant schools in the same districts (Exhibit II.5). Schools in the study had much higher rates of poverty and non-White enrollment than other schools in their same district. In some cases—including two large urban districts in California, urban districts in Georgia and Wisconsin, and a rural district in Louisiana—the differences are substantial, at 10 to 40 percentage points. These differences are consistent with the distribution of nontraditionally certified teachers generally.

We can conclude that districts and schools hiring AC teachers face much different circumstances than districts and schools that do not—a conclusion that holds even among schools in the same labor market (i.e., a particular school district). This observation is critically important, for two reasons. First, it highlights the limited population to which this study can be generalized. Perhaps even more importantly, it offers useful insight into the TC teachers that serve as the study's counterfactual, or "control" group.

TC teachers in schools staffed with AC teachers are unlikely to be representative of TC teachers in the general population, and they may not even be representative of TC teachers in their own districts. Schools that hire AC teachers typically do so out of need. If these schools are troubled, high-turnover organizations, they do not have the luxury of choosing from among many qualified applicants. Instead, it is likely that even their TC staff suffers from lower-than-average quality. In fact, most of the existing literature confirms this: schools with high concentrations of poor or minority students are disproportionately staffed with less effective, less experienced, and less academically talented teachers.[22]

Selection of Grades

The sampling design of the Mathematica report also yields an unusually skewed distribution of teachers over grade levels. As Table 20.1 shows, nearly 56% of all teachers in the study were kindergarten and first grade instructors; 71% were concentrated in Grades K-2.

There are a number of plausible explanations for this over-representation of early grade teachers. As the report shows, schools hiring from AC programs have higher shares of poor and minority students, greater turnover, and fewer qualified teaching staff.[23] In a high-stakes testing environment—such as that under No Child Left Behind—an under-resourced school may rationally assign its most capable and effective teachers to the tested Grades (3-8), leaving more AC teachers and—even more importantly—weaker-than-average TC teachers in the early grades.[24]

There are several reasons why the study's overreliance on early grade teachers is important. First, as with the nonrandom sample of schools, it limits the population to which its results can be generalized. Second, if TC teachers assigned to early grades are among the least qualified or effective in the school, comparisons between AC and TC teachers in the earlier grades will be least likely to find differences in effectiveness.[25] Third, as noted in the previous section, the existing literature has little to say about teacher effects in the early grades. Finally, the nature of instruction differs markedly between the early and middle grades. If early grade

Table 20.1. Distribution of Teachers by Grade

	# of Teachers	% of Matched Pairs
K	20	22.2
1	30	33.3
2	14	15.6
3	9	10.0
4	11	12.2
5	6	6.7

educators are more likely to follow rote lesson plans or otherwise have less control over their curriculum, few outcome differences between AC and TC classrooms might be expected.

Selection of Teachers

The Mathematica report sought to compare "relatively novice" AC and TC teachers providing instruction to the same grade level within a school. The report's sampling design also sought to include roughly half "low-coursework" and half "high-coursework" AC teachers. As it turned out, finding a sufficient number of teacher pairs who met these criteria proved difficult. In the first year of the experiment, when "relatively novice" was defined as three or fewer years of experience, only 25 AC teachers and 24 TC teachers were available for inclusion (pp. 14-15). In order to obtain a sufficient sample size, the authors in the second year retained as many teachers as possible from the first year, and broadened their definition of "relatively novice" to five or fewer years of experience. This allowed for many more matched pairs; over the 2 years combined, 87 AC and 87 TC teachers participated.

As a result of this expanded sampling procedure, the average teacher in the study had a relatively high average experience level, about 3.1 years of "study-eligible teaching experience."

Given random assignment of teachers to students, why should the average experience of participating teachers matter? We offer two reasons. First, AC teachers may have a higher rate of turnover than TC teachers in their first few years of teaching. To the extent that exiting AC teachers are less effective than the ones who stay, the average quality of remaining AC teachers will be higher. If this is the case, the study would overlook the potential negative effect that AC teachers have on students in their first year of teaching. Second, many of the policy discussions surrounding alternate certification relate to the potential risk of hiring under-prepared and inexperienced teachers who have not completed

Table 20.2.   Average Teacher Experience

	AC	TC	Combined (Weighted Average)
Low coursework	2.7	3.3	3.0
High coursework	3.3	3.0	3.2
Combined (weighted average):	3.0	3.2	3.1

their formal training. (The authors cite this as one of their central motivations for the study.) But as the above table shows, participating teachers already have demonstrated longevity in the classroom. The bulk of teachers were recruited in the second year under the less stringent definition of novice teachers, and 14 of the study's teachers were retained and observed for 2 years in a row (p. 14). Even these teachers were a select sample, given that many teachers in the first year of the study were unavailable for the second year.

Recent empirical evidence finds that less effective teachers are more likely to transfer schools or exit teaching in their first few years than are more effective teachers.[26] Further, some research shows that AC teachers have a higher rate of turnover than TC teachers in their first few years.[27] This should not be too surprising, as TC teachers have already revealed a potentially greater commitment to the profession by investing in a more time-consuming educational program than AC teachers. The same argument may differentiate low- and high-coursework AC teachers.

Selective Emphasis of Results

A careful read of Mathematica's report reveals a large number of relevant findings that received little or no attention in the executive summary, or in press coverage of this study. We briefly highlight several that caught our attention:

1. The authors reported that there was no difference between the math performance of AC and TC teachers, and that there was no variation in the effects of AC versus TC teachers across grade levels. Yet the authors excluded scores from half of the math tests administered to students in Grades 2-5 ("Math Computation") from the analyses reported in the body of the study.[28] Excluding these scores from their primary analyses is a surprising design choice, given that their Exhibit A.9 demonstrates that *the students of alternatively certified teachers from low coursework programs scored <u>significantly lower on math computation</u>, and the magnitude of this <u>effect is substantial in size</u> (Effect size = −.18 of a standard deviation)*. This finding not only suggests that students in Grades 2-5 are harmed by exposure to alternatively certified teachers, but that there is important variation in the effects of alternative certification across grades.

2. A central concern with AC programs is how the timing of teacher-education coursework affects student outcomes. The Mathematica study found that the *students of alternatively certified teachers currently*

taking coursework—43% of all alternatively certified teachers—performed worse in math (ES = -.09).

3. The report's findings are also sensitive to the inclusion or exclusion of students and teachers who exited during the study. The authors find that after excluding students and teachers who left during the year from the analysis, the students of *alternatively certified teachers from high-coursework programs scored lower on math, and these differences were statistically significant (ES = −.08).*

4. There are potentially important geographic variations in the effects of alternative certification that were not attended to in the press release or executive summary. The authors found that overall *the students of AC teachers in California performed worse in math than the students of TC teachers (ES = −.13).* They further determined that this effect is driven by the 62% of California AC teachers currently enrolled in coursework (ES = −.16).

5. The authors underplay the finding that on all instructional dimensions observed in the classroom, *high-coursework AC teachers were rated substantially worse than high-coursework TC teachers.* The reason they de-emphasize this is that many of these large effects do not reach statistical significance. But the lack of statistical significance is not surprising, since the study had a very small sample size, allowing the researchers to detect only what were (by the standards of educational research), enormous differences between groups. The difference between high coursework TC and AC teachers ranges from .22 to .37 standard deviations in reading, and it ranges from .27 to .33 standard deviations in math—but the only difference between TC and AC high-coursework teachers that reached statistical significance was on literacy culture (and it registered a remarkable difference of .40 standard deviations).

6. Finally, the authors underplay that AC teachers received lower principal ratings—some of them a great deal lower—on every dimension. Again, because the sample size is small, even large differences—for example, the .42 standard deviation TC advantage over high-coursework AC teachers in classroom management—do not reach statistical significance.

These results (points 5 and 6) do not reach statistical significance because the comparisons are (appropriately) made at the level of the teacher (n =188) rather than the student. However, when a study using relatively small sample sizes produces results showing large effect sizes that fall short of statistical significance, it is important to bear in mind what tests of statistical significance are intended to do—provide readers with an estimate of the probability of a difference between two groups occurring simply by chance. The smaller the sample, the more likely it is that even differences of practical significance—differences that are substantively important for education policy—will not be statistically significant. As many other researchers have argued,[29] discussing both the effect size and the statistical significance of effects is particularly important in the case of "low-power tests," tests of statistical significance where the sample size is small.

REVIEW OF THE VALIDITY OF THE FINDINGS AND CONCLUSIONS

Throughout the Mathematica report, the authors argue that their findings on student achievement will be "relevant to principals faced with a choice between hiring an AC or a TC teacher." They add that their results on low- or high-coursework training programs will provide guidance "to policymakers and designers and administrators of teacher training programs in their efforts to identify the training characteristics and certification requirements that are related most positively to student achievement" (pp. xvi-xvii, 3-4, 12). It is unclear to us that the report's findings are useful to either of these ends.

With respect to informing the hiring of teachers, even if this study were perfectly executed, its findings would apply only to very select population of districts, schools, grades, and geographic regions of the country. The schools that provided the study's sample are disproportionately poor, heavily minority, low-performing schools located in central cities of urban areas, with histories of hiring at least moderate numbers of AC teachers. Furthermore, the vast majority of teachers in the study were K-2 teachers, and 71% were from California or Texas.

Moreover, it is unclear what information the study can provide even to the select population of districts, schools, and grades for which it is relevant. The AC "treatment" as operationalized here is not easily differentiated from the "control," and the training routes themselves were not randomly assigned to teachers but governed by self-selection and state requirements. The study assumes that AC and TC teachers in the same grade and the same school do not cooperate, and thus do not influence each others' practice and outcomes, which we find highly implausible.

Unfortunately, despite these limitations on the report's external and internal validity, the authors elected not to provide the necessary cautions to their readers.

REPORT'S USEFULNESS FOR GUIDANCE OF POLICY AND PRACTICE

Policymakers and other readers of the Mathematica report will surely be looking for a simple answer to a simple question: "Is alternative teacher certification a *bad thing* or a *good thing?*" They will also surely be interested in an important corollary to this question: "If alternative certification does no harm, is traditional teacher certification even *necessary?*" Notwithstanding suggestions to the contrary in the report's press release and executive summary, the report is unable to provide a satisfactory or general answer to either of those questions.

In this review we have addressed some of the ways in which the Mathematica study provides a weak test of the AC "treatment effect." We have also emphasized the very limited population to which the study's findings can be generalized and pointed to de-emphasized results that suggest negative AC outcomes, contradicting the report's broad conclusions.

The study's limitations are not completely disregarded by the report's authors. The executive summary contains the following key observation:

> An important distinction of this design is that because certification routes are not randomly assigned to teacher trainees, the estimates of the effects on student achievement and classroom practices of teachers who were trained through different routes to certification pertain to those *who chose to participate in these programs*. Because of likely differences in the types of people who attend various certification programs, *the results cannot be used to rigorously address how a graduate of one type of program would fare if he or she had attended another type* (p. xxi, emphasis added).

Teacher candidates self-select into training programs that are traditional or alternative, low-coursework or high-coursework. In the absence of random assignment of teachers to training routes, we cannot determine whether AC programs add value or not, or if lower-coursework programs are as effective as higher-coursework programs. All one can say is that for the types of schools and grade levels studied, students of those teachers who decided to go through AC routes may have performed no worse in reading and somewhat worse in math (in some instances) than those who were taught by teachers who selected traditional routes. The study is fundamentally unable to provide evidence about a counterfactual world in which traditional certification ceases to exist, or is not the default.

The report fails to recognize other limitations. For instance, another critically important source of non-random variation is the certification requirements imposed by states, but the report's introduction states:

The increased variation in the teacher preparation approaches created by the existence of various AC and TC programs offers an opportunity to examine the effect of different components of training on teacher performance.... We can exploit this type of variation to examine whether the form of training is associated with differences in teacher performance. (p. xv)

But, of course, state requirements for AC programs are not randomly assigned. States set requirements for a reason. A state with particularly dire teaching shortages may elect to set a very low bar for alternative certification. On the other hand, a state with exceptionally high standards for teacher quality may set a higher bar. Either way, these requirements will be related to the average quality of schools and teachers.

Finally, this study can make no claims about the long-term effects of a wholesale movement away from traditional teacher certification. The fact that a small number of AC teachers in a select population of schools, grades, and states performed only somewhat worse than TC teachers in the same schools cannot help us learn about the systemic changes in teacher quality, selection, and instruction that would arise under a wholly different system. Unfortunately for fans of randomized control trials, no amount of randomized assignment will answer such questions.

NOTES AND REFERENCES

1. Constantine, J., Player, D, Silva, T., Hallgren, K., Grider, M., & Deke, J. (2009, Feb.). *An Evaluation of Teachers Trained Through Different Routes to Certification: Final report*. Princeton, NJ: Mathematica Policy Research. Retrieved March 9, 2009, from http://www.mathematica-mpr.com /publications/PDFs/Education/teacherstrained09.pdf

2. Gladwell, M. (2008, Dec. 15). Most likely to succeed. *The New Yorker*.

3. Kristof, N. (2009, Feb. 14). Our greatest national shame. *The New York Times*. Retrieved March 4, 2009, from http://www.nytimes.com/2009/02/15/ opinion/15kristof.html

4. Mathematica Policy Research. (2009, Feb. 9). Study evaluates different routes to teacher certification. Press release by Author. Retrieved March 4, 2009, from http://www.mathematica-mpr.com/press%20releases /alternativecertifcation_2_9_09.asp

5. Mathematica Policy Research. (2009, Feb. 9). Press release.

6. Shadish, W. R., Cook, T. D., & Campbell, D. T. (2003). *Experimental and quasi-experimental designs for causal inference*. Boston, MA: Houghton-Mifflin. Schneider, B., et al. (2007). *Estimating causal effects: Using experimental and observational designs*. Washington, DC: American Educational Research Association.

7. Randomized control trials are valued for their ability to remove the confounding effects of nonrandom selection into treatment and control

groups. Because subjects are randomly assigned to these groups, we can assume that "all else is held constant," and infer that differences between groups (short of randomness) are due solely to the treatment.

8. Murnane, R. J., & Nelson, R. R. (2005, Dec.). Improving the Performance of the education sector: The valuable, challenging, and limited role of random assignment valuations. *National Bureau of Economic Research Working Paper* #11846

Deaton, A. S. (2009, Jan.). Instruments of development: Randomization in the tropics, and the search for the elusive keys to economic development. *National Bureau of Economic Research Working Paper* #14690.

9. This excluded some high-profile but selective AC programs like Teach for America, based on the rationale that the vast majority TC comparison teachers are not put through comparable selective screens.

10. For example, see Lankford, H., Loeb, S., & Wyckoff, J. (2002). Teacher sorting and the plight of urban schools: A descriptive analysis. *Educational Evaluation and Policy Analysis, 24*(1).

Clotfelter, C. T., Ladd, H. F., & Vigdor, J. (2005). Who teaches whom? Race and the distribution of novice teachers. *Economics of Education Review, 24*(4).

Clotfelter, C. T., Ladd, H. F., & Vigdor, J. (2006a). The Academic Achievement Gap in Grades 3 to 8. *National Bureau of Economic Research Working Paper* #12207.

11. Teach for America and New York City Teaching Fellows teachers (both selective AC programs).

12. Nye, B., Konstantopoulos, S., & Hedges, L. (2004). How large are teacher effects? *Educational Evaluation and Policy Analysis, 26*(3), 237-257. Retrieved March 9, 2009, from http://www.sesp.northwestern.edu/docs/publications/169468047044fcbd1360b55.pdf

For a cross-sectional study of teacher effectiveness in the early grades, based on the Early Childhood Longitudinal Study, see: Croninger R. G. et al. (2007). Teacher qualifications and early learning: Effects of certification, degree, and experience on first-grade student achievement. *Economics of Education Review, 26*(3).

13. Boyd, D., Lankford, H., Loeb, S., & Wyckoff, J. (2008). The impact of assessment and accountability on teacher recruitment and retention. *Public Finance Review, 36*(1).

14. California accounts for 22% of the sample used in the study (p. 15).

15. Eight of 28 sponsoring institutions of AC programs "also operated TC programs whose graduates were in the same study" (pp. 25-27). Surprisingly, the authors "did not systematically explore potential connections or similarities between AC and TC programs operated by the same institution such as the extent to which they required the same courses or the extent to which they shared instructors" (p. 27).

16. One report highly critical of existing AC programs argues that there is fundamentally no difference between TC and AC programs in the United States. In the forward to this report, Chester Finn and Michael Petrilli write, "[This report's] findings confirm our fears and suspicions. Two-

thirds of the [AC] programs that they surveyed accept half or more of their applicants. One-quarter accept virtually everyone who applies. Only four in ten programs require a college GPA of 2.75 or above—no lofty standard in this age of grade inflation. So much for recruiting the best and brightest. Meanwhile, about a third of the [AC] programs for elementary teachers require at least 30 hours of education school courses—the same amount needed for a master's degree. So much for streamlining the pathway into teaching; *these programs have merely re-ordered the traditional teacher-prep sequence without altering its substance, allowing candidates to take this burdensome course load while teaching instead of before"* [emphasis added]. See: Walsh, K., & Jacobs, S. (2007). *Alternative certification isn't alternative.* Thomas B. Fordham Institute and National Council on Teacher Quality.

17. Rubin, D. B. (1980). Discussion of "Randomization Analysis of Experimental Data in the Fisher Randomization Test." *Journal of the American Statistical Association, 75.*

18. Clotfelter, C. T., Ladd, H. F., & Vigdor, J. L. (2006b). Teacher-student matching and the assessment of teacher effectiveness. *Journal of Human Resources, 41,* 778-820.

   Dee, T. S. (2004). Teachers, race and student achievement in a randomized experiment. *Review of Economics and Statistics, 86*(1), 195-210.

   Ehrenberg, R. G., & Brewer, D. J. (1994). Do school and teacher characteristics matter? Evidence from high school and beyond? *Economics of Education Review, 13,* 1-17.

   Ehrenberg, R. G., & Brewer, D. J. (1995). Did teachers' verbal ability and race matter in the 1960s? Coleman revisited. *Economics of Education Review, 14,* 1-21.

19. Normal Curve Equivalent differences for Black students are 3.45 in math, $p = 0.09$, and 2.35 in reading, $p = 0.17$.

20. It is not possible to determine the exact number of schools in the study that are in urban areas. However, 15 of the 63 schools are in California, where all of the study's districts are in urban areas, and 27 of the 63 are in Texas, where all but one of the study's districts is in an urban area. All of Georgia and Wisconsin's study districts are in urban areas, as are two of New Jersey's three sampled districts.

21. Authors' calculations using the Common Core of Data 2004-05.

22. For example, see Lankford, Loeb, & Wyckoff (2002); see note 10.

   Clotfelter, Ladd, & Vigdor,(2005); see note 10.

   Clotfelter, Ladd, & Vigdor (2006a); see note 10. Clotfelter and his colleagues show that over two-thirds of the Black-White gap in exposure to novice teachers can be attributed to within- rather than between-district differences.

23. See Exhibits II.4 and II.5, and page 21 of the report.

24. There is very little empirical evidence on schools' staffing responses to testing and accountability, but one recent paper found that teachers assigned to teach fourth grade in New York State were less likely be inexperienced once mandatory fourth grade tests were implemented. See Boyd, Lankford, Loeb, & Wyckoff (2008); see note 13.

25.   It is possible, of course, that these schools assign the most effective AC teachers to the tested grades, in addition to the most effective TC teachers. In that case, there's an assignment bias issue on both sides of the equation.

26.   For example, see Goldhaber, D., Gross, B., & Player, D. (2007). Are public schools losing their "best?" Assessing the career transitions of teachers and their implications for the quality of the teacher workforce," *Center on Reinventing Public Education Working Paper #2007-2*.

27.   There is very thin empirical evidence on this pattern. But one legislative study from Texas on this subject can be found. See Herbert, K. S. & Ramsay, M. C. (2004, September). *Teacher Turnover and Shortages of Qualified Teachers in Texas Public School Districts, 2001-2004: Report to the Senate Education Committee*. State Board for Educator Certification. Retrieved March 5, 2009, from http://www.sbec.state.tx.us/SBECONLINE/reprtdatarsrch /ReportforSenateEducationCommittee.pdf
The turnover rate among teachers was high in the Mathematica study: 7 of 93 AC teachers in the study (7.5%) left *during the school year*, while 5 of 95 TC teachers did (5.3%).

28.   The math test administered to students in grades 2-5 included two components, "Math Concepts and Applications" and "Math Computation." However, because the Math Computation test was not available for students in K-1, the authors used only the "Math Concepts" score in the analyses reported in the primary body of the report, "for comparability across grades" (p. A-4).

29.   McCloskey, D., & Ziliak, S. (2008). *The cult of statistical significance: How the standard error costs us jobs, justice, and lives*. Ann Arbor, MI: University of Michigan Press.

CHAPTER 21

GIVING STUDENTS THE CHAFF

How to Find and Keep the Teachers We Need

Raymond Pecheone and Ash Vasudeva

Review of Marie Gryphon's "Giving Students the Chaff: How to Find and Keep the Teachers We Need," published by the Cato Institute. This is a modified version of a review originally published on October 25, 2006.

INTRODUCTION

In the disputatious area of research on teacher quality, establishing common ground between scholarship from the left and right could potentially loosen policy logjams and allow federal, state, and local educators and policymakers to support a unified educational agenda that strengthens teaching and improves student learning. Unfortunately, common ground is hard to find. The CATO Institute report, *Giving Kids the Chaff: How to Find and Keep the Teachers We Need*, falls short.

That report begins on solid ground, noting that teachers affect student achievement and that teacher quality is an important factor in improving educational outcomes, especially among poor children. It also finds that

Think Tank Research Quality: Lessons for Policy Makers, the Media, and the Public, pp. 301–310

school choice and pay are levers to improve teacher quality and student achievement. The author then argues that competition and choice induce improved hiring practices and more flexible compensation policies, which in turn attract and retain high-quality teachers.

To reach this conclusion, the report cites only a narrow band of research literature. In the end, the report's failure to consider alternative interpretations of empirical research on hiring and compensation undermines the validity of its findings and conclusions, as does the failure to address research that does not corroborate an "achievement effect" for charter and private schools. The report's conclusions are accordingly of mixed usefulness in guiding policy.

FINDINGS AND CONCLUSIONS OF THE REPORT

The article presents the following conclusions concerning the importance and means of attracting and retaining high-quality teachers:

- The best predictor of student success is the quality of the teacher;
- Higher quality teachers appear to leave the profession at a greater rate than lesser quality teachers;
- The problem with attracting high-quality teachers is greatly exacerbated by bureaucratic and restrictive public school systems that distort and undermine the hiring practices of school administrators;
- Salary compression and the lack of flexibility to differentiate pay dissuade the best teachers from entering the profession;
- Merit pay systems as they are currently structured cannot change teaching because they do not target or reward the best teachers;
- Increased competition will improve teacher quality;
- Private and charter schools are much more successful at attracting and hiring high-quality teachers; and
- Under a system of school choice, teacher quality will be greatly improved—and through marketplace competition, school administrators will have an incentive to hire the best teachers.

RATIONALES SUPPORTING THE FINDINGS AND CONCLUSIONS OF THE REPORT

The report's rationale for connecting competition and choice to teacher quality is based on a review of empirical studies of school and district policies and practices in traditional public schools, public charter schools, and private schools. The report first identifies research linking teacher quality to student performance. Next, literature is identified suggesting that traditional hiring and compensation systems offer few incentives to attract and retain high-quality teachers. Finally, research on two areas—(1) districts with high levels of competition, and (2) charter and private schools—is used to suggest that when faced with competitive pressure, administrators select higher quality teachers and use differentiated compensation systems to promote retention.

THE REPORT'S USE OF RESEARCH LITERATURE

Cato's report is undermined by its narrow use of the research literature. Even on the central (and widely accepted premise) of CATO's policy analysis—that teachers matter and thus teacher quality matters for improving student achievement—the report references just a narrow band of research (primarily the work of the Rivkin group[1]). The excluded evidence base suggests that teacher effectiveness matters *and* that proxy measures for quality extend far beyond the prospective teachers' standardized test scores discussed in CATO's analysis.[2] This literature suggests that CATO's claims about teacher hiring overstate the importance of standardized test scores as a proxy measure for teacher quality and understate the importance of other measures such as teacher preparation, certification, professional development and mentoring.

Numerous studies conducted at the individual classroom, school, district, and state levels have found that students' achievement is significantly related to whether their teachers are fully prepared or certified in the field they teach.[3]

In addition to certification, teacher variables that have been found to have an impact on student achievement include: professional development,[4] graduation from a high-quality university;[5] quality of the teacher-preparation program, quality of mentoring of beginning teachers, and the teacher's knowledge of teaching and learning.[6]

Several variables have been found to influence student achievement in some studies, but not in others: (a) lower class sizes;[7] (b) route to credential and type of teacher preparation;[8] (c) teachers' verbal abilities;[9] (d) whether the teacher's race is the same as student's race;[10] (e) the extent to which instruction is aligned to the test[11] (also referred to as, "topic by cognitive demand"); and (f) general measures of ability or academic talent, such as an ACT, SAT or exam scores on the Texas licensing test of basic skills, the Texas Examination of Current Administrators and Teachers (TECAT).[12]

Given the large number of methodologically diverse studies that support CATO's thesis that "higher quality teachers can significantly improve educational outcomes, especially among poor students" (p. 1), it seems neither fair nor balanced to exclude studies suggesting a range of possible indicators of teacher quality other than standardized test scores. The report also neglects to mention other direct assessments of teaching, beyond test scores, that are arguably more accurate indicators of teacher quality. For example, an assessment developed by the National Board for Professional Teaching Standards (NBPTS) directly measures both content and pedagogy by documenting a teacher's actual practice (planning, teaching, and assessment) and objectively testing the teacher's content/ pedagogical knowledge in his or her content area. Several studies have found that the NBPTS assessments predict teachers' effectiveness as measured by their students' learning gains.[13] These studies add to the rich body of research that suggests multiple factors that affect and demonstrate teacher quality. By giving short shrift to studies of such variables as teacher preparation, licensure, and professional development, CATO's analysis appears to be highly selective and limited to those references that lend support to CATO's teacher quality argument.

REVIEW OF THE VALIDITY OF THE FINDINGS AND CONCLUSIONS

CATO's report accurately captures two fundamental challenges facing K-12 education—"identifying the highest quality teaching applicants and finding policies that will keep them in the classroom" (p. 2)—but offers little compelling evidence for how competition and choice would improve either one. Specifically, the report does not consider alternative interpretations of the empirical evidence on hiring and compensation. Further, it understates the importance of working conditions and fails to acknowledge existing monetary and nonmonetary incentives to retain high-quality teachers. Finally, it ignores data suggesting that educational sectors with presumed advantages in both hiring and compensation policies—charter and private schools—do not demonstrate clear and consistent academic advantages over public schools. In particular, the absence of a strong empirical advantage for either charter schools or private schools over the noncharter public sector suggests that CATO's claims about the link between teacher quality, choice, and competition are guided by ideological presumption rather than empirical reality. Each of these issues is discussed below.

Hiring Policies and Working Conditions

The teacher-effects literature emphasizes the importance of recruiting, supporting, retaining and motivating talented teachers. Many of CATO's claims about the problems afflicting teacher hiring policies and practices find support in that literature. Public school systems can be bureaucratic and rigid and sometimes provide few or no incentives to attract and support quality teachers.[14] Similarly, compensation systems governed by seniority rules and lock-step salary increments often fail to reward the most committed and effective teachers.[15] Therefore, few would dispute that bureaucratic structures can prevent school districts from attracting and hiring high-quality teachers and that "teacher quality can be improved dramatically when administrators understand the attributes that make for good teachers and are given the right incentives to make good hiring decisions."[16]

Less transparent and more contentious are CATO's claims about the predictive value of standardized test scores as a proxy measure for teacher quality. CATO's treatment of test scores as a predictor of teacher success is internally inconsistent and overly narrow. On one hand, CATO's report acknowledges that the attributes of good teachers are neither readily apparent nor quantifiable, that "teachers' scores can explain only a portion of the large difference in achievement [attributed] to teacher quality" (p. 4), and that "most of the teacher effect remains a mystery" (p. 4). On the other hand, the report criticizes the hiring practices of principals and school district administrators by stating, "Those gatekeepers systematically fail to hire the most capable candidates" (p. 5). Hiring the most capable candidates should involve far more than standardized test score data. Other important factors that could (and should) have an impact on hiring decisions, but which go unmentioned in the article, include certification, quality of teacher education program, professional development, and measures of teacher's knowledge of content and pedagogy, such as NBPTS assessments.

In addition to overstating the importance of standardized test scores in hiring decisions, the CATO report suggests that performance-based pay coupled with unrestricted hiring practices and compensation systems would reduce bureaucratic rigidity and help attract and retain high-quality teachers. Empirical evidence casts doubt on these assumptions. For example, in recent years several states have experimented with accountability systems that provide for bonuses or salary increases directly tied to student test scores. The early research on these systems are not encouraging; they do show an overall increase in scores on standardized tests used by states for accountability, but these gains do not carry over to other tests that measure the same content.[17] This disconnect should be understood in light of evidence that tests used for accountability can be—and are—gamed.[18] Neal observed that to establish a fair and equitable test-based performance system would incur considerable test costs and engage students in significantly more testing, taking away time that might be better used for instruction.[19]

The report's assumption that schools competing for talented teachers will demonstrate improved hiring practices has another problem. It potentially conflates teachers' individual employment decisions with hiring managers' practices and policies. Although the report cites research suggesting "administrators in competitive districts gave quality higher priority in the hiring and retention process" (p. 10), there is no mention of a simple and arguably more compelling explanation for any variation in teacher quality in these districts: teachers' self-selection into schools with better working conditions.

The implications of this alternative interpretation are subtle but significant. If teacher self-selection into schools (rather than managerial hiring policies and practices) is chiefly responsible for placement, then improving school working conditions should be the priority. While it may be argued that schools will improve working conditions to attract talented teachers, this ignores resource disparities between and across schools and districts as well as the communities in which they are located. An arguably more efficient policy mechanism to attract talented teachers to high-needs schools may be targeted assistance for facilities development, program enhancement, and teacher incentives.

Compensation Policies and Private/Charter School Comparisons

The CATO report also flags problems in the area of teacher compensation policies and practices, and this contention does have empirical support. For example, public school compensation policies often do underpay many of the most promising potential teachers, and there are indeed limitations to the effectiveness of across-the-board salary increases or merit pay systems in retaining high-quality teachers.

CATO's report suggests that pay compression (via salary schedules that link pay to such factors as years of experience and education/professional development) drives higher-quality teachers out of the profession while retaining mediocre teachers. These analyses seem to exclude the role of non-monetary incentives in retaining high-quality teachers. For example, there is no discussion of how high-quality teachers may be rewarded through choice of teaching assignments, additional support for professional learning activities, and classroom or other building-level preferences. Working conditions, arguably the most important non-monetary incentive influencing teachers, are relegated to the notes, which state that "Some other interesting research suggests that teachers tend to prioritize good working conditions far more highly than salary" (p. 13). Again, a clear weakness of the report is that it does not identify and discuss strategies to directly improve working conditions—beyond choice and competition—as potential strategies for recruiting and retaining high-quality teachers.

Throughout the report, private and charter schools are praised for having superior hiring and compensation policies. Consider, for example, the following two assertions: "A seemingly mystical property of private and charter schools is their ability to simultaneously keep teaching quality high and student/teacher ratios low, all while spending less on salaries per teacher than the public system" (p. 10); and "[private and charter schools] have more resources available to reward high-performing teachers" (p. 10). These claims are only supported by a few references to a narrow slice of empirical research.

While hiring and compensation policies and other "mystical" properties may be different in charter and private schools than public schools, they do not necessarily conjure up improvements in student achievement. In fact, three recent analyses of National Assessment of Educational Progress (NAEP) data collected by the National Center for Educational Statistics suggest no "achievement effect" of private and charter schools relative to public schools.[20] Applying hierarchical linear modeling to NAEP data in mathematics and reading, researchers at the Educational Testing Service and at the University of Illinois each independently found minimal achievement differences across sectors. Where statistically significant differences did exist (in fourth-grade mathematics and eighth-grade reading), they did not consistently favor one sector over the other. In fact, the analyses of math scores by Lubienski and Lubienski showed public schools doing better than charter schools, while both did better than private schools.[21] Given that private and charter schools play a central role in linking competition and choice to teacher quality and ultimately to student performance, CATO's policy analysis should at least address studies that suggest more tenuous linkages between these variables.

USEFULNESS OF THE REPORT FOR GUIDANCE OF POLICY AND PRACTICE

While one key element of CATO's policy analysis—the growing acceptance by researchers across that policy spectrum that teachers and teacher quality matters—provides important guidance for policy and practice, other elements are undermined by a propensity to filter the evidence base in favor of a particular point of view. Specifically, the report's conclusion on the role of competition in teacher hiring and compensation is poorly linked to any supporting evidence base, disregards alternative explanations for the evidence cited, and fails to identify and address contradictory or confounding evidence. Although competition and choice are essential elements of a robust educational system, CATO's analyses fall short of establishing a strong connection between those elements and teacher quality via hiring and compensation systems.

NOTES AND REFERENCES

1. Rivkin, S. G., Hanushek, E. A., & Kain, J. F. (2002). *Teachers, schools and academic achievement* (No. 6691). Cambridge, MA: National Bureau of Economic Research.
2. Cochran-Smith, M. (2003). The unforgiving complexity of teaching: Avoiding simplicity in the age of accountability. *Journal of Teacher Education, 54*, 3-5.
3. Betts, J. R., Rueben, K. S., & Danenberg, A. (2000). *Equal resources, equal outcomes? The distribution of school resources and student achievement in California*. San Francisco, CA: Public Policy Institute of California.
    Darling-Hammond, L. (2000). Teacher quality and student achievement: A review of state policy evidence. *Education Policy Analysis Archives, 8*(1).
    Darling-Hammond, L., Holtzman, D. J., Gatlin, S. J., & Heilig, J. V. (2005). *Does teacher preparation matter? Evidence about teacher certification, Teach for America, and teacher effectiveness*. Palo Alto, CA: School Redesign Network
    Ferguson, R. F. (1991). Paying for public education: New evidence on how and why money matters. *Harvard Journal on Legislation, 28*(2), 465-498.
    Fetler, M. (1999). High school staff characteristics and mathematics test results. *Education Policy Analysis Archives, 7*(9).
    Fuller, E. J. (1999). *Does teacher performance matter? A comparison of TAAS performance in 1997 between schools with low and high percentage of certified teachers*. Austin, TX: Charles A. Dana Center, University of Texas at Austin.
    Goe, L. (2002). Legislating equity: The distribution of emergency permit teachers in California. *Education Policy Analysis Archives, 10*(42).
    Goldhaber, D. D., & Brewer, D. J. (2000). Does teacher certification matter? High school teacher certification status and student achievement. *Educational Evaluation and Policy Analysis, 22*(2), 129-145.
    Hawk, P., Coble, C. R., & Swanson, M. (1985). Certification: It does matter. *Journal of Teacher Education, 36*(3), 13-15.
    Strauss, R. P., & Sawyer, E. A. (1986). Some new evidence on teacher and student competencies. *Economics of Education Review, 5*(1), 41-48.
4. Porter, A. C. (2002). Measuring the content of instruction: Uses in research and practice. *Educational Researcher, 31*(7), 3-14.
    Wenglinsky, H. (2002). How schools matter: The link between teacher classroom practices and student academic performance. *Education Policy Analysis Archives, 10*(12), 32.
5. Goldhaber, D., & Brewer, D. E. (1997). Evaluating the effect of teacher degree level on educational performance. In W. Fowler (Ed.), *Developments in school finance*. Washington, DC: US Department of Education.

Summers, A. A., & Wolfe, B. L. (1975). *Which school resources help learning? Efficiency and equality in Philadelphia public schools. Business Review.* Philadelphia, PA: Federal Reserve Bank of Philadelphia.

Wayne, A., & Youngs, P. (2003, March). Teacher characteristics and student achievement gains: A review. *Review of Educational Research*.

Wenglinsky, H. (2000). *Teaching the teachers: Different settings, different results.* Princeton, NJ: Educational Testing Service.

6.   Darling-Hammond (2000); see note 3.

Darling-Hammond, L. (2005). *A good teacher in every classroom: Preparing the highly qualified teachers our children deserve.* San Francisco, CA: Jossey-Bass.

Wilkerson, J. R., & Lang, W. S. (2003). Portfolios, the pied piper of teacher certification assessments: Legal and psychometric issues. *Education Policy Analysis Archives, 11*(45).

7.   Ferguson (1991); see note 3.

Rivkin, Hanushek & Kain (2002); see note 1.

8.   Darling-Hammond (2005); see note 6.

Darling-Hammond, L., Chung, R., & Frelow, F. (2002). Variation in teacher preparation: How well do different pathways prepare teachers to teach? *Journal of Teacher Education, 53*(4), 286-302.

Laczko-Kerr, I., & Berliner, D. C. (2002). The effectiveness of "Teach for America" and other under-certified teachers on student academic achievement: A case of harmful public policy. *Education Policy Analysis Archives, 10*(27).

Raymond, M. E., Fletcher, S. H., & Luque, J. (2001). *Teach For America: An evaluation of teacher differences and student outcomes in Houston, Texas.* Washington, DC: Thomas Fordham Foundation.

9.   Ehrenberg, R., & Brewer, D. (1995). Did teachers' verbal ability and race matter in the 1960s? Coleman revisited. *Economics of Education Review, 14*(1), 1-23.

Hanushek, E. A. (1992). The trade-off between child quantity and quality. *Journal of Political Economy, 100*(1), 84-117.

10. Dee, T. S. (2001). *Teachers, race and student achievement in a randomized experiment.* (Vol. 8432). Cambridge, MA: National Bureau of Economic Research.

Ehrenberg & Brewer (1995).

Ladson-Billings, G. (1994). *The dreamkeepers: Successful teachers of African American children.* San Francisco, CA: Jossey-Bass.

11. Porter (2002); see note 4.

Rowan, B., Correnti, R., & Miller, R. J. E. (2002). *What large-scale, survey research tells us about teacher effects on student achievement: Insights from the "Prospects" study of elementary schools* (No. RR-051). Philadelphia, PA: Consortium for Policy Research in Education.

12. Ferguson (1991); see note 3.

Ferguson, R. F., & Ladd, H. F. (1996). How and why money matters: An analysis of Alabama schools. In H. F. Ladd (Ed.), *Holding schools accountable: Performance-based reform in education* (pp. 265-298). Washington, DC: Brookings Institution.

13.   Ladson-Billings, G., & Darling-Hammond, L. (2000). *The validity of National Board for Professional Teaching Standards (NBPTS)/Interstate New Teacher Assessment and Support Consortium (INTASC) assessments for effective urban teachers*. Washington DC: National Partnership for Excellence and Accountability in Teaching.
Bond, L., Smith, T., Baker, W., & Hattie, J. (2000). *The certification system of the National Board for Professional Teaching Standards: A construct and consequential validity study*. Greensboro, NC: Center for Educational Research and Evaluation at the University of North Carolina at Greensboro.
Goldhaber, D., & Anthony, E. (2004). *Can teacher quality be effectively assessed?* Seattle, WA: University of Washington and the Urban Institute.
Cavaluzzo, L. (2004). *Is National Board Certification an effective signal of teacher quality?* (National Science Foundation No. REC-0107014). Alexandria, VA: The CNA Corporation.
Vandevoort, L. G., Amrein-Beardsley, A., & Berliner, D. C. (2004). National board certified teachers and their students' achievement. *Education Policy Analysis Archives, 12*(46), 117.
14.   Neal, D. (2002). How vouchers could change the market for education. *Journal of Economic Perspectives, 16*(4), 25-44.
15.   Ballou, D., & Podgursky, M. (1995). Recruiting smarter teachers. *Journal of Human Resources, 30*(2), 326-328.
16.   Gryphon, M. (September 25, 2006). *Giving kids the chaff: How to find and keep the teachers we need*. CATO Institute Policy Analysis Number 579. Washington, DC: CATO Institute, p. 12.
17.   Koretz, D. (2002). Limitations in the use of achievement tests as measures of educators' productivity. *Journal of Human Resources, 37*(4), 752-777.
18.   Baker, G. P. (2002). Distortion and risk in optimal incentive contracts. *Journal of Human Resources, 37*, 728-51.
Heckman, J. J., Heinrich, C., & Smith, J. (2002). The performance of performance standards. *Journal of Human Resources, 112*(4), 1127-1161.
19.   Neal (2002); see note 14.
20.   Braun, H., Jenkins, F., & Grigg, W. (2006a). *Comparing private schools and public schools using hierarchical linear modeling* (NCES 2006-461). U.S. Department of Education, National Center for Educational Statistics, Institute for Education Sciences. Washington, DC: U.S. Government Printing Office.
Braun, H., Jenkins, F., & Grigg, W. (2006b). *A closer look at charter schools using hierarchical linear modeling* (NCES 2006-460). U.S. Department of Education, National Center for Educational Statistics, Institute for Education Sciences. Washington, DC: U.S. Government Printing Office.
Lubienski, S.T., & Lubienski, C. (2006). School sector and academic achievement: A multi-level analysis of NAEP mathematics data. *American Educational Research Journal, 43*(4), 651-698.
21.   Lubienski & Lubienski (2006).

CONCLUSION

Junk Social Science:
Its Patrons and Its Audience

Kevin G. Welner and Alex Molnar

Scientists and economists have been offered $10,000 each by a lobby group funded by one of the world's largest oil companies to undermine a major climate change report due to be published today.

Letters sent by the American Enterprise Institute (AEI), an ExxonMobil-funded thinktank with close links to the Bush administration, offered the payments for articles that emphasise the shortcomings of a report from the UN's Intergovernmental Panel on Climate Change (IPCC).

*Travel expenses and additional payments were also offered. * * ***

The AEI has received more than $1.6m from ExxonMobil and more than 20 of its staff have worked as consultants to the Bush administration. Lee Raymond, a former head of ExxonMobil, is the vice-chairman of AEI's board of trustees.[1]

This incident, as reported by *The (UK) Guardian*, brought unwanted attention to a powerful private think tank and illuminated the nature of a key think-tank activity: producing and publishing advocacy research. The primary goal of advocacy research publications is not a search for truth—it is to create the impression that a favored policy position has authoritative intellectual and scientific support. These publications are not meant to bear critical scrutiny any more than, for example, is any science behind the claim that four out of five dentists recommend sugarless gum for their patients who chew gum. This junk science is what Susan Sarnoff calls "sanctified snake oil," and it is a key way that money is used to drive policy.[2]

What the AEI incident reveals is a corporate-sponsored organization recruiting sympathetic scientists to create persuasive materials friendly to their patron's perspective. It represents business as usual: wealthy interests use (and even create) private think tanks to impart to the public the impression that their position on a topic is favored by a large number of disinterested scientists. While these kinds of activities are not illegal, they are unethical. They corrupt the process of scientific inquiry. In this instance the corruption is revealed most clearly by the AEI project research guidance for scientists seeking funding, apparently requiring that, for scholars to receive funds, their findings *must* be critical of the UN Intergovernmental Panel on Climate Change.

It is no doubt true that unbiased research is difficult to produce in a setting where only certain conclusions will be funded or published. Many think tanks are simply not designed to produce or encourage objectively valid analyses. Even so, the problem revealed by the *Guardian* report is much more complex than a corporation paying a third party to produce self-serving reports promoted as disinterested science. Our concerns should extend beyond well-funded think tanks like AEI, to policymakers and the media. They are the targets and the crucial enablers, and they have legitimized a policymaking process subject to heavy influence by self-interested research.

One of the reasons research publications produced by think tanks have become so widely accepted by policymakers and the media in this "pay for play" policy environment is because there is no effective mechanism for subjecting those reports to outside quality controls. If every document labeled as "research" is received and reported without review or critique by independent experts, then its value is not derived from its quality and rigor—these become relatively beside the point. Value is instead tightly linked to the ability of the research to gain attention and influence policy. Private think tanks accordingly become, from a business standpoint, sensible investments for corporate influence-seekers. It is thus hardly surprising that the most well-funded think tanks tend to be those perceived to have the greatest influence with the media and policymakers. In fact, these prominent private think tanks are so proficient at packaging and marketing their publications that many of their reports have attained greater prominence than articles addressing the same issues that are published in the most rigorous and respected research journals. This is the context for the Think Tank Review Project (TTRP).

Simply put, we began the TTRP because the public, the media and policymakers had nowhere to turn for expert analyses of the strengths and weaknesses of the non-peer-reviewed education reports published by private think tanks. The project's goal has never been to serve as the final arbiter of the value of these reports. Rather, we intend to bring as many think tank reports as possible into a scholarly discussion. Such discussions proceed based on recognized principles for organizing, conducting and reporting rigorous, high-quality research. The TTRP holds the think-tank reports to standards and procedures comparable to those required of other research in the field. We think it beyond debate that a policymaker reading a TTRP review alongside the non-peer-reviewed report it assesses will be in a much better position to make sound and informed judgments about the report's usefulness than if she or he had read the report alone.

In the introductory chapter, we quoted the Mackinac Center's Nathan J. Russell, who clearly articulated the key strategy of free-market think tanks: to transform the "political climate" so that future legislative and legal debates would be more hospitable to their favored policies.[3] We also quoted former Olin Foundation executive director James Piereson's statement that a successful conservative movement "need[s] to wage an ongoing battle of ideas."[4] As policy researchers, we welcome battles over ideas. The value of such battles depends, however, on maintaining the focus on ideas and the quality of the research that supports them. If instead the influence of a research publication derives from the amount of money spent promoting it and the ability of its sponsors to access powerful media and political networks, then "research" can easily become simply a label slapped onto the latest advocacy statement prior to a media marketing campaign.

The Think Tank Review Project attempts to raise the issue of research quality to prominence in this battle over ideas. If a report is dressed up with the trappings of research but fails to address basic elements of research quality, then policymakers should understand this. Similarly, policymakers benefit if the quality of a think tank report can be confirmed by an independent, third-party, expert reviewer. And we all benefit when experts exchange ideas, critiques and opinions about a given research study. As social scientists we are committed to the idea of scholarly checks and balances—that research findings should always be subject to an ongoing, critical discussion. Accordingly, the TTRP has helped move non-peer-reviewed reports published by private think tanks into such a discussion.

Along the way, the Project has highlighted harmful patterns and practices that permeate the research publications of advocacy think tanks. These include the selective use of earlier research to bolster what appear to be predetermined findings, methodological weaknesses such as failure to account for selection bias or the confusion of correlation for causation, failure to provide the data on which the report's findings are based, overstated conclusions, and unsupported recommendations often based on improbable inferential leaps.

In report after report from market-oriented think tanks, privatization reforms in particular have been offered as the preordained solution for any number of educational problems, from school funding to high school drop-out rates to the weaknesses of the No Child Left Behind law. Indeed, a person reading these reports could not fail to conclude that the public nature of public education is the root cause of all that ails schools, that everything else is just a symptom. Time after time, our reviewers identified analyses that led inexorably to a prescription for school privatization. Even reports that began with a reasonable policy analysis would suddenly and groundlessly leap to claim the need for vouchers or other forms of privatization as the key policy implication of their findings. As we pointed out in a 2008 commentary published in *Education Week*:

> In purely political and ideological (if not social science) terms, biased think tank reports are understandable. Reports intended primarily to be vehicles for advancing the ideological preferences of the think tanks will view data, logic, and experience as mere tools to be manipulated to serve policy goals. Nuanced ... policy analysis is a notoriously unreliable tool for advocates. A nuanced analysis of voucher research might conclude, for example,
>
> *Overall, voucher research shows both positive and negative outcomes. On the one hand, means-tested voucher programs provide new choices for families with very limited options, and those families receiving vouchers tend to be happy with their choices. In addition, many students who attend private schools using vouchers undoubtedly gain an academic benefit.*
>
> *On the other hand, the research shows that on average these voucher recipients show little or no academic benefit, as measured by standardized exams. Further, the research shows that even for means-tested voucher programs, the policies often result in stratification, with parents in voucher families tending to be more educated. Moreover, the transaction costs of a full-scale voucher program may make voucher plans more costly than other, more educationally potent alternatives.*
>
> Admittedly, that's not much of a sales pitch and pretty cold soup for an ideologue. As for policymakers, they will have to decide whether false clarity is more valuable than messy truths. The evidence provided by the Think Tank Review Project suggests that they can not have it both ways.[5]

Currently, think tank reports remain very effective in attracting attention and in exerting influence in policy debates. Their conclusions are disseminated through mainstream media outlets as well as through new media such as blogs. To a remarkable degree, they have shaped and driven news coverage as well as the way key education issues are discussed in legislatures. This is their great coup: findings from think tank reports can become part of the conventional wisdom without ever having been subject to expert review. As we argued several years ago, this may be good partisan politics, but it is terrible social science, and it harms efforts to improve the nation's schools.[6]

The Think Tank Review Project entered its fifth year in 2010, having produced 58 reviews. Some reviews have offered praise for the research reviewed; most have not. As of yet we can find no improvement in the quality of the reports; reviews of reports in 2009 revealed the same problems as did the reviews in 2006. The relentless regularity with which advocacy think tanks repeat these flaws has not been noticeably moderated by the efforts of our expert reviewers, nor (with one or two minor exceptions) have these think tanks attempted to refute the critiques.

In some respects this silence is not surprising. If the research publications reviewed are seen by think tanks not as social science but rather as advocacy documents, then responding to our reviews makes little sense. A response would bring greater attention to the reports' flaws and would begin to draw advocacy think tanks into a serious scholarly discussion of their work, undermining their effectiveness. In academic journals, publishing corrections and debate over research methods and findings is part of the peer-review process. But our experience with the TTRP suggests that the problems with much of the research published by advocacy think tanks are the result of active deception, not carelessness or lack of knowledge.

This brings us back to the question of the intended audiences for the reports from advocacy think tanks. These reports are generally not aimed at experts in the field, who know the other research in the area or can easily recognize methodological flaws. Instead, they are aimed at policymakers, reporters, bloggers and others who are either predisposed towards their ideological conclusions and recommendations or are simply receptive to using "research" that is slickly produced and well-packaged. It is likely that think tanks will continue to brush off our reviews until we succeed in raising the awareness of policymakers and reporters of common flaws in these reports and the dangers of uncritically accepting, distributing, or acting on their findings. While non-peer-reviewed reports may at times contribute to our social-scientific knowledge base and to sound policymaking, each such report should be subjected to careful examination and judged on its merits. As our free-market friends would caution, *caveat emptor.*

NOTES AND REFERENCES

1. Sample, I. (2007, February 2). Scientists offered cash to dispute climate study. *The (UK) Guardian.* Retrieved December 30, 2009, from http://www.guardian.co.uk/environment/2007/feb/02/frontpagenews.climatechange

2. Sarnoff, S. K. (2001). *Sanctified snake oil: The effect of junk science on public policy.* Westport, CT: Praeger.

3. Russell, N. J. (n.d.). *An introduction to the Overton Window of Political Possibilities.* Mackinac Center for Public Policy. Retrieved December 30, 2009, from http://www.mackinac.org/7504

4. Piereson, J. (2005, May 27). Investing in the Right Ideas: How philanthropists helped make conservatism a governing philosophy. *Commentary Magazine.* Retrieved December 30, 2009, from http://www.opinionjournal.com/extra/?id=110006723

5. Welner, K. G., & Molnar, A. (2008, February 20). The Privatization Infatuation. *Education Week, 27*(24), 28-29.

6. Welner, K. G., & Molnar, A. (2007, March 28). Truthiness in education. *Education Week, 26*(25), 32, 44.

ABOUT THE AUTHORS

Bruce D. Baker is Associate Professor in the Department of Educational Theory, Policy and Administration at Rutgers University where he teaches courses in school finance policy and district business management. His recent research focuses on state aid allocation policies and practices, with particular attention to the equity and adequacy of aid for special student populations.

W. Steven Barnett is board of governors professor of education and codirector of the National Institute for Early Education Research at Rutgers, the State University of New Jersey. Dr. Barnett is an economist who studies the costs, benefits, and effects on children and families of early care and education programs and policies. His research includes statewide program evaluations and long-term follow-up studies of preschool program impacts.

Clive R. Belfield is associate professor of economics at Queens College, City University of New York. He is also codirector of the Center for Benefit-Cost Studies in Education, Teachers College, Columbia University. His professional interests are in economic evaluation of educational policy, cost-benefit analysis, and early education reforms.

Derek Briggs is chair of the Research and Evaluation Methodology Program at the University of Colorado at Boulder, where he also serves as an associate professor of quantitative methods and policy analysis. His research agenda focuses upon building sound methodological approaches for the valid measurement and evaluation of growth in student achievement. His research interests include the critical evaluation of methods that purport to estimate and/or generalize causal inferences in the context of quasi-experimental research designs.

Sean P. Corcoran is assistant professor or educational economics at New York University. He is an affiliated faculty member of the Institute for Education and Social Policy at NYU, and in 2005-06 was a visiting scholar at the Russell Sage Foundation. His research emphasizes the economics of school funding, school choice, and the labor market for teachers.

Bruce Fuller is a professor of education and public policy at the University of California at Berkeley, and codirector of policy analysis for California Education (PACE), a research center based at Berkeley and at Stanford University. His current work focuses on decentering of public interests and government programs, including charter schools, early education, and welfare reform.

Gene V Glass is Regents' Professor in the Mary Lou Fulton Institute and Graduate School of Education at Arizona State University. He is the editor of *Education Review,* an open access electronic journal of book reviews. In 2008, he published *Fertilizers, Pills & Magnetic Strips: The Fate of Public Education in America* published by Information Age Publishing.

Patricia H. Hinchey is associate professor of education at Penn State. Formerly director of PSU's Jack P. Royer Center for Learning and Academic Technologies, she frequently conducts professional development for educators at all levels. Her research interests include critical pedagogy and educational policy.

Ernest R. House is professor emeritus, University of Colorado, specializing in evaluation and policy. He is a recipient of the Lasswell Prize in policy science and the Lazarsfeld Award for evaluation theory.

Kenneth Howe is a professor in the School of Education, University of Colorado at Boulder. He has published articles on a variety of topics in education policy, ethics, and social justice. His recent research has focused on the controversies surrounding the methodology and politics of "scientifically-based" educational research.

Luis A. Huerta is an associate professor of education and public policy at Teachers College-Columbia University. He teaches courses in policy analysis and implementation, school finance and organizational sociology. His research and scholarship focus on school choice reforms (including charter schools, homeschooling, tuition tax credits and vouchers) and school finance policy.

Jennifer Jennings is assistant professor in the Department of Sociology at New York University. Her research focuses on the effects of accountability systems on racial, gender, and socioeconomic inequality in educational outcomes; teacher and school effects on noncognitive skills such as motivation and self-control; and the effects of noncognitive skills on cognitive outcomes.

Jaekyung Lee is an associate professor of education, State University of New York at Buffalo, and a 2009-10 Fellow of the Center for Advanced Study in the Behavioral Sciences, Stanford University. He is an associate editor of American Educational Research Journal (Social and Institutional Analysis Section). He specializes in educational policy research and evaluation.

Christopher Lubienski is an associate professor of education policy and Fellow with the Forum on the Future of Public Education at the University of Illinois, where he is affiliated with the Institute of Government and Public Affairs. His research focuses on education reform, access, and the political economy of education, with particular interests in organizational responses to competitive conditions in local education markets.

Gary Miron is professor of education at Western Michigan University. He has extensive experience evaluating school reforms and education policies. Over the past 2 decades he has conducted several studies of school choice programs in Europe and in the United States, including nine state evaluations of charter school reforms. In recent years, his research has increasingly focused on the education management organizations and efforts to create systemic change in urban schools in Michigan and rural schools in Louisiana.

Lawrence Mishel came to the Economic Policy Institute in 1987 and became president in 2002. He is principal author of The State of Working America (published even-numbered year since 1988), which provides a comprehensive overview of the U.S. labor market and living standards. He also leads EPI's education research program and has published on charter schools, teacher pay, and high school graduation rates.

Alex Molnar is professor of education policy and director of the Education Policy Research Unit (EPRU) at Arizona State University. His principal research interests are commercializing influences on schools and children and education privatization, subjects about which he has written numerous articles, research reports, and other publications.

Ray Pecheone is the director of the Stanford Center for Assessment Learning and Equity (SCALE). He has held various leadership roles and had published extensively on topics including teacher quality and assessment as well as student performance assessment and data use.

Ash Vasudeva is coexecutive director of Stanford University's School Redesign Network (SRN). He develops partnerships with districts, school developers, and intermediary organizations and heads up SRN's portfolio of research, evaluation, and leadership development initiatives.

Kevin G. Welner is professor at the University of Colorado at Boulder School of Education and director of the National Education Policy Center (NEPC). He is the author of *NeoVouchers: The Emergence of Tuition Tax Credits for Private Schooling* (2008, Rowman & Littlefield) and *Legal Rights, Local Wrongs: When Community Control Collides With Educational Equity* (2001, SUNY Press).

John T. Yun is an associate professor in the Gevirtz Graduate School of Education and director of the University of California Educational Evaluation Center (UCEC). His research focuses on issues of equity in education, specifically: patterns of school segregation; the effects of school context on educational outcomes; the importance of integrating evaluation into everyday school practice; and the educative/countereducative impacts of high-stakes testing.

LaVergne, TN USA
30 June 2010
187962LV00002B/15/P